RACE AND ETHNICITY IN
NEW YORK CITY

RESEARCH IN URBAN SOCIOLOGY

Series Editor: Ray Hutchison

RESEARCH IN URBAN SOCIOLOGY   VOLUME 7

RACE AND ETHNICITY IN NEW YORK CITY

EDITED BY

JEROME KRASE

Brooklyn College of the City University of New York, USA

RAY HUTCHISON

University of Wisconsin, Green Bay, USA

2004

ELSEVIER

JAI

Amsterdam – Boston – Heidelberg – London – New York – Oxford
Paris – San Diego – San Francisco – Singapore – Sydney – Tokyo

ELSEVIER B.V.
Radarweg 29
P.O. Box 211
1000 AE Amsterdam
The Netherlands

ELSEVIER Inc.
525 B Street, Suite 1900
San Diego
CA 92101-4495
USA

**ELSEVIER Ltd
The Boulevard, Langford
Lane, Kidlington
Oxford OX5 1GB
UK**

ELSEVIER Ltd
84 Theobalds Road
London
WC1X 8RR
UK

First edition 2004

British Library Cataloguing in Publication Data
A catalogue record is available from the British Library.

ISBN: 0-7623-1149-5
ISSN: 1047-0042 (Series)

⊗The paper used in this publication meets the requirements of ANSI/NISO Z39.48-1992 (Permanence of Paper). Printed in The Netherlands.

Working together to grow libraries in developing countries

www.elsevier.com | www.bookaid.org | www.sabre.org

ELSEVIER   BOOK AID
International   Sabre Foundation

CONTENTS

LIST OF CONTRIBUTORS

David A. Badillo	Lehman College, City University of New York, USA
Evrick Brown	State University of New York at Albany, USA
Sherri-Ann P. Butterfield	Rutgers University – Newark, USA
Jeffrey Geiger	Essex University, UK
Holger Henke	Caribbean Research Center, Medgar Evers College, City University of New York, USA
Tarry Hum	Queens College, City University of New York, USA
J. A. George Irish	Caribbean Research Center, Medgar Evers College, City University of New York, USA
Anna Karpathakis	Kingsborough Community College, The City University of New York, USA
Michel S. Languerre	University of California at Berkeley, USA
Philip F. Napoli	Brooklyn College, The City University of New York, USA
Mohúbolú Olúfúnké Okome	Brooklyn College, The City University of New York, USA
Victor Roudometof	University of Cyprus
Timothy Shortell	Department of Sociology, Brooklyn College, CUNY, USA

INTRODUCTION

With changes in immigration law and increased migration in the last decades of the 20th Century the United States is more diverse than at any time in its history. While the actual number of immigrants is less than that of peak years of the Great Migration at the beginning of the 20th Century, the high level of immigration has lasted longer and has brought more diverse groups to American shores. In 2000, there were 28.4 million foreign born persons living within the United States, more than 10% of the total population (Lollack, 2001). For the country as a whole, these developments have resulted in substantial increases among many groups that were virtually unknown in even the recent past: while the Chinese population has increased from 435,000 persons in 1970 to 2,730,000 in 2000, and the Filipino population increased from 343,000 to 2,360,000 during the same period, the Korean population grew from 69,000 to 1,200,000 persons, and the Laotian (largely Hmong) population, not included in the 1970 census, in 2000 numbered some 1,230,000 persons. Similarly, the Mexican-origin population has nearly doubled each decade since 1960, and Latinos now are largest minority population, surpassing the African American population shortly after the 2000 census.

As was true of the earlier Great Immigration, the majority of recent immigrants have settled in urban areas. In 2000 there were some 29 million immigrants living in metropolitan areas across the country, an increase of 10 million immigrants from just 10 years earlier (Logan, 2003). More than half of the foreign-born population in the United States is found in just 13 metropolitan areas, and this increase is not bounded by the geography of earlier immigrant neighborhoods. By 2000 fully 25% of the suburban population was comprised of minority populations, due in large part to the movement of immigrants into suburban communities and, in some cases, into suburban ethnic enclaves: the increase of immigrant populations in the suburbs (a 4.8 million increase from 1990 to 2000) far surpassed their increase in central cities (a 3.5 million increase). Many cities – and suburbs – have undergone visible change in population and neighborhoods. In Chicago, for example, the Hispanic and Asian populations have doubled each decade since 1950. In the 1960s it made sense to speak of Chicago as a white and black city; in the 1970s one had to refer to Chicago as a white, black, and Hispanic (largely Mexican) city, while in the 1990s and into the present Chicago has become a multi-cultural city with distinct white, black, Hispanic, Asian, and European immigrant communities across the metropolitan area.

While Chicago has long served as the convenient and well-studied model for urban sociology, in the 1990s Ed Soja and others argued that Los Angeles had replaced Chicago as the focus of urban study – that while Chicago was the appropriate model for the industrial city, Los Angeles had become the focal point for the postmodern heteropolis and was in fact the model for the city of the future. This journey has taken us from the reassertion of space in critical social theory (Soja, 1989) to the thirdspace of Los Angeles and other real and imagined places (Soja, 1996; whatever else one may say about the contents, the subtitles give a good reading of the Los Angeles School). In between has been an ambitious and self-conscious effort to promote a research agenda to supplant the Chicago School of Urban Sociology with the Los Angeles School of Urban Studies; note that Scott and Soja's (1996) collection is titled *The City: Los Angeles and Urban Sociology at the End of the Twentieth Century* after Robert Park's earlier essay titled *The City: Suggestions for the Investigation of Human Behavior in the Urban Environment*, from the edited volume by Park, Burgess, and MacKenzie (1925) titled simply *The City*.

It is interesting that New York City has largely remained outside the general focus of urban study. As the nation's largest city and the focal point for business and commerce, as symbolized in both the rise and fall of the Twin Towers, New York has long provided us with a mosaic of social worlds comparable to that of Chicago, and today presents us with an ethnic diversity comparable to that of Los Angeles. In addition to long established Chinese, Italian, Jewish, African American, and Puerto Rican communities, the last several decades have brought many newer ethnic groups to the city. The result is increasingly visible communities of Dominicans (in Manhattan), Haitians and Jamaicans (in Brooklyn), and Asians of all sorts (in Queens). One can also find the Indian subcontinent in Staten Island, pockets of Albanians (in The Bronx) as well as continuing immigration of Middle Eastern Moslems who inexplicably mix with new groups of Jews in Orthodox communities (in Brooklyn). Perhaps because New York City seems less of a recognizable mosaic and more of a free form, almost splatter of ethnic locales that it is seldom thought of a "model" for other urban society. It is not that ethnicity and ethnic groups in New York City are not written about. There are many excellent works on the various individual ethnic groups that have made or are making their mark on Gotham's physical and social landscape, but few since Glazer and Moynihan's Beyond the Melting Pot: The Negroes, Puerto Ricans, Jews, Italians and Irish of New York City (1970) that has had a global scope. One that immediately comes to mind is Nancy Foner's From Ellis Island to JFK: New York's Two Great Waves of Immigration (2000), which attempts to make up for, so to speak, lost time.

We began this volume with the idea that while the development of ethnic communities in Los Angeles is certainly of interest for urban sociology, this is not the only area of the country where heteropolis can be observed and studied. Indeed, most cities across the country have experienced a pattern of growth similar to that of Los Angeles, and we have much to learn for studying the emergence of ethnic communities in other metropolitan areas. So, alongside the Los Angeles school, we felt it was incumbent that urban sociologists not confine themselves to the study of urban geography in Southern California, but to expand that perspective to include both established and emerging ethnic and racial communities in other metropolitan areas. The twelve articles presented in this volume represent both older and established ethnic and racial communities as well as new and emerging groups in New York City. These include Italian communities, African American, as well as newer Jewish, Caribbean, and Asian groups.

"Navigating Ethnic Vernacular Landscapes" by co-editor Jerome Krase is in a sense a spatial semiotic and visual challenge to a venerable sociological tradition of community study. The tradition begins when Robert Ezra Park and Ernest Burgess published their relatively primitive ecological research on Chicago describing "how" residential neighborhoods follow a distinct pattern. Since that time consecutive generations of urban sociologists have disagreed about "why" they are spatially distributed. This essay employs Visual Sociology techniques in a study of ethnicized vernacular urban landscapes to suggest how cultural identities of neighborhood residents are reflected on the streets. A visual approach, it is argued, can build a bridge between those disciplines focusing on metropolitan form and function. The discussion of often-competing models is illustrated by a small selection of ethnically iconic photographs taken in Brooklyn, New York. During the previous century the neighborhoods have been a "virtual Roman fountain of ethnic transitions." Notably, during that time over one third of the population of the borough has been foreign born. Classical American urban sociologists would many of the oldest and newest residents of Brooklyn such as Chinese, Italians, Jews, and Poles. However one would be hard pressed to find concentrations of Bangladeshis, Egyptians, and Koreans in the concentric circles of any early twentieth century American city.

Krase synthesizes ideas from the old and new urban sociology via the insights of John Brinckerhoff Jackson who brought attention to the value of understanding the ordinary in the built environment. Concretely, he argues that urban theoreticians and practitioners of all sorts can greatly benefit by a visual and semiotic approach to the urban environment to better comprehend the results of Census 2000. Since the 1960s there have been major real and imagined changes in the structure and appearances of America's metropolitan areas. Globalization brings with it new technologies, increased trade, concentration of economic control, a reduced welfare state, spatial integration of economic activities, and most important for this essay; movement of both capital, and people. De-industrialization, as well as the decline of the importance of ports and railroads, have drastically changed the structure and appearance of the city. Concomitant with this has been the spread of the "city" toward the fringes and suburbs. The ethnic flavors of the city are enhanced by new immigration increasing the diversity of residents. Large numbers of undocumented aliens have further enhanced the diversity of neighborhoods. Given the increasing complexity of our already overly complex metropolitan areas new methodological techniques such as visual sociology and theoretical perspectives such as spatial semiotics are a welcome addition to the repertoire of those who study the New York City scene.

In "Immigrant Global Neighborhoods in New York City" by Tarry Hum we are graphically shown that New York City's status as a majority "minority" city is reflected in many local neighborhoods that exemplify the racial and ethnic diversity of the urban landscape in the 21st century. It was part of a Ford Foundation study of immigrant global neighborhoods in New York, and introduces these neighborhoods via a review of demographic data that indicates various local transformations. The careful analysis of census data shows what might seem as paradoxical trends both toward diversity and segregation. The influx of Post-1965 immigrants has resulted in the creation of new, and in some cases expansion of older, multi-ethnic neighborhoods. Interestingly, these localities composed primarily of mixtures of Asians, Latinos, and non-Hispanic Whites, are largely absent of Blacks. One finds Blacks in neighborhoods comprised nearly exclusively of Blacks and Latinos. The global neighborhoods which are the focus of this study are Sunset Park in the borough of Brooklyn, and Richmond Hill, and Elmhurst in Queens. Hum uses these communities to introduce and illustrate several factors and perspectives which are important to the study of multi-ethnic immigrant settlements: (1) neighborhood definition; (2) neighborhood opportunity structures; (3) defining "communities of interests"; and (4) the role of local institutions in promoting prospects for a multiracial democracy.

The paper forcefully shows how New York City continues to be an immigrant city, where the proportion of foreign-born in the population is approaching that of the turn of the twentieth century. While old and new immigrants represent virtually the whole of the global spectrum residential segregation continues to be a feature of the urban landscape. For African Americans especially segregation has actually increased. Ironically Hum offers that the "racial balkanization of New York City, however, is tempered by the expansion of 'polyethnic' or 'global' neighborhoods." Such diverse neighborhoods can be found throughout much of the city but she notes that they are concentrated in the borough of Queens. In addition, she argues that the magnitude of ethnic diversity in these neighborhoods is great today than at any time in the past.

Hum illustrates the immigrant geography of New York City – new enclave formations, multi-racial, multi-ethnic neighbourhoods – by categorizing more than 2,200 census tracts into a neighborhood typology. The typology is defined by dominant race tracts and multi-racial tracts. The resulting spatial geography shows persistent settlement patterns and global neighborhoods. This paper argues that the notion of an immigrant global neighborhood as part of a typology of immigrant neighborhoods shows how they are mediating incorporation strategies and transforming the landscape of New York City.

In "The Muslim Chronopolis and Diasporic Temporality" Michel S Laguerre begins with two observations about the social integration of the Muslim week into mainstream civil time in New York City. On the one hand, Muslim immigrants engage in social practices that are regulated by civil society and that follow the rhythms of the civil week, inhabiting a diasporized, and Americanized Muslim temporality. On the other hand they continue to live in a temporal enclave or chronopolis connecting them to global Islam. This is possible because of an Islamic calendar that gives direction to believers daily, weekly, and annual activities. These social temporalities often intersect and crisscross each other. Therefore it is necessary to look at the Muslim week in American society to understand the mechanisms of the constitution and transglobalization of the American Muslim chronopolis.

In New York City, the Muslim week undergoes a transformation in order to accommodate to the constraints of the workplace, state regulations, as well as the local rhythms of the week. The Muslim week also allows for a locally distinct yet global temporal identity characterized by the cultural content of its global flows, influence of transnational networks, and the temporal rhythms. Laguerre examines the nature of these double identities here in terms of their internal restructuring and their relations with larger society. Muslim immigrants come from distinct cultural and national backgrounds. While some lived in Muslim states with an Islamic calendar and New York presents them for the first time with a need to adapt to a civil or Western calendar, others have already adapted in their country of origin. Even these latter immigrants, however most were able to engage freely in their weekly Friday communal prayers. In contrast, public and private organizations in New York City have not yet adjusted to the different social and temporal requirements of the immigrant Muslim week. This creates challenging constraints for both groups in their adjustment to the West.

The focus in this study is exclusively on the immigrant population from the Persian Gulf states, and not on Caribbean, African, or Afro-American Muslims. It concerns itself with these immigrants specifically because of the traditional emphasis they place on Friday congregational prayers. In countries, such as Saudi Arabia, Friday is the official day of rest. In others, such as Turkey, Sunday is the official day of rest because pressures to readjust or replace their national calendar with the Western calendar because of international trade requirements and interstate relations. Even though Sunday might be designated in their homeland as a day of rest, Friday continues to play a predominant role in their secular weekly activities because of the Koranic prescription of noon prayers at a mosque on that day. The Islamic week is distinguished from other weeks not simply by its distinct peak day but also because it forms a distinct "temporal domain." By its rhythm, cadence, and mode of organization, the Islamic week organizes everyday life. By promoting structure and order, life becomes more predictable. The analysis of the Muslim day and week thus calls for both an interpretation of their reconstitution in New York City, and an examination of how the temporality unique to this group fractures the geometry of the urban social system. Laguerre does this through an examination of the temporal niche expressed in the physical landscape which Muslims occupy in this immigrant and simultaneously modernist city.

Jeffrey Geiger's " 'The game behind the game': Spatial Politics and Spike Lee's He Got Game" begins his essay with the irony of two "two portentous events" of the year 1896; Edison's introduction of large-screen projection, which led to film viewing as a mass audience phenomenon and the *Plessy vs. Ferguson* decision giving federal imprimatur to "separate but equal" facilities for blacks and whites. Thus the American communal cinematic experience for the next six decades would be divided into black and white factions and also gave rise to black independent cinema. It also suggests that segregation is at the root of film viewing and production. Theaters were segregated in the South and also in cities such as Chicago and New York where separate entrances and seating areas for whites and blacks could be found well into the 1930s. Exclusionary Hollywood distribution practices underpinned the "race picture" business, and the films themselves codified segregated screen spaces, and encoded images with representations of racial division and dominance.

Geiger carefully examines issues related to segregated space and power in cinema, leading to a consideration of topographies of African American urban life in Spike Lee's 1998 film "He Got Game." He shows how Lee wove spatial metaphors into the narrative to make visible the ongoing, double-sided relationship between African Americans and the space of "America." Much of his references might be new to sociologists, but well worth reading. For example, in this essay we learn from Philosopher and film theorist Noël Carroll that the film metaphor gestures beyond itself, carrying signifying properties similar to verbal metaphors while relying on visual codes. These codes as "homospatiality," or the collapsing of separate objects or spaces into a single setting; "noncompossibility," or the bringing together of objects and images that are logically incompatible; and "intelligible correspondence," or an understanding between director and audience that the juxtaposition of dissimilar objects or spaces can generate new meanings. Film metaphors are a form of "shared recognition," dependent on the filmmaker's belief that his or her image has "heuristic value." In spatial metaphors, film metaphors politicize cinematic space because they draw attention to how both "actual" and represented spaces are socially produced and negotiated within a field of power relations. A good example of a spatial metaphor appears in *He Got Game*'s opening credits, in which Lee uses the game of basketball as an overarching trope connecting America's various discrete, racialized zones: the farm and the trailer park, the suburb and the ghetto. Geiger convincingly argues that Lee connects the experience of concrete space to the space of the imagination by forging visual and symbolic links between the prison and the university, the basketball court and the board room.

In "Being Racialized Ethnics: Second Generation West Indian Immigrants in NYC" Sherri-Ann P. Butterfield tackles the issue of "Blackness" which has long plagued American society. In the extensive social science literature it has been treated as a taken-for-granted, and only occasionally problematized. Her essay reports on in-depth interviews of second generation West Indian adults in New York City and examines how their own Blackness, both racially and ethnically is conceived by them. New York is an important urban context that almost mandates the creation of an ethnic identity for any population. The greater or lesser assimilation of second generation West Indians in discussed in relation to the socioeconomic status and gender of interviewees. The results show West Indians strongly identify with both their racial and ethnic identities. Butterfield strongly argues that this demands a reconceptualization of "Blackness." Her research also points to New York City as a space of cross-cultural integration. The city is a place where identity formation is strongly influenced by the presence of other immigrants, as well as their children. For example, the residential segregation of some NYC neighborhoods and residential integration of others places put native born and immigrant communities of color together. She also suggests that this phenomenon makes possible a "pan-immigrant" or "pan-ethnic" identity among many young city residents. The proximity and integration of various immigrant communities is fostering a new identity among the second generation. The complex identity construction of West Indians shown in this essay here problematizes how those who study immigration conceive of the process of assimilation. When referring to "assimilation," social scientists imagine that immigrants are merely being absorbed by the mainstream culture. Butterfield makes a strong case for New York's West Indians as following, if not creating, a new model. As a national cultural center for the country as well as home to millions of immigrants, New York City has a special impact on the development of ethnic identity within the second generation immigrant population. She calls for the continuation of in-depth research to discover how New York City, politics, roles, cultural dynamics, and personality types, contribute to the development of ethnic identity.

Most readers this volume about ethnicity in New York City when they see the author's name "Badillo" will expect to found some reference in the text to U.S. Congressman Herman Badillo. They will not be disappointed. Congressman Badillo is best known for his ethnically bruising loss to Abraham Beame in the Democratic mayoral primary in New York City in 1973. David A. Badillo in his sensitively analytic biographical essay "Titi Yeya's Memories: A Matriarch of the Puerto Rican Migration" relates that: "Yeya found herself on a steamer bound for New York with two eleven-year-old boys – her eldest son Jose Luis and nephew Herman, now her unofficially adopted *hijo de crianza* (foster son). Remarkably, her sister's boy would grow up to become a four-term U.S. Congressman."

We learn through the at times tortuous journey of Titya that for better and often for worse, female Puerto Rican migrants provided a wide range of options for their immediate and extended families. Often they were breadwinners and fundraisers for their kin and also cemented internal networks. They also were active and forceful outside of the immediate family and impacted community institutions as well. The tenacity and resourcefulness of Puerto Rican women often led to their becoming leaders in the community. Even though Badillo focuses on a single family during their intricate migration, he deftly places that family in the context of origin and destination. By doing so he offers to the reader a broader view of history across generations and places. This gives a rare insight into otherwise commonplace urban and social developments. The life of one person and her family also provides a critical point of reference from which to appreciate subsequent migrations of individuals and groups to New York City from the Hispanic Caribbean. Titi Yeya (the author's great aunt Aurelia), was born almost a century ago in Cayey, Puerto Rico. She left her homeland early in 1941 and lived for fifteen years mostly in New York City's Spanish Harlem (El Barrio). From there she moved to California, returned to Puerto Rico, and for the last few years has been living in a senior center in the Bronx. Her complex story reveals much about the immigrant and ethnic dimensions of the Puerto Rican saga. In an example of excellent sociology and biography her grand nephew demonstrates how "She refused to accept limitations imposed in her environment by hardship and death, and struggled long and hard for her own survival, as well as the regeneration of her family in a strange land." This essay could be a model for other social scientists to explore their own ethnic histories.

Even the most cursory look at the collection of essays in this volume would lead the casual reader to conclude that it offers an extremely varied array representing the diverse demographic composition of the Big Apple. The collection is also extremely diverse in its theoretical and methodological orientations as well ranging from the almost classic participant observations of Evrick Brown to the cutting edge visual analysis of Jeffrey Geiger. "The Decline of the Public Sphere: A Semiotic Analysis of the Rhetoric of Race in New York City" by Timothy Shortell is probably the most innovative and offers the most for future analysis of texts which chronicle the important discourses of New York City social, political, and cultural life.

He notes that Juergen Habermas' theory of the structural transformation of the public sphere has been a major platform from which theoretical debate has been launched during the latter half of the 20th century. For Habermas, as for others, the source of the decline in intelligent public discussion of collective interests can be found in the capitalistic production of a post-industrial consumer culture. Where at one time the public sphere was a location for rational-critical discursive activity, today conversation about public life is more of a commercialized spectator sport. It is therefore to be expected that corporate mass media have reduced the possibility of critical debate in the general public of pressing social issues, including race.

Shortell try to show how public discussions of race in New York City have changed. He does this via a comparison of nineteenth-century and contemporary discourse. The nineteenth-century texts are from *The Weekly Advocate* and *The Colored American*, which were black Abolitionist New York City newspapers between 1837 and 1841. This particular discourse both attacks slavery and calls for civil rights. Therefore it combines analysis of the violence of racism and the nature of racial inequality. A parallel to this discourse is found in 1998 newspaper articles dealing with contemporary racial issues from *New York Times*. The author then employs an innovative semiotic content coding strategy to describe the conceptual network and ideology of public discussions of race in New York City. It is this theoretically informed methodology that offers great potential for future analyses.

"Emergent African Immigrant Philanthropy in New York City" by Mojúbàolú Olúfúnké Okome, introduces us to the little researched area of African Philanthropic Traditions and African Immigrants. According to African traditional mores, a central requirement of being "a good person" is philanthropy. Therefore it should be expected that various forms of African philanthropy permeate the social, economic and political lives of African immigrants in New York City. Conceptually speaking some of the key, as well as sociologically interesting features of these practices are the informality of the institutions and their invisibility to outsiders.

Ironically, Okome notes the growing interest in United States foreign policy toward Africa which is the subject of much debate while at the same time the increasing presence of African immigrants is virtually ignored in policy advocacy circles. Globalization shapes the decision of Africans, as others, to emigrate and the location chosen for settlement. Philanthropic organizations help people face challenges in both the home country and country of recent settlement.

Most people expect that many African immigrant organizations are male dominant in leadership and decision making. However, the nature of African philanthropy is also affected by many other less known factors. Old stereotypes from Africa die hard, therefore unity across old, divisive national and ethnic boundaries is elusive in America. Elders are privileged for positions of authority and in these organizations there are attempts to build structures that perpetuate and favor distinct interests. Gender, class, religion, prestige, and ethnicity are some of the cross-cutting variables that delineate lines of power. These interests are ameliorated by attempts to persuade members that those few who control decision making within the group both understands and works actively to promote interests of the group at large. As might be expected, dissenters are punished by exile or other alienation from the group.

Okome describes some of the many forms of philanthropy among African immigrant communities. It exists in the form of mutual aid for friends, extended family, lineage, and fictive kin. Fictive kin are those who are not from an individual's ethnic group, or even from their country of origin. Philanthropy is also to be found in the form of kindness and generosity toward strangers. At the highest level philanthropy is expressed in the corporatization of community-based efforts to develop the human and material resources among African ethnic groups in New York City. The literature indicates numerous studies of African urbanization that indicate how newly urbanized Africans create hometown organizations that perform social and philanthropic functions. This assistance includes material and moral support in times of social celebration as well as crisis. Assistance is given for education, home construction, local infrastructure, and other development efforts. In New York City, the efforts of African immigrants closely follow the patterns described of newly urbanized Africans on the home continent. The patterns are so ubiquitous as to warrant a claim of their emergence from a philosophical orientation toward philanthropy in African society.

In "Relations between the Jewish and Caribbean American Communities in New York City: Perceptions Conflict and Cooperation" Holger Henke and J. A. George Irish explore the interesting history of conflict and cooperation between New York City's Caribbean-Americans and Jews. The authors warn that inter-group relations between these two complex ethnic groups should not be viewed simply as per usual "Black/Jewish relations" Because of the complexity of the topic, and to counter the usual over generalizations which plague such inter ethnic studies, they dive the article into two parts. The first of these sections is dedicated to an exploration of the historical trajectory of relations between the two groups largely by focusing on the Crown Heights district in Brooklyn. For those not familiar with Brooklyn geography, Crown Heights is nestled between two better know neighborhoods of Bedford-Stuyvesant to the north and Flatbush on the south.

Crown Heights is home to a variety of immigrants from the Caribbean. It is the center of settlement and organization for the Jewish Lubavitcher Hasidic community. Henke and Irish survey a wide range of historical material which shows that in the late 1960s and early 1970s, the peaceful coexistence between the two groups was increasingly tested by issues relating to community spaces and resources. The nadir for relations between the two groups came in 1991 with the "Crown Heights unrest," (some referred to it at the time as a riot and even a "pogrom") which shocked the city and this large urban neighborhood in the center of Brooklyn during several days of violence. It is in the second part of the paper that the authors attempt to demonstrate how local issues such as crime, and differential access to resources and political influence, as well as significant cultural differences continue to affect relations between the groups in the community. By looking at the dynamics of additional cultural factors they try to show how these often ecologically competitive ethnic groups manage to reduce conflict and restore more productive relationships.

Evrick Brown presents us with a fascinating and innovative "ground up" approach to the study of ethnic politics in "The Caribbean nation-state in Brooklyn Politics." The simple subtitle: "An Examination of The Una Clarke Major Owens Congressional Race" belies its complexity.

In 2002, New York City Councilwoman Una Clarke ran against the incumbent Congressman Major Owens, a man she once strongly supported, and thereby displayed a new stage of ethnic politics in the city. Brown argues that the substantial presence of Caribbean voters in Brooklyn challenged the hegemony of the essentially African American Democratic Party faction. Caribbean politicians and leaders no longer uncritically support African American politicians, and instead, have sought create a separate political space for themselves. They do this by exploiting their ties to island "home" in their appeals to Afro-Caribbeans for support. Brown intensively researches this hotly contest political campaign in Brooklyn between an African American incumbent and a Caribbean insurgent. The study also makes a contribution to the growing literature on transnationalism by illustrating how the cultural or social capital of immigrants' continuing bonds to their home countries while living abroad can be used politically. New York as a complex collection of immigrants and ethnic neighborhoods becomes clearer during political campaigns. One important aspect of Immigrants becoming "Ethnics" is their comprehension of and demand for their rights as naturalized citizens of the United States. They then enter into the political arena and challenge others for scant resources.

Brown points out that the prior ethnic political history of Brooklyn was primarily among white ethnics with blacks receiving minor patronage and holding political posts under the watchful eye of the former. The increasingly Black demographic profile of the Brooklyn landscape made it possible for Black politicians and political clubs to gain an independent foothold. As the West Indian population grew, especially post-1965, it became the African Americans' turn to defend their niche in the Kings County Democratic organization. Here, Brown notes the establishment of an African American political machine. The West Indian population in Brooklyn represents an attempt of another "Black" group to establish their claim to political efficacy based on ethnicity or ethnic identity, as opposed to or in addition to race.

There have been many more or less classical studies of Italian American neighborhoods. In the 1950s and 1960s few introductory sociology students could avoid at least a passage from the likes of Wiliam F. Whyte's Street Corner Society or Herb Gans' Urban Villagers. "Little Italy: Resisting the Asian Invasion, 1965–1995" by Philip F. Napoli represents a new generation of ethnic neighborhood studies. One of this volumes co-editors (Jerome Krase) has borrowed extensively from historical and literary sources to write on the subject of Little Italy as a semiotic of ethnicity. This paper shows how sociology can make a valuable contribute to the scholarly repertoire of an urban historian. Napoli begins his paper on New York's Little Italy with a quote of Pietro Di Donato, from his Depression Era novel "Christ in Concrete" which ends with "Sure I like it here. Why should I leave, I'm with my own people. Is there any place better?" One might expect then the conclusion that Little Italy never changes. He notes to the contrary that the answer for many Italian-Americans the answer was "Yes," to the point that slowly but surely actually, but not virtually, it has dissappeared. From a stereotypical ethnic enclave it is today a tourist destination. What Krase has called an Ethnic Theme Park, and an even larger part of which is Chinatown and a diverse Asian community. The area also offers wholesale, upscale and downscale retail, and even some remnants of its light industrial past. In short, Napoli argues "Manhattan's Little Italy is many things at present, but it is not an ethnic Italian community."

The transition however was neither a smooth nor an easy process. The paper traces the struggle by some Italians and Italian American organizations to not only remain in the community but to maintain its Italian identity and resist what Napoli refers to as the "Asian invasion" for over 30 years. It begins with an outline of the demographic changes which have occurred over the decades and then shifts gears to narrate the story of local Italians responding in various ways to the threat of ethnic and other changes in their defended neighborhood. He suggests what the Italian response to the "Asian invasion" may tell us about the nature of Italian ethnic identity in the late 20th century and concludes with brief remarks about the continuing transformation of the area.

In "Changing Racial Conceptualizations: Greek Americans in NYC" by Anna Karpathakis and Victor Roudometof we get an analysis of ethnicity and globalization from sociologists in both America and Greece. Although most approaches to globalization look at increasing economic, political, military and social interrelations between societies, here a variety of methods are used to trace the evolution of changing racial ideologies. Historical secondary sources, interviews of both immigrants and Greeks in Greece, and content analysis of poems, popular songs and electronic discussion groups are examined to see the changing nature of racial classifications.

While Castells (1996, 1998), and others have written on export of cultural products from core to semi-peripheral and peripheral economies, this exportation of cultural products and populations also occurs in reverse. Research on immigrant incorporation into American society in many ways ignores the history of the immigrants in their home society. Immigrants are seen as arriving without political, economic and social histories. The case of Greek immigrants shows this is clearly not the case. The politics of the Greek immigrants' home society and its history are important factors in how they acculturate in America and how they interpret uniquely American cultural constructions of race.

In this chapter, Karpathakis and Roudometof discuss the incorporation of American racial ideologies into the racial repertoires of Greek immigrants. Greek Americans create a unique national/racial framework which combine institutions and ideologies of home and host society. Immigrants arrive with national and racial identities and narratives that have their sources in Greek national and political life of the past few centuries. In the U.S., Greeks must construct a new set of group narratives forged out of complex interactions of the immigrants being citizens and members of two distinctive "imagined communities," interactions between Greece and the U.S. in cultural and political markets, and immigrants' attempts to remain faithful to their motherland while maximizing their group interests in the host country. These group narratives and identities occur through both formal and informal institutions. The authors conclude that it is in this form of a "transnational cultural/political" space that Greek immigrants combine elements of home society, political and national narratives, along with American racial conceptualizations to create a "potpourri" of group identities.

One striking feature of these studies is the variety of methodological perspectives that are brought to the study of ethnic and racial communities by urban sociologists. These range from the historical content analysis of ethnic and establishment press, film analysis, visual sociology, and participant observation and personal interviews. Indeed, no two of the articles in this volume use the same methodological techniques, attesting to both the variety and vitality of research in the field. This stands in contrast to the research often published in mainstream sociology journals, which most often present quantitative studies making use of survey data, the analysis of census data, and the like. These are complementary methodologies, and it may be useful to think that articles published in the other sources provide us with a general framework for observing trends and comparing urban areas, while the methodologies present in the following chapters provide us with substantive information about the goings-on of particular neighborhoods or ethnic communities within the city. They answer some questions that have been posed in earlier studies – providing us with detailed information about the origins of the Puerto Rican community and others, as well as an understanding of ethnic and racial conflict among Jews and African Americans.

The chapters also raise interesting questions. The study of the ethnic and immigrant press goes back to W. I. Thomas and Robert Park of the Chicago School, but there has been little follow through in subsequent urban or ethnic research. The information presented here is interesting in documenting a shift from public to private discourse – but also raises important questions. What if our comparison had been the African American press in the Abolitionist period and the African American press during the Civil Rights era? Or the present? Or if the comparison had been the major news media during the period? Is the change of discourse presented in the results here an artifact of the newspapers selected for study – or would similar change in discourse be found in a comparison of African American newspapers, or mainstream media, across comparable time periods? What if this methodology were applied to the ethnic press more generally – to the issues presented and discussed in the Italian, Jewish, or Chinese press in New York City?

CONCLUSION

Some chapters provide us with a snapshot (intentional) of ethnic community across the city. Others look closely at a particular place. Still others look across the whole ethnic landscape of the city. Neither individually nor as a whole collection do they form a complete picture. But perhaps because they are so eclectic maybe they form a challenge to urban sociology to exam not just macro level change in urban form and metropolitan space, but to apply other methodologies to better understand the increasingly complex, unfocused mosaic of social worlds in the American city.

REFERENCES

Foner, N. (2000). *From Ellis Island to JFK: New York's two great waves of immigration.* Yale University Press.

Glazer, N., & Moynihan, P. (1970). *Beyond the melting pot. The Negroes, Puerto Ricans, Jews, Italians and Irish of New York City.* Cambridge, MA: MIT Press.

Logan, J. R. (2003). *America's newcomers.* Albany, NY: University at Albany, Lewis Mumford Center for Comparative Urban and Regional Research.

Lollack, L. (2001). *The foreign-born population of the United States: March 2000*. Current Population Reports, P20–534, U.S. Census Bureau, Washington, DC.

Park, R. (1966 [1925]). The city: Suggestions for the investigation of human behavior in the urban environment. In: R. Park, E. Burgess & R. MacKenzie (Eds), *The City* (pp. 1–46). Chicago: University of Chicago Press.

Park, R., Burgess, E., & MacKenzie, R. (Eds) (1925). *The city*. Chicago: University of Chicago Press.

Scott, A. J., & Soja, E. W. (1996). *The city: Los Angeles and urban sociology at the end of the twentieth century*. Berkeley: University of California Press.

Soja, E. W. (1989). *Postmodern geographies: The reassertion of space in critical social theory*. London: Verso.

Soja, E. W. (1996). *Thirdspace: Journeys to Los Angeles and other real-and-imagined places*. Oxford: Blackwell.

Jerome Krase
Ray Hutchison
Editors

VISUALIZING ETHNIC VERNACULAR LANDSCAPES

Jerome Krase

Race and Ethnicity in New York City
Research in Urban Sociology, Volume 7, 1–24
Copyright © 2004 by Elsevier Ltd.
ISSN: 1047-0042/doi:10.1016/S1047-0042(04)07001-1

ABSTRACT

Ever since Robert Ezra Park and Ernest Burgess published their classic research on Chicago which described "how" residential neighborhoods follow a distinct ecological pattern, generations of urban practitioners and theoreticians have been arguing about "why" they are spatially distributed. This essay is designed to demonstrate the utility of Visual Sociology and the study of Vernacular Landscapes to document and analyze how the built environment reflects the changing cultural identities of neighborhood residents. It is strongly suggested that a visual approach can also help build a bridge between various theoretical and applied disciplines that focus on the form and function of the metropolis. While discussing some of these often-competing models, the text is illustrated by a selection of photographs taken in Brooklyn, New York whose neighborhoods over the past century have been a virtual Roman fountain of ethnic transitions. Although many of the oldest and newest residents of Brooklyn such as Chinese, Italians, Jews, and Poles would be familiar to Park and Burgess, others such as Bangladeshis, Egyptians, and Koreans would not. Ideas about Old and New cities from the "classical" to the "post-modern"; from Park and Burgess to Harvey and Lefebvre are also synthesized via the insights of J. B. Jackson.

INTRODUCTION

Urban theoreticians and practitioners of all sorts are anxiously awaiting the results of Census 2000, some to test their hypotheses about the city and others to use the new data in order to better plan for it. If recent past history is any indication, by the time the information is analyzed, many of the facts on the ground will contradict those in the book. Since the 1960s there have been major, real and imagined changes in the structure and appearances of America's metropolitan areas. Social scientists debate the role of markets and governments in accounting for these changes. The term "globalization" is often used to describe a combination of factors, changing values and norms that are spread across the world. These include new technologies, increased trade, concentration of economic control, a reduced welfare state, spatial integration of economic activities, and most important for this essay; movement of both capital, and people. Another term that has entered our Post-modern vocabulary is "de-industrialization," referring in general to the reduced importance of manufacturing, movement abroad of heavy industry, as well as the decline of historically important urban ports and railroad centers. Concomitant with this has been increased reliance on air, auto, and truck transportation resulting in the spread, perhaps even better – the "displacement," of the city toward the fringes and suburbs. The ethnic flavors of the city are accounted for by changes in American immigration laws that have made possible an increasing diversity of permanent and temporary immigrants, as residents of our cities. Large numbers of undocumented aliens have further enhanced the diversity of neighborhoods, and workforces, in recent decades.

In a simpler time, Ernest W. Burgess' Concentric Zone diagram from "The Growth of the City"[1] provided students of urban life with "The" semiotic for "The" City. Since then much "urban" research continued to be focused on the domains and denizens of the "Inner City" or other euphemisms for what Ernest W. Burgess called the "Zone of Transition." There one found roomers, hobos, addicts, poor folks, non-white minorities, and lower class immigrants who lived in real and symbolic places called the Ghetto, Slum, Black Belt, Chinatown, Underworld, Vice, and Little Sicily. At the turn of the century, tens of thousands of immigrants flooded Chicago and mobilization for WWI brought with it a large number of southern blacks. Urban Ecology, the study of the spatial distribution of human activity, developed as a way to make sense of what was for the period an amazingly complex ethnic and racial mosaic. Simply put, the Chicago School of Urban Sociology had borrowed an analogy from biology ecology in the principles of cooperation and competition for space and resources, to inadvertently create an icon for urban development.

Heuristically powerful notions such as "Natural Areas," and "Invasion and Succession" well served those who sought to understand racial segregation, as well as immigrant and ethnic enclaves. Increasingly, however, the accepted wisdom that the stability and change of the metropolis was merely "natural" as opposed to the consequence of the way that powerful people and institutions think and plan became contested. The discipline of Urban Ecology was seen by more radical analysts as too timid (e.g. "conservative") for honest analyses of White flight, Urban Blight, Redlining, not to mention simultaneous Gentrification and Dis-investment. [2] In my opinion, however, its basic descriptive principles continue today to have a great deal of value when contemporized by studious attention to more analytic notions such as "Circuits of Capital" and "Spatial Semiotics." Under these newer rubrics the same immigrant and ethnic enclaves are treated not as much as merely "natural " but nevertheless "inevitable." Today's major urban models and paradigms continue the sociological profession's tradition of place names such as the Los Angeles and New York City "Schools." One must ultimately agree that no concrete entity can adequately serve as an abstract concept. That being said, whether it is Ferdinand Toennies Eurocentrically using *Gemeinde*, or me, Brooklyn, as an "illustration," we must recognize the value of ideas that are grounded in empirical geographical realities and re-presented as images or semiotics.

A recent look at Chicago by Erick Howenstine is a literal case of *déjà vu* "Eighty years ago the ethnic mosaic of Chicago was defined primarily on the basis of first and second generation European groups settling in inner-city neighborhoods. Thirty years ago, a large population of first and second-generation Black internal migrants from the South changed the character of that mosaic. Today immigrant groups are again changing the mosaic, this time from Latin American and Asia. Today's ethnic mosaic has extended to suburban territory. Details of the specific settlement and segregation patterns, as shone in these analyses, continue to change. Nonetheless Chicago continues to be an ethnically diverse and also, to an important extent, a racially segregated urban area."[3] Note here the use of the visually meaningful term "mosaic," as opposed to neat concentric rings to enhance the factual description of demographic facts.

Compared to 1900, in 2000 the proportion of the total U.S. population that is foreign-born is not nearly as great. In contrast to the simpler times and spaces of the past, the changing uses of urban spaces today gives the appearance to some that newer immigrant settlements follow no pattern whatsoever. It is more likely, however that the patterns are simply not seen as such. Many of the most recent poor and working-class migrants to American cities are no longer found near the expected, stereotypical, places where jobs for newcomers were found in decades past because that "traditional" work is no longer done in those places. In addition, many of the historical areas of first settlement immigrant are concurrently being gentrified. Yet in order to find new immigrant and ethnic enclaves we still must take into account the same factors that have always been part of location formulas such as public transportation routes, proximity to work, rental rates, ethnic markets, and ethnic institutions.

Whether or not "globalization" "de-industrialization," "post-industrialism," and/or "post-Fordism" have produced what Ronald Van Kempen and Peter Marcuse considered a "New Spatial Order" for the "Global City." They cautioned that no uniform pattern can be expected as "The functional, social, and cultural divisions we expect to find is one of consistent and general tendencies expressed in widely varying contexts, along widely varying lines, with widely varying results."[4] And to those who are suggesting the decreasing value of the traditional "neighborhood" in the new city, they offer contemporary residential community forms in the "citadels of the rich," gentrified areas, middle-class suburbs, tenement areas, ethnic enclaves, and what is to them a "new type" of ghetto.[5]

In a related way, Robert A. Beauregard and Anne Haila note that Postmodern urbanists tend to ". . . portray the contemporary city as fragmented, partitioned, and precarious, and as a result, less legible that its modernist precursor." Discussing Modernist and Post Modernist, Fordist and Post-Fordist Cities they write that "No one would dispute that the city of the late 20th century differs spatially from the city of the early to mid-20th century. The multiple business centers, transformed waterfronts, gentrified neighborhoods, and hollowed-out zones of manufacturing distinguish the contemporary U.S. city from its precursors."[6] They conclude however that a distinctly "postmodern" city has not displaced the modern one despite a more complex patterning of old and new, and of continuing trends and new forces. Urban areas have always been changing in response to the entrance of "strangers." The difference today is the rapidity and variety of that change which produce different kinds of segregation and different logics of location. Especially important is the uneven spatial competition that lower class immigrants face with more privileged members of society. Gentrification of areas which once offered good-paying blue collar jobs, industrial loft conversions for artists, and coop and condo conversions of workingmen's houses create inner city neighborhoods where visible indications of ethnicity are merely a part of the local "ambiance."

For those who study the city there are two essential questions. The first is Descriptive: "Who or what is where in the city?" The second is Analytic: "How and why" they got there. The purely descriptive models of Classical Urban Ecology come from a biological analogy. In the city, equilibrium is expressed through the interaction of human nature with geographical and spatial factors producing "natural" areas. This view is seen by as ideologically conservative as others more to the left, see these same ecological zones as the result of "uneven development" or perhaps even planned cycles of decay and renewal. On a theoretical plane Sharon Zukin discusses two schools of thought about the urban environment. "One, identified with political economy, emphasizes investment shifts among different circuits of capital that transfer the ownership and uses of land from social class to another. Its basic terms are land, labor, and capital. The other school of thought, identified with the symbolic economy, focuses on the representations of social groups and visual means of excluding or including them in public and private spaces. From this view, the endless negotiation of cultural meanings in built forms – in buildings, streets, parks, interiors – contributes to the construction of social identities."[7] Zukin suggests using both to interpret landscapes of culture and power in the city.

Another tool for deciphering the complex metropolis is spatial semiotics, defined by Mark Gottdiener as "the study of culture which links symbols to objects."[8] A spatial semiotician would recognize that social and cultural meanings are attached to urban landscapes as well as to the people and activities observed on the scene. According to him the most basic concept for urban studies study is the *settlement space* which is both constructed and organized. Looking at an immigrant ethnic neighborhood in this way, as part of national and global systems, "It is built by people who have followed some meaningful plan for the purposes of containing economic, political, and cultural activities. Within it people organize their daily actions according to meaningful aspects of the constructed space."[9] Semiotic and sociospatial analysis makes it possible to see the most powerless of urban dwellers as a social "agent" in the local reproduction of regional, national, and global societal relations. In this regard, it is important to note that perceptions and valuations of residential neighborhood spaces, for example, may be significantly different for insiders as opposed to outsiders. For the casual passersby, foreign language shop signs are easily noticed, but understanding the meanings of the spaces they define requires sensitivity and understanding of the particular culture that creates, maintains, and uses the re-signified space.

Most of this work is framed in the terms of Henri Lefebvre's "Spatial Practices" as presented by David Harvey. Harvey recognizes that those who have the power to command and produce space are therefore able to reproduce and enhance their own power. It is within the parameters outlined by these practices that the local lives of ordinary urban dwellers take place. "*Material social practices* refer to the physical and material flows, transfers, and interactions that occur in and across space in such a way as to assure production and social reproduction." "*Representations of space* encompass all of the signs and significations, codes and knowledge, that allow such material practices to be talked about and understood, no matter whether in terms of everyday common sense or through the sometimes arcane jargon of the academic disciplines that deal with spatial practices." "*Spaces of representations* are social inventions that seek to generate new meanings of possibilities for spatial practices." *Accessibility and distanciation* speaks to the role of the "friction of distance" in human affairs. Distance is both a barrier to and a defense against human interaction. It imposes transaction costs upon any system of production and reproduction. "The *appropriation of space* examines the way in which space is used and occupied by individuals, classes, or other social groupings. Systematized and institutionalized appropriation may entail the production of territorially bounded forms of social solidarity." "The *domination of space* reflects how individuals or powerful groups dominate the organization and production of space so as to exercise a greater degree of control either over the friction of distance or over the manner in which space is appropriated by themselves or others."[10]

WHY VERNACULAR LANDSCAPE?

The study of the vernacular landscape lends itself to both the new and old urban sciences. As a sociologist, I must admit that one can't go further than John Brinckerhoff Jackson in appreciating what ". . . lies underneath below the symbols of permanent power expressed in the "Political Landscape."[11] His perceptive work neatly complements Sociology's interest in how and why groups are where they are in the city, and how space effects their social interactions and opportunities. According to Helen Lefkowitz Horowitz: "Jackson always asserted that to interpret landscapes accurately we must turn to the common places of ordinary people rather than to the rarefied designs of architects and planners . . .." "The side of him that recognized his own 'commonness' insisted the landscape shaped by the needs and tastes of average working people was more important than that created by architects and planners. In this vein, he argued that we should consider the houses and places of work of the poor as well as the rich, of those on the margin as well as those at the center. In essays that others have criticized as being too accepting of contemporary blight, Jackson insisted that we are not rejecting the common landscape but seek to understand and love it."[12]

Jackson noted that what people do in a particular physical territory and how they use objects therein are critical for understanding the space. Writing about gentrification, and the displacement of the activities of the poor from the streets and city spaces in 18th and 19th century England, he noted that "in brief, much of the traditional play, popular with working class citizens, located at the center of town where the players lived and worded, was driven out, either by the shortage of space or by police decisions to improve traffic circulation and promote order."[13] As to why the study of vernacular, as opposed to "polite," architecture has become more valuable for insight into social history he argued that since the 19th century, "Innumerable new forms have evolved, not only in our public existence – such as the factory, the shopping center, the gas station, and so on – but in our private lives as well."[14] Especially valuable for our purposes here, Jackson commented on the visual competition of commercial streets that he believed represented "a new and valid form of what can be called commercial vernacular."[15] In the same way Dolores Hayden recognized the potential contribution of immigrant and ethnic vernacular urban landscapes for urban planners in helping to make city life more livable, equitable and at the same time visually interesting.[16]

Harvey is in synch with Jackson, and Hayden, when he writes that: "Different classes construct their sense of territory and community in radically different ways. This elemental fact is often overlooked by those theorists who presume a priori that there is some ideal-typical and universal tendency for all human beings to construct a human community of roughly similar sort, no matter what the political or economic circumstances."[17] For those lacking power (especially "low-income populations") "the main way to dominate space is through continuous appropriation. Exchange values are scarce, and so the pursuit of use values for daily survival is central to social action. This means frequent material and interpersonal transactions and the formation of very small-scale communities. Within the community space, use values get shared through some mix of mutual aid and mutual predation, creating tight but often highly conflictual interpersonal social bonding in both private and public spaces. The result is an often intense attachment to place and 'turf' and an exact sense of boundaries because it is only through active appropriation that control over space is assured."[18]

For Puerto Rican residents of New York City, folklorist Joseph Sciorra provides a radical framework for the vernacular. "It is within this imposed economic, political and social marginality that poor people of color struggle to change the existing conditions in with they live by creating spaces of their own design that serve as locations of resistance to a system of inequity and domination."[19] In the South Bronx, East Harlem, and the Lower East Side they ". . . clear the detritus of urban decay to cultivate bountiful gardens and construct wood-frame structures typical of the Caribbean. These transformed sites serve as shelter for the homeless, social clubs, block associations, cultural centers, summer retreats and entrepreneurial ventures. The cultural production of vernacular horticulture and architecture create local landscapes of empowerment that serve as centers of community action where people engage in modes of expressivity that are alternatives to those imposed from above by the dominant culture. In turn these concerted actions pose a direct challenge to official notions pertaining to the status of public land and its future use. These vernacular forms are united temporally and spatially with the historic dispossession of laboring people by the forces of a global capitalist economy."[20] My own more radical approach recognizes the power of ordinary people to change the meaning of spaces and places merely by being in them.

VISUAL SOCIOLOGY

Anthony D. King[21] speaks of cities as "text" to be read. Ethnic Vernacular Landscapes are crucial, yet often ignored parts of that text. In basic agreement, Zukin noted the emphasis and interest by urbanists has been on the geographic battles over access and representations of the urban center. "Visual artifacts of material culture and political economy thus reinforce – or comment on – social structure. By making social rules 'legible' they represent the city."[22] As a sign of decline for example, "In the long run vacant and undervalued space is bound to recede into the vernacular landscapes of the powerless and replaced by a new landscape of power."[23] "In Henri Lefebvre's framework, New York is an example of abstract space: simultaneously homogeneous and fragmented, subordinated to the flows and networks of world markets, and divided into units of exchange by real estate developers."[24] "In this enigmatic text immigrant shopping strips sometimes fare better than Madison Avenue and combative ethnic groups maintain uneasy coexistence in Brooklyn neighborhoods."[25]

Manuel Castells provides us with another view of how real and imagined urban spaces are used, contested, and transformed by different social groups. For him power is information, and networks of information or "Spaces of Flows" supercede "Spaces of Places." Along with this comes the tribalization of local communities. As local identities lose meaning, place based societies and cultures (cities, neighborhoods) also lose power. Castells proposes that this momentum toward the total disempowerment of urban dwellers can be reversed by the reconstruction of place-based meaning via social and spatial projects at cultural, economic, and political levels. Territorially defined ethnic groups, for example, can preserve their identities and build on their historical roots by the "symbolic marking of places," preservation of "symbols of recognition," and the "expression of collective memory in actual practices of communication."[26]

Visual attention to Vernacular Landscapes allows us to read conflict, competition, and dominance at a level not usually analyzed. Just think of how more useful Lefebvre's notions of "accessibility" and "distanciation" become when we visualize discrimination in local housing markets. How better to explain ethnic or class-based neighborhoods than when Harvey writes: "Successful control presumes a power to exclude unwanted elements. Fine-tuned ethnic, religious, racial, and status discriminations are frequently called into play within such a process of community construction."[27] Seeing other productions of Symbolic Capital, defined by Bourdieu as "The collection of luxury goods attesting to the taste and distinction of the owner,"[28] might help us to understand the gentrification of immigrant ethnic enclaves during a later phase in the second circuit of capital when they become shabbily chic "in" places to live.

WHAT IS VISUAL SOCIOLOGY?

Jon Prosser informs us that: "Over the last three decades qualitative researchers have given serious thought to using images with words to enhance understanding of the human condition. They encompass a wide range of forms including films, photographs, drawings, cartoons, graffiti, maps, diagrams, signs and symbols. Taken cumulatively images are signifiers of a culture; taken individually they are artefacts that provide us with very particular information about our existence. Images provide researchers with a different order of data, and, more importantly, an alternative to the way we have perceived data in the past."[29] John Grady adds that Visual Sociology is an organized attempt to investigate "how sight and vision helps construct social organization and meaning and how images and imagery can both inform and be used to manage social relations." Most valuable for us in studying vernacular urban landscapes is "how the techniques of producing

Fig. 1. Orthodox Jewish Balcony.

and decoding images can be used to empirically investigate social organization, cultural meaning and psychological processes."[30] In addition, Jon Rieger noted that among its many other advantages "Photography is well-suited to the study of social change because of its capacity to record a scene with far greater speed and completeness than could ever be accomplished by a human observer taking notes."[31]

Given that rapidly changing metropolitan landscapes are often the venues for sociological reconnaissance of globalization and de-industrialization, Visual Sociology can be a valuable adjunct to "normal" urban research and reportage. For example, we can use photographic surveys in comparison with historic photographic archives to see and record how differing constructions of space and spatial practices the landscape of new immigrants transform the city. We can photograph, film, or video ethnic enclaves to both document and illustrate how particular spaces are changed by their new occupants. Of special interest might be the ways by which public areas are used. Visual methods make it easier to examine new construction, as well as the alterations of existing spaces (Figs 1 and 2).

Fig. 2. West Indian Stone Work.

The power of the visual is clearly demonstrated by Steven A Camarota. Noting stories of immigrant businesses revitalizing neighborhoods are a staple of local news coverage used by immigration advocates to show "... that immigrants infuse the country with an entrepreneurial spirit unmatched by natives." However data show that immigrants are not more likely to be self-employed than natives. People are more likely to encounter immigrant entrepreneurs than immigrant workers. "The immigrant restaurant owner who greets customers is much more likely to be remembered than are the immigrant cooks and dishwashers, whom the patron never sees." And, "most Americans have much more personal contact in their

Fig. 3. Chinese New Year.

daily lives with self-employed immigrant street vendors or kiosk operators than with immigrant farm labors or construction workers. Since most people make generalizations based on their own experience, it is not surprising that they see immigrants as particularly entrepreneurial."[32]

As an aside to ethnic impressions created by commercial streets in immigrant neighborhoods, I note that many "Indian" restaurants in New York City are operated by Bangladeshis, as "Japanese" restaurants are run by Koreans, and "Mexican" eateries by other-than-Mexicans. In addition to the obvious décor and menu, the ethnic authenticity of the establishment rests on the visual competency of the patron *vis-à-vis* the staff. There is of course a special relevance of race (and racism) for the visualized spatial structure of cities – For most Americans, Blackness, Latinoness, Asianess, are generalized visual values that are partial explanations for why some areas look more "dangerous," "inviting," and/or at least "exotic" (Fig. 3).

BROOKLYN AND THE WORLD

With a population of almost two and a half million people, Brooklyn is a huge social laboratory. It has always been a city of immigrants. During the 20th century Brooklyn, almost a third of its residents have been foreign-born. Most dramatic, and visible, and are the changes in racial composition of the population over the most recent decades. Since 1940, the non-Hispanic Black population in Brooklyn has grown from slightly over one-hundred-thousand to almost eight-hundred-thousand persons; or from 4% of the borough's total population to 35%. In broader racial terms, Brooklyn has gone from having a 96% white non-Hispanic majority to having a 40.1% white non-Hispanic minority. Along with these basic demographic changes have been significant shifts in immigration trends, especially in the last two recent decades, which have created an almost bewildering socio-cultural panorama.

As might be expected, immigrant and racial residential transitions are not uniform across the borough. In some sections of Brooklyn more than half of the population is foreign-born. Residential and commercial segregation by ethnic, racial, and/or religious groupings is common. Some neighborhoods are virtually all-white; others all-black. Brooklyn's black population is large enough for it to be further segregated by nativity. In the borough one can find a variety of Afro-Caribbean as well as Afro-American neighborhoods. The greatest proportional increase, and most "visible," has been the more than doubling of the "Asian" population. If we were able to include the estimates of the numbers of "undocumented" it might have trebled or even quadruped. Although the Chinese, and Bangladeshis have produced the most striking changes, there is also a multiplication of Latinos on top of their already impressive base populations. Within the span of a decade large areas have taken on distinct new ethnic characters. The ethnic dimension was visible long before the publication of Census 2000 announces the spectacular transformation to those who have not

Fig. 4. Russian Brighton Beach.

Fig. 5. Lech Welesa Square.

already witnessed it. As a paean to the New Urbanists, I note that the demographic shifts do not follow the "usual" historical patterns; slowly moving from the downtown center city outward and in their wake creating zones of transition. New immigrants appear to settle and move to specific parts of the borough, defying the Classical Ecology of place. In some cases immigrant communities leap frog each other as if directed by unseen, but understandable, forces. An important case in point was the "sudden" emergence of a Russian enclave in Brighton Beach. Since 1940 minority groups moved southward in Brooklyn, filling in the housing vacuum left by exiting (sometimes fleeing) white European middle-class families. A half-century old densely over-built residential area, Brighton Beach had been projected by housing experts to become a low-income black and Hispanic community (Fig. 4).

It would be erroneous to assume that the ethnic transformation of Brooklyn's urban landscape is essentially the consequence of more or less radical changes in immigration law, international labor migrations, or simply international transportation and communication technologies. The Pre- and Post-Duvalier chaos in Haiti, Civil Wars in Central America and West Africa, the Rescue of Soviet Jews and the collapse of the Soviet Union, the Polish Solidarity Movement, and the change-over of Hong Kong from British to People' Republic sovereignty are just some of the global events which have helped fill once residentially marginal spaces (Fig. 5).

VISUALIZING THE "NOT SO NEW" SPATIAL ORDER IN BROOKLYN

Global political and economic restructuring has resulted in increasing and diversifying forms of labor and capital mobility. In response, Curtis C. Roseman, Hans Dieter Laux, and Guenter Thieme have identified five general types of major migration systems that help to understand the emergence of "EthniCities": internal migration; regional international migration; global migration; illegal migration; and refugee migration all of which can be "seen" or are "legible" in Brooklyn (1996, p. 33).[33] Although Marcuse and van Kamp saw no single new spatial order for what they term the "Globalized City" they noted some varied patterns and common trends which also might inform our discussion here: strengthened structural spatial division among quarters of the city; quarters of those excluded from the globalizing economy; increasing walling among the quarters; increased totalization of life within each quarter; and continuing formation of immigrant enclaves of lower-paid workers both within and outside the global economy.[34]

In addition, John Logan argued that the impact of the de-industrialization, global financial, transnational linkages, and service industries of the 1970s and 1980s on New York's occupational structure has been "minor" and that what is seen today is substantially an outgrowth of old patterns. His central thesis is that "...key features of inequality in New York are traceable not so much to the city's new function in the world economy as to the continuing and expanding function as a receptor of peoples."[35] As to Residential Segregation, Logan compared the present to 1920 and finds much higher levels of segregation between Europeans and non-Europeans, and Blacks from whites. Separation between Puerto Ricans and whites is still about the same. In addition, Afro-Caribbean's and Dominicans even more highly segregated from whites than either Blacks or Puerto Ricans. Interestingly, Asian segregation from whites is the least. Minorities are also highly segregated form each other. "These unique identities of these national origin ethnic groups are clearly preserved and reflected in urban space. These results taken together undercut the viability of interpreting New York along a simple white-non-white dimension."[36]

There are many parts of Brooklyn which belie any "simple dimension." One of the best is Kensington a neighborhood shared most remarkably by Moslems, and Orthodox Jews, Middle Easterners, Bangladeshis, Russians, and residual European "white ethnics." There within walking distance of each other can be see mosques, synagogues, shuls, mikvahs, male-only Sweet Shops, as well as Halal and Kosher butcher shops. The competition for dominance of the area is demonstrated in the constantly changing panorama of national colors, flags, foreign language signs, and religious symbols along the main commercial strip of the neighborhood. Another contested marketplace is the busy intersection of Flatbush and Church Avenues, which centuries ago, was the center of the Dutch town of Flatbush. Today it is a busily diverse Afro-American and Afro-Caribbean "downtown" shopping center replete with car and van services competing for passengers, and a myriad of colorful street vendors surrounded by jostling, bargaining patrons.

Some semiotics are obvious, while other signs are much more cryptic. In the center of Brooklyn's new Chinatown is a "Lute Fisk" sign in a run-down storefront window. It is one of the last traces of "Scandinavian" Bay Ridge. Nearby, on the border of Borough Park, an international center for Orthodox Jewry, one comes across a *Agencja* sign in a corner office window which recruits the Polish women who are "preferred" for Orthodox Jewish household work. At busy intersections on the edges of declining industrial areas in Brooklyn one can easily spot the ethnically segregated informal male labor markets – Bangladeshis here, Poles there, and Mexicans in yet another place. Well-developed ethnic neighborhoods also have their "own" car services – Acapulco, Carmel, and

Fig. 6. Lute Fisk.

Fig. 7. Western Union Sign.

Tel Aviv are a few more or less obvious examples. Finally, in most enclaves one finds at least one local shipping, phone, and wire-services business, for sending goods, messages, and of course remittances to families "back home." The language of the storefront sign is a general clue, and the specially advertised destinations a more specific indicator of places of origin for community residents (Figs. 6 and 7).

Ethnic enclaves are products as well as sources of both social and cultural capital. When immigrants alter the territory allowed to them, they simultaneously become part of the transformed urban landscape. The images they create eventually come to represent them and in the process they lose their autonomy. In some cases, the enclave comes to symbolize its imagined inhabitants and is also commodified. For example for the delight of tourists, the expropriated cultural capital of Caribbeans, and Italians, are turned into "Ethnic Theme Parks"[37] like the West Indian Day Carnival Parade in Crown Heights, and a *festa* in Bensonhurst's Little Italy. Visual study can show how what I have termed "Traces of Home"[38] and Lefebvre's "material spatial practices," are transformed via "representations of space" into "spaces of representation" (Fig. 8).

Fig. 8. Festa on 18th Avenue.

SUMMARY

Theoreticians and practitioners in the field of urban sociology are faced with a wide range of apparently competing theories and methods for describing and analyzing the post-modern metropolitan urban scene. Because the main focus in urban studies is "space," explaining how these actual and virtual spaces are used, contested, and transformed by different social groups is a crucial task. All the "urban" disciplines use visual approaches more or less explicitly whether through mapping, architectural rendering, photographic surveys, or land use and building condition surveys. In architecture and planning the visual has always been important in documentation, presentation, research and teaching. Historical photographic archives are used in the processes of Historical Landmark research, restoration, and preservation. "Windshield" surveys, conducted with eyes, cameras, and camcorders have a long tradition in urban studies.

In most cases visual techniques are used in qualitative, or descriptive studies. It can be argued that generalizations can also be made from visual surveys and employed in hypothesis testing. The simplest types of analytic studies would be longitudinal studies of physical changes as a consequence of specified variables. In any case the method used and the link between the evidence presented in "before and after" photographs for example would have to be quite explicit. At the least, as a purely qualitative method, such research ought to produce delightful insights even if of limited generalizability. My own procedure has been to treat observations and photographs as I do other information, such as interviews, or demographic data which are specific to areas, neighborhoods, streets, organizational boundaries, and census tracts. I should note here that my snap shots attempt to be as close as I can get to what an ordinary person might see as they traverse a space. They are not attempts at artist representation, but are intended to document visual surveys.

In addition to the general utility of this visual approach as, there are, I believe, distinct advantages of documented visual surveys for social research, urban planning, as well as informing policy makers. Findings from visual surveys can differ significantly from census or other published data. In addition to the general enumeration taking place only every ten years, Census and other data may not be as up to date as needed when dealing with ethnically, racially, or culturally sensitive issues. Much published data tend also not to be specific to the smaller pieces of territory that one might study such as a single intersection or cluster of buildings. As one moves to the block level in Census data, for example, the categories become less meaningful. Also official immigration data does not accurately show, or locate, the undocumented, most data is reported by Zip Code for registration of resident aliens. In my experience the visible presence of the undocumented is considerable in certain areas, as are the homeless, and other "statistically invisible" populations.

We can add to this the simple observations of illegal business and other activities that can be made in these same places, and which contradict official portraits.

Finally, in some cases seeing is the only way of knowing. Ethnic groups can be quite concentrated in small "pockets" but because of the geography of census, or other maps, the numbers can be shared between two or more units. In a related vein, on the basis of published data and casual observation, substantial residential concentrations of ethnic groups can be missed. It is common for people to falsely assume the ethnic character of a neighborhood by reading the symbolic environment of its commercial streets. Such was the case of Brooklyn's Eight Avenue in Sunset Park. Even though Chinese dominated the residential scene for at least a decade it became a virtual "Chinatown" only after the stores on the commercial strip announced their hegemony. Ironically, whereas at first the Chinese were invisible in Sunset Park, other Asians (Burmese, Cambodian, Korean, Laotian Pakistani, Turkish, and Vietnamese) who share some of the territory with them now merely blend into the background. Similarly, in 2000 there were well over a half a million Latinos in Brooklyn. Seeing "differences" among Spanish-speaking people from let us say Mexico and The Dominican Republic in the barrios they share, can be as easy as deciphering Productos Mexicanos from Productos Dominicanos. Recognizing the national flags, cultural emblems, and religious effigies such as those of La Vergine de Guadalupe are more challenging. Most difficult is noting the variations of native dress worn by the newest arrivals to the neighborhood.

NOTES

1. Ernest Burgess, "The Growth of the City," in *The City*. Park, Robert E. Ernest W. Burgess, and Roderick D. McKenzie, eds. (Chicago: University of Chicago Press, 1925), 114–123.

2. Joe R. Feagin, *The New Urban Paradigm: Critical Perspectives on the City* (Lanham, Maryland: Rowman and Littlefield, 1998), 19.

3. Erick Howenstine, "Ethnic Change in Chicago," in *EthniCity: Geographic Perspectives on Ethnic Change in Modern Cities*, eds. Curtis C. Roseman, Hans Dieter Laux, and Guenter Thieme, (Lanham, Maryland: Rowman and Littlefield, 1996), 47.

4. Ronald Van Kempen and Peter Marcuse, eds. "The Changing Spatial Order in Cities," Vol. 41. No 3. *American Behavioral Scientist*, November/December, (1997), 293.

5. Van Kempen and Marcuse, 4.

6. Robert A. Beauregard and Anne Haila, "The Unavoidable Continuities of the City," in Marcuse and Van Kempen, (2000), 23.

7. Sharon Zukin, "Space and Symbols in an Age of Decline," in *Re-Presenting the City: Ethnicity, Capital and Culture in the Twenty-First Century Metropolis*, ed. Anthony D. King, (London: Macmillan, 1996), 43.

8. Mark Gottdiener, *The New Urban Sociology* (New York: McGraw—Hill, 1994), 15–16.

9. Gottdiener, 16.

10. Henri, Lefebvre, *The Production of Space* (Oxford: Blackwell, 1991), 261–64.

11. John Brinckerhoff Jackson, *Discovering the Vernacular Landscape* (New Haven: Yale University Press, 1984), 6.

12. Helen Lefkowitz Horowitz, ed., *Landscape in Sight: Looking at America/John Brinckerhoff Jackson* (New Haven: Yale University Press, 1997), xxx–xxxi.

13. Jackson, 11.

14. Jackson, 118–119.

15. Jackson, 246.

16. Dolores Hayden, "The Potential of Ethnic Places for Urban Landscapes," *Places* Vol. 7, no. 1 (1991), 17.

17. David Harvey, *The Urban Experience* (Baltimore: John Hopkins University Press, 1989), 265.

18. Harvey, 265–266.

19. Joseph Sciorra, "Return to the Future; Puerto Rican Vernacular Architecture in New York City," in King (1996), 61.

20. Sciorra, 61–62.

21. Anthony D. King, ed., *Re-Presenting the City: Ethnicity, Capital and Culture in the Twenty-First Century Metropolis* (London: Macmillan, 1996).

22. Zukin, 44.

23. Zukin, 49.

24. Zukin, 50.

25. Zukin, 50.

26. Manuel Castells, *The Informational City* (Oxford: Blackwell, 1989) and Manuel Castells. "Conclusion: The Reconstruction of Social Meaning in the Space of Flows," in *The City Reader* eds. Richard T. LeGates and Frederic Stout, 494–98. London: Routledge, 1996.

27. Harvey, 266.

28. Pierre Bourdieu, *Outline of a Theory of Practice* (New York: Cambridge University Press: 1977), 188.

29. Jon Prosser, ed. *Image-based Research: A Sourcebook for Qualitative Researchers*, (London: Falmer Press, 1998), 1.

30. John Grady, "The Scope of Visual Sociology." *Visual Sociology* Volume 11, Number 2 (Winter) 1996, 14.

31. John H. Rieger, "Photographing Social Change," *Visual Sociology*. Volume 11, Number 1 (1996), 6.

32. Steven A. Camarota, "Reconsidering Immigrant Entrepreneurship: An Examination of Self-Employment Among Natives and the Foreign-Born." January 2000, ISBN 1–881290–05–0 < http://www//cis.org.

33. Curtis C. Roseman,, Hans Dieter Laux, and Guenter Thieme, eds. *EthniCity: Geographic Perspectives on Ethnic Change in Modern Cities* (Lanham, Maryland: Rowman and Littlefield, 1996), xviii.

34. Peter Marcuse and Ronald Van Kempen, eds. *Globalizing Cities: A New Spatial Order?* (Oxford; Blackwell, 2000), 271.

35. John R. Logan, "Still a Global City: The Racial and Ethnic Segmentation of New York," in *Globalizing Cities: New Spatial Order?*, eds. Peter Marcuse and Ronald Van Kempen, (Oxford: Blackwell, 2000), 159–160.

36. Logan, 178.

37. Jerome Krase, "The Spatial Semiotics of Little Italies and Italian Americans," in *Industry, Technology, Labor and the Italian American Communities*, eds. Mario Aste, et al. (Staten Island, New York: American Italian Historical Association, 1997), 98–127.

38. Jerome Krase, "Traces of Home," *Places: A Quarterly Journal of Environmental Design* Vol. 8, No.4 (1993): 46–55.

ACKNOWLEDGMENTS

Reproduced with permission of the Journal of Architectural and Planning Research from the 2002 volume (i.e. 19n4). Published by Locke Science Publishing Co. Inc.

REFERENCES

Beauregard, R. A., & Haila, A. (2000). The unavoidable continuities of the city. In: P. Marcuse & R. Van Kempen (Eds), *Globalizing Cities: A New Spatial Order?* (pp. 22–36). Oxford: Blackwell.

Bourdieu, P. (1977). *Outline of a theory of practice*. New York: Cambridge University Press.

Burgess, E. (1925). The growth of the city. In: R. E. Park, E. W. Burgess & R. D. McKenzie (Eds), *The City* (pp. 114–123). Chicago: University of Chicago Press.

Camarota, S. A. (2000). Reconsidering immigrant entrepreneurship: An examination of self-employment among natives and the foreign-born. January, ISBN 1–881290–05–0 <http://www//cis.org.

Castells, M. (1989). *The informational city*. Oxford: Blackwell.

Castells, M. (1996). Conclusion: The reconstruction of social meaning in the space of flows. In. R. T. LeGates & F. Stout (Eds), *The City Reader* (pp. 494–498). London: Routledge.

Feagin, J. R. (1998). *The new urban paradigm: Critical perspectives on the city*. Lanham, Maryland: Rowman and Littlefield.

Gottdiener, M. (1994). *The new urban sociology*. New York: McGraw–Hill.

Grady, J. (1996). The scope of visual sociology. *Visual Sociology, 11*(2), 10–24.

Harvey, D. (1989). *The urban experience*. Baltimore: John Hopkins University Press.

Hayden, D. (1991). The potential of ethnic places for urban landscapes. *Places, 7*(1), 11–17.

Horowitz, H. L. (Ed.) (1997). *Landscape in sight: Looking at America/John Brinckerhoff Jackson*. New Haven: Yale University Press.

Howenstine, E. (1996). Ethnic change in Chicago. In: C. C. Roseman, H. D. Laux & G. Thieme (Eds), *EthniCity: Geographic Perspectives on Ethnic Change in Modern Cities* (pp. 31–47). Lanham, MD: Rowman and Littlefield.

Jackson, J. B. (1984). *Discovering the vernacular landscape*. New Haven: Yale University Press.

King, A. D. (Ed.) (1996). *Re-presenting the city: Ethnicity, capital and culture in the twenty-first century metropolis*. London: Macmillan.

Krase, J. (1993). Traces of home. *Places: A Quarterly Journal of Environmental Design, 8*(4), 46–55.

Krase, J. (1997). The spatial semiotics of little Italies and Italian Americans. In: M. Aste et al. (Eds), *Industry, Technology, Labor and the Italian American Communities* (pp. 98–127). Staten Island, New York: American Italian Historical Association.

Lefebvre, H. (1991). *The production of space*. Oxford: Blackwell.

Logan, J. R. (2000). Still a global city: The racial and ethnic segmentation of New York. In: P. Marcuse & R. Van Kempen (Eds), *Globalizing Cities: New Spatial Order?* (pp. 158–185). Oxford: Blackwell.

Marcuse, P., & Van Kempen, R. (Eds) (2000). *Globalizing cities: A new spatial order?* Oxford; Blackwell.

Park, R. E., Burgess, E. W., & McKenzie, R. D. (Eds) (1925). *The city.* Chicago: University of Chicago Press.

Prosser, J. (Ed.) (1998). *Image-based research: A sourcebook for qualitative researchers.* London: Falmer Press.

Rieger, J. H. (1996). Photographing social change. *Visual Sociology, 11*(1), 5–49.

Roseman, C. C., Laux, H. D., & Thieme, G. (Eds) (1996). *EthniCity: Geographic perspectives on ethnic change in modern cities.* Lanham, MD: Rowman and Littlefield.

Sciorra, J. (1996). Return to the future; Puerto Rican vernacular architecture in New York City. In: A. D. King (Ed.), *Re-Presenting the City: Ethnicity, Capital and Culture in the Twenty-First Century Metropolis* (pp. 60–92). London: Macmillan.

Sharon, Z. (1996). Space and symbols in an age of decline. In: A. D. King (Ed.), *Re-Presenting the City: Ethnicity, Capital and Culture in the Twenty-First Century Metropolis* (pp. 43–59). London: Macmillan.

Van Kempen, R., & Marcuse, P. (Eds) (1997). The changing spatial order in cities. *American Behavioral Scientist, 41*(3).

IMMIGRANT GLOBAL
NEIGHBORHOODS IN NEW YORK CITY

Tarry Hum

INTRODUCTION

New York City's status as a majority "minority" city is reflected in many local neighborhoods that exemplify the racial and ethnic diversity of the urban landscape in the 21st century. In this quintessential immigrant city, the relative share of foreign-born has reached levels not seen since the historic immigrant wave at the turn of the last century (Foner, 2000; Scott, 2002). While "all the nations under

Race and Ethnicity in New York City
Research in Urban Sociology, Volume 7, 25–55
Copyright © 2004 by Elsevier Ltd.
ISSN: 1047-0042/doi:10.1016/S1047-0042(04)07002-3

heaven" are represented among old and new New Yorkers, researchers find that patterns of residential segregation persist and in fact, have worsened especially for African Americans (Beveridge, 2001; Logan, 2001). The racial balkanization of New York City, however, is tempered by the expansion of "polyethnic" or "global" neighborhoods. These racially and ethnically diverse neighborhoods are found throughout New York City but their concentration in the borough of Queens is notable. Moreover, the magnitude of ethnic diversity in these neighborhoods has "no parallel in previous waves of immigration" (Foner, 2000, p. 58).

Spatially defined neighborhoods remain central to shaping local opportunity structures, resident life chances, and quality of daily lives (Galster et al., 1999; Wilson, 1987). For immigrants, neighborhoods serve a critical role in shaping their "context of reception" (Portes & Rumbaut, 1990). Fundamental national and regional shifts to a post-industrial, service-based economy contributes to a social and economic context that presents distinct opportunities and challenges that differentiate contemporary and historic periods of mass immigration. The local expressions of these demographic and economic restructurings are evident on the neighborhood level.

While historic ethnic neighborhoods remain central ports of entry, the immigrant geography of New York City includes new enclave formations as well as numerous multi-racial, multi-race neighborhoods. By categorizing New York City's more than 2,200 census tracts into a neighborhood typology defined by dominant race tracts and multi-racial tracts, and mapping the results, the spatial geography of New York City reveals both persistent racial settlement patterns and the notable presence of global neighborhoods. Although the immigration literature emphasizes enclave formations, increasingly, immigrants are settling in racially and ethnically diverse neighborhoods. This paper proposes that the typology of immigrant neighborhoods should include and develop the concept of an immigrant global neighborhood not solely because of its diverse demography but rather, because these neighborhoods are an important part of the multiple and varied ways that immigrant-driven urbanization is mediating incorporation strategies and transforming the landscape of New York City.

This paper is part of a Ford Foundation funded study of New York City global neighborhoods. As this project has just started, this paper introduces NYC's immigrant global neighborhoods by reviewing the demographic evidence for neighborhood transformations. Key findings confirm the paradoxical trend of increasing diversity and persistent segregation. While the influx of post-1965 immigrants has facilitated the emergence and expansion of multi-race neighborhoods comprised of Asians, Latinos, and non-Hispanic Whites, this neighborhood-level diversity is largely absent of Blacks except for neighborhoods comprised nearly exclusively of Blacks and Latinos. The paper introduces three

NYC global neighborhoods – Sunset Park, Richmond Hill, and Elmhurst – to illustrate several research areas important to the study of multi-race immigrant settlements: (1) neighborhood definition; (2) neighborhood opportunity structures; (3) defining "communities of interests"; and (4) the role of local institutions in promoting prospects for a multiracial democracy.

THE MEANING OF NEIGHBORHOOD AND PLACE

Neighborhoods are an integral aspect of the immigration experience (Logan et al., 2002). Local, territorially defined spatial neighborhoods remain central to how people organize their daily lives (Gottdiener & Hutchison, 2000). The seminal work of Alejandro Portes and his colleagues developed the concept of a "context of reception" to describe the key mechanisms that shape the incorporation of new immigrants (Portes, 1981; Portes & Bach, 1985; Portes & Rumbaut, 1990; Portes & Zhou, 1992). Immigration is a social process facilitated by ethnic-based networks and these largely informal networks also promote a particular set of conditions for socioeconomic integration in the host country though the formation of immigrant enclaves and occupational niches (Portes & Bach, 1985; Portes & Rumbaut, 1990; Waldinger, 1996). A critical component of the context of reception is the establishment of an ethnic community especially one with a large co-ethnic entrepreneurial base. Immigrant enclaves serve as "stepping stone" or "port of entry" communities providing necessary social, economic, and cultural resources to help facilitate the settlement and integration of new immigrants and subsequent generations (Marcuse, 1997; Portes & Bach, 1985; Portes & Rumbaut, 1990).

While the spatial agglomeration of immigrant-owned businesses is an important defining characteristic, the benefits of enclave residence and employment is an outcome of ethnic-based social structures which mediate labor market processes and community institutions (Waldinger, 1996; Zhou, 2002). Enclave economies provide opportunities for social mobility through informal hiring and training practices, flexible work environments, self-employment possibilities as well as protection from interracial competition, discrimination, and government surveillance and regulations (Zhou, 1992). As Sassen (2000) notes, ". . . immigrant communities offer an advantage, given the intensity of their networks and the channeling of newly arrived and long-term resident immigrants into immigrant-dominated labor markets" (p. xii).

Proponents of immigrant enclaves contend that the reproduction of these communities do not necessarily indicate the persistence of involuntary segregation, but underscores the capacity of ethnic solidarity and social networks to facilitate economic mobility, community life, and cultural continuity (Li, 1999; Zhou, 1992;

Zhou & Logan, 1991). Enclave residence is not the sole option for new immigrants but rather, a superior one since enclaves provide "a means of enhancing their economic, social, political, and/or cultural development" (Marcuse, 1997, p. 225).

Logan and his colleagues (2002) proposed that there are different types of ethnic neighborhoods; immigrant enclaves and ethnic communities. A key distinguishing quality of these neighborhood types is that immigrant enclaves are similar to ghettos since "both exhibit a prevalence of cheap and densely populated housing stock, inner city location, poverty, and other indicators of dependency" (Logan et al., 2002, p. 301). In contrast, ethnic communities are often located in suburban settings and/or neighborhoods with improved socioeconomic characteristics. Termed an ethnoburb or ethnic suburb, Monterey Park in California's San Gabriel Valley is often cited as an example due to the suburban location, middle-class composition, and ethnic economy that serves a local and transnational market (Li, 1999). The key factor in these community formations is ethnic preferences that result in voluntary segregation for both immigrants that need enclave neighborhood resources as well as for upwardly mobile immigrants who form ethnic concentrations "due to individual tastes and preferences" (Logan et al., 2002).

Others view immigrant community formations on a continuum of urban and social restructurings rather than as a process of ecological and economic successions (Kwong, 1987; Lin, 1998; Sassen, 1991). Enclaves represent sites of production and social reproduction that are integral to an evolving landscape of urban inequality. These scholars reject voluntary segregation and note that ethnicity often masks class divisions and conflicts. Immigrant enclaves are concentrated in marginal industries where minimal profits for risk-taking immigrant business owners are based on squeezing labor. The spatial agglomeration of ethnic resources and institutions does not necessarily promote upward mobility but buffers unemployment and underemployment, and the impacts of working poverty (Ong, 1984). The social isolation of immigrant enclaves enables ethnic institutions to dominate community politics and business development (Kwong, 1987). Rather than bounded solidarity, class divisions in enclave communities are evident in the degree of labor exploitation found in many workplaces (Light & Bonacich, 1988).

The limitations of "neighborhood opportunity structures" in immigrant enclaves were recently examined by George Galster and his colleagues (1999). They found evidence to suggest "higher residential exposure to other members of one's immigrant group is associated with greater increases in poverty, and perhaps, smaller gains in employment for that group" (p. 123). While ethnically concentrated neighborhoods offer employment opportunities to low-skill workers, these neighborhoods are typically characterized by overcrowded public schools, poor neighborhood services, and substandard housing conditions that affect the institutional infrastructure and life chances of local residents.[1] These studies on immigrant communities highlight the importance of local "neighborhood effects" that structure economic opportunities and mobility strategies.

Current research on immigrant incorporation focus on continuing ties with the home country and how multiple forms of transnational practices mediate daily lives and the processes of incorporation into mainstream society (Codero-Guzman et al., 2001; Levitt, 2002). Rejecting a simple assimilationist trajectory, transnationalist scholars document and theorize "an alternative form of adaptation" that entails "cross-border economic, political, and cultural activities" (Portes et al., 2002). While transnationalism elaborates on how the compression of time and space made possible by technology facilitates continuing involvement in the home country and shapes immigrant identities and experiences (Foner, 2001; Levitt, 2002), the significance of locality i.e. how neighborhood matters and influences transnational practices and processes, is underdeveloped.

A growing field of community studies investigates the meaning of race and ethnicity in neighborhood dynamics in New York City. These important neighborhood ethnographies have focused on a single racial and/or ethnic group (Gregory, 1998; Kasinitz, 1992; Kwong, 1987; Lin, 1998; Muniz, 1998; Zhou, 1992), or on established white residents' reception and reactions to the settlement of African Americans or new immigrants (Rieder, 1985; Sanjek, 1998; Winnick, 1990). Another important research trend in community studies looks at the emergence of racially diverse neighborhoods and supporting social, political, and economic conditions. Studies on racially integrated neighborhoods emphasize African American and white integration (Ellen, 1998; Nyden et al., 1998). With the exception of a few case studies in Nyden et al.'s 1998 national survey of racially and ethnically diverse neighborhoods, the impacts of post-1965 immigration in facilitating and sustaining neighborhood diversity has not been fully investigated.

Theorizations of immigrant enclaves and ethnic communities are increasingly inadequate to describe neighborhood dynamics in pluralistic settings because these concepts emphasize ethnic and racial homogeneity that do not provide the analytical tools to study neighborhood dynamics in a multi-race context. Immigrant global neighborhoods raise important questions for urban and community studies. Are immigrant global neighborhoods a "mosaic of little social worlds which touch but do not interpenetrate" (Park, 1925, p. 47)? Do immigrant global neighborhoods represent a phase in neighborhood succession? Will contemporary racialized immigrant groups replicate the assimilation trajectory of earlier immigrant groups? How does a multi-race neighborhood context mediate ethnic resources, networks, and institutions? Are there shared neighborhood concerns and issues that promote "communities of interests"? Does neighborhood life hold promising signs for co-existence in a pluralistic society? Does the multi-race composition of global neighborhoods provide a venue to compare and contrast transnational practices undertaken by different immigrant groups within a shared neighborhood context?

THE GEOGRAPHY OF A MAJORITY "MINORITY" CITY

New York City transitioned into a majority "minority" city during the mid-1980s. The percent of non-Hispanic whites progressively declined from over half (52%) of NYC's population in 1980 to 35% by 2000 (Table 1). A second notable trend is that the numbers of Latinos have surpassed African Americans making them the city's second largest population group in 2000. Numbering over 2 million, Latinos represent 27% of the citywide population edging out African Americans at 1.9 million or 25% of New Yorkers. These demographic shifts are fueled by the influx of Caribbean and Latin American immigrants. Immigration has also made Asians the fastest growing racial group. Increasing their numbers by 55% in the past decade, Asian Pacific Americans now represent 10% of NYC's population at close to 800,000.

These racial shifts are accompanied by a tremendous ethnic diversification of New York City's population. A growing share of New York City's Black population is foreign born with significant numbers of newcomers from the West Indies and Haiti (Kasinitz, 1992). While Puerto Ricans remain the largest Latino ethnic group, their numeric dominance is declining with rapidly growing numbers of Dominicans, Mexicans, and South and Central Americans namely Colombians, Ecuadorians, and Salvadorans. The same pattern is found for Asians – although the Chinese remain the largest ethnic group, South Asians including Asian Indians, Pakistanis, Bangladeshis, and Sri Lankans, are the fastest growing group as their numbers more than doubled in the past decade from 106,349 to 214,146. Adding to the diverse ethnic composition of Asian New Yorkers are sizable numbers of Koreans and Filipinos.

In the past decade, nearly one million immigrants settled in New York City making it the top metropolitan destination for newcomers.[2] Immigration to New York City is marked by two distinguishing qualities: diversity in sending countries and geographic concentration in key neighborhoods. Listing the top twenty source countries of immigrants indicates that no one group clearly dominates (Table 2). Although immigrants from the Dominican Republic and the former Soviet Republics are the two largest groups, they represent less than one-third of all newcomers to NYC during the 1990s. New York City receives immigrants from all over the world and the top twenty sending countries include countries in the Caribbean, Asia, Latin America as well as Europe.

Table 1. Racial Composition and Change in New York City, 1980–2000.

	1980	1990	2000	1980 Pop Comp (%)	1990 Pop Comp (%)	2000 Pop Comp (%)	% Change 1980–1990	% Change 1990–2000
New York City	7,071,639	7,322,564	8,008,278	100	100	100	4	9
Non Hispanic White	3,703,203	3,178,712	2,801,267	52	43	35	-14	-12
African American	1,694,505	1,874,892	1,962,154	24	26	25	11	5
Asian	245,759	510,549	787,047	3	7	10	108	54
Latino	1,406,389	1,723,665	2,153,736	20	24	27	23	25
Other	21,783	34,746	78,925	0.3	0.5	1	60	127
Multi-Race[a]	–	–	225,149	–	–	3	–	–
Queens	1,891,325	1,951,598	2,229,379	100	100	100	3	14
Non Hispanic White	1,183,038	941,890	752,895	63	48	33	-20	-22
African American	341,261	394,170	422,831	18	20	19	16	7
Asian	99,132	238,818	391,500	5	12	18	141	64
Latino	263,548	365,805	554,408	14	19	25	39	52
Other	4,346	10,915	35,234	0.2	1	2	151	223
Multi-Race[a]	–	–	92,511	–	–	4	–	–
Brooklyn	2,230,936	2,300,664	2,465,326	100	100	100	3	7
Non Hispanic White	1,095,946	928,255	854,532	49	40	35	-15	-8
African American	688,405	806,864	848,583	31	35	34	17	5
Asian	46,217	111,148	185,818	2	5	8	140	67
Latino	393,103	444,918	486,351	18	19	20	13	9
Other	7,265	9,479	21,354	0.3	0.4	1	30	125
Multi-Race[a]	–	–	68,688	–	–	3	–	–

Table 1. (Continued)

	1980	1990	2000	1980 Pop Comp (%)	1990 Pop Comp (%)	2000 Pop Comp (%)	% Change 1980–1990	% Change 1990–2000
Manhattan	1,428,285	1,487,536	1,537,195	100	100	100	4	3
Non Hispanic White	721,588	728,563	703,873	51	49	46	1	–3
African American	290,561	264,717	234,698	20	18	15	–9	–11
Asian	75,652	110,168	144,538	5	7	9	46	31
Latino	335,247	377,728	416,569	23	25	27	13	10
Other	5,237	6,360	8,573	0.4	0.4	1	21	35
Multi-Race[a]	–	–	28,944	–	–	2	–	–
Bronx	1,168,972	1,203,789	1,332,650	100	100	100	3	11
Non Hispanic White	401,856	276,221	193,651	34	23	15	–31	–30
African American	349,961	380,670	416,338	30	32	31	9	9
Asian	17,412	33,696	40,120	1	3	3	94	19
Latino	395,138	506,118	643,143	34	42	48	28	27
Other	4,605	7,084	12,189	0.4	1	1	54	72
Multi-Race[a]	–	–	27,209	–	–	2	–	–
Staten Island	352,121	378,977	443,728	100	100	100	8	17
Non Hispanic White	300,775	303,783	316,316	85	80	71	1	4
African American	24,317	28,471	39,704	7	8	9	17	39
Asian	7,346	16,719	25,071	2	4	6	128	50
Latino	19,353	29,096	53,265	5	8	12	50	83
Other	330	908	1,575	0.1	0.2	0.4	175	73
Multi-Race[a]	–	–	7,797	–	–	2	–	–

Source: 1980, 1990, and 2000 SF1, U.S. Census Bureau.

[a]Multi-Race is a new category in the Census 2000 and includes persons of multiple racial identities.

Table 2. Immigration to New York City, 1990–1998.

	New York City	Brooklyn	Queens	Manhattan	Bronx	Staten Island
Total immigrants	963,121	343,531	293,791	180,180	105,500	14,569
	(100%)	(36%)	(31%)	(19%)	(11%)	(2%)
Dominican Republic	173,239	31,049	23,470	68,605	49,847	268
	(100%)	(18%)	(14%)	(40%)	(29%)	(0.2%)
Former Soviet Republics	123,858	89,590	25,513	4,446	3,152	1,157
	(100%)	(72%)	(21%)	(4%)	(3%)	(1%)
China	83,339	23,594	23,709	32,854	2,295	887
	(100%)	(28%)	(28%)	(39%)	(3%)	(1%)
Jamaica	55,022	23,781	13,095	1,729	16,228	189
	(100%)	(43%)	(24%)	(3%)	(29%)	(0.3%)
Guyana	48,610	19,543	21,066	881	6,963	157
	(100%)	(40%)	(43%)	(2%)	(14%)	(0.3%)
Poland	28,395	18,983	6,776	1,788	273	575
	(100%)	(67%)	(24%)	(6%)	(1%)	(2%)
Trinidad	26,764	16,199	7,123	1,157	1,961	324
	(100%)	(61%)	(27%)	(4%)	(7%)	(1%)
India	26,355	3,032	17,985	2,160	1,733	1,445
	(100%)	(12%)	(68%)	(8%)	(7%)	(5%)
Haiti	26,130	18,257	6,182	1,261	365	65
	(100%)	(70%)	(24%)	(5%)	(1%)	(0%)
Ecuador	25,716	5,948	12,174	3,673	3,730	191
	(100%)	(23%)	(47%)	(14%)	(15%)	(1%)
Phillipines	25,508	4,494	11,227	5,050	3,692	1,045
	(100%)	(18%)	(44%)	(20%)	(14%)	(4%)
Bangladesh	25,267	6,185	13,766	2,490	2,753	73
	(100%)	(24%)	(54%)	(10%)	(11%)	(0%)
Colombia	17,831	1,990	13,453	1,334	825	229
	(100%)	(11%)	(75%)	(7%)	(5%)	(1%)
Pakistan	17,603	7,232	7,797	1,098	963	513
	(100%)	(41%)	(44%)	(6%)	(5%)	(3%)
Korea	14,053	1,178	10,175	1,338	816	546
	(100%)	(8%)	(72%)	(10%)	(6%)	(4%)
Ireland	13,877	1,333	5,836	2,915	3,574	219
	(100%)	(10%)	(42%)	(21%)	(26%)	(2%)
Hong Kong	11,524	3,687	3,896	3,340	196	405
	(100%)	(32%)	(34%)	(29%)	(2%)	(4%)
Peru	10,856	1,506	6,817	1,275	1,081	177
	(100%)	(14%)	(63%)	(12%)	(10%)	(2%)
Honduras	9,553	2,592	1,458	1,234	4,031	238
	(100%)	(27%)	(15%)	(13%)	(42%)	(2%)
United Kingdom	8,259	1,802	1,886	3,372	1,020	179
	(100%)	(22%)	(23%)	(41%)	(12%)	(2%)

Note: Settlement patterns of top twenty groups.

Source: 1990–1998 Immigrant Public Use Tapes, U.S. Dept. of Justice, Immigration and Naturalization Service.

While a majority two thirds of newcomers to New York City settled in Brooklyn or Queens, immigration patterns are quite distinct for each borough. Nearly two-fifths (38%) of the immigrants who settled in the Bronx or Manhattan during the 1990s are from the Dominican Republic. The second largest group settling in the Bronx are from Jamaica while newcomers from the People's Republic of China are the second largest group settling in Manhattan. Former Soviet Republic immigrants constitute the largest immigrant group settling in Brooklyn at 26%. In contrast, the nearly 300,000 immigrants to Queens are so diverse that no one sending country comprises 10% or more of the newcomers which includes large numbers from the Dominican Republic, former Soviet Republics, People's Republic of China, Guyana, India, Bangladesh, and Colombia.

The settlement patterns of immigrant groups suggest distinct neighborhood preferences. These patterns reflect in part the social process of chain migration as newcomers settle near family and friends, and/or find their residence through informal networks. The dominance of immigrants from the former Soviet Republics among the newcomers settling in Brooklyn is underscored by the observation that nearly three-quarters settled in Brooklyn in the past decade. Similarly, a majority of immigrants from Haiti (70%) and Poland (67%) settled in Brooklyn whereas a majority of immigrants from India (68%), Korea (72%), Colombia (75%), and Peru (63%) settled in Queens. Among the largest immigrant groups, Manhattan is a key destination for Dominicans and Chinese immigrants although Dominicans also settle in sizable numbers in the Bronx while comparable numbers of Chinese choose Queens and Brooklyn.

By categorizing New York City's 2,217 census tracts as dominant race tracts or multi-race tracts and mapping the results, the spatial geography of New York City reveals both persistent racial settlement patterns and the notable presence of global neighborhoods.[3] Dominant tracts are defined as census tracts comprised of 50% or more of one racial group and where no other racial group comprises more than 25% (Table 3). For example, dominant Asian tracts are census tracts where Asians constitute 50% or more of the tract population, and where NHWs, Blacks, and Latinos comprise less than 25% of the population, respectively. Multi-race tracts are differentiated into two types. One is "polyethnic" tracts where at least three racial groups comprise a minimum of 20% of the tract population.[4] The second type of multi-race tract is categorized according to the two racial groups that comprise the tract population's majority. For example, a multi-race tract is comprised of at least one racial group that makes up 40% or more of the tract population and another racial group that represents at least 25% of the census tract.

The racial geography of New York City indicates persistent residential segregation amidst increasing racial and ethnic diversity. A majority (64%) of NYC census tracts are dominant race tracts in that one racial group comprises

Table 3. Definitions of Census Tract Categories.

Census Tract Type	Definition
Dominant NHW	NHW ≥ 50% and no other group ≥25%
Dominant Black	Black ≥ 50% and no other group ≥25%
Dominant Latino	Latino ≥ 50% and no other group ≥25%
Dominant Asian	Asian ≥ 50% and no other group ≥25%
Poly-Ethnic	At least three racial groups ≥20%
Multi-Race, Asian-NHW	Asian or NHW ≥ 40% and Asian or NHW ≥25%
Multi-Race, Latino-Black	Latino or Black ≥ 40% and Latino or Black ≥25%
Multi-Race, Latino-NHW	Latino or NHW ≥ 40% and Latino or NHW ≥25%
Multi-Race, Latino-Asian	Latino or Asian ≥ 40% and Latino or Asian ≥25%
Multi-Race, Asian-Black	Asian or Black ≥ 40% and Asian or Black ≥25%
Multi-Race, Black-NHW	Black or NHW ≥ 40% and Black or NHW ≥25%

50% or more of the census tract population (Tables 4 and 5). This represents a slight decline from a decade ago when more than two-thirds (69%) were dominant race tracts. This decline is the result of the continuing out-migration of NHWs reflected in the 25% decrease in the number of dominant NHW tracts. In contrast, dominant Black, Asian, and Latino census tracts increased in number and as a relative share of NYC census tracts.

Nearly two-fifths of NYC census tracts are multi-race representing a 17% increase in the past decade. Much of this growth is due to the influx of Asian immigration since the greatest increase is noted in multi-race tracts with a large Asian presence. The number of multi-race Asian-NHW tracts grew by 197%, while multi-race Asian-Latino tracts doubled. Poly ethnic tracts (i.e. at least three racial groups comprise a minimum of 20% of the tract population) also increased significantly. Reflecting their greater numbers, the most common type of multi-race tracts are Latino-Black and Latino-NHW. Overall, the likelihood of Latinos and Blacks residing in multi-race tracts with a large NHW presence is declining. The high level of Black segregation is evident in the concentration of Black New Yorkers in two neighborhood types – dominant Black or multi-race Latino-Black. The small number of Black-NHW tracts declined by nearly half such that the largest cluster of Black-NHW tracts represent Starrett City, a Mitchell-Lama housing complex comprised of 46 residential buildings developed in the 1970s in Canarsie, Brooklyn. Several Black-NHW tracts buffer dominant Black and dominant NHW neighborhoods in Brooklyn while the remaining few includes a tract in Crown Heights, a site of racial conflict during the 1990s.

The notable residential integration of Asians does not include neighborhoods with a significant presence of Blacks. This heightened social distance between Asians and Blacks is evident in that there is only one multi-race Asian-Black

Table 4. Census Tract Categories by Borough, 1990–2000.

	New York City					Manhattan					Brooklyn				
	1990	90dist	2000	00dist	%Chge	1990	90dist	2000	00dist	%Chge	1990	90dist	2000	00dist	%Chge
Total census tracts[a]	2,216	100%	2,217	100%	0%	298	100%	296	100%	-1%	789	100%	783	100%	-1%
Dominant race tracts	1,487	69%	1,373	64%	-8%	212	73%	216	76%	2%	590	77%	552	72%	-6%
NHW	924	62%	694	51%	-25%	144	68%	147	68%	2%	343	58%	267	48%	-22%
Black	405	27%	431	31%	6%	40	19%	32	15%	-20%	194	33%	219	40%	13%
Latino	151	10%	223	16%	48%	23	11%	30	14%	30%	53	9%	62	11%	17%
Asian	7	0.5%	25	2%	257%	5	2%	7	3%	40%	0	0%	4	1%	–
Multi-race tracts	664	31%	774	36%	17%	78	27%	70	24%	-10%	180	23%	213	28%	18%
Poly-Ethnic	73	11%	124	16%	70%	4	5%	6	9%	50%	14	8%	19	9%	36%
Asian-NHW	39	6%	116	15%	197%	5	6%	6	9%	20%	7	4%	42	20%	500%
Latino-Black	257	39%	270	35%	5%	31	40%	33	47%	6%	73	41%	74	35%	1%
Latino-NHW	195	29%	172	22%	-12%	27	35%	18	26%	-33%	52	29%	38	18%	-27%
Latino-Asian	26	4%	52	7%	100%	5	6%	5	7%	0%	1	1%	8	4%	700%
Asian-Black	1	0.2%	1	0.1%	0%	0	0%	0	0%	–	0	0%	0	0%	–
Black-NHW	73	11%	39	5%	-47%	6	8%	2	3%	-67%	33	18%	32	15%	-3%

	Queens					Bronx					Staten Island				
	1990	90dist	2000	00dist	%Chge	1990	90dist	2000	00dist	%Chge	1990	90dist	2000	00dist	%Chge
Total census tracts[a]	673	100%	673	100%	0%	355	100%	355	100%	0%	101	100%	110	100%	9%
Dominant race tracts	445	68%	346	53%	-22%	157	46%	173	51%	10%	83	85%	86	80%	4%
NHW	286	64%	152	44%	-47%	70	45%	44	25%	-37%	81	98%	84	98%	4%
Black	139	31%	137	40%	-1%	30	19%	41	24%	37%	2	2%	2	2%	0%
Latino	18	4%	43	12%	139%	57	36%	88	51%	54%	0	0%	0	0%	–
Asian	2	0.4%	14	4%	600%	0	0%	0	0%	0%	0	0%	0	0%	–
Multi-race tracts	210	32%	305	47%	45%	181	54%	165	49%	-9%	15	15%	21	20%	40%
Poly-Ethnic	43	20%	88	29%	105%	10	6%	2	1%	-80%	2	13%	9	43%	350%
Asian-NHW	27	13%	67	22%	148%	0	0%	1	1%	–	0	0%	0	0%	0%
Latino-Black	19	9%	25	8%	32%	131	72%	133	81%	2%	3	20%	5	24%	67%
Latino-NHW	85	40%	82	27%	-4%	31	17%	29	18%	-6%	0	0%	5	24%	0%
Latino-Asian	20	10%	39	13%	95%	0	0%	0	0%	–	0	0%	0	0%	–
Asian-Black	0	0%	1	1%	–	1	1%	0	0%	–	0	0%	0	0%	–
Black-NHW	16	8%	3	1%	-81%	8	4%	0	0%	-100%	10	67%	2	10%	-80%

[a] The sum of dominant and multi-race census tracts do not add up because open space tracts and tracts with a population of 100 or less were omitted from the categorizations. Forty-six census tracts with a total population of 1,345 were omitted.

Table 5. Racial Composition and Change in NYC's Global Neighborhoods, 1980–2000.

	1980	1990	2000	1980 Pop Comp (%)	1990 Pop Comp (%)	2000 Pop Comp (%)	% Change 1980–1990	% Change 1990–2000
Elmhurst								
Total Population[a]	83,472	94,710	114,154	100	100	99	13	21
Non Hispanic White	36,731	24,427	16,109	44	26	14	-33	-34
African American	1,950	2,319	1,537	2	2	1	19	-34
Asian	17,423	34,691	44,042	21	37	39	99	27
Latino	27,338	32,606	48,704	33	34	43	19	49
Multi-Race[b]	–	–	3,071	–	–	3	–	–
Richmond Hill								
Total Population[a]	57,335	62,399	78,399	100	100	94	9	26
Non Hispanic White	42,616	32,801	19,003	74	53	24	-23	-42
African American	1,911	6,678	6,554	3	11	8	249	-2
Asian	1,555	5,638	15,011	3	9	19	263	166
Latino	11,063	16,626	24,578	19	27	31	50	48
Multi-Race[b]	–	–	8,354	–	–	11	–	–
Sunset Park								
Total Population[a]	89,440	96,978	116,436	100	100	100	8	20
Non Hispanic White	39,839	29,301	20,001	45	30	17	-26	-32
African American	1,906	3,184	2,882	2	3	2	67	-9
Asian	4,712	16,360	31,507	5	17	27	247	93
Latino	42,628	47,613	57,628	48	49	49	12	21
Multi-Race[b]	–	–	3,346	–	–	3	–	–

Source: 1980, 1990 STF3 and 2000 SF1, U.S. Census Bureau.

[a]The small numbers who selected Other are not reflected in this table.

[b]Multi-Race is a new category in the Census 2000 and includes persons of multiple racial identities.

census tract in NYC. This tract is located in Jamaica Hills which is part of a multi-race neighborhood corridor stretching along the northern border of a concentrated cluster of Black middle-class neighborhoods in Southeast Queens. The racial geography of NYC tells a paradoxical story of diversity and persistent patterns of racial segregation. Although multi-race neighborhoods comprised largely of Asians, Latinos, and some NHWs are increasing, the concentration of Blacks in dominant Black or Black-Latino neighborhoods is particularly acute. Moreover, the likelihood of NHWs residing in neighborhoods with Latinos or Blacks is declining.

By mapping these census tract categories, the spatial contours of New York City's racial geography are apparent [refer to Map]. While large sections of the city are predominantly non-Hispanic White, African American, or Latino, multi-race tracts, i.e. global neighborhoods, are a significant part of the spatial geography of New York City, especially in the borough of Queens. Three-quarters or more of the census tracts that comprise Manhattan, Brooklyn, and Staten Island are dominant race tracts. Nearly all Staten Island census tracts are dominant NHW underscoring how it remains the only NYC borough with a majority NHW population. More than two-thirds of Manhattan's dominant race tracts are dominant NHW, however, notable clusters of dominant Black tracts make up the historic uptown neighborhood of Harlem, and dominant Latino tracts are concentrated in neighboring East Harlem, Washington Heights, and Inwood. In contrast, Brooklyn's dominant race tracts are divided fairly evenly in the affluent dominant NHW neighborhoods of Windsor Terrace, Kensington, Park Slope, Borough Park, Bay Ridge, Bensonhurst, and Sheepshead Bay, and dominant Black tracts that define the historic Central Brooklyn neighborhoods of Brownsville, Bedford-Stuyvesant, Crown Heights, East Flatbush, Flatbush, and Canarsie. Notably, four dominant Asian tracts are now part of Brooklyn's landscape and are clustered in the multi-race neighborhood of Sunset Park which also encompasses the majority of Brooklyn's dominant Latino tracts.

The neighborhood composition of Queens and the Bronx is much more diverse as indicated by the lower share of dominant race tracts relative to the other three boroughs. Like Brooklyn, dominant race tracts in Queens are divided into significant NHW and Black neighborhood clusters. Dominant Black tracts concentrate in the middle-class neighborhoods of Southeast Queens including Jamaica, S. Jamaica, Springfield Gardens, Rosedale, Laurelton, Cambria Heights, Hollis, and St. Albans. Queens' dominant NHW tracts form two neighborhood clusters: the northeastern section of College Point, Whitestone, Clearview, Douglaston and Littleton, and Glen Oaks, and a midwestern section of Maspeth, Middle Village, Forest Hills, and Glendale. Rego Park, Kew Garden Hills, Howard Beach are also dominant NHW neighborhoods in Queens. Howard Beach is

New York City Spatial Patterns

Racial Composition of Census Tract

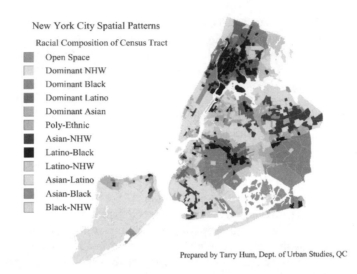

- Open Space
- Dominant NHW
- Dominant Black
- Dominant Latino
- Dominant Asian
- Poly-Ethnic
- Asian-NHW
- Latino-Black
- Latino-NHW
- Asian-Latino
- Asian-Black
- Black-NHW

Prepared by Tarry Hum, Dept. of Urban Studies, QC

infamous for the 1986 death of Michael Griffith who was hit by a car as he and two friends fled from a group of white teenagers armed with baseball bats. Recently, a dominant NHW neighborhood in the Far Rockaway section of Queens noted for its residential concentration of NYC police and firemen, was in the news for a racial bias incident involving a white resident charged with the verbal and physical assault of a Latino child visiting friends in the neighborhood (Healy, 2003).

The majority of NYC's dominant Asian tracts are located in Queens. These tracts form the pan-Asian Flushing neighborhood that elected the first Asian American to the New York City Council in 2001. The racial geography of the Bronx is distinguished by its majority Latino population evident in the concentration of multi-race Latino-Black census tracts surrounded by dominant Latino census tracts in the neighborhoods of Mott Haven, Longwood, and Hunt's Point. Dominant Black tracts cluster in the northern Bronx neighborhoods of Williamsbridge, Coop City, Eastchester, Baychester, and Wakefield. A few notable affluent NHW enclaves such as Fieldston and Riverdale are also located in the Bronx.

Multi-race neighborhoods are located throughout New York City but their concentration and diversity in Queens is unparallel. The exceptional racial and ethnic diversity of Queens is evident in the northwestern neighborhoods of Elmhurst, Jackson Heights, Long Island City, Sunnyside, and Woodside comprised largely of poly-ethnic, Asian-Latino, and Latino-NHW census tracts. Latino-Black tracts cluster in East Elmhurst adjacent to dominant Latino Corona. Surrounding the dominant Asian tracts that concentrate in Flushing in the northeastern section of Queens are many neighborhoods with multi-race Asian-NHW tracts including East Flushing, Queensboro, Auburndale, Bayside, Oakland Gardens, Bellerose and Floral Park, Jamaica Estates, Hillcrest. Buffering these Asian-NHW neighborhoods from the dominant Black neighborhoods in southeastern Queens is another series of multi-race neighborhoods stretching across the borough from its western to eastern border including Queens Village, Hollis, Jamaica Hills, Briarwood, Richmond Hill, South Ozone Park, Ozone Park, and Woodhaven. These multi-race neighborhoods are comprised of Asian-Latino tracts and poly-ethnic tracts.

Multi-race neighborhoods in the Bronx are largely Latino-Black neighborhoods clustered in central Bronx. The few notable exceptions include the Latino-NHW neighborhoods of Throgs Neck and Pelham Bay Park, and a single Asian-NHW census tract that is the center of the Southeast Asian community in Northwest Bronx (Nguyen, 2001). The influx of Asian immigrants has facilitated the dramatic increase of multi-race Asian-Latino tracts in southwest Brooklyn's Sunset Park neighborhood and Asian-NHW tracts clustered in distinct sections of the heavily Italian neighborhoods of Dyker Heights, Bensonhurst, and Sheepshead Bay. Latino-NHW tracts comprise a significant part of the Red Hook and Gowanus neighborhoods also located along southwest Brooklyn's industrial waterfront. These tracts may indicate neighborhoods in transition as the numbers of Latino-NHW tracts are declining overall due to gentrification spilling over from neighboring areas such as Park Slope. Brooklyn's Latino-Black tracts cluster in historic Black neighborhoods such as Bedford-Styvesant, East New York, and Bushwick. Staten Island's multi-race census tracts are concentrated along its northern shore and a large share of its minority population resides in these neighborhoods, for example, over half of Staten Island's Black population resides in a multi-race tract.

Driving New York City's demographic transformation is the influx of new immigrants and the continuing out-migration of NHWs. Countering the city-wide decline in dominant NHW census tracts, however, is Manhattan and Staten Island. In both boroughs, dominant NHW neighborhoods consolidated and expanded. For example, 97% of the dominant NHW tracts in Manhattan in 1990 continued to be dominant NHW ten years later. The neighborhood type that experienced the greatest demographic change in Manhattan is multi-race tracts as many became dominant NHW in 2000, an indication of neighborhood gentrification in the East Village, Battery Park, Soho, Chelsea, and lower Harlem. In Staten Island, several Black-NHW tracts transitioned to dominant NHW tracts in 2000.

While Manhattan's dominant NHW neighborhoods consolidated in the last decade, Brooklyn's dominant NHW census tracts shrank as one in four tracts transitioned mostly to Asian-NHW tracts reflecting the significant immigrant influx into historic white neighborhoods. In contrast, nearly all dominant Black tracts

in Brooklyn remained dominant Black, however, the percentage of foreign born
in these tracts increased 8 percentage points to 35% representing a sizable and
growing immigrant Caribbean population.

The dramatic racial and ethnic transformation of Queens in the past decade is
evident as nearly one-half (46%) of dominant NHW tracts transitioned to multi-race
tracts with the most common types being poly-ethnic, Asian-NHW, and Latino-
NHW. Similar to the other NYC boroughs, dominant Black and dominant Latino
tracts were quite stable with 90% remaining so in 2000.

The distribution of New Yorkers among these census tract categories further
indicate the relative concentration and isolation of NHWs and Blacks, and
the greater likelihood for Asians and Latinos to reside in multi-race tracts.
Figure 1 indicates nearly three-quarters of NHW New Yorkers resides in a
dominant NHW neighborhood. NHWs are, in fact, the most segregated racial
group in NYC followed by 57% of Blacks who are similarly concentrated in a
dominant Black neighborhood. In contrast, residence in a multi-race census tract
is the most common experience for Asian and Latino New Yorkers. Although
enclave neighborhoods figure prominently in studies of Asian residential patterns,

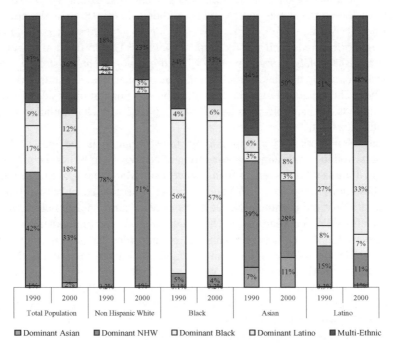

Fig. 1. Locating Global Neighborhoods in a Majority "Minority" City.

Asians are more likely to reside in a multi-race or dominant NHW census tract. Nonetheless, the share of Asians in enclave or dominant Asian tracts increased in the past ten years from 7 to 12%.

This overview of NYC's racial geography disaggregated on the census tract level underscore several important trends shaping the urban landscape: persistent segregation of Blacks in neighborhoods that experienced little change in racial composition while incorporating large numbers of Afro-Caribbean and African immigrants; dominant NHW neighborhoods have consolidated in Manhattan and Staten Island; and the influx of Asian and Latino immigrants have transformed numerous Queens and Brooklyn neighborhoods. Even dominant race tracts are experiencing greater diversity compared to ten years ago. For example, NHWs comprised 82% of the population in dominant NHW tracts in 1990 but this population share declined slightly to 76% in 2000. This pattern is found for dominant Latino, Asian, and Black tracts as well. Nevertheless, the striking observation about the racial geography of New York City is the concentration of minority groups in multi-racial, multi-race neighborhoods where the presence of NHWs is comparatively low. Moreover, multi-race neighborhoods are quite stable as nearly three-quarters remained multi-race ten years later.

NEW YORK CITY'S IMMIGRANT GLOBAL NEIGHBORHOODS: SUNSET PARK, ELMHURST, RICHMOND HILL

The spatial and demographic analysis underscores how multi racial immigrant neighborhoods are a prominent feature of NYC's geography. By introducing three global neighborhoods – Brooklyn's Sunset Park, Elmhurst and Richmond Hill in Queens – this paper describes how the context of reception for new immigrants is defined by a post-industrial economy and unprecedented multi-race, multi-racial local neighborhood settings. Clearly, these neighborhoods defy simplistic characterizations as immigrant enclaves.

Sunset Park, located along a two mile stretch of southwest Brooklyn's waterfront, exemplifies the dramatic post-1960s demographic and economic restructuring of many urban neighborhoods. Once a vibrant industrial waterfront neighborhood, the deleterious effects of massive deindustrialization, the relocation of maritime activities, and the destruction caused by urban renewal culminated in Sunset Park's designation as a federal poverty area in the 1970s. Sunset Park's decline, however, contained the seeds for its rebirth including a plentiful supply of cheap housing, weak resistance to newcomers, and proximity to public transportation.

Sunset Park is simultaneously referred to as a "satellite" Chinatown reflecting its status as the third largest concentration of Chinese in the New York metropolitan area following Manhattan Chinatown and Flushing, Queens (Lin, 1998; Matthews, 1997; Oser, 1996), as well as a "full" Latino neighborhood along with Washington Heights in Manhattan and Hunts Point in the Bronx (Hansen, 1996). Sunset Park's majority Puerto Rican population is now joined by numerous Latino immigrant groups including Dominicans, Mexicans, and Central Americans. A sizable and growing Middle Eastern population as well as a small but renewing Polish community adds to its rich ethnic landscape.

Frequently cited as an exemplar of immigrant-driven neighborhood revitalization, Asian and Latino immigrant capital and sweat equity pumped new life into a "dying neighborhood," and in the process, transformed decaying urban spaces into vibrant marketplaces and streetscapes. This new economic prosperity, however, is countered by the uneven growth systemic of ethnic economies. Immigrant working poverty, the expansion of a sweatshop economy, and casualization of employment relations are also prominent features of economic life in Sunset Park.

Historically, Sunset Park provided entry level manufacturing jobs to European and Scandinavian immigrants. Their occupations as sailors, shipbuilders, dockworkers, construction workers, laborers, cargo handlers, harbor pilots, and maritime related officers, reflected the prominence of waterfront development and city building activities. Representing the largest port economy in the nation, New York's waterfront was central to its economic vitality until the 1960s (Freeman, 2000). A significant segment of the neighborhood economy remains based on manufacturing. According to the New York State DOL, nearly a third (27%) of Sunset Park workers are employed in manufacturing industries in contrast to 7% city-wide. However, these jobs are increasingly in downgraded manufacturing industries such as apparel and furniture making (Hum, 2003).

Sunset Park's waterfront, home to Bush Terminal, a model industrial park development comprised of nearly 200 acres of piers, warehouses, and manufacturing firms which in its heyday included the American Can Company and Bethlehem Steel Shipyard, continues to hemorrhage unionized employment as indicated by a recent New York Times article, "Where Blue Collars Grow Endangered: Factory Jobs Decline in Sunset Park."[5] Job opportunities in Sunset Park are increasingly centered on an immigrant sweatshop economy that has been documented in a series of public testimonials conducted by State Assemblyman Felix Ortiz and compiled into two monographs, *Behind Closed Doors: A Look Into the Underground Sweatshop Industry* in 1997 and a follow-up in 1999, *Behind Closed Doors II: Another Look into the Underground Sweatshop Industry*.

Photojournalist Jacob Riis, author of the classic publication, *How the Other Half Lives: Studies among the Tenements of New York*, a timeless and vivid testament to the extreme inequalities of urban life at the end of the 19th century, lived in the comforts of Victorian Richmond Hill as he prepared his book. A rural retreat in Queens, Richmond Hill provided bucolic farmlands and beautiful estates to those with the means to escape the conditions captured in Riis' photographs. Although majority NHW up to the 1990s, the Asian population exploded in Richmond Hill in the past decade, nearly tripling their numbers. While the largest Asian ethnic group are Asian Indians, Richmond Hill reflects the rich intra-ethnic diversity and the multiple streams of the South Asian Diaspora.

Richmond Hill is the residential and commercial center of a vibrant and expanding Indo-Guyanese and Indo-Trinidadian community concentrated in South Central Queens including neighboring Ozone Park, South Ozone Park, and Jamaica. Indo-Caribbeans are the descendants of Indian migrants who lived in the Caribbean nations of Guyana, Trinidad and Tobago, for well over 100 years. The fusion of Caribbean and Indian culture is dominant along Liberty Ave also known as Little Guyana. Sari shops, Trinidadian roti restaurants, CD shops playing calypso music, jewelry stores specializing in Guyana Gold, and the ubiquitous ethnic markets that offer fruits and vegetables from the home country are evidence of a vibrant enclave economy. Similar to the transnational practices of Afro-Caribbeans, several store fronts specialize in shipping barrels filled with daily household items to family members remaining in the Caribbean. New community groups such as Agenda 21 formed to promote the economic development of Richmond Hill and envision Liberty Ave as a tourist destination just as Canal Street in Manhattan Chinatown is a must see for NYC visitors.

Richmond Hill stands out with a high percentage of individuals who defined themselves as multi-racial for Census 2000. Relative to only 3% of New Yorkers who selected multi-racial, 11% of Richmond Hill residents identified as multi-racial. Upon closer examination, it is apparent that many of these individuals are part of the Indian diaspora from the Caribbean. More than half of those identifying as multi-racial chose Asian in combination with another race. Nearly all multiracial Asians chose two combinations with the most common being Asian and other race; Asian and Black or African American, and Asian and American Indian or Alaska Native. During the administration of Census 2000, concerns were expressed by community advocates regarding the potential undercount of the growing Indo-Caribbean population due to limited racial categories (Paul, 2000). The Indo-Caribbean Task Force for Census 2000 instructed the Indo Caribbean population to check Asian and other race, and then list Indo-Caribbean.

The South Asian population of Richmond Hill also includes a significant Sikh community. Established in the early 1970s, the Richmond Hill Sikh Cultural

Society is housed in a converted Christian church and is one of the oldest and largest Sikh temples, or gurdwaras, on the East Coast. A relatively young religion, Sikhism was founded approximately 500 years ago in the Punjab province of India, and the word "Sikh" means disciple in the Punjabi language. One of the key tenets of Sikhism rejects the caste system of Hinduism and promotes full equality among people of different races, religions, and sex. As symbols of their faith, men wear turbans and beards, and are given the surname Singh while women's surname is Kaur. There are an estimated 70,000 Sikhs in New York City with many residing in Richmond Hill.

The aftermath of the 9/11 tragedies brought the Sikh community into the public eye as many innocent Sikhs were mistaken for Muslim or Arab and targeted in racially biased attacks (Banerjee & Leung, 2001). In response, the Richmond Hill Sikh Cultural Society produced an educational leaflet with attached patriotic ribbons of red, white, and blue, and organized its distribution citywide to inform the public about the Sikh population. In the midst of the ongoing effort to raise public awareness of the Sikh community, the Richmond Hill Sikh Cultural Society was destroyed in an accidental fire that started in the temple's kitchen (Fries, 2002). Until the temple is rebuilt, a temporary altar has been set up in a house next door that is owned by the cultural society and continues to accommodate 300–400 worshippers daily.

Frequently referred to as the most diverse neighborhood in the world, Elmhurst was a multi-race, multi-racial community by the late 1970s. Since then, the Asian and Latino populations have grown dramatically and now constitute an overwhelming majority (82%) reflecting numerous ethnic groups including Chinese, Asian Indian, Korean, Filipino, Mexican, Colombian and Ecuadorian. Despite its racial composition, Elmhurst has not elected a person of color to the New York City council. The most recent round of political redistricting has failed to approve city council district boundaries intended to advance an Asian/Latino coalition district.

Every ten years following the decennial census, political district lines must be redrawn to contain approximately equal numbers of people in order to adhere to the constitutional mandate of "one person, one vote." As guaranteed by the Fourteenth Amendment to the U.S. Constitution and the 1965 Voting Rights Act, the redrawing of districts must not dilute the voting strength of racial, ethnic, and language minorities, and must provide full and fair opportunities for these minorities to elect candidates of their choice. Since the 1991 redistricting, the United States Supreme Court has also held that districts must include "communities of interest" defined as groupings of people with "actual shared interests." The courts, however, have never precisely defined this concept.

Elmhurst is part of New York City Council District 25 which also includes parts of Jackson Heights, East Elmhurst, Corona, Rego Park, and Woodside, and is currently represented by Helen Sears, a white woman, formerly the Director for Government and Community Affairs at Elmhurst Medical Center. Recognizing the majority Asian and Latino populations and their continuing growth, community organizations including the Asian American Legal Defense and Education Fund (AALDEF) sought to keep the pan-Asian populations of Elmhurst intact by pulling in census tracts to the south and west where much of the population was expanding but was split among different city council districts. To advance the common interests among Asians and Latinos in Elmhurst, AALDEF's proposed boundaries for District 25 included the growing pan-Asian population as well as the majority Latino population in and around Elmhurst.

Public testimonies before the New York City Districting Commission provided much evidence of shared concerns among the multi-race Asian and Latino populations, and the need to create a city council district that promotes a fair opportunity to elect an individual representative of these largely immigrant communities. In his testimony, Elmhurst resident Youngjae Kim noted,[6]

> Latinos and Asians in these areas are relatively recent immigrants who have shown common interest and basic needs such as quality education, affordable housing, public safety, access to health care, and immigrant services.

Underscoring a community of interest among Asians and Latinos, resident Lester Diaz noted,

> In order for our community to participate and advocate for its needs, they need to be united . . . Redistricting of Council Districts 21 and 25 as proposed by the Commission would dilute the ability of these groups from effectively participating. It encourages division. It will constantly pit the various groups to compete against each other.

Resident Jeffrey Van Baemer argued, "Removing a whole section of the neighborhood and placing it into yet a third Council District will only serve to disempower the residents of Elmhurst." He concluded "This cannot be good for the people of Elmhurst, and may dilute the voting strength of racial and ethnic minorities in the district."

Despite the community appeal to keep the Elmhurst neighborhood whole, and adopt district boundaries that encompass the growing Asian and Latino populations who represent multi-race communities of interest, the New York City Districting Commission approved district lines that protected the incumbent by accommodating census tracts to the north which are largely white rather than the Asian/Latino concentrations to the south and west. Reactions expressed disappointment about the dashed opportunity to politically empower Asian and Latinos even in NYC's oldest multi-race, multi-racial neighborhood (AALDEF, 2003).

CONCLUSION

Demographic trends underscore the impact of post-1965 immigration in reshaping the spatial and social contours of the local neighborhoods that make up New York City. Asian and Latino immigrants are transforming the urban landscape by

Table 6. Asian and Latino Ethnic Composition in NYC Global Neighborhoods, 2000.

	Sunset Park	Elmhurst	Richmond Hill
Total Population	116,436	114,154	78,399
Non Hispanic White	17%	14%	24%
African American	2%	1%	8%
Asian	27%	39%	19%
Latino	49%	43%	31%
Multi-Race[a]	3%	3%	11%
Other	1%	1%	6%
Total Asian Population	31,507	44,042	15,011
Chinese	84%	43%	8%
Asian Indian	6%	17%	77%
Korean	0.5%	16%	1%
Filipino	2%	10%	7%
Pakistani	1%	2%	3%
Bangladeshi	1%	4%	1%
Japanese	0.2%	1%	0.4%
Other[b]	4%	7%	3%
Total Latino Population[c]	57,628	48,704	24,578
Mexican	19%	20%	5%
Puerto Rican	39%	6%	26%
Dominican	16%	9%	18%
Colombian	2%	21%	9%
Ecuadorian	6%	20%	10%
Central American[d]	12%	7%	19%
Peruvian	1%	4%	3%
Cuban	1%	2%	1%
Other[e]	4%	10%	9%

Source: 2000 SF1, U.S. Census Bureau.
[a] Multi-Race is a new category in the Census 2000 and includes persons of multiple racial identities.
[b] Other Asian includes Southeast Asians, Thais, Malaysians, Burmese.
[c] Latino figures reflects the adjusted numbers.
[d] Central American includes Central American, Costa Rican, Guatemala, Honduran, Nicaraguan, Panamanian, Salvadoran, and other Central American.
[e] Other Latino includes Argentinean, Bolivian, Chilean, Paraguayan, Uruguayan, Venezuelan, other South American, and Other Hispanic.

rejuvenating and creating vibrant public spaces. This brief introduction to Sunset Park, Richmond Hill, and Elmhurst highlights several important new directions in community studies. These neighborhoods defy simplistic characterizations as immigrant enclaves. Table 6 indicates how the Asian and Latino populations in these neighborhoods are not ethnically homogenous. Even when one ethnic group is the largest as in the case of Asians in Richmond Hill and Sunset Park, there are tremendous religious, regional, and linguistic differences which Census racial categories fail to capture.

Immigrant neighborhoods are clearly differentiated by class composition and resources. Table 7 summarizes several variables that indicate similar socioeconomic conditions among Asians and Latinos within a neighborhood. Will a shared class position lead to cross-racial alliances as seen in the public testimonials that recognized the common interests of Asians and Latinos in Elmhurst? Depending on class resources, will these common concerns be articulated as neighborhood quality of life issues, or as issues of immigrant and workers rights? Will significant class differences among ethnic groups in different neighborhoods affect the formation of pan-ethnic alliances that transcend spatial boundaries?

Towards an analytical framework to study the multi-faceted processes of community and social formation in multi-race neighborhoods, this paper concludes with a preliminary outline of research areas that may contribute to understanding how global neighborhoods shape immigrant trajectories and prospects for building community.

Neighborhood Definition

While neighborhoods are spatial entities, defining neighborhood boundaries is highly subjective and dependent on many social factors including class, age, gender, race and ethnicity (Chaskin, 1995). Are neighborhoods a viable unit of immigrant identity? In immigrant global neighborhoods, what are the micro-level patterns of segregation and how are internal neighborhood "borders" established and maintained? How does the built environment shape neighborhood dynamics and boundaries, influence social interactions, and symbolize cultural and political practices? What defines ethnic spaces? The imposition of externally defined neighborhood borders in terms of political jurisdictions may or may not be consistent with resident definitions of their neighborhood. The example of NYC Council District 25 points to how a neighborhood is divided among several districts resulting in the disenfranchisement of Asian and Latino voters. The ability to define neighborhood spaces and boundaries is critical in community building.

Table 7.   Select Characteristics of Latino and Asian Residents New York City's Immigrant Global Neighborhoods.

Characteristics	Sunset Park		Elmhurst		Richmond Hill	
	Latino	Asian	Latino	Asian	Latino	Asian
Population	57,628	31,507	48,704	44,042	24,578	15,011
% of Neighborhood population	(49)	(27)	(43)	(29)	(31)	(19)
Growth rate 1990–2000 (%)	21	93	49	27	48	166
% Immigrant	41	81	73	82	48	79
% Population below poverty level	29	35	21	17	19	13
Median family income	$28,274	$27,606	$37,810	$37,480	$40,179	$45,351
Homeownership rate (%)	14	28	12	31	33	49
Labor force participation[a] (%)	54	56	62	59	61	59
Unemployed (%)	11	6	10	8	10	
Industry						
Educational, health, social services (%)	16	10	10	12	16	15
Manufacturing (%)	16	28	11	11	8	9
Retail trade (%)	11	8	10	13	10	12
Accommodation and food services (%)	10	19	17	15	9	6
Professional and managerial (%)	7	4	7	7	9	7
Construction (%)	6	3	8	3	5	7
Other services (%)	6	6	10	8	8	6
Finance, real estate, insurance (%)	6	5	5	7	8	7
Transportation and warehousing (%)	5	4	5	6	10	14
Wholesale trade (%)	5	4	4	6	3	6
Other industries[b] (%)	11	9	13	11	14	10
Occupation						
Professional and managerial (%)	14	16	12	28	17	23
Service (%)	25	24	34	21	26	15
Sales and office (%)	26	20	21	29	30	29
Construction (%)	10	4	12	4	10	10
Production (%)	15	29	13	11	8	10
Transportation (%)	10	6	8	7	9	13
% Adults did not complete high school[c]	54	59	42	28	38	35

Source: Census 2000 SF3, U.S. Census Bureau.
[a] Labor Force Participation Rate for 16 years and older.
[b] Other Industries includes Public Administration, Repair and Maintanance, and Private Households.
[c] Adults defined as 25 years and older.

Neighborhood Opportunity Structures

While earlier periods of industrialization and city building provided scores of entry-level jobs for non-English speaking immigrants, immigrants now confront a post-industrial urban economy with weakened institutions such as unions. Much of the emphasis on immigrant economies in both the scholarly and policy arenas highlight their "exceptionalism" in generating entrepreneurship, ethnic solidarity, and economic opportunities, and propose to replicate small business development as a strategy for asset-building in other disadvantaged communities.

Sunset Park is frequently cited as an exemplar of immigrant driven neighborhood revitalization (Kadet, 2000; Oser, 1996; Winnick, 1990). However, the poverty rates among Sunset Park's Asians and Latinos are alarming (Table 7). The relatively high concentration of low-wage employment in immigrant niches such as manufacturing and food services is key to working poverty. While the impact of jobless poverty on neighborhood life and institutions is well theorized and documented by William Julius Wilson and his colleagues, these insights are less developed for working poor neighborhoods.

Although immigrants secure employment in an ethnic economy, their attachment to the labor force is concentrated in marginal sectors where workers are isolated from the mainstream economy due to language barriers and/or lack of information, informal networks, and skills. Recent research on post-9/11 impacts on immigrant garment workers documented limited social networks and ties (Chin, 2003). What are the impacts of working poverty on family and neighborhood life, and opportunities for mobility? Moreover, immigrant neighborhood economies now include growing numbers of transnational businesses. What are the consequences for enclave practices of informal skills training, reliance on social networks, and reciprocity which mediate the conditions and benefits of employment in marginal industry sectors? Will labor and employer relations become more transparent in transnational businesses as the mediating effects of ethnic social ties are weakened?

Locating "Communities of Interest"

It is commonly understood that while neighborhoods are a spatial or geographic unit, communities are not necessarily place-based. In global neighborhoods, locating "communities of interest" that may bridge ethnic diversity is necessary to promote community building. Do Asian and Latino immigrants in spatially disparate neighborhoods constitute a "flexible post-Fordist politics of networked (ethnic) communities" (Sassen, 2000, p. x) or is there a basis for shared concerns and interests that are grounded in the experiences of a particular locality that may promote a collective identity or interest among multi-race populations? A recent survey of Asian community stakeholders conducted by the Asian American Legal Defense and Education Fund found that common neighborhood issues and concerns are not ethnic-specific as they pertained to employment, housing conditions, and neighborhood services. Are these concerns shared among the multi-race populations in global neighborhoods or do minority groups view each other as competitors for scarce resources? (Johnson & Oliver, 1989).

Building Community in Global Neighborhoods

While multi-race immigrant neighborhoods are not a new phenomenon (Binder & Reimers, 1995), post-1965 immigrant neighborhoods are "global" in unprecedented ways that go beyond encompassing ethnically diverse "multiple publics." Most important, post-1965 immigrant groups are racialized non-white minorities. Non-white immigrants from Asia, Latin America, and the Caribbean are, moreover, racialized in distinct ways. This is evident in Louis Winnick's (1990) description of Sunset Park's Latino population as a "socially disorganized" (p. 167) underclass whose "fate [was] to depress more deeply an already depressed community" (p. 94). In contrast, Asian immigrants were portrayed as a model minority whose "penchant for saving and investment" (p. 122) facilitated business and home ownership. While many European ethnic groups were initially perceived as racially distinct with dire consequences culminating in the 1924 National Origins Quota Act, European immigrant groups eventually became "white" (Brodkin, 1998; Ignatiev, 1995; Steinberg, 1981).

In a multi-race neighborhood context, what are the individual and institutional efforts and capacity to foster a cohesive community identity and a sense of "social connection" among a diverse residential population (De Souza Briggs & Mueller, 1997). What are potential converging or divergent interests? While crisis often serves as the basis to unite different population groups, what are the sustained, daily social, political, and cultural practices that create and/or promote bridging and bonding social capital and relationships? As Jane Jacobs noted, "The cross-links that enable a district to function as a Thing are neither vague nor mysterious. They consist of working relationships among specific people, many of them without much else in common than that they share a fragment of geography" (1961, p. 133). How do the social worlds of global neighborhoods "touch" and "interpenetrate" in public spaces including streets, markets, open spaces, and work environments, housing markets, and public schools? How do these interactions evolve into working relationships? Given linguistic barriers and distinct social histories and conditions, do community institutions play a particularly important role in promoting neighborhood identity and providing venues for interaction and exchanges? What type of community leadership is necessary to address these challenges in immigrant global neighborhoods?

NOTES

1. The Asian American Legal Defense and Education Fund conducted a survey on defining neighborhood boundaries and concerns among Asian New Yorkers, and found that key issues are poor employment and housing conditions, overcrowded schools, and neighborhood quality. Refer to AALDEF's website for further information – http://www.aaldef.org.

2. For the past five years, INS data is deflated by more than 100,000 per year due to a backlog in application processing resulting from amnesty provisions in immigration laws. Moreover, immigration figures do not reflect a true "flow" of new immigrants since some are "adjustment of status" and are actually already residing in U.S. but lack legal status. Moreover, INS data only reflects legal immigration and does not include thousands of undocumented immigrants.

3. My categorization of NYC's census tracts is consistent with the methodology employed by Lobos, Flores, Salvo in their 2002 Urban Affairs Review article on Hispanic settlement with the exceptions that of the categorization of multi-race tracts. While Lobo, Flores, and Salvo defined their multi-race tracts by Hispanics in combination with other racial groups, I was also interested in neighborhood typologies that included Asians, NHWs, and Blacks in combination with both Hispanic and other racial groups.

4. Lobo, Flores and Salvo (2002) call these "melting pot" tracts. Some studies use less stringent definitions of multi-ethnic neighborhoods. Nyden et al. (1998) study of racially and ethnically stable neighborhoods in the US defined diverse neighborhoods as those areas with a racial and ethnic composition that approaches the average mix for the city as a whole (p. 14).

5. Diane Cardwell. 2003. New York Times, June 24, p. B1.

6. Quotations are taken from the transcript from the New York City Districting Commission public hearing held on November 24, 2002 at Queens. The transcript is available online at http://home.nyc.gov/html/nydc/pdf/hearing_11_26_02.pdf.

REFERENCES

Asian American Legal Defense and Education Fund (2003). Media release: Asian Americans oppose New City Council Districts. February 6.

Banerjee, N., & Leung, A. (2001). South Asians face violent backlash after WTC attacks. *AsianWeek* (September 20–26), 8.

Beveridge, A. (2001). *Immigration, ethnicity, race in Metropolitan New York, 1990–2000.* Unpublished Paper.

Brodkin, K. (1998). *How Jews became white folks and what that says about race in America.* New Brunswick: Rutgers University Press.

Chin, M. (2003). Moving on: Chinese garment workers after 9/11. Working Papers Series, Russell Sage.

Codero-Guzman, H. R., Smith, R. C., & Grosfoguel, R. (Eds) (2001). *Migration, transnationalization, and race in a changing New York*. Temple University Press.

De Souza Briggs, X., & Mueller, E. with Sullivan, M. (1997). *From neighborhood to community: Evidence on the social effects of community development*. Community Development Research Center, Robert J. Milano Graduate School of Management and Urban Policy, New School for Social Research.

Ellen, I. G. (1998). Stable racial integration in the contemporary United States: An empirical overview. *Journal of Urban Affairs, 20*(1), 27–42.

Foner, N. (2000). *From Ellis Island to JFK: New York's two great waves of immigration*. Yale University Press.

Foner, N. (2001). Transnationalism then and now: New York immigrants today and at the turn of the twentieth century. In: H. R. Codero-Guzman, R. C. Smith & R. Grosfoguel (Eds), *Migration, Transnationalization, and Race in a Changing New York*. Temple University Press.

Fries, J. H. (2002, March 9). Fire destroys a Sikh temple in Queens, injuring 6 priests. *New York Times*.

Galster, G., Metzger, K., & Waite, R. (1999). Neighborhood opportunity structures of immigrant populations, 1980 and 1990. *Housing Policy Debate, 10*, 395–442.

Gottdiener, M., & Hutchison, R. (2000). *The new urban sociology*. McGraw-Hill.

Gregory, S. (1998). *Black Corona: Race and the politics of place in an urban community*. Princeton University Press.

Jacobs, J. (1961). *The death and life of great American cities*. New York, NY: Vintage Books.

Healy, P. (2003). Bias-crime claim puzzles beach enclave in Queens. *New York Times* (July 29), B1.

Hum, T. (2003). Mapping global production in New York City's garment industry: The role of Sunset Park, Brooklyn's immigrant economy. *Economic Development Quarterly, 17*(3), 294–309.

Ignatiev, N. (1995). *How the Irish became white*. Routledge Press.

Johnson, J. H., & Oliver, M. L. (1989). Interethnic conflict in urban America: The effects of economic and social dislocations. *Urban Geography, 10*, 449–463.

Kadet, A. (2000). New dawn in Sunset Park. *Brooklyn Bridge* (February–March).

Kasinitz, P. (1992). *Caribbean New York: Black immigrants and the politics of race*. New York: Cornell University Press.

Kwong, P. (1987). *The new Chinatown*. New York: Hill and Wang.

Levitt, P. (2002). *The transnational villages*. University of California Press.

Li, W. (1999). Building ethnoburbia: The emergence and manifestation of the Chinese ethnoburb in Los Angeles' San Gabriel Valley. *Journal of Asian American Studies, 2*, 1.

Light, I., & Bonacich, E. (1988). *Immigrant entrepreneurs: The Koreans in Los Angeles, 1965–1982*. University of California Press.

Lin, J. (1998). *Reconstructing Chinatown: Ethnic enclave, global change*. University of Minnesota Press.

Lobo, P. A., Flores, R., & Salvo, J. (2002). The impact of Hispanic growth of the racial/ethnic composition of New York City neighborhoods. *Urban Affairs Review, 37*, 703–727.

Logan, J. (2001). *Ethnic diversity grows, neighborhood integration is at a standstill*. Lewis Mumford Center for Comparative Urban and Regional Research, SUNY Albany, Available online at http://www.albany.edu/mumford.

Logan, J. R., Alba, R., & Zhang, W. (2002). Immigrant enclaves and ethnic communities in New York and Los Angeles. *American Sociological Review, 67*(April), 229–322.

Marcuse, P. (1997). The enclave, the citadel, and the ghetto: What has changed in the post-Fordist U.S. City. *Urban Affairs Review, 33*, 228–264.

Muniz, V. (1998). *Resisting gentrification and displacement.* Garland Publishing.

Nyden, P., Lukehart, J., Maly, M. T., & Peterman, W. (1998). Neighborhood racial and ethnic diversity in U.S. cities. *Cityscape: A Journal of Policy Development and Research, 4*(2), 1–17.

Ong, P. (1984). Chinatown unemployment and ethnic labor markets. *Amerasia Journal, 11*(1).

Oser, A. S. (1996). Immigrants again renew Sunset Park. *New York Times* (December 1).

Paul, J. (2000). The importance of being counted – correctly. Available online: http://www.rediff.com/us/2000/mar/06us1.htm.

Portes, A. (1981). Modes of structural incorporation and present theories of immigration. In: M. M. Kritz, C. B. Keely & S. M. Tomasi (Eds), *Global Trends in Migration* (pp. 279–297). Staten Island, NY: Center for Migration Studies Press.

Portes, A., & Bach, R. (1985). *Latin journey: Cuban and Mexican immigrants in the United States.* Berkeley, CA: University of California Press.

Portes, A., Guarnizo, L. E., & Haller, W. J. (2002). Transnational entrepreneurs: An alternative form of immigrant economic adaptation. *American Sociological Review, 67*(April), 278–298.

Portes, A., & Rumbaut, R. G. (1990). *Immigrant America: A portrait.* UC Press.

Portes, A., & Zhou, M. (1992). Gaining the upper hand: Economic mobility among immigrant and domestic minorities. *Ethnic and Racial Studies, 15*(4), 491–522.

Rieder, J. (1985). *Canarise: The Jews and Italians of Brooklyn against liberalism.* Harvard University Press.

Sanjek, R. (1998). *The future of us all: Race and neighborhood politics in New York City.* Cornell University Press.

Sassen, S. (1991). *The global city.* Princeton University Press.

Sassen, S. (2000). Forward. In: V. M. Valle & R. D. Torres (Eds), *Latino Metropolis.* University of Minnesota Press.

Scott, J. (2002). Foreign-born in U.S. at record high. *New York Times* (February 7).

Steinberg, S. (1981). *The ethnic myth: Race, ethnicity and class in America.* Beacon Press.

Waldinger, R. (1996). *Still the promised city?* Harvard University Press.

Wilson, W. J. (1987). *The truly disadvantaged.* University of Chicago Press.

Winnick, L. (1990). *New people in old neighborhoods.* New York, NY: Russell Sage.

Zhou, M. (1992). *Chinatown: The socioeconomic potential of an urban enclave.* Temple University Press.

THE MUSLIM CHRONOPOLIS AND DIASPORIC TEMPORALITY

Michel S. Laguerre

Two observations can be made concerning the social integration of the Muslim week into mainstream civil time by the Muslims in New York City, irrespective of these diasporic citizens' country of birth.[1] On the one hand, Muslim immigrants

Race and Ethnicity in New York City
Research in Urban Sociology, Volume 7, 57–81
Published by Elsevier Ltd.
ISSN: 1047-0042/doi:10.1016/S1047-0042(04)07003-5

engage in social practices that are regulated by civil society and that follow the rhythms of the civil week. They thus inhabit a diasporized Muslim temporality that has been Americanized. At the same time, however, they also inhabit a temporal enclave or chronopolis that links them to worldwide Islam via an Islamic calendar that gives direction to their daily, weekly, and annual activities. These two sets of social temporalities often intersect and crisscross each other, which makes it important to analyze the Muslim week in American society if we are to understand the mechanisms of the constitution and transglobalization of the American Muslim chronopolis.[2]

The Muslim week as practiced in the country of origin undergoes a transformation that adjusts it to the constraints of the workplace in New York, the regulations of the state, and the conventional rhythms of the civil week. But the Muslim week also affords the basis for a locally distinct globalized temporal identity that is characterized by the cultural content of its global flows, the direction and spatiality of its transnational networks, and the temporal rhythms that cadence these flows. The nature of these double identities will be examined here in terms of their internal restructuring and their external relations with the rest of society. Here again, as in our study of the Jewish week in New York, and throughout, our concern is with the nature of the interactions of the subalternized temporality with hegemonic mainstream temporalities.

Muslim immigrants are an even less homogeneous group than Jewish immigrants. They come from distinct cultural and national backgrounds as diverse as Iran, Egypt, India, Morocco, Turkey, Lebanon, Pakistan, and Syria.[3] While some immigrants have lived in a Muslim state where the Islamic calendar is hegemonic (for example, Iran or Saudi Arabia) and diasporization constitutes their first adaptation to a civil or Western calendar, others, such as Turkish immigrants, have adapted to this adjustment in their country of origin prior to immigration into the United States. Even in this latter case, they were accommodated at home by the public and private sectors so as to be able to engage freely in their weekly Friday communal prayers. In contrast, the municipal government and the business community in New York City have yet to come up with ways of accommodating the different temporal deployment of the immigrant Muslim week. In this sense, for both groups of Islamic practitioners, their adjustment to the West is a novel experience that has challenging constraints unknown to them before their emigration from their homeland.

In this study of the Muslim week in New York, the focus is exclusively on the immigrant population from the Persian Gulf states, and not on Caribbean, African, or Afro-American Muslims. Since African American Muslims or members of the "Nation of Islam" hold their religious services on Sunday, we will not deal with the temporal rhythms of their weekly activities. This study concerns itself with Gulf states' immigrants precisely because of the traditional emphasis they place on Friday congregational prayers. In some of these countries, such as Saudi Arabia, Friday is the official day of rest of the civil population. However, in other Muslim states, such as Turkey, Sunday has become the official day of rest as a result of external pressures to readjust or replace their national calendar with the hegemonic Gregorian calendar of the West because of international trade requirements and interstate relations.[4] Even though, for some, Sunday is designated in their homeland as a day of rest, Friday continues to play a predominant role in their secular weekly activities because of the Koranic injunction to attend the noon prayers at a mosque on that day. Observing this injunction retroactively affects the flow of business practices during the week.

The Islamic week is distinguished from other weeks not simply by its distinct peak day – Friday – but also because it forms a distinct "temporal domain." By its rhythm, cadence, and mode of organization, the Islamic week contains the basic characteristics that organize daily life. As Zerubavel puts it, "through imposing a rhythmic 'beat' on a vast array of major activities (including work, consumption, and socializing), the week promotes the structuredness and orderliness of human life, making it more regular and thus more predictable."[5]

We saw in the study of the Jewish week in New York a diaspora engaged in a series of negotiations with the temporalities of the mainstream culture over temporal identities, employing a series of strategies adapted to the particular subaltern identities involved. In the Muslim diaspora, we encounter a different set of such negotiations, with strategies adapted to different identities – to different forms of assimilation and also to the production of a different kind of enclave, ghettoized or dispersed, that has a cultural rhythm on a par with that of the original homelands and that thus constitutes a different kind of transglobalized chronopolis, a global city with its own distinct temporal orientation. This latter strategy may disrupt the temporal harmony of mainstream society by inserting its temporality in the fabric of the social system. This practice implies that the diaspora establishes its temporality as a guidepost for the cultural life of the group, as a barometer to measure and judge its adaptations to city life, as a collection of strategies used to bend city ways in areas in which the immigrant group is unwilling to compromise, and as an infrastructure for the American Muslim chronopolis.

The analysis of the Muslim day and week thus calls for both an interpretation of their reconstitution in New York City and an examination of how the temporality unique to this group fractures the geometry of the urban social system. These analyses will be carried out through an examination of the temporal niche expressed in the physical landscape the Muslims occupy in this immigrant and modernist city. To understand that, we must examine the place of Friday, the peak day, in the structure of the Islamic week, and also the nature of the Islamic day as I observed them at a makeshift mosque in mid-Manhattan.

When I arrived at the mosque, there were about three hundred people in the basement of this modern office building, attending the Friday congregational prayers. This group of Muslims had been renting this basement since 1991 for between $3,000 and $5,000 per month. The basement is the only spot they occupy in the building, The rest of the space in the building is occupied by law firms and other professional offices.

New York Muslims do not come to the mosque for all the prayers. They recite some while at work. At the workplace, they lay their carpets in some corner, sometimes in public view, sometimes in their offices, to pray facing east. At first, co-workers find the practice strange, but as time goes by, they adjust to it. So Muslim workers have brought a new religious dimension to secular Manhattan. Like the Orthodox Jews before them, they have carved a niche for the performance of their daily rituals.

On this Friday, Muslims were assembled in the main hall of the basement, in the small office of the imam, in the corridors, and on the steps leading to the exit door on the first floor. The basement was packed with worshippers. Some who could not get in at all were praying in front of the building on the sidewalk. Those outside the building laid their carpets, took off their shoes, faced east, and performed their prostrations and prayers. Some passersby, perhaps tourists, were amused at seeing them praying so publicly without being disturbed by onlookers.

While in some areas one national group or another dominates by their numbers in attendance, in most urban mosques, the congregation is rather diversified. It was found in New York City that "most of the city's mosques attract an amalgam of regular congregants, shopkeepers from the local neighborhood, or perhaps a few cab drivers in the vicinity during *Juma'a*."[6] Diversity certainly characterized this Manhattan mosque. I was told that on a weekly average, about eight hundred people come to this mosque for daily prayers and meditation, mostly individuals who work nearby and taxi drivers. Every day they come from all walks of life: street vendors, mostly from West Africa, operators of food carts, mostly from Egypt, Pakistani and Bangladeshi office workers, cab drivers from everywhere, who complain about the difficulty of finding a place to park their vehicles, Indonesian immigrants, overseas Chinese, Albanians, North Africans, and students from Turkey. I spoke at length with the imam (an Egyptian American), an elder (a Turkish American), and an attendant (from West Africa) who works at the *New York Times*.

My impression was that in terms of social class, the membership of the congregation was mixed, from the bourgeois to poor daily workers, but once they were in the basement with their shoes off, it was difficult to distinguish them by class. It was notable, however, that there was only one woman in attendance (an

African American woman), who was confined to the office of the imam. Gender separation, gender exclusion, and gender marginalization transpire through the strengths of the male membership.

FRIDAY AND THE STRUCTURE
OF THE ISLAMIC WEEK

For the Muslim faithful, the Islamic week indirectly derives from an act of "divine revelation" for the Prophet Muhammad that directs them to use Friday as a congregational day of prayer.[7] The Koran is strict about this prescription and presents it as an obligation to the faithful. Verses 9 to 11 from chapter 62 provide the social context and religious meaning of the peak day of the Islamic week.[8]

> 9. O you who believe, when the call is sounded for prayer on Friday, hasten to the remembrance of Allah and leave off traffic. That is better for you, if you know.
> 10. But when the prayer is ended, disperse abroad in the land and seek of Allah's grace, and remember Allah much, that you may be successful.
> 11. And when they see merchandise or sport, they break away to it, and leave thee standing. Say: what is Allah is better than sport and merchandise. And Allah is the Best of Providers.

The exegesis of verses 9 and 11 reveals or implies that the day of congregation is a work day and that Muslims, upon hearing the call for prayer, must leave all their earthly activities – commerce, sport, or any other – and attend the gathering (*Juma'a*) at the mosque. So work is permitted before the congregational prayer. Verse 10 also indicates that after prayer, one may return to work, confident that entreprencurial activities may be successful because of the grace of Allah. Friday thus is parceled out in three distinct moments according to the Koran: the half-day's work in the morning, the prayer time around noon, and the later half-day's work in the afternoon. It is the only day of the week that is thus fractured.

The centrality of Friday resides in the fact that it is the culmination of the week, when the faithful communicate their joys, sorrows, and intentions to Allah, when they experience fellowship with other fellow believers, and when they are spiritually reenergized for the following week. Hence, the three characteristics of the Friday *Juma'a* can be summarized as congregational prayer, fellowship, and the infusion of spiritual energy for the next weekly cycle.

What distinguishes the Islamic week from the other weeks is that it has no prescribed day of rest. The day of rest in Muslim countries, be it Friday or Sunday, is imposed by the state, and not by Islam. In a sense, the Islamic week is a continuous week, and one weekly cycle touches the other without a day of rest in between the two. In the context of the Islamic week, one is not prevented from earning money on Friday, as happens in the case of the Jewish Sabbath. The justification for working on Friday is from the Koran: "Allah is active every day, He never rests." In my observations in New York, I have found that after the congregational prayer, most Muslim workers indeed return to their jobs.

Friday thus is not even strictly speaking a *day* of worship, but rather a midday worship period in which prayer is proposed for a specific time of the day – around noontime, or in the early hours of the afternoon. However, following Friday prayers, the afternoon is often taken at a slow pace. And while congregational prayer is required of males on Friday, women are not obligated to partake in this ritual.

Although Friday is the most important day for the Muslims, the congregational prayer meeting cannot always be attended on that day by some congregants because of conflict with workplace schedules. The distance of the mosque from the workplace also may hinder one's ability to attend such services. The absence of any nearby congregation of Muslims is sometimes a handicap. This sort of problem concerns the individual in his or her devotional activities, not in adherence to Friday as the peak day of the week. At the Manhattan mosque, I learned that people are likely to attend the mosque near the location they happen to be on the day of congregational prayer – be it at home or at their workplace. This mosque is attended almost exclusively by people who work on Friday in Manhattan. Those who take a day off on Friday, following the customs of their homeland, attend the mosque near their places of residence.

While some Muslims do not adhere strictly to the daily prayers, they may nevertheless attend the Friday prayers at a nearby mosque. The latter have been referred to as the "Muslims of Friday," distinguishing them from the daily practitioners and from the "*Eid* Muslims," who show up for prayers only during the high holy days.[9] According to a Saudi Arabian immigrant:

> Friday is only for those who go to pray. But most people don't, and those who do, [it] is not that they are faithful – it is a tradition that if you pray on Friday, God would hear you more than any other day. *Juma'a* is "Friday" in Arabic and means "group." So people get together on Friday as a group. Friday is like Sunday morning for Christians. You go and pray.

There are several interpretations of the choice of Friday as the Muslim weekly holy day. The first is purely conjectural and refers to the needs for Muslims to worship on a day different from the holy days of the Jews and Christians. Since the Jews have Saturday and the Christians Sunday, this conjecture argues, Friday was selected to give a different and distinct identity to the Islamic faith and its followers.[10] It was an institutional choice to identify, separate, and consolidate one faith from the others by way of de-Judaizing and de-Christianizing it.[11]

The second interpretation is theological and refers to the Islamic narrative of the creation of the world by Allah. In that tradition, Friday becomes a holy day, a day of excellence, because of what Allah undertook on that day. The principal reasons for the holiness of Friday are that, according to Muslims "it was on Friday that Adam was created,"[12] that he entered into Paradise, and that he was sent down to Earth. For these reasons, it is believed that judgment day will occur on Friday. Because of this, congregational prayers are held on Friday, and people are encouraged to give money to charity on this day. As a result of the sanctity of Friday, it is widely believed by the faithful that prayers offered to Allah on that day bear immediate fruit and one's sins are ipso facto forgiven.

The theological explanation of why Friday is not constructed in Islam as a day of rest stems from the fact that Muslims are not asked to subscribe to the belief that Allah got tired after he had created the universe in six days. For Muslims, being tired and in need of rest is the consequence of one's sins, and would imply imperfection and finitude if applied to Allah. This interpretation, according to two Egyptian American imams and one Palestinian American imam I spoke to for clarification on that question, is unacceptable to Muslims.

The third reason is contextual and sociological. According to Goitein, Friday was selected as a holy day in reference to "the instructions given by Muhammad to his representative in Medina to hold the public service on the day when the Jews bought their provisions for their Sabbath."[13] Since Friday was a market day in Medina – the day of preparation for the Jews and a day for restocking merchandise for others – the injunction for Friday prayers implies that the people were already in town, and services should be held before they return home. For Goitein, "the market in Arabia breaks up soon after noon, so that everybody attending it is able to reach his home before nightfall . . . Therefore, the proper time for the public worship was at noon, shortly before people dispersed to get to their homes, and thus it has remained until the present day."[14] This sociological interpretation provides a plausible explanation for both the choice of Friday and the midday prayer.

THE "DAY" IN THE MUSLIM CALENDAR

The definition of the day in the Islamic calendar is not the same as in the civil calendar because among Muslims, the day starts at sunset and ends at sunset.[15] The day has a rhythm provided by the five prayers, while the rhythm of the week leads to the peak day – Friday – after which a new weekly cycle begins.

Similarly, the day in the Muslim week is not defined in the same way as the day in the Christian week. The Christian day is not astronomical, but is conventionally based on the rotation of the clock from midnight to midnight. In contrast, as in the case of the Jewish day, the Muslim day goes from sundown to sundown. That is, it comprises a full period of dark and a full period of daylight consecutively. The Christian day contains or covers the second half of the period of dark, a full period of daylight, and the first half of the following period of dark. In practice, the Christian day does not fully coincide with the Muslim day. As Freeman-Grenville[16] notes, "in correct Arabic . . . the Christian 7 p.m. is 1 o'clock in the evening . . . and what to the Muslim is Sunday evening is to the Christian still Saturday evening." Locating the end of the day at sunset, rather than at midnight, provides a different temporal rhythm that syncopates the life of the Muslim with a different beat than that of the mainstream citizen.

Because Friday is a peak day in the Muslim calendar, the rest of the week tends to rotate around it. Friday separates the week to come from the preceding week in the same way that Sunday does in the Gregorian calendar used by the civil week. The communal prayer mandated by the Koran for that day both spiritually reinvigorates the faithful and is an experience of fellowship. The Muslim turns to Friday as the day of completion, the rendezvous with Allah. This is why the day is considered by the faithful to be "holy."

Although Friday is not a day of rest in some Muslim countries it still shares a number of characteristics with the Jewish Sabbath and the Christian Sunday. It is a day different from the other days of the week because of the obligatory communal worship, the required cleanliness of the body, the purification of the soul, and the fellowship with the faithful. In the external manifestation of the exceptionality and singularity of the day, the clothes that one wears and the food that one eats differ from the routine practices of daily life.

THE AMERICANIZATION OF THE ISLAMIC WEEK

The Muslim week has not simply been transplanted to the five boroughs. It has been Americanized in several different ways. However, despite its adaptation to urban life in the United States, and although it frequently intersects with the civil week, it does not collide with the civil week and continues to maintain its distinct identity. Studying how the Islamic week is reconstituted in New York will also allow us to identify and explain the mechanisms of operation of this chronopolis there.

The Islamic week is Americanized in three ways: because of the constraints of immigrant life in a non-Islamic state, because of the way Muslim immigrants adjust to the system of the Western week that is heavily influenced by Western European Christianity, and because of the new identity that it forges due to these external factors and the internal urge to conform to traditional Islamic ways.

By "Americanization," we mean that the week contains features of both the homeland week and the American week and is a hybrid product. This is why one cannot speak of it as being a transplantation, but rather as a new production or new creation. Full cultural continuity would have implied structural continuity, which is not the case here.

Instead, the organization of the civil week, with Sunday as a day of rest, influences the structure of the Muslim week. The civil week is not simply a matter of sequence of days, it is also the rhythm of daily life in terms of peak days, the obligation to take Sunday off as a day of rest, and the concentration of leisure activities during the weekend. Immigrant children, for example, must adjust to a different rhythm for the school week. Those who come from Saudi Arabia and Iran, where school is closed on Friday, but open on Sunday, must adjust to the temporal deployment of the American civil week. Children who were not accustomed to going to school on Friday must adjust to a situation in which they have to do so. Those who used to go to school on Sunday must adjust to the fact that Sunday is a rest day during which regular schools are closed. Likewise, the religious education of Muslim children takes place more and more on Sunday as they use the Christian day of rest for Sunday school. In U.S. cities with large Muslim immigrants from the Gulf states, Sunday school has become a main activity at the mosque, irrespective of the immigrants' Shi'ite or Sunni backgrounds. This is one area where the Americanization of the Muslim faith has become most visible.

The fact that secular society stops working on Sunday also forces Muslims to do likewise because non-Muslims are not available on Sunday for business, especially in the morning. The ideology for some Muslims then becomes: Let's worship on Friday and let's rest on Sunday. As one Muslim immigrant businessman put it:

Yes, most often business merchants will take one day off, and that's possibly Sunday. And there are a combination of reasons: one is if he has children, the children are off school on this day, second, the business is very slow, so they can afford to take the day without losses, and third, most activities, going to the park, taking kids to recreational things, gatherings, Sunday seems to be the day for all of that, so definitely there is a shift.

You could say that the weekend definition that applies to Americans applies to Muslims, as well. There is no difference in many instances.

He conceded that "there are some that do take the day off as Friday" – he mentioned a dentist of his acquaintance – and "some stores also close on Friday, but that's not the majority, that would be the minority. In this area, around the *Masjid* [the mosque], the businesses are open, they close for two hours, and they will attend to the Friday prayers."

"The weekend definition that applies to Americans applies to Muslims" in the structuring of activities other than formal labor – activities as diverse as weddings and the scheduling of academic conferences. As one informant put it,

> In traditional Muslim societies, most often Thursday evenings would be the time for the community to gather, like a wedding would occur on Thursday evening, an engagement party, a celebration of a newborn child, any type of community festivity or religious festivity, or any community attempt for gathering, public meetings, usually they would take place on Thursday evenings, and sometimes would go onto Friday evenings. Now in the U.S., that is completely altered, most of the gatherings that occur in the Muslim community, and here we're talking about the majority of them, are on Saturday evening. Some would occur on Friday evening, and some would occur on Sunday. Conferences, without any exception, would take place on Saturday and Sunday, and some would begin Friday, after Friday prayer, or Friday evening; so they'll begin at seven in the evening and go onto Saturday and Sunday. This is also completely different, because most conferences, let's say in the Muslim world, if they want to start, they'll start on maybe Wednesday evening, if they're two days or more, Wednesday evening, Thursday, and then Friday, with the major gathering being around Friday.

Because of the temporal practices of mainstream society, Sunday rest for Muslims thus simply becomes a practical matter, especially in states where Sunday rest is legislated by blue laws, as in New York. And to the extent that the Christian and secular calendars coincide, the Islamic week reacts and adjusts to the Christian calendars, as well. There are Christian holidays, such as Christmas, that are also secular holidays of the state.

Just as we have seen in the case of the Jewish adaptation to the temporalities enforced by the hegemony of the civil and Christian week, "reform" Muslims have sought to accommodate the temporalities of worship to the temporalities of the mainstream society by moving the day of congregational worship from Friday to Sunday.[17] Such a move solves two problems at once. Sunday is the time when people are free to attend congregational prayer. Using Sunday, instead of Friday, also saves time, since the family may have to come to the mosque to bring the children for Sunday school. Elkholy,[18] who studies the Sunday noon prayer among the Muslim community in Toledo, interprets it as representing "a kind of over-all religious integration with the American environment."

But as with Reform Judaism's shift of the Sabbath, the transfer of the congregational prayers from Friday to Sunday by "reform" Muslims has consequences for the content of the faith itself. Since the belief system underlines the importance of Friday as the day of the birth of Adam, which gives a theological justification to the temporal structure, moving the time of congregational worship from Friday to Sunday disentangles the theological justification from the temporal location that gives it its spiritual and eschatological meaning. The maintenance of the day of worship on Sunday by reformists thus somewhat distances them from traditional Islam and constitutes a major point of theological contention among believers.

However, in general, the shift of congregational worship from Friday to Sunday remains a practical matter, not a theological one: Those who attend the Sunday prayers do so because of their inability to leave the workplace or because they have children they bring to the mosque for Sunday school. Those who are not handicapped by these two constraints, as well as the old or unemployed, attend the Friday service.[19] While in Reform Judaism, Sunday Sabbath replaces the Saturday Sabbath, in the Muslim context, as Haddad puts it, "Sunday services . . . serve only as alternative meetings and do not replace Friday worship."[20] As the study of Muslim worship practices in the Southend found, "Because of the difficulties encountered in leaving work to worship on Fridays, the weekly communal prayer has traditionally been observed only by the elderly and retired men of the Southend. . . . The Friday communal prayers . . . almost disappeared as the custom of Sunday worship became the preferred norm."[21]

Research carried out in Quincy, Massachusetts, found that for reasons of convenience, not theology or ideology, attendance of congregational worship on Friday was heavier during the summer months than during the rest of the year, when it was heaviest on Sunday. This was because he faithful came in large numbers on Sunday, when Sunday school was held, to bring their children to school, while during the summer months, when Sunday school was not held, they came in large numbers to the Friday services.[22]

Because Sunday congregational worship is a matter of convenience, not of theology, and because Sunday worship lacks a theological justification, it is easy for worshippers to move back and forth in their devotional practices. They are fervent believers in attending the mosque on Friday, but are ready to shift in order to accommodate themselves and their children. They are simply accommodating themselves to the rhythms of the civil week.

And because the accommodation is practical, not ideological, it can be reversed, just as we have seen a similar accommodation of the Jewish Sabbath to the rhythm of the civil week reversed in a Reformed Jewish congregation in San Francisco. The recent history of the Southend Muslim community, for example, reveals that following the change from the Friday prayer to the Sunday services, worshippers returned to Friday congregational prayers as new settlers reinvigorated the traditional practices of the community: "In recent years, a group of men of varying ages . . . can be found attending the Friday communal prayer. In contrast to the past, this attendance represents a virtual revival of the Friday prayer. . . . To a large extent, the revival of the mosque is a direct result of the influx of a large number of new immigrants to the Southend."[23] The new immigrants serve as a catalyst for the reproduction of the transnational relations of the community with the homeland and for the revival of the disappearing old culture in the diasporic neighborhood.

While the disjunction between theology and practical matters means that the Americanization of the Muslim week via "reform" strategies for locating the day of congregational worship is relatively easy and relatively easy to abandon, the conflict between Muslim and civil temporalities in the Americanization of the Islamic weekly cycle is felt more acutely in the deployment of the day itself. Diasporans must attempt to combine and mesh together the features of both the Islamic day and civil day because of the dual religious and secular obligations to which they must attend. The singularity of the Islamic day rests with the scheduling of the five daily prayers. While the morning (fajr/dawn) and evening (maghrib/sunset and isha/night) prayers do not present any problem because they can be done in the privacy of one's home, the daylight prayers, (zuhr/noon and asr/afternoon) for those who work outside their home, require some adjustment, because they must be done while one is still at the workplace. Indeed, the struggle to accommodate the prayers in the workplace when "there is usually no area at the place of employment where it is appropriate to prepare for and perform them"[24] is the single most important issue that characterizes the adaptation of the Muslims to the civil day.[25] Because of workplace constraints, these prayers are not always fulfilled in the strict order prescribed by traditional Islamic tradition. Instead, their temporal locations are sometimes adjusted to the rhythmic cadence of urban life through via prayer clustering.[26] Prayer clustering is a strategy for accommodating religious obligations to the demands of secular social life, a strategy that is permitted under Islamic law. It consists of relocating unsaid prayers to a different moment when they can be combined with the prayer of the hour.

Midday and afternoon prayers have been the best candidates for such clustering. An Iranian woman reflecting on her life in New York, remarks that:

> In the morning and evening, I have no problem to recite my prayers on time. But the only problem I have is with the middle of the day prayers [asr and maghrib]. We are allowed to combine sets of daily prayers together. I don't know how to explain it. You can ask there is a reason for that. You just pray in the evening, but you say that this is for past prayers. There is a rule for that, but you are not supposed to do that all the time.

Another Iranian American woman interviewed in San Francisco was more casual and less scrupulous about doing the prayers at an exact time. For her,

> it is an interval of time so as long as you have an idea of what time it is to pray, you know the sun is going down at 5:30, you know you need to get your afternoon prayer done before then. It is better to do it earlier, but it is okay if you do it before sunset. So it is an interval, it is very easy to fit into your life.

Difficulties presented by the sequence of the prayers during the winter months, when sunset falls at an early period, fade away during the summer, and prayer clustering as a way of fulfilling one's religious obligations then is used less often by the faithful.

The temporal location of two of these prayers (*zuhr*/noon and *asr*/afternoon) corresponds to the moment when the practitioner may be at work. The part of the Muslim day that culturally does not correspond to the civil day provides the rhythm for these prayer activities, but at the same time places the Muslim in conflict with the routine flow of work of the civil day. Here, the Muslim is the integrating site where the hybridization of the logics of two different days occurs. There is a back-and-forth motion whereby the Muslim penetrates the secular day for his labor, but reverses on occasion to the Muslim day for devotional purposes. In this new temporal regime, some Muslims thus have developed a flexible identity that is compatible with both the teaching of the Koran and the constraints of daily life in New York. Although from the standpoint of the actor, the secular and Muslim days are not parallel days, but a single integrated day, with prayer times punctuating the routine of daily life in the civil day, what one actually sees here is the deployment of the Muslim day side by side with the deployment of the secular day and their periodic intersection.

Perhaps the best example of the way in which the Muslim week and the civil week proceed in parallel is the way in which the peak day of the Muslim week remains gendered, while the civil week is differently gendered. Gender differences are sustained by a temporal infrastructure, and not simply by a spatial one. Gender is temporized precisely because it is spatialized. Because of the spatial distance that exists between males and females as a result of their different positions in American Muslim society, women occupy different temporalities from men.[27] Muslim gender positioning does not coincide with gender positioning in the hegemonic Anglo community because these two agencies belong to different temporal cycles and proceed from different logics toward different goals.

As we have seen, the Muslim week allocates spheres of public worship in terms of gender by making it mandatory for men – and not for women – to participate in the communal prayer on Friday. This peak day constructs the private realm as the sphere of women and the public mosque as the sphere of men. In relation to mosque attendance on Friday, an Iranian Muslim woman has the following to say:

> Well, for the sisters, it's not as big of an issue as it is for the brothers, because it's not something that they must do, but for the brothers, it is something they need to partake in every week. The women, they are invited to come? Oh, of course, it's best if you do, but it's not necessary. So for the brothers, the few brothers that I know, they just take their lunch-hour break and they manage to come and pray and leave.

The fact that men, but not women are mandated to attend the Friday prayers opens a spatial division that distances each group from the other and reinforces the ideology that confines women to the domestic sphere.

Gender division also is present in the mosque in the physical separation of men and women worshippers, which reflects the different positions that both men and women occupy in society. This division is spatially asymmetrical and reflects spatially that social asymmetry. These gendered practices reinforce and reproduce the gendered ideology that is necessary to justify the asymmetry. The production of these gendered practices is a male project that is part of the effort to reproduce in New York City gendered Islamic identities and ethnicities[28] that devalue diasporic Muslim women and that lead to what Rowbotham calls "women's partial citizenship."[29]

The Muslim woman's social position of course is also asymmetrically temporized vis-à-vis the mainstream community because of the minority status of the group. While in the first instance, the inequality factor was the result of different positions of individuals in the same group, here, the disparity is between the majority and the minority communities. These two forms of subjugation are also inscribed in the week. Emancipation in such a situation would imply the implementation of some form of "differentiated citizenship."[30]

Male and female attendance on Friday reflects the tradition of the country of attendees. While in some Muslim countries, it is customary for males only to attend these prayers, in others, both men and women attend. As a consequence of these cultural practices, gender representation in mosque attendance on Friday reflects the diversity of customary practices among Muslims in the United States.[31] In this light, adaptation to American society also implies adaptation to other Muslim practices and the diasporic regendering of the week according to different ethnic practices.

In addition, however, the changes experienced by diasporized Muslim women as part of the process of adaptation to the New York social landscape bring about a temporal difference between them and the women in the original country. Temporal change as a result of their participation in the Americanized Islamic week and the social mores of the American city dissociates them from temporal social practices in the homeland. So time is an issue that fractures the transnational relations between Americanized Muslim women and the homeland.[32]

THE MUSLIM TEMPORAL ENCLAVE

The social processes at work among Muslim immigrants in New York City in part result in the periodic assimilation of these diasporas into the mainstream temporalities of the city. However, because the temporalities remain parallel, the opposite process also is at work. The subaltern temporalities are also transglobal. The presence of the transglobal in the local regime resists assimilation and leads over time to the transformation of the diasporans into an enclave city or chronopolis shaped by the modulations of Islamic temporal practices. This chronopolization takes various forms because of the interplay between the global and the local in the diasporans' specific localized niche.

The insertion of the five prayers within or into the interstices of the civil day gives Muslims "a very basic sense of Islamic identity"[33] separate from that imposed by the hegemonic civil day. Identity is not expressed in a temporal vacuum, and in the case of Muslims, not in any type of weekly arrangement. By giving a tempo to the day, the prayers constitute an infrastructure for the expression of that Islamic identity. The Islamic day, week, month, and year are all part of the architecture of this identity.

Islamic time is not civil time. The Islamic week and the civil week proceed from different assumptions, evolve according to different rhythms, and emphasize different aspects of the week. Naff[34] writes that "it had long been apparent to Muslims in the United States that the American time schedule and calendar were not adjusted to the Islamic way of life." The time of the "noon" prayer (*zuhr*), for example," varies from season to season or depending on the month of the year. The noon prayer was calculated to be held at 11:53 a.m. for November 1, 1998 and at 2:59 p.m. for September 29 of the same year for Muslims in the San Francisco Bay Area.

In the absence of the call to prayer by the muezzin, as happens in the Middle East, therefore, the Muslim immigrant in New York City becomes very attached to his or her watch and to the Islamic calendar, with its subdivision of daytime hours, to help locate when the prayers should be done. This calendar is needed not only to determine the time of midday prayers, because this does not always coincide with noon in the Western clock, but to identify the precise date and time of the beginning and ending of Ramadan and to verify the beginning of daylight in areas where fog can obstruct one's ability to see and determine the exact time of sunrise for morning prayers. The American Muslim calendar provides the time on the Western clock when the Muslim midday occurs and the precise time when each of the five prayers should be offered to Allah. The Western clock thus becomes an auxiliary for the identification of prayer times according to Muslim calculations. The temporal enclave of Muslim time takes precedence over civil time, and transglobal subaltern time displaces hegemonic time.

The disjunction between Islamic time and civil time is thus not simply a product of different histories, it is contemporary, as well.[35] Muslim temporalities and those of the hegemonic mainstream do not always mesh well, and the two cannot always be reconciled on the part of the subaltern community by strategies such as prayer clustering. While some employers are willing to let Muslims have time off for the Friday prayer because it is mandatory and because it happens once a week, for example, they are not always ready to allow time for the daily prayers. Unlike the congregational Friday prayers, the daily prayers are acts of personal devotion and may not be noticeable to persons in the mainstream because of the shorter amount of time they require. In contrast, the two to three hours prayer on Friday require a longer and more visible absence from the workplace.

A Moroccan construction worker who is a regular at a recently constructed mosque in upper Manhattan – The Islamic Cultural Center of New York – informed me that he takes his day off on Friday so that he can come to the mosque for the congregational prayers. He claims that he is not able to do his prayers at work because the boss complains about the ten minutes he loses (or "wastes each time"), since he is not allowed to work extra time because the office closes at 5:00 p.m. It would be impractical for the manager to expand his own hours to accommodate him. However, he indicated to me that those who work for Arab American employers or even some Jewish American employers are allowed to take time off for their prayers.

In some instances, though, strategies of temporal substitution are possible and help assimilate Muslim to non-Muslim temporalities. The manager of a textile store in Brooklyn who is of Palestinian origin, but who does not own the store, informs me that he carefully mixes Muslim with non-Muslim workers to prevent conflict on Friday and during the month of Ramadan. On Friday, both the manager and the Muslim workers leave the store at noon to attend the midday prayers in a nearby mosque, and the non-Muslims run the store while they are away. With this strategy, no profit is lost, and the Muslim workers are able to fulfill their religious duties. In some cases, arrangements are made on an ad hoc basis. That is, an employee may request from an employer to start early on Friday so that he can take time off at midday or may do overtime to compensate for time lost at work. Similarly, a Turkish American faculty member at a New York university had arranged with the college to teach at 3:00 p.m. or in the morning so that he could attend the Friday prayers at the nearby mosque in Manhattan. In the same vein, students enrolled in universities try not to take classes that meet at midday and early afternoon on Friday: "Very few," said a doctoral student at one of the local universities, who is himself a devout Palestinian Muslim, "unless that's the only class so that you might graduate, they'll do it, so most will not take class on Friday, usually after Friday prayer, that's when students gather, so you'll most often see that will be the time of lunchtime gathering."

However, pursuing these strategies is not always possible. There are real problems associated with the practice of the Friday prayer. Haddad and Lummis[36] report that:

> Muslims . . . hesitate to ask their employers for time off to attend the Friday noon prayer service. This is due to the fear that such a request might hurt their chances of promotion or might be refused. One imam reported that his request for release from his job for two hours on Fridays

to lead the Friday prayer was denied even though he was willing to have the necessary amount deducted from his salary.

A Saudi Arabian immigrant who has been living in the United States for the past thirty years confirms the incompatibility of Islamic and mainstream temporalities and the consequences that have flowed from them:

> If you want to pray on time you could probably get fired. Recently, they have been saying that there should be tolerance of Moslems if they want to pray, but until very recently, you could not pray during working hours unless you wanted to lose your job. And most of the time people do, from what I hear; it has never happened to me because I never prayed anyway. If you can't do it, Islam is flexible; you can pray later in the day or whenever you have the chance. So, even if you want to pray and feel good about your prayers, there is no place to go to. It is not allowed in the buildings; it is not allowed in the school. So, it is very lonely and intimidating if you are a practicing Moslem and you want to go pray at noon or at one o'clock. Your boss would not let you go; you would lose your job. And if the other two are available, there is no place where you could feel that you are at peace when you are praying.

Another Saudi confirmed this sense that the hegemonic culture is overtly hostile to the expression of Muslim temporalities:

> The Saudis who pray feel lonely when it comes to prayer time, extremely lonely, because they are in the environment that nobody prays except themselves. Maybe you will find one person hiding behind a tree or behind a building praying on campus, and he also (mostly he, not she) knows that praying is being ridiculed in this culture. When you pray and you go to wash, when you go and do these rituals. So he is aware of two things: the fact that nobody next to him is praying, he does not even know if he is praying correctly or not. And he knows that the culture and the society are against Islam because of how Islam is being depicted in the American media, American TV, political campaigns, and stuff like that. So the ones who are actually faithful have a hell of a time praying in this country and normally some of them go back based on these kind of premises; because they cannot practice their faith freely like they do back home. I am not sure if it is freely, but safely. You know, in Saudi Arabia, everything stops at prayer time, and you go to pray whether you like it or not. Shops close, traffic stops . . . everything stops, and you go to the mosque. Here, you don't have that kind of collective prayers, efforts, and stuff like that.

Increasingly, however, there has been a recognition and acceptance of the fact that the temporalities of Islamic identity cannot be reduced to mainstream temporalities and that Islamic time forms a transglobalized enclave within mainstream time. As a result, American society has been bending its old ways to make room for Muslims[37] by providing space at the workplace for the congregational prayers and by converting work time in nonwork time so that the faithful can attend these prayers. Husain and Vogelaar have found that "most universities and colleges in Chicago provide rooms for Muslim students to offer Friday prayers. Many businesses and hospitals also provide space to conduct Friday prayers or allow time off to their Muslim employees to attend these prayer services."[38] For this to happen, there must be sufficient Muslim workers in the workplace or students attending the university for their request to be taken into consideration. either because of humanitarian concerns or because of a threat of discriminatory suits. Such a request may be granted irrespective of the existence of a nearby mosque and with the understanding that this disruption of work will not negatively affect the productivity of the operation.

Winning recognition as a legitimate temporal enclave has required negotiations in the workplace and in the broader fields of law, politics, and society. An imam who heads a mosque in the San Francisco Bay Area summed up the problem thus:

> I know that Oracle provides the room for Muslims who work in there as engineers, to pray in Silicon Valley. I know it has come up with many Muslims having to negotiate an hour or two to attend the prayer, and I think that's standard, and CAIR (Council on American Islamic Relations) has a whole advisory on worker's rights – which is this organization, and they have it on their Web site, their advice on how to approach and deal with this issue, and we have a list of the cases that they actually have won with companies that provided permission for their workers to attend the private prayer, and also issues of dress, beard, all those items. So they have many cases where the companies have agreed to that, it's a workers rights under religious need that the companies have to work with the workers to try to provide them that. Now there are definitely cases where the companies have difficulty accepting this and that's where the legal intervention has to be. But I know that Oracle does that and other companies in Silicon Valley, because there are large numbers of Muslim workers there.

In some places, the Muslims have been able to carve out micro-Islamic communities inside mainstream U.S. society as a way of recouping the Islamic day and giving it a hegemonic status in their enclaved chronopolis. In Detroit's Southend, for example, just as in Arabic communities in the Middle East, calls for prayer "are now carried across a public address system, which can be heard throughout the area, reminding the Muslim residents of their obligations."[39] In Dearborn, Michigan, where the Muslim community is ghettoized, the call to prayer has become a permanent feature, which has occasioned objections by the surrounding community against the noise level in the area. Muslims in San Diego had also faced such a challenge. Hermansen[40] reports that "in the course of acquiring permission to build from the city a series of hearings were held" in which objectors "feared that the call to prayer would disturb the neighborhood." The presence of such a chronopolis not only establishes itself on the basis of its temporal difference, it thus affects the rest of the city as it pursues strategies to maintain its temporal distinctness.

In enclaves such as these, the subaltern day has emerged as an alternative to the hegemonic day, wholly recognized by the formal system to the extent that it has been able to impose its way in this specific niche.[41] Such enclaves, whether fully or only partially realized, function as genuine communities within communities

– transglobalized chronopolises with links not shared with mainstream society. In my observations in two Manhattan mosques, I have found that the site of the Friday prayer is used as the place where the community meets as a group and where information about the community, discount stores, and political meetings affecting both the diaspora and the homeland are provided and shared. This phenomenon is not peculiar to New York. Those who have studied Muslim communities in other parts of the country have reported similar observations. For example, Fisher and Abedi[42] note that "prayer ends. Fliers are distributed: Five Star Groceries announces special prices; A&N Automobile and Body Shop, 10 percent off; Visit Shamania Sweets; Granny's Buffet invites everyone to a complete 'Id program with poetry and music. . . .' There is no Iranian newspaper table. Rumor has it, they are at a demonstration today."

The difference between the weekly cycles of the enclave community and the mainstream society is manifest in the operation of stores located nearby mosques, where the owners anticipate clients will show up after Friday prayers. For these enclave businesses, Friday is a peak commercial day. One Muslim immigrant noted that:

> after the Friday prayer usually what happens is the businesses that are closely located around the mosque experience an increase in sales, an increase in commercial transactions; this is due to the proximity to the mosque, a lot of people attend the prayer, it affords them time to go to shop for the necessities, or what you call "ethnic food," or ethnic items that are not carried by the mainstream stores.

THE TRANSGLOBAL CHRONOPOLIS

As we have seen, because the Muslim diaspora follows a weekly cycle different from that of the civil week, both in its adaptations to that week as it runs parallel to it and in the resistances that constitute it as an enclave, it moves to its own rhythms engendered by Islamic temporal logic. This temporality structures the pace of life of the community and also affects various aspects of social and institutional life of the mainstream community. In addition, however, as we have also seen, the chronopolis it forms is not simply a local entity, but is also and foremost a transglobal production. Globality implodes in the local structure and in the process temporizes its behavioral expression.

The Muslim week has a global content in both its forward orientation and its backward posture. It is a continuation of the structure of the homeland week. Immigration simply implies a continuity of that practice, and in a sense transnationalizes and globalizes it. The Muslim living in New York is in temporal harmony with the homeland and with Muslims throughout the world as they are

united by the temporal rhythms of their practice. The week is also global by
the position of the faithful during the communal prayer facing Mecca, thereby
recognizing the locational and spatial origin of their faith. One prays as if one
were in Mecca, acknowledging the physical distance between here and there, but
still in communion with the faithful everywhere and recognizing the geographical
roots of one's faith.[43] Also, international connections with the homeland are
sometimes maintained because some receive cassettes of sermons from abroad
and listen to them on Friday at home or at the workplace, as some taxi drivers in
New York do.

The distinct identity of the chronopolis is expressed at the local level when the
entire community isolates itself from the mainstream for the purpose of fulfilling
its religious obligations. At times during the course of the week, a good segment
of New York city sets itself aside because Muslim workers are not available to
carry out secular activities for themselves or mainstream employers. In this sense,
their different temporal lifestyle fractures the social landscape, slowing down some
activities in the formal economy and at the same time raising the intensity level of
some sectors of the informal economy.

Three types of overt global intervention can be detected as they influence the
form and content of the American-Muslim day. Perhaps the most visible sign of
the implosion of the global in the local is manifest in the influence held by the
homeland government over its overseas diasporas. The Saudi government goes as
far as to provide the departee with a compass so that he or she may adequately
locate geographically Mecca for the daily prayers:

> Well, the Saudis give everybody this compass back home before they leave the country, and it
> shows you where Mecca is. So, wherever that compass needle refers to you go and pray; even if
> the compass is false, and the needle is directing them to the east, they would still pray wherever
> the needle shows them to pray.

Another way that the homeland government and clergy exert an overt presence
in the transglobalized American Muslim chronopolis is by issuing the Islamic
prayer calendar, which indicates the moments of the day and night when they are
to be held, literally minute by minute. The calendar for the New York region was
prepared by the Department of Survey and Geodesy of Cairo, Egypt and distributed
in a booklet form to the faithful.[44]

The third form of overt intervention by the homeland is through the governance
of the main mosque in Manhattan.[45] This influential mosque, which is a central
point of gathering for Muslims living or working in New York City, is under the
control of the Islamic states. The most visible sign of this control by the homelands
is manifest through the role of its board of trustees, whose membership is made up
of the permanent representatives of the Muslim countries at the United Nations.

They have been influential in the selection and appointment of the imams, directors, and staff at this mosque. This type of managerial transnationality is consolidated by other types of diasporic transglobality (familial, grass-roots, congregational, professional, and industrial) among the rank and file of the chronopolis.

More covert interventions of the temporalities of the homeland in the Americanized Muslim chronopolis exist, as well. As one Iranian female student in the San Francisco Bay Area noted:

> sometimes I'll see little flyers on the table when I'm walking out of the Friday prayer area, or when I'm at school, they have books and cassettes that you can borrow and bring back, but they're all related back to Islam and Muslim countries, there was an Internet printout – not something about sales or something that had nothing to do with what kind of building that you are in, it's really if it's about politics, it's about Islamic politics, relating to Muslims.

Such unofficial irruptions of the homeland in the diasporized chronopolis can provide occasions for political opposition to and resistance directed at the forces governing the homeland. Because the Friday congregational prayer brings a large group of people to the mosque, it provides an opportunity for activists to promote opposition politics. In one of the San Diego mosques, "after one Friday prayer in 1993, for example, a leaflet was distributed by some disaffected persons (falsely) accusing this institution of being sponsored by the Saudi Arabian secret police."[46] The use of the congregational prayer both to spread state political propaganda or for opposition politics has always been a factor in the history of this institution.[47] Diasporization has not eclipsed such a practice. It has simply given diasporans one central means to reach the faithful and sensitize them to the political realities of the homeland, especially in communities that do not have their own radio programs and local newspapers.

Although opposition politics is one aspect of the politicization of the mosque, the faithful also use it to engage in what might be called "allegiance politics" and to support the government in office. Far from reducing the faithful to their religious dimension, the Friday service provides a site where the affairs of state are discussed among practitioners. It is the foremost site in the diaspora where Muslims with different ideological orientations address their political vision of the state.[48]

The informal economy also represents a covert presence of the homeland within the transglobalized diaspora. On Friday, from 10:00 a.m. to 3:00 p.m., the informal economy is alive and well in the areas in front of the main entrance of the Upper Manhattan Mosque. Vendors display their merchandise (Islamic books, carpets, jewelry, women clothing, incense, candles, videos, tape-recorded music, beads, and other homeland items) and attract a captive clientele to their ware. One finds here an ephemeral marketplace where homeland goods that are not available at this location in other days of the week can be purchased. Conversely, some mainstream secular or economic activities in the city are affected on Friday by the Muslim stores that are not available and professional offices that are not open for business. Thus, as in the Jewish American chronopolis, but in distinctively different ways, the adaptations and resistances of transglobalized diasporic Muslim temporalities within the structure of the subaltern week constitute a separate temporal enclave within the civil society of New York City.

NOTES

1. This chapter is a revised version of a paper presented at the International Conference "Diasporas: Transnational Identity and the Politics of the Homeland" organized by the William Saroyan Chair in Armenian Studies and the Berkeley Program in Soviet and Post-Soviet Studies and held at the University of California at Berkeley, November 12–13, 1999. I am grateful to Hatem Bazian, Hamid Algar, Beshara Doumani, Ali H. Alyami and Stephan H. Astourian for their thoughtful contribution to this chapter.

2. It is not only in New York that Muslim places of worship are mushrooming (see The Muslim World Day Parade and Storefront Mosques of New York City, in *Making Muslim Space in North America and Europe* edited by Barbara Metcalf. Berkeley: University of California Press, 1996, pp. 204–216). A similar phenomenon has been observed in the San Francisco Bay area as well. Hermansen (1994, p. 190) provides a profile of the Muslim organization in the San Francisco Bay Area "The overall Muslim community in the San Francisco Bay area comprises over one hundred thousand persons with a total of perhaps fifteen functioning Islamic Centers or mosques including Masjid al-Islam (Oakland), Hussaini Center (San Jose), Masjid Muhammad (Oakland), Masjid An-Noor (Santa Clara), Masjid Jamea (San Francisco), Masjid Nur (Richmond), Islamic Center of San Jose, Hayward Masjid, Islamic Center of San Francisco, Islamic Center of Freemont, American Muslim Mission (San Francisco), Fiju Muslim Mosque (South San Francisco). Masjid Abi Bakr al-Siddiq (Berkeley), and two student groups at the University of California at Berkeley."

3. Jane I. Smith, *Islam in America*. New York: Columbia University Press, 1999.

4. On the reasons given for the shift from Friday to Sunday as a day of rest in Muslim countries, see for Lebanon, Khalid Ziyadah, *Vendredi, Dimanche*. Arles, France: Sindbad/Actes Sud, 1996; for Turkey, see Andrew Rippin, *Muslims: Their Religious Beliefs and Practices*. New York: Routledge, 1993, Vol. II, p. 131.

5. Eviatar Zerubavel, *The Seven Day Circle: The History and Meaning of the Week*. New York: The Free Press, 1985, p. 4.

6. Marc Ferris, "To Achieve the Pleasure of Allah: Immigrant Muslims in New York City, 1893–1991," in *Muslim Communities in North America*, op. cit., p. 220.

7. For a genealogy of the Friday prayer, see S. D. Goitein, "Djum'a," in *The Encyclopedia of Islam* edited by B. Lewis, Ch. Pellat and J. Schacht. Leiden: E. J. Brill, Vol II, 1983, pp. 592–594; and S. D. Goitein, "Le Culte du Vendredi Musulman: Son Arriere-Plan Social et Economique." *Annales, Economies, Societes, Civilisations*, pp. 488–500, 1958.

8. *The Holy Qur'an* edited by Maulana Muhammad Ali. Lahore, Pakistan: Ahmadiyyah Anjuman Isha'at Islam, 1991.

9. See on this, Marc Ferris, "To Achieve the Pleasure of Allah: Immigrant Muslims in New York City, 1893–1991," in *Muslim Communities in North America* edited by Yvonne Yazbeck Haddad and Jane Idleman Smith. Albany: State University of New York Press, 1994, pp. 209–230; and Yvonne Yazbeck Haddad and Adair T. Lummis, *Islamic Values in the United States: A Comparative Study*. New York: Oxford University Press, 1987.

10. S. D. Goitein, "The Origin and Nature of the Muslim Friday Worship," in *Studies in Islamic History and Institutions*. Leiden: E. J. Brill, 1966, p. 111.

11. G. H. Bousquet and G. W. Bousquet-Mirandolle. *Revue Africaine*, *98*, 85–112, 1954.

12. Hugh Goddard, *Christians and Muslims: From Double Standards to Mutual Understanding*. Surrey: Curzon Press, 1995, p. 89.

13. S. D. Goitein, "The Origin and Nature of the Muslim Friday Worship," in *Studies in Islamic History and Institutions*. Leiden: E. J. Brill, 1966, p.112.

14. S. D. Goitein, "The Origin and Nature of the Muslim Friday Worship," in *Studies in Islamic History and Institutions*. Leiden: E. J. Brill, 1966, p. 120.

15. E. G. Richards, *Mapping Time: The Calendar and its History*. New York: Oxford University Press, 1998, p. 234.

16. G. S. P. Freeman-Grenville, *The Muslim and Christian Calendars*. London: Oxford University Press, 1963, 9. 3.

17. Canadian Muslims have also made use of Sunday for similar reasons. It is reported that "in some cities, a Sunday noon gathering is held that at least allows them an unofficial congregational prayer on the one day all Muslims are theoretically free to attend" (Murray Hogben, "The Socio-Religious Behavior of Muslims in Canada: An Overview," in *The Muslim Community in North America* edited by Earle H. Waugh, Baha Abu-Laban, and Regula B. Qureshi. Edmonton: The University of Alberta Press, 1983, p. 113.

18. Abdo A. Elkholy, *The Arab Moslems in the United States: Religion and Assimilation*. New Haven: College and University Press, 1966.

19. Yvonne Haddad, "Arab Muslims and Islamic Institutions in America: Adaptation and Reform," in *Arabs in the New World: Studies on Arab-American Communities* edited by Sameer Y. Abraham and Nabeel Abraham. Detroit: Wayne State University Press, 1983, p. 73; and Sameer Y. Abraham, Nabeel Abraham, and Barbara Aswad, "The Southend: An Arab Muslim Working-Class Community," in *Arabs in the New World*, op. cit., p. 173.

20. Yvonne Haddad, "Arab Muslims and Islamic Institutions in America: Adaptation and Reform," in *Arabs in the New World*, op. cit., p. 76.

21. Sameer Y. Abraham, Nabeel Abraham, and Barbara Aswad, "The Southend: An Arab Muslim Working-Class Community," in *Arabs in the New World*, op. cit., p. 173.

22. Mary Lahaj, "The Islamic Center of New England," in *Muslim Communities in North America*, op. cit., p. 309.

23. Sameer Y. Abraham, Nabeel Abraham, and Barbara Aswad, "The Southend: An Arab Muslim Working-Class Community," in *Arabs in the New World*, op. cit., p. 173.

24. Carol L. Anway, "American Women Choosing Islam," in *Muslims on the Americanization Path* edited by Yvonne Yazbeck Haddad and John L. Esposito. Atlanta: Scholars Press, 1998, p. 188.

25. Not all Muslims see these obstacles as inconveniences in a negative light. Some prefer to see them as challenges that can draw one closer to Allah because of the extra effort that is needed to accomplish the prayers, see Barbara Metcalf, "Introduction," in *Making Muslim Space in North America and Europe* edited by Barbara Metcalf. Berkeley: University of California Press, 1996, pp. 1–27.

26. In her interview with French Muslims, Cesari was told a number of circumstances that may justify the jamming of the prayers (workplace constraints, menstrual period, postpartum period, to name a few). See Jocelyne Cesari, *Etre Musulman En France Aujourd'hui*. Paris: Hachette, 1997, p. 137; and Alain Boyer, *L'Islam en France*. Paris: Presses Universitaires de France, 1998, p. 190.

27. For analyses of gendered time, see for example K. Davies, *Women and Time: The Weaving of the Strands of Everyday Life*. Aldershot: Avebury, 1990; F. J. Forman and C. Sowton, eds., *Taking Our Time: Feminist Perspectives on Temporality*. Oxford: Pergamon Press, 1989; J. Kristeva, Women's Time. *Signs* 1: 16–35, 1981; and O. Sullivan, "Time Waits for no (Wo)man: An Investigation of the Gendered Experienced of Domestic Time." *Sociology* 31, pp. 221–239, 1997.

28. For an elaboration of this argument, see Rachel Bloul, "Engendering Muslim Identities: Deterritorialization and the Ethnicization Process in France," in *Making Muslim Space in North America and Europe*, edited by Barbara Metcalf. Berkeley: University of California Press, 1996, pp. 234–250.

29. S. Rowbotham, *The Past is Before Us*. London: Pandora Press, 1989, p. 148.

30. Iris Marion Young, Polity and Group Difference: A Critique of the Ideal of Universal Citizenship, in *The Citizenship Debates* edited by Gershon Shafir. Minneapolis: University of Minnesota Press, pp. 263–290, 1998.

31. M. K. Hermansen, "The Muslims of San Diego," in *Muslim Communities in North America* edited by Yvonne Yazbeck Haddad and Jane Idleman Smith. Albany: State University of New York Press, 1994, p. 180.

32. For some background materials on the framing of the gender issue among Muslim women, see Jane I. Smith, *Women in Contemporary Muslim Societies*. Lewisburg: Bucknell University Press, 1980.

33. Andrew Rippin, *Muslims: Their Religious Beliefs and Practices*. New York: Routledge, 1993, p. 131.

34. Alixa Naff, *Becoming American: The Early Arab Immigrant Experience*. Carbondale: Southern Illinois University Press, 1985.

35. Yvonne Yazbeck and Adair T. Lummis, *Islamic Values in the United States: A Comparative Study*. New York: Oxford University Press, 1987, p. 19.

36. Yvonne Yazbeck Haddad and Adair T. Lummis, *Islamic Values in the United States: A Comparative Study*. New York: Oxford University Press, 1987, p. 77.

37. John O. Voll, "Islamic Issues for Muslims in the United States," in *The Muslims in America* edited by Yvonne Yazbeck Haddad. New York: Oxford University Press, 1991, p. 207.

38. Asad Husain and Harold Vogelaar, "Activities of the Immigrant Muslim Communities in Chicago," in *Muslim Communities in North America* edited by Yvonne Yazbeck Haddad and Jane Idleman Smith. Albany: State University of New York Press, 1994, p. 246.

39. Sameer Y. Abraham, Nabeel Abraham, and Barbara Aswad, "The Southend: An Arab Muslim Working-Class Community," in *Arabs in the New World: Studies on Arab-American Communities* edited by Sameer Y. Abraham and Nabeel Abraham. Detroit: Wayne State University, 1983, p. 166.

40. M. K. Hermansen, "The Muslims of San Diego," in *Muslim Communities in North America* edited by Yvonne Yazbeck Haddad and Jane Idleman Smith. Albany: State University of New York Press, 1994, p. 178.

41. The Muslim population in Paris provides a point of comparison with the occurrences in New York. In Paris, the Muslim population has maintained a presence in the city for over a century. To reach the brethren both in the city or the nearby suburbs, the call to prayer is announced through Islamic radio programs choreographed by Muslim activists. Kepel speaks of the effort of the workplace to harmonize industrial time with Islamic time and explains how the Renault company has installed mosques and prayer rooms in its factories and how the upper echelon of management has been sensitized to that issue to the extent that such a factor is integrated in their long-range planning and labor-relations policies. He also observes that similar policies were being implemented at Citroen and Simca, two other well known French firms. Kepel further notes that the institution of the Friday prayer has led to the transformation of the district where a popular mosque is located. He remarks that the Jean Pierre Timbaud Street becomes a very busy street on Friday. Many use the occasion to do their shopping in the Muslim stores, restaurants, bookshops, and meat shops. The area between the Couronne subway station and the location of the mosque is littered with Muslim commercial sites, and non-Muslim shops are being slowly pushed out to be replaced by Muslim stores. Gilles Kepel, *Les Banlieues de l'Islam. Naissance d'une Religion en France*. Paris: Editions du Seuil, 1987, pp. 9, 10, 150, 192. The establishment of a mosque in a neighborhood is a sure sign of the Arabization or Muslimization of the area.

42. Michael M. J. Fischer and Mehdi Abedi, *Cultural Dialogues in Postmodernity and Tradition*. Madison: The University of Wisconsin Press, 1990, p. 311.

43. E. Allen Richardson, *Islamic Cultures in North America*. New York: The Pilgrim Press, 1981.

44. Abdel-Rahman A. Osman, *The Islamic Calendar 1420 A. H*. New York: The Islamic Cultural Center of New York, 1999, p. 4. In the San Francisco Bay Area, the Islamic calendar and prayer times calculations are distributed around the Iranian New Year (March 21) and in the other Muslim communities around the Ramadan period. The Islamic Calendar and Prayer Times are also published every Islamic year in *The Greater California American Muslims Fast Yellow Pages: Business Telephone Directory* edited by C. A. Mahmood. Fremont: Expressions-Printing/Publishing, 1998.

45. For background discussion on Islamic globalism, see B. S. Turner, Politics and Culture in Islamic Globalism, in R. Robertson and W. R. Garrett (eds.), *Religion and Global Order*. New York: Paragon House, 1991.

46. M. K. Hermansen, "The Muslims of San Diego," in *Muslim Communities in North America* edited by Yvonne Yazbeck Haddad and Jane Idleman Smith. Albany: State University of New York Press, 1994, p. 194.

47. See, for example, Soheib Bencheikh, *Marianne et le Prophete: L'Islam dans la France Laique*. Paris: Grasset, 1998, p. 9.

48. Yvonne Haddad, "Arab Muslims and Islamic Institutions in America: Adaptation and Reform," in *Arabs in the New World: Studies on Arab-American Communities* edited by Sameer Y. Abraham and Nabeel Abraham. Detroit: Wayne State University Press, 1983, p. 72.

"The game behind the game": SPATIAL POLITICS AND SPIKE LEE'S *HE GOT GAME*

Jeffrey Geiger

Race and Ethnicity in New York City
Research in Urban Sociology, Volume 7, 83–105
© 2004 Published by Elsevier Ltd.
ISSN: 1047-0042/doi:10.1016/S1047-0042(04)07004-7

Where's the game in life behind the game behind the game? – Public Enemy, "He Got Game."

The late James Snead made a thought-provoking observation when he linked the birth of black independent cinema to "two portentous events" that occurred in 1896. The first was Thomas Edison's commercial decision to phase out the Kinetoscope and introduce large-screen projection, which helped to shift film viewing from an individuated activity towards a mass audience phenomenon. The second occurred less than a month later, when the Supreme Court decision in *Plessy vs. Ferguson* supported "separate but equal" facilities for blacks and whites, initiating nearly 60 years of federal compliance with legislated segregation. The origins of cinema viewing as a communal experience in the U.S. thus coincided with the division of the filmgoing community into black and white factions. This confluence of events, Snead argues, helped give rise to the necessity for black independent cinema (Snead, 1995, p. 366).

But these facts also suggest that the segregationist tendencies of cinema inhere in its very roots. Theaters were not just segregated in the South: in Northern cities such as New York, separate entrances and seating areas for whites and blacks could be found well into the 1930s (Gomery, 1992, p. 159). This racializing of film exhibition space was underpinned by the structure of the film business and, especially in the South, by the existence of black and white movie houses. Hollywood's exclusionary distribution practices helped to impel the rise of the "race picture" business, while Hollywood films were themselves codifying a segregated screen space, encoding film images with an ongoing history of racial division and power.[1] Snead argues, "It is one of the bitter ironies of American history, then, that motion picture technology, with its singular potential for good or evil, grew to perfection during the same time period (1890–1915) that saw the systematic, determined, and almost hysterical persecution and defamation of blacks and other minority groups" (1995, p. 365).

This essay will look at issues related to segregated space and power in cinema, leading to a consideration of a film that draws attention to topographies of African American urban life at the end of the twentieth century: Spike Lee's *He Got Game* (1998). Because it carefully weaves into the narrative a series of what I would call spatial metaphors, *He Got Game* can be seen to make visible the ongoing, double-sided relationship between African Americans and the space of "America": itself a socially constructed utopian space dependent upon the Hollywood dream machine that fashions and refashions it.

Noël Carroll describes the film metaphor as an image or sequence that gestures beyond itself, carrying signifying properties similar to verbal metaphors while relying on visual codes. Carroll defines these codes as "homospatiality," or the collapsing of separate objects or spaces into a single setting; "noncompossibility," or the bringing together of objects and images that are logically incompatible; and "intelligible correspondence," or an understanding between director and audience that the juxtaposition of dissimilar objects or spaces can generate new meanings. "Through homospatiality," Carroll writes, "our film metaphors identify disparate objects and/or link disparate categories that are not physically compossible, in terms of what we know about the universe." Film metaphors are a form of "shared recognition," dependent on the filmmaker's belief that his or her image has "heuristic value" (1996, pp. 214–215). Particularly in the case of what I am calling spatial metaphors, film metaphors can be seen to politicize cinematic space by drawing attention to the ways that various spatial formations – both "actual" and represented spaces – are socially produced and negotiated within a field of power relations.

An example of a spatial metaphor appears in *He Got Game*'s opening credits, in which Lee uses the game of basketball as an overarching trope that connects various scenes depicting America's discrete, racialized zones: the farm and the trailer park, the suburb and the ghetto. The end of the film sums up these images in the form of a visual postscript. The protagonist, Jake Shuttlesworth (Denzel Washington), a prisoner at Attica, is shown shooting hoops at an outdoor prison court. When he steps over a line on the pavement that designates the "no go" zone adjoining the court, he is out of bounds in more ways than one. A guard posted on a wall above him levels his rifle and threatens to shoot, but he refuses to move. Staring at the concrete barrier interposed between his gaze and the outside world, Jake finally hurls the basketball over the prison wall. The ball traces a wide arc, landing on an indoor basketball court where Jake's son, Jesus (Ray Allen), is practicing.

In a concise gesture, Lee bridges the gap between closeness and distance, freedom and enclosure, and connects the experience of concrete space to the space of the imagination. The film forges visual and symbolic links between spheres that are rarely meaningfully brought together in mainstream cinema: the prison and the university, the basketball court and the board room. Yet it is tempting to read the spatial imagery in *He Got Game* as more broadly re-framing a history of cinematic segregation: the ways that mainstream cinema has historically not only elided blackness, but confined it to certain spaces – to the margins of the screen, to the sides or rear of the movie theater, or, as in the case of "race pictures," to the outer limits of Hollywood's distribution practices.

As Carroll's definition would suggest, Jake's basketball becomes an object that knits together disparate spatial categories, contravening the logic that sees cross-cutting as a mode of narrative continuity and spatial discontinuity by making visible the simultaneity of spaces *within* the frame. Lee's metaphor utilizes cinematic space to create a more complex awareness of emplacement, of the individual's relationship to concrete and social space. Though Jake's point of view is restricted and heavily policed, he comes to recognize social dynamics hidden by the everyday limits of spatial awareness. His revelation behind concrete walls points to more abstract limitations on any embodied point of view: the enclosures, modes of surveillance, and geographical divisions that define the lives of so many Americans. U.S. cinema history is dominated by images of white mobility and black containment. Yet Manthia Diawara suggests that the work of black filmmakers has often revealed an acute awareness of the power of spatial representation, illustrating how the screen can provide a critically transformative space (1993, pp. 8–19). Paula J. Massood's recent work takes this suggestion further, providing a detailed social and historical map to the ways in which spatial tropes of mobility and entrapment have been central to black films "from their very inception" (2003: 201).

SCREEN SPACE

Cultural visibility is closely linked to physical and social mobility, and access to – or denial of – free movement through private and public spaces powerfully shapes individual and social identities. As Liam Kennedy has shown in the context of urban space, "the operations of power are everywhere evident in space: space is hierarchical – zoned, segregated, gated – and encodes both freedoms and restrictions – of mobility, of access, of vision" (2000, pp. 169–170). A consideration of how film articulates a relationship between space and identity might thus begin by breaking down the concept of space itself into three distinct yet interconnected areas of analysis: first, the notion of socially produced space, as shown in the work of Henri Lefebvre and others; second, the idea of audience space or the architectural space of the theater; and finally, the theory of film space or the space of the screen. Given this essay's limited scope, the latter will be examined in more detail than the first two, but I would like to stress the underlying interconnectedness of the three. While, for example, formalist studies of film aesthetics may be just as valuable as in-depth studies of changing viewing habits, audience demographics, and exhibition technologies, film interpretation should strive to keep in view the variety of spatial formations and conditions that might come to bear on any particular visual text.

With respect to the first area of analysis, Lefebvre's work has demonstrated the notion that the spaces inhabited in everyday life, in particular (though not limited to) the architecture of urban spaces, are part of a network of socially produced space (1991, 1996). While not contesting the essential concept of mathematical space that emerged in post-Cartesian philosophy, Lefebvre has provided the groundwork for viewing the social production of space as ideological; therefore the analysis of social space can be seen as inherently political. Lefebvre argues, "Marx replaced the study of things by the critical analysis of the productive activity. Resuming the initiative of the great economists (Smith and Ricard) and connecting to it the critical analysis of the mode of (capitalist) production, he extended knowledge to a higher level. Today a similar approach is necessary with regard to space" (1996, p. 196). Underlying my discussion is the related work of Edward Soja, who, through a critique of Marx and Lefebvre, has argued for the reassertion of spatial analysis in materialist readings of culture. Soja cites John Berger's observations on the increasing presence of a "lateral" comprehension of events in modernity, as opposed to a temporally-based, linear historicism, noting that modern subjects are aware of constant interventions, of the "simultaneity and extension of events and possibilities" (1989, p. 23). Though no study of spatial relations can disassociate itself from issues of temporality – for movement through space presupposes time (and film study in particular is predicated on theorizing the space-time continuum) – a deconstruction of human geography reveals the interconnectedness of the shifting boundaries of the personal and political, social and economic, local and global. Soja further stresses that the relationship of space to social formations is always dialectical. "Space in itself may be primordially given," he argues, "but the organization and meaning of space is a product of social translation, transformation, and experience" (1989, pp. 79–80).[2]

The fabric of African American life has always been marked by hierarchies determined by shifting geographical relations. These are grounded in the forced displacements of slavery, in the migration in the early decades of the twentieth century, and in the Second Great Migration (1940–1970) from the rural South to the industrialized, urban regions of the North and West. As Ed Guerrero has argued, "The negotiation of racial images, boundaries, and hierarchies has been part of our national life from its beginnings" (1993, p. 41). Post-war urban housing policies, in particular, engendered ongoing geopolitical problems of ghettoization, targeted neighborhoods where police employ "paramilitary tactics," and economic redlining (Hayden, 2000; Hirsch, 2000). Los Angeles has been seen as a blueprint for this emerging politics of urban space, exemplified by "fortress identities" and "spatial ghettos" which continue to hinder the physical and social mobility of economic and racial others.[3] On the East coast, practices such as male motorists being stopped for what Patricia Williams has referred to as "driving while black" (2001), as well as police shootings and racial profiling in the "mosaic city" of New York, have drawn renewed attention to the racialized policing of public space.[4] In the 1980s, Marshall Berman noted that New York had undergone a long-term transformation "into a place where capital from anywhere in the world is instantly at home, while everybody without capital is increasingly out of place" (Kennedy, 2000, p. 20). The problems of postindustrial urban space have only intensified throughout the 1990s and into the present decade, as a period of sustained economic growth yielded an increased disparity between zones of excessive wealth and extreme poverty.[5]

The movie theater, though often viewed as a safe or neutral space for fantasy and imaginary transport, is also a socially produced architectural space that has hardly been immune to the social contingencies outside its walls. Exhibition conditions have undergone renewed attention with recent work in audience studies, which has contextualized the rise of the film industry, examining the history of the theater, the changing demographics of film audiences, and the impact that these and other factors have had upon the production and consumption of film images.[6] Robert F. Arnold, for example, has cited the necessity of examining the conditions of spectatorship in order to avoid reductive or universalizing theories that tend to posit notions of an ideologically unified or ideal spectator. Citing the work of James Spellerberg and Norman Bryson, Arnold suggests that unitary approaches fail to fully take into account not only the heterogeneity of cultural formations over time, but also the crucial role that spectatorship plays in determining spatial meanings generated by works of art, photography, or film. "The complex ideological give and take in the conditions of spectatorship," Arnold argues, "cannot be reduced to a formal definition of a single apparatus and/or assumed across a variety of historically and functionally distinct practices" (1990, p. 51).

Such an approach not only helps to break down a linear, chronological history of spectatorship, but opens the door to a consideration of the heterogeneity of viewing positions within particular historical contexts. Several questions are raised by this approach: How have actual spatial limits imposed by hierarchical viewing positions effected the navigation of virtual space? Or, to put this differently, what ways of seeing are produced from the cinema's balcony (where black patrons were often seated) as opposed to the main floor? The implications of hierarchical viewing positions and the ways these might determine not only audience responses, but the very meanings produced during film viewing, are hinted at by the white critic G. William Jones, who recalls the experience of segregated theaters in the South. He writes, "although I cannot remember ever hearing them laughing or cheering at the screen like we [white] boys did down below, I knew they were there, because I could occasionally hear them, before the show started, moving around the backless benches they had to sit on while we sat in the comparative comfort of wooden, bolted-to-the-floor rows of folding seats which curved to fit the body" (1991, p. 185).

My intention is not merely to engage questions of human geography as a backdrop for readings of cinematic narratives, but to perform a closer interrogation of cinematic space while looking at a local example – Lee's *He Got Game* – of how racial politics can be configured on the screen. In the years since the publication of André Gardies's *L'Espace au cinéma* in 1993, spatial analysis has become an increasingly important component of film theory, leading to the more recent question, "is space just the latest fashionable frame of reference in the academic world, just as gender or race may have been just a few years ago? Or is it what founds film's identity?" (Konstantarakos, 2000, p. 6). As the recent work of Massood (2003) and others has begun to demonstrate, it may not be so much a matter of replacing studies of race or gender in cinema with space as of exploring the inextricable links between race, gender, and the politicized spaces that these cultural identities inhabit.

Influential analyses of film space are fewer than one might at first imagine, though a number – among them the work of Noel Burch, Stephen Heath, André Bazin, Yurij Lotman, and Gilles Deleuze – have recently found renewed interest. In Burch's reading of Jean Renoir's *Nana* (1926) in *Theory of Film Practice*, the screen is described as creating two different kinds of space: space within and space outside the frame. Burch further divides off-screen space into six "segments": the four areas that project from the four sides of the frame, the space "behind the camera," and finally the space behind the set, which is just beyond the limits of the spectator's gaze; that is, the space beyond the door through which a character passes, the space beyond the corner a character has gone around, and so on (1973, p. 17). Burch's spatial typology was revisited by Stephen Heath in the influential essay "Narrative Space," which foregrounds the dialectic between visual form and narrative content. Developing his argument from a discussion of the perspective system developed in the Italian Renaissance, Heath suggests that cinema may flatten pro-filmic space into two dimensions and bound it by a four-sided frame, but its prime achievement is that it creates an "impression of reality" which is neither absolutely two-dimensional nor absolutely three-dimensional (1981, p. 31). Heath imports the theoretical apparatus of psychoanalytic and ideological criticism to bear on Burch's argument, arguing that classical narrative cinema works to order, control, and unify both on-screen and off-screen space through the construction of looks, exchanges, and objects seen (1981, pp. 45–46). Narrative cinema thus plays on the assumptions of point-of-view to create a stable subject position, endowing the spectator with an imaginary position of authority. Developing the concept of the "suture," Heath argues that film can elide or suture over any potential ruptures that might endanger a sense of spatial unity, while it posits the spectator at the center as the producer of meaning.

Mark Garrett Cooper's discussion picks up where Heath's leaves off, attempting to more carefully examine "the subdivision of the visual field into distinct spaces within and across frames," and interrogating the ways that characters' looks work to organize cinematic space (2002, pp. 145, 148). Indirectly linked to these formulations of the ways that on-screen and off-screen space are controlled in cinema is the work of Yurij Lotman, who focused more closely on the dynamic produced within the boundaries of the frame, helping to articulate what David Forgacs aptly calls the different kinds of "pressure" created within the frame: "when [the frame] is filled with objects or emptied, when three-dimensional depth and "planes of action" are replaced by flatness and surface, when a human figure is positioned at its extreme edges or in extreme close up or long shot" (Konstantarakos, 2000, p. 108).

Before these studies appeared, André Bazin described the screen as creating something more akin to a "centrifugal" space: "The frame of a painting polarizes space inwards. On the contrary, what the screen shows us seems to be part of something prolonged indefinitely into the universe" (1967, p. 166). Deleuze appears to take up a similar notion, denying that film space necessarily produces a closed system of ordered and controllable meanings, and adopts a radical stance towards the potential disruptions of off-screen space (the "out-of-field"). He suggests that Burch's formulation of on-screen and off-screen does not sufficiently consider the different kinds of out-of-field spaces towards which film images might gesture, such as opening on to "a new unseen set, on to infinity" (1986, p. 17). The out-of-field may be prefigured by a set or system of signification already defined within the visible field of the frame, but it might just as well hint at a more disturbing presence: something that is not necessarily part of the established mise-en-scène and therefore "does not belong to the order of the visible" (*ibid.*, p. 17). The latter idea might be seen to point towards psychoanalytic readings of racial visibility and invisibility in mainstream cinema, according to which even those films which seem to completely elide racial images from the frame, banishing racial difference not only to off-screen space but to a liminal space beyond the logical system of signification constructed in the film narrative, can be seen as haunted or marked by a return of repressed racial otherness. The classical Hollywood film, in general, might be said to be haunted by this perpetual "out-of-field."

Critical discussion of black film has often centered on the political dimensions of screen space, and has been concerned with the dialectics of center and periphery, the visible and the hidden. Guerrero expresses this process succinctly, arguing that mainstream American film has long engaged in a spatial project of "framing blackness": a historical tendency to relegate African Americans to a space of otherness. Hollywood strives to "construct black people as other and subordinate, while it naturalizes white privilege as the invisible but sovereign 'norm' " (1993, p. 5). As an ideological construct, film not only re-presents the lived experience of spatiality, but restructures it within the realm of virtual space, often burying or transforming actual spatial relations. In his study of *Daughters of the Dust* (1991), Diawara mentions the "hierarchical disposition of objects on the screen," pointing to a connection between screen space, mise-en-scène, and issues of power: "space is related to power and powerlessness, in so far as those who occupy the center of the screen are usually more powerful that those situated in the background or completely absent from the screen" (1993, p. 11).[7]

But questions of visibility are rarely straightforward, and the navigation of screen space tends to function dialectically. As films from *Hallelujah!* (1929) to *The Color Purple* (1985) have shown, cinematic visibility has not always translated into control over dominant patterns of signification. Alternatively, Hollywood cinema has sometimes reworked the frame's margins to elliptically draw attention to sublimated political issues, as in Douglas Sirk's version of Fannie Hurst's *Imitation of Life* (1959). One reading of the latter might link elements of film space and mise-en-scène (set arrangements, color, framing, deep focus) to narrative allusions and the melodramatic plot convention of hierarchical reversal, revealing that the blonde actress Nora Meredith (Lana Turner) is, arguably, finally upstaged by the sacrifices of her saint-like friend, Annie Johnson (Juanita Moore). But examples of the latter type are relatively rare. As Jane Gaines has suggested of the duplicity of American "white culture" more generally, it "offers the opportunity of belonging on the one hand and withdraws all offers with the other" (1996, p. 181). Though subject to the vagaries of spatial relations, including the actual space of the segregated theater and the virtual space of the segregated screen, it should be remembered that cinematic narratives have not just reflected given spatial relations, but have also produced new spatialities and new modes of perception.

VIRTUAL MOBILITY

As Tom Gunning (1995) has shown, the cinema has not been just a medium of mimesis but of movement: furnishing spectators with new forms of virtual mobility. Anne Friedberg has further mapped new forms of virtual mobility provided by early cinema projections, and posits the emergence of a "mobilized virtual gaze" that evolved over the course of the pre-cinematic, cinematic, and televisual eras, which induced "a gradual and indistinct tear along the fabric of modernity" (1995, p. 60).[8] Friedberg grounds her discussion in the work of Walter Benjamin's meditations on Baudelaire and the nineteenth-century Parisian *flâneur*, who typifies the modern subject wandering through urban space "in a daze of distraction" (*ibid.*, p. 61). Emphasizing the role of the *flâneuse* – the female shopper who became an urban fixture with the mid-nineteenth century rise of the department store – Friedberg stresses the important links between mobile acts of looking, commodity fetishism, gender, and the emergence of the cinema. She argues,

> The newly conjoined *mobilized and virtual* gaze of the cinema answered the desire not only for temporal and spatial mobility but for gender mobility as well. The spectator-shopper – trying on identities – engages in the pleasures of a temporally and spatially fluid subjectivity. Theories of

spectatorship that imply a one-to-one correspondence between the spectator position and gender, race, or sexual identity – as if identity were a constant, consistent continuum unchallenged by the borrowed subjectivity of spectatorship – do not consider the pleasures of escaping physically bound subjectivity (*ibid.*, p. 65, italics in original).

Friedberg posits a concept of mobile spatial relations in film against previous static theories of spectatorship, suggesting at the same time that race, like gender or sexual identity, might serve as a commodity "worn" during film viewing, then potentially discarded after leaving the theater. Her ideas are useful in noting how cinema space interacts with heterogeneous viewing positions, producing the potential for mobile identification. But Friedberg's ideas also give rise to the question of whether the mobilized and virtual gaze might be limited by the contingencies of space: in particular, the frequently racialized realms of theater and screen. Friedberg has convincingly argued that there need not be a direct equivalence between spectators and actors on the screen to produce forms of identificatory investment. Still, what happens to the mobile gaze when viewers are restricted by social-spatial conditions? As I have suggested, up through the Civil Rights period, segregation was endemic to the black viewing experience, not only on the screen – as formalized by the addenda to the Production Code in 1930, which forbade references to miscegenation – but in the segregation of audiences and through the "back door" policies of white theater owners (Streible, 1993, p. 224). As Massood notes: "the segregated space on the screen was replicated in the experiences of black audiences in the theater" (2003, p. 15).

As Diawara (1993, pp. 215–217) has suggested, the gaze of the black male spectator has often been constituted as much by prohibition and the denial of pleasure as by the promise of mobile identification. E. Ann Kaplan further expands notions of spectatorship by incorporating issues of race, gender, and the barriers that have been set up around mobile looking relations (1997, p. 6). Studies of the relationship of race to film viewing have often focused on images of containment and captivity rather than on the mobile navigation of cinema space. "One 'shoots' film, one 'captures' images, and one is 'captivated' by spectacles of celluloid," begins Gwendolyn Audrey Foster in *Captive Bodies* (1999, p. 1). Opening her essay on the "oppositional gaze," bell hooks also lingers on images of suppression and containment: "Thinking about Black female spectators, I remembered being punished as a child for staring," she writes, and the moment is associated with the denial of subjectivity enforced by master/slave looking relations (1993, p. 288). But the containment of the gaze encouraged by dominant filmmaking practices does not automatically reduce marginal viewers to passive immobility. On the contrary, hooks argues, by enforcing an active, critical gaze, by "looking and looking back," black women can combat the process of "cinematic negation" enforced by hegemonic looking relations (*ibid.*, p. 300–302). This and other more positive amplifications of W. E. B. Du Bois's notion of "twoness" have posited an actively self-reflexive process of seeing, and critiquing, cinematic processes with a "third eye" (Rony, 1996, pp. 3–5). This rather different kind of mobilized gaze twins the viewing experience with a simultaneous recognition of a film's textuality – its interrelation to other historical narratives, images, and spaces.

In the world of Hollywood-financed filmmaking, the gaze of the spectator who does not share in cinema's dominant perspectives can encounter obstacles. Films like the *Indiana Jones* trilogy (1981–1989), *Gorillas in the Mist* (1988), or *The Green Mile* (1999), to name just a few, have promised imaginative transport through adventure, travel, or spiritual redemption, respectively, while grounding their narratives in a series of racial allusions, exclusions, and stereotypes (Modleski, 1991, 2000). The screen might appear as a democratic, infinitely expandable space available to the discerning gaze of the spectator-flâneur, but this subject of modernity may also be narrowly defined and monitored. The screen might be seen less as a neutral space than as a kind of bounded space or territorial enclosure; and territory, as Michel Foucault has suggested, is "no doubt a geographical notion, but it is first of all a juridico-political one: The area controlled by a certain kind of power" (1980, p. 68). The virtual space of the popular screen is an "ideal" rather than "actual" space that has been dominated by images sprung from the Hollywood imagination. Yet as Soja has pointed out, Hollywood is "itself a façade . . . [though] there is much more being screened behind it" (1989, p. 227).

THE CONTINGENCIES OF SPACE:
SPIKE LEE'S *HE GOT GAME*

In her Introduction to *Representing Blackness*, Valerie Smith notes that D. W. Griffith's *The Birth of a Nation* is "considered by many to be the symbolic, although not the literal, origin of U.S. cinema, [and is] frequently offered up by film critics and historians as the inaugural moment of African American cinema as well" (1997, p. 1). As Smith asserts, the problem with *The Birth of a Nation* is not so much its fictional status as cinema's "origin," but its seemingly monolithic quality for African Americans: a grand spectacle that refuses to go away. When asked to respond to criticism that *Do the Right Thing* (1989) made white viewers uncomfortable, Spike Lee responded: "How do you think Black people have felt for 80 years watching stuff like *Birth of a Nation* . . . and we go on and on. Black people have to had to live under this thing for 400 years . . . We made [*Do the Right Thing*] so we could put the spotlight on racism and say that everything is NOT okay, that this is not the land of milk and honey and truth and justice" (Jones, 1989, p. 13).

Though it may appear worlds away from the urban geographies of *He Got Game*, it is useful to briefly look at *The Birth of a Nation*'s place in the cinematic canon in advance of considering Lee's potential "answer," since the problematic status of Griffith's film stems from the ways it dramatizes fundamental tensions invoked by the mobilization of racial discourses. *Birth* literally and metaphorically conflates "race" with "culture" and "nation," depicting segregation as the only way to preserve the sacred dream of the American Adam and the domain of whiteness (Gaines, 1996). In so doing, it naturalizes a racialized map of human geography, twinning racial determinism with an essentialist concept of space. Struggles over spatial freedoms and constraints – which encompass the control of land, property, and, crucially, the symbolic space of the white female body – are primary narrative catalysts in Griffith's film. Introductory intertitles set the stage for the battle, omitting any reference to slavery while laying blame for the loss of the Edenic South on the "introduction of the African to American Shores" which "laid the seeds of national tragedy." As Clyde Taylor notes, this claim performs the geographical feat of shifting "the essential scene of national development to the South instead of colonial New England or the Western frontier" (1996, pp. 20–21). For Thomas Cripps (1978), the film relocates to the rural South of the past the bitter contests that were then going on in American urban centers as a result of African American migration. The film thus conjoins two threats posed by racial mobility, one topographical (the movement of peoples across national and cultural space), and the other biological (miscegenation, which threatens to disturb scientific and social taxonomies of race). The viewer is left to infer that the black menace – both during Reconstruction and in the present moment – stems not from color per se but from boundary crossings: those who once occupied their allotted place are now roaming freely across the land.

After the defeat of the South, Griffith equates new black freedoms with spatial invasions. The territorial battles of the Civil War are encapsulated in scenes depicting black men jostling whites off the sidewalks of Piedmont, overtaking and desecrating the halls of government (authenticated as "historical facsimile"), and preying on white women. As demonstrated in the famous scene in which Gus (Walter Long, in blackface) chases "Little Sister" Cameron (Mae Marsh) through the forest, spatial politics are rendered visible through Griffith's framing. Gus's darkened face and eyes are shot in tight close-up and partial shadow, dominating and then exceeding the frame, while long shots of Little Sister running through the forest emphasize her smallness, her figure bounded by a frame now controlled by Gus's lascivious gaze. The film's climactic scenes similarly intensify the territorial conflict, suggesting that the unbearable result of black liberation is that whiteness has been marginalized and now is, quite literally, imprisoned. The remnants of the Cameron clan are confined to a cabin while the advancing black mob threatens to vanquish the symbolic remnants of the white race. The trajectory from freedom to confinement serves as a metaphor not only for the story of the Camerons, but for the history of white Southerners in general. The film's final scenes consolidate the return of social "order," illustrated by images of black voters timidly backing out of the frame as they retreat from public polling places guarded by the Klan. An alternative ending showed the invasive "others" sent back to Africa; as Gaines notes, they end up "where they 'belong' – that is, they are returned to their 'own' culture, nation, and family" (1996, p. 179).

The project of answering these images, attempted unsuccessfully in a film like *The Birth of A Race* (1918),[9] is not limited to presenting a corrective to previous "negative" images, but involves reconfiguring a racial geography naturalized by Hollywood. As the struggles of black independent filmmakers like Oscar Micheaux have shown, the difficulty has been to highlight the hidden consequences that cross and recross the cinematic text, to develop codes of representation that might redress on-screen elisions and stereotypes and their assumed extension to off-screen space (Bowser, 2000; Green, 2000). Part of this struggle was to rupture the unified myth of the rural South while drawing attention to the emerging urban realities of the Northeast and West. This growing concern is a theme that runs through Micheaux's independent films (1918–1931), as well as his and other white-financed "race movies." It appears with renewed force in the blaxploitation genre, the Los Angeles School of black filmmakers (such as Charles Burnett), and more recently in the "new ghetto cinema" of John Singleton, Albert and Allen Hughes, and Matty Rich (Massood, 1996, 2003). Though the latter has been criticized for furnishing African American stereotypes for the voyeuristic pleasures of white audiences, the genre might also suggest an attempt to utilize screen space to transform blackness from a unitary and hegemonically "framed" concept into a provocative, polyvalent circulation of images and ideas.[10]

Yet few African American filmmakers have attained the status and influence of Spike Lee. Popularizing the phrase "guerrilla filmmaking" in his early career, Spike Lee has often cast himself as working in direct opposition to a racist status quo and a legacy of cinematic "white space." Working primarily in the locale of his "home town," Brooklyn, his work in the 1980s and early 1990s constructed a kinetic cinematic space charged with racial tensions and divisions. Films like *School Daze* (1988), *Do the Right Thing*, and *Jungle Fever* (1991) employed the screen as a hot space, saturated with light and intense color, where inter- and intra-ethnic tensions were acted out, often brutally. Lee's desire to politicize the space of the screen through explicit references to restraints on African American freedoms and mobilities was nowhere more visible than his decision to intercut the videotaped beating of Rodney King into the opening credits of *Malcolm X* (1992).

With few exceptions, such as *She's Gotta Have It* (1986), *Get on the Bus* (1996) and *Four Little Girls* (1998), Lee has worked as a crossover artist, playing the game within Hollywood modes of production and distribution. Critics who construct a dichotomy between assimilation and accomodation on the one hand, and counter-hegemonic work that challenges received images on the other, most often have placed Lee in the former camp. William Lyne, for example, praises *Do The Right Thing*, but generally considers Lee to be a corporate sellout who maintains "a veneer of militant dissent" (2000, p. 39). Critiques of Lee's sociopolitical outlook often focus on Lee's narrative content (Baraka, 1993; Lyne, 2000; Reid, 1993), still, a close look at Lee's visual and spatial sensibility may not necessarily end the debate. It has become clear that, with or without Spike Lee, some of the most radical elements of oppositional cinema to survive the postmodern upheavals of recent years have been appropriated into the mainstream. Vertov's cinematic immediacy can be viewed nightly on MTV, while Eisenstein's montage praxis of collision long ago became a Hollywood mainstay (and can now be seen in commercials for headache remedies). What is at stake no longer is the question of whether narrative or formal innovation can produce revolutionary ways of seeing, but whether the cinema experience even resembles its former self, or can any longer be considered an effective site for a radical politics of transformation.

Though arguably Lee has never worked from a position of undiluted political or aesthetic resistance, his films, in both content and form, have attempted to address some of the stickier questions regarding film as a medium for reflecting and constructing political realities. His films gesture beyond direct social commentary to draw attention to the socially produced concrete, social, and virtual spaces his characters inhabit. For Massood, Lee "places complex characters into a fully defined setting that is not easily readable as a ghetto, thus suggesting that the space itself requires a different narrative from those [blaxploitation films] from the preceding decade" (2003, p. 130). Moreover, his work has "transformed African American city spaces and black filmmaking practices," thus influencing "African American filmmaking as a whole" (2003, p. 122). Yet *He Got Game* was not well received; *Sight and Sound* even called it an "awkward and fraught" film marred by obvious product placement and overt sexism (Falcon, 1998, p. 45). Formally, the New York City setting, restless camera work, saturated colors, and persistent musical score identify *He Got Game* as a Spike Lee film, while a narrative that focuses almost exclusively on issues of black male desire and responsibility is consistent with much of his previous work. The film, as noted earlier, opens with a spatial metaphor, as the opening credit sequence presents a slow-motion montage of diverse basketball players, suggesting that the game might knit together the geographically, economically, racially, and sexually divided space of America, while the court serves as a stage where personal and political tensions are acted out. The musical score – drawn from both the "Dean of American music," Aaron Copland, and Public Enemy – reinforces Lee's efforts to project a more inclusive, multi-racial image of America. The credit sequence ends with a shot that suggests the relationship between real and imaginary spaces: recalling images from the film's documentary predecessor, *Hoop Dreams* (1994), the camera follows an elevated train – a trope closely associated with broader issues of physical and social mobility – passing above an inner-city court.[11] The viewer is likewise shifted from an idealized America to the "actual" spaces, the prison and the housing projects, that the film explores.

He Got Game begins with the story of Jake Shuttlesworth, who faces fifteen years in Attica state prison for murdering his wife. Jake also happens to be the father of an amazingly talented high school basketball player named Jesus, known as "the number one prospect in these United States." At the beginning of the film, Jake is called from the confines of his cell to see Attica's warden, who informs him that the governor, an alumnus of "Big State" university, would consider reducing his prison time if Jake can convince his son to attend the governor's alma mater. Jake is given one week to return to Coney Island and win over his estranged son.

The obvious implausibility of the plot, with its Christian subtext, suggests that the film might be read more convincingly as allegory. Allegory might be said in the simplest sense to spatialize narrative by simultaneously operating on different levels of signification. Historical allegories signify or tell a literal story of fictional characters and events while at the same signifying a parallel story of "actual" historical characters and events; the sustained "allegory of ideas," on the other hand, employs personification to point to abstract entities such as virtues, vices, states of mind, modes of life, and types of character (Abrams, 1988, p. 5). Here, the name "Jesus" begins this conceptual migration from the literal to its multiple layers of signification. Lee, with cinematographer Malik Hassan Sayeed and editor Barry Alexander Brown, manipulates the film's early scenes to divert attention away from the surface narrative towards its allegorical implications. Cross-cutting in the film's early scenes fractures a linear structure, gesturing to the artifice of a plot that constantly seems to verge on disintegration. During the discussion between the warden and Jake, the subterranean darkness of the prison seems both to embody and alienate the sensibilities of its inhabitants. In the meantime, words and phrases in the dialogue appear to provoke a series of circular images that both flash back and flash forward in time. As the two speak, the spatial logic of shot/counter shot is ruptured as images appear of a second narrative space: Jake in his cell, his illness, and his release from prison. Unlike Griffith's "Gus chase" scene, which also combines associative editing with cross-cutting, this scene troubles the spectator's absorption into the literal narrative by rupturing the diegesis with seemingly unmotivated cuts, constantly taking the viewer to spaces outside assumptions of spatial and temporal unity.[12]

These disruptions no doubt form part of Lee's "messiness" and "incoherence," adjectives which have frequently been applied to his films. Stuart Klawans, writing in the *Nation*, notes that the world of *He Got Game* "becomes a random explosion of sounds and images, opportunities and demands . . . At its best, *He Got Game* tosses you into this big, crazy, wide-open America and lets you feel how it spins through Jesus Shuttlesworth's head – or maybe Spike Lee's" (1998, p. 21). Allegory is, by its very nature, a messy way to tell a story, though it is seldom employed at random. Similar to a sustained literary allegory, *He Got Game* strives to produce multiple and overlapping spaces of signification built around the narrative skeleton of a spiritual journey. The question of who, or what, can redeem a disunified America is paralleled by numerous Christian allusions: Jesus battles with temptation; his girlfriend Lala becomes a Judas; he at first decries the hypocrisy of religion, but finally delivers a speech in which he thanks God. Basketball is the medium of the new messiah: the ghetto's solution to a world of stock market gamblers and "dot com" millionaires. The name Jesus invites not only obvious, sensationalist linguistic plays on the part of the press – "Jesus Saves [the game]"screams at least one headline in the film – but as the son, Jesus forms part of a fallen trinity which includes his father and the "holy spirit" of his dead mother, Martha. Martha's mythic presence conjures up other saintlike figures from both national (Martha Washington) and cinematic (Martha, the dead mother of *The Searchers* (1956)) memory. Within the neighborhood, Jesus is a potential savior, one of the few due to be delivered from the confines of the projects, and who hopefully will deliver (socially, financially) those who stand by him.

But Jake is, on the other hand, a constant reminder of restrictions that guard a limitless mobility. Constrained by an ankle bracelet and under electronic surveillance, his presence recalls the prison. Whereas in films such as *Do the Right Thing*, police surveillance is physically represented by cruising squad cars (the street equivalent of the Los Angeles chopper), here the surveillance is virtual, distant, yet ever-present: "we will track you down," states one of his guarding officers. Jake thus reminds Jesus that escape is never a sure thing, reminding him: "Moses parted the Red Sea, not Jesus." Lee's allegory works to disperse the space of unified narrative into a constellation of interconnected, sometimes contradictory, myths and images.

With few exceptions, Lee's films have surveyed a contained geographical area. Brooklyn is the setting for *She's Gotta Have It*, *Do the Right Thing*, *Crooklyn* (1994), *Clockers* (1995), and *Summer of Sam* (1999), though he has wandered as far as Harlem for *Jungle Fever* and *Mo' Better Blues* (1990). A mostly-white (and occasionally Jewish or ethnic European) image of Manhattan occupies a dominant place in the cinematic imagination, while the black inner city, as Carby has observed, is "the symbolic space of suburban anxiety" (1998, p. 170). Lee has attempted to transform both the narrow geographical conception of "New York" and received images of black urban life, though his own image of Brooklyn has been called "a highly selective vision" (Pouzoulet, 1997, p. 33).[13] Again in *He Got Game*, Lee demonstrates sensitivity to the subtleties of place and location, juxtaposing Attica's enclosed cells and corridors with Coney Island's visually similar, yet paradoxically "open" apartment blocks. These are inhabited places, yet few suggest permanency or rootedness. Further images of confinement are mixed with fleeting shots of the horizon and soaring overhead camera work rarely seen in the Bedford-Stuyvesant films, representing Coney Island as a crossroads, a place signifying both stagnation and transformation. Shots of the Wonder Wheel and the ghostly shell of the old Cyclone roller coaster, rebuilt to serve the ever-increasing demands for thrills, suggest a world of discovery and transition, continuity and change, not only for Jesus but for the people who surround him.

Yet the Coney Island setting is also the very home of what Gunning has called the "aesthetic of attractions" that paralleled the early cinema's cult of virtual shocks and thrills. Location in this case encourages a deeper reflection on the status of *He Got Game* as cinema, and points to the direction that the cinema ride might be taking at the end of the century. While early cinema transported sensation-seeking viewers through virtual space, simulating Coney Island's roller coasters and stimulus rides, the challenge to cinema is to address intensified forms of perception produced in emerging virtual realities that threaten, at best, to redefine film's cultural role or, at worst, to render it obsolete. In a film about corruption, masks, false impressions, and virtual identities, the amusement park is still the "dreamworld home of attractions," a place where Jesus finds idealized love with Lala, and where the prostitute in the room next to Jake's goes for a brief respite, to ride the Cyclone and the Wonder Wheel. Yet as Gunning relates, when Maxim Gorky visited Coney Island in 1906, he found only "a slavery to varied boredom . . . an amazement in which there is neither transport nor joy" (1995, p. 126). Coney Island's thrill rides were a symptom of a deepening lack at the heart of the culture of modernity, corresponding to "the radical restructuring of spatial and temporal relations" in modern life. Similarly, cinema was in fact a weak compensation for the drying up of experience: Siegfried Kracauer would call cinema part of a "cult of distraction" which signaled the increasing fragmentation of human perception (1987, p. 91).

With its visual and narrative allusions to MTV, digital video, Playstation games, and pornography, *He Got Game* seems to recognize that a cinema of attractions continues to share space with the classical Hollywood narrative. But Lee's use of cinematic space also makes visible both the intensification and the restructuring of the gaze in African American life. Though Jesus appears to be the ideal flâneur at the "shopwindow of life," calmly "weighing his options" for the future, he is also a product of the Coney Island projects, assaulted by luxury goods always held just beyond reach. The acquisition of "real" power, as Friedberg suggests, might be limited to identities adopted in virtual space, an idea made visible when Jesus's sister, Mary, trumps her male cousin at a Sony Playstation. At the same time, Jesus is being made over into a commodity himself, to be bartered in virtual space. The higher he goes, the more he is absorbed into the hierarchies of the "show me the money" world of white hegemony: the false paternalism of his white high school coach; the brilliantly white interior of a sports promoter's home with its promise of cars, Rolexes, and cash; and finally the world of Tech University, where the sexual advances of white women are viewed as the highest form of flattery, and black women are pushed to the margins. In this multi-leveled world of masks and endlessly reflecting mirrors, it seems impossible that Jesus, or the viewer, could still discern (as the Public Enemy title song suggests), "the game of life behind the [con] game behind the game [of basketball]." The screen is frequently overrun with interview sound bites, infotainment news stories and promotional videos about the up-and-coming star, which break into the narrative and subsequently begin to invade the integrity of the film's realist framework. Real-life sports deities from Dick Vitale to Michael Jordan rally around the fictional character of Jesus, while the casting of Ray Allen, an NBA player with the Milwaukee Bucks, further gestures to a media culture in which traditional distinctions between the fictional and the real have virtually collapsed.

Many reviewers were critical of Lee for fictionalizing narrative and structural elements from Steve James, Peter Gilbert, and Fred Marx's *Hoop Dreams*, one of the most successful documentaries of all time. But the echo of *Hoop Dreams* is consistent with Lee's effort to blur the line between reality filmmaking and Hollywood realism. Lee's appearance in James's film, lecturing to student players about the real divisions of labor behind the game, underlines the intertextual relationship between the films. In a scene that directly glosses *Hoop Dreams*, Jesus is led into a massive college basketball court, surrounded by empty seats. A hyperactive announcer's voice introduces Jesus to an imaginary crowd. The scoreboard shows a series of images: Jesus in his basketball jersey with a crown of thorns, images of the disciples from George Stevens's *Greatest Story Ever Told*, Jesus on the cover of *Sports Illustrated*, depicted as a crucified Christ. The sequence induces a painful sense of irony, in which Jesus's pleasure in seeing his name in lights also suggests a disturbing doubling and estrangement from the self. The film within the film produces a mise-en-abyme, revealing that the agent of the narration is not merely the cinematic apparatus, but the commercial machinery behind it; meanwhile the self reflected back to Jesus is precisely *not* his own dream, but a media simulacrum of the imagined self. The narcissism promised by Jesus's voyeuristic identification with his own image is further fractured by the surreal images themselves, which make visible his exploitation and sacrifice to the gods of capital. Jesus's talent provides him with the mobility he will need to move from the projects to the utopia of the university and NBA riches, but, as in *Hoop Dreams*, one is constantly reminded of the inauthenticity of this mobility – it remains unclear whether this allegorical escape can ever be actualized.[14]

Lee's mise-en-scène points to the ongoing commodification of life, and art – which includes both basketball and filmmaking. One of the final images in the film, marking the closure of the narrative and the beginning of the metaphorical postscript discussed earlier, frames Jesus reading a letter sent from his father in prison. The last two close-ups of Jake and his son are compressed by an anamorphic lens, lengthening their figures as in a wide-screen film broadcast on television. In recalling the transformation of the aspect ratio of widescreen space into a televisual or video commodity, the gesture is at once nostalgic (when credit sequences of widescreen epics and westerns were compressed for television broadcast) and cynical, given Lee's much-maligned tendency towards the consumer packaging of his own art. But in another sense, the shots also reflect one of the film's broader messages: that the myth of America as a space of possibility is itself an outmoded widescreen construction, and might be headed straight to video.

He Got Game carries with it numerous cautions. Ultimately, Jesus is blessed with the desire to "do the right thing," and, for better or worse, the didacticism that runs through most of Lee's work returns here to rescue the film from moral ambiguity. A problematic element of Lee's film is that the pressing social and political contexts of the story, explored more fully in *Hoop Dreams*, might be buried here in a narrative that ultimately subsumes social context to an exploration of Jesus's personal and moral dilemma.[15] But perhaps Lee is attempting to address the medium as well as the message: the struggle for African American cinema is not simply about "getting game" and registering a "positive image" on the screen. Black film artists hoping to make a popular impact will inevitably come up against a complex web of hegemonic socio-economic interests (or, in this case, "Hollywood") that threatens their autonomy. As in basketball, white power brokers absorb the innovations of black talent and then sell it back to them as a product, and the small number who reap the rewards only perpetuate an apparatus predicated upon the systematic exclusion of others. Hegemony makes space only to reframe the periphery, and even oppositional, transformationist cinema, in whatever form it might take, rarely escapes being appropriated into the mainstream.

And perhaps Lee's participation in this process is one of the film's chief ironies.

NOTES

1. Daniel Bernardi (1996, pp. 115–116) considers segregated mise-en-scène in "The Voice of Whiteness: D.W. Griffith's Biograph Films."

2. Related to these discussions is the classic distinction between "space and place" in Edward Casey's work, which describes the transformation of space inhabited by real or imagined bodies into place. See Casey (1993). For a critique of Soja's methods as universalist, see Derek Gregory (1990), "Chinatown Part Three: Soja and the Missing Spaces of Social Theory," *Strategies*, *3*, pp. 40–104. Further reading on the relationship of space, place, and identity would include the considerable output of the journal *New Formations*, selected in James Donald, Judith Squires, and Erica Carter, eds., *Space and Place: Theories of Identity and Location* (1997), including the work of Gail Ching-Liang Low, Iain Chambers, and others.

3. See for example Anderson (1996, pp. 342–346); Soja (1989, pp. 190–217); Davis (1990); Gooding-Williams (1993); Hannigan, (1998).

4. When unarmed African immigrant Amadou Diallo was killed by the New York Street Crimes Unit in 1999, visitors who later came to the scene were struck by the smallness of the vestibule into which police fired 41 bullets. Diallo appeared to have been killed like a caged animal: "they [the police] could have just about touched him as he stood here," one visitor observed. Associated Press (2000), "Shooting Scene Becomes Shrine," *Rochester Democrat and Chronicle* (February 25): B5. Williams has expanded her ideas in the wake of the post-September 11th patriot act: See Williams (2001).

5. Between 1973 and 1996, U.S. individuals with incomes over $100,000 rose from 6 to 11% of the total, while incomes under $10,000 rose from 6 to 8%. The poverty level stands at $16,000. See Solow (2000, pp. 20–21).

6. See for example: Streible (1993); Gomery (1992); Stokes and Maltby (1999); Stacey (1994).

7. Massood (1996, p. 89) also cites Diawara, offering a useful reading of spatiality and the African American "urban realist" film.

8. Friedberg expands on these ideas in *Window Shopping: Cinema and the Postmodern* (1993), Los Angeles: University of California Press.

9. The film began as an NAACP project but quickly and awkwardly evolved into a piece of wartime propaganda. Cripps documents its "considerable failings" (1996, pp. 38–55).

10. See Massood (2001, 2003); Kennedy (2000, pp. 115–127). It is worth noting that the following keywords appear on an internet search for Rich's *Straight Out of Brooklyn* (1991): "African American, drug dealing, poverty, New York, domestic violence, housing project, robbery, tragedy," perhaps summing up the focus of the genre. See Internet Movie Database http://us.imdb.com/Keywords?0102989.

11. Massood examines the cinematic trope of train travel in Lee's *Clockers* (2003, pp. 175–205).

12. Kennedy (2000, p. 159) points to a similar effect in Lee's *Clockers* (1995); see also Massood (2001, 2003).

13. Massood suggests that Lee might be responsible for the construction of a "Brooklyn chronotope," expanding on Robert Stam's cinematic application of Mikhail Bakhtin's theorization of the chronotope (2003, p. 130).

14. This ambiguity is thematized in other Lee films. Kennedy (2000, p. 162) notes a similar pattern at the end of *Clockers*.

15. On *Hoop Dreams*, see Hooks (1996); Kennedy (2000, p. 101).

REFERENCES

Abrams, M. H. (1988). *A glossary of literary terms* (5th ed.). Philadelphia: Holt, Rinehart and Winston.

Anderson, S. (1996). A city called heaven: Black enchantment and despair in Los Angeles. In: A. J. Scott & E. W. Soja (Eds), *The City: Los Angeles and Urban Theory at the End of the Twentieth Century* (pp. 336–364). Los Angeles: University of California Press.

Arnold, R. F. (1990). Film space/audience space: Notes toward a theory of spectatorship. *The Velvet Light Trap*, 25(Spring), 44–52.

Baraka, A. (1993). Spike Lee at the movies. In: M. Diawara (Ed.), *Black American Cinema* (pp. 145–153). New York: Routledge Press.

Bazin, A. (1967). *What is cinema?* Vol. 1. Hugh Gray (Trans.). Berkeley: University of California Press.

Bernardi, D. (Ed.) (1996). *The birth of whiteness: Race and the emergence of U.S. cinema*. New Brunswick, NJ: Rutgers University Press.

Bowser, P., & Spence, L. (2000). *Writing himself into history: Oscar Micheaux, his silent films, and his audiences*. New Brunswick, NJ: Rutgers University Press.

Burch, N. (1973). *Theory of film practice*. H. R. Lane (Trans.). New York: Praeger.

Carby, H. V. (1998). *Race men*. Cambridge: Harvard University Press.

Carroll, N. (1996). *Theorizing the moving image*. Cambridge: Cambridge University Press.

Carter, E., Donald, J., & Squires, J. (Eds) (1997). *Space and place: Theories of identity and location*. London: Lawrence and Wishart.

Casey, E. (1993). *Getting back into place: Toward a renewed understanding of the place-world*. Bloomington: Indiana University Press.

Cooper, M. G. (2002). *Narrative spaces*. Screen 43(Summer), 139–157.

Cripps, T. (1978). *Black film as genre*. Bloomington: Indiana University Press.

Cripps, T. (1996). The making of *The Birth of a Race*: The emerging politics of identity in silent movies. In: D. Bernardi (Ed.), *The Birth of Whiteness* (pp. 38–55). New Brunswick, NJ: Rutgers University Press.

Davis, M. (1990). *City of quartz: Excavating the future in Los Angeles*. London: Verso.

Deleuze, G. (1986). *Cinema 1: The movement-image*. Hugh Tomlinson and Barbara Habberjam (Trans.). Minneapolis: University of Minnesota Press.

Diawara, M. (1993). Black American cinema: The new realism. In: M. Diawara (Ed.), *Black American Cinema* (pp. 3–25). New York: Routledge Press.

Falcon, R. (1998). Review of *He Got Game*. Sight and Sound, 8(10), 45.

Foster, G. A. (1999). *Captive bodies: Postcolonial subjectivity in cinema*. Albany: State University of New York Press.

Foucault, M. (1980). *Power/knowledge: Selected interviews and other writings, 1972–1977*. C. Gordon (Trans., Ed.). New York: Pantheon.

Friedberg, A. (1995). Cinema and the postmodern condition. In: L. Williams (Ed.), *Viewing Positions: Ways of Seeing Film* (pp. 114–133). New Brunswick, NJ: Rutgers University Press.

Gaines, J. (1996). *The Birth of a Nation* and *Within Our Gates*: Two tales of the American South. In: R. H. King & H. Taylor (Eds), *Dixie debates: Perspectives on southern cultures* (pp. 177–192). New York, NY: University Press.

Gomery, D. (1992). *Shared pleasures: A history of movie presentation in the United States.* Madison: University of Wisconsin Press.

Gooding-Williams, R. (Ed.) (1993). *Reading Rodney King/reading urban uprising.* New York: Routledge Press.

Green, J. R. (2000). *Straight lick: The cinema of Oscar Micheaux.* Indianapolis: University of Indiana Press.

Guerrero, E. (1993). *Framing blackness: The African American image in film.* Philadelphia: Temple University Press.

Gunning, T. (1995). An aesthetic of astonishment: Early film and the (in)credulous spectator. In: L. Williams (Ed.), *Viewing Positions: Ways of Seeing Film* (pp. 59–83). New Brunswick, NJ: Rutgers University Press.

Hannigan, J. (1998). *Fantasy city: Pleasure and profit in the postmodern metropolis.* London: Routledge Press.

Hayden, T. (2000). LAPD: Law and disorder. *The Nation, 270*(April 10), 6.

Heath, S. (1981). *Questions of cinema.* Bloomington: Indiana University Press.

Hirsch, A. R. (2000). Choosing segregation: Federal housing policy between *Shelley* and *Brown*. In: J. F. Bauman, R. Biles & K. M. Szylvian (Eds), *From Tenements to the Taylor Homes: In Search of an Urban Housing Policy in Twentieth-Century America* (pp. 206–225). University Park: Pennsylvania State University Press.

hooks, bell (1993). The oppositional gaze: Black female spectators. In: M. Diawara (Ed.), *Black American Cinema* (pp. 288–302). New York: Routledge Press.

hooks, bell (1996). *Reel to real: Race, sex, and class at the movies.* New York: Routledge Press.

Jones, G. W. (1991). *Black cinema treasures, lost and found.* Denton: University of North Texas Press.

Jones, J. (1989). Spike Lee's look at the realities of racism. *Black Film Review, 5.2* (Spring), 13–14.

Kaplan, E. A. (1997). *Looking for the other: Feminism, film, and the imperial gaze.* London: Routledge.

Kennedy, L. (2000). *Race and urban space in contemporary American culture.* Edinburgh: Edinburgh University Press.

Klawans, S. (1998). Fanfares (Review of *He Got Game*). *The Nation, 266*(June 1), 35–36.

Konstantarakos, M. (Ed.) (2000). *Spaces in European cinema.* Exeter: Intellect Press.

Kracauer, S. (1987). *Cult of distraction: On Berlin's Picture palaces* [1927]. New German Critique 40(Winter), 91–96.

Lefebvre, H. (1991). *The production of space.* Donald Nicholson-Smith (Trans.). London: Blackwell.

Lefebvre, H. (1996). *Writing on cities.* Eleonore Kofman and Elizabeth Lebas (Ed. and Trans.). London: Blackwell.

Lyne, W. (2000). No accident: From black power to black box office. *African American Review, 34*(1), 39–59.

Massood, P. J. (1996). Mapping the hood: The genealogy of city space in *Boyz N the Hood* and *Menace II Society. Cinema Journal, 35*(2), 85–97.

Massood, P. J. (2001). Which way to the promised land? Spike Lee's *Clockers* and the legacy of the African American city. *African American Review, 35*(2), 263–279.

Massood, P. J. (2003). *Black city cinema: African American urban experiences in film.* Philadelphia: Temple University Press.

Modleski, T. (1991). *Feminism without women*. London: Routledge.

Modleski, T. (2000). In Hollywood, racist stereotypes can still earn Oscar nominations. *The Chronicle of Higher Education, 46*(28), B9–B10.

Pouzoulet, C. (1997). The cinema of Spike Lee: Images of a mosaic city. In: M. A. Reid (Ed.), *Spike Lee's Do the Right Thing* (pp. 31–49). Cambridge: Cambridge University Press.

Reid, M. A. (1993). *Redefining black film*. Berkeley: University of California Press.

Rony, F. T. (1996). *The third eye: Race, cinema and ethnographic spectacle*. Durham: Duke University Press.

Smith, V. (1997). *Representing blackness: Issues in film and video*. New Brunswick, NJ: Rutgers University Press.

Snead, J. (1995). Images of blacks in black independent films. In: M. T. Martin (Ed.), *Cinemas of the Black Diaspora: Diversity, Dependence, and Oppositionality* (pp. 365–375). Detroit: Wayne State University Press.

Soja, E. W. (1989). *Postmodern geographies: The reassertion of space in critical social theory*. London: Verso.

Solow, R. M. (2000). Welfare: The cheapest country. *The New York Review of Books, 48*(5), 20–21.

Stacey, J. (1994). *Star gazing: Hollywood cinema and female spectatorship*. New York: Routledge.

Stokes, M., & Maltby, R. (Eds) (1999). *American movie audiences: From the turn of the century to the sound era*. London: BFI.

Streible, D. (1993). The Harlem theater: Black film exhibition in Austin, Texas, 1920–1773. In: M. Diawara (Ed.), *Black American Cinema* (pp. 221–236). New York: Routledge Press.

Taylor, C. (1996). The re-birth of the aesthetic in cinema. In: D. Bernardi (Ed.), *The Birth of Whiteness* (pp. 38–55). New Brunswick: Rutgers University Press.

Williams, P. (2001). By any means necessary: The new USA Patriot Act. *The Nation, 273*(November 26), 11.

BEING RACIALIZED ETHNICS: SECOND GENERATION WEST INDIAN IMMIGRANTS IN NEW YORK CITY

Sherri-Ann P. Butterfield

ABSTRACT

While the issue of "Blackness" has long pervaded American society, it has rarely been problematized in social science literature and treated as a taken-for-granted. This article utilizes in-depth interviews with second generation

Race and Ethnicity in New York City
Research in Urban Sociology, Volume 7, 107–136
© 2004 Published by Elsevier Ltd.
ISSN: 1047-0042/doi:10.1016/S1047-0042(04)07005-9

*West Indian adults in New York City to examine the ways in which they
conceive of their Blackness, both racially and ethnically. New York City
is viewed as an important urban context that in many ways facilitates the
formation of identity for this population. The assimilation process, or not, of
second generation West Indians is also considered in terms of socioeconomic
status and gender. The results indicate that second generation West Indians
strongly identify with both their racial and ethnic identities, which in turn
calls for a reconceptualization of "Blackness". There is also evidence that
points to New York City as a space of cross-cultural integration where identity
formation is significantly impacted by the presence of other immigrants (and
their children) that leads to a pan-immigrant or pan-ethnic identity among
young New Yorkers.*

I wish that they would stop assuming that everyone with dark skin is African American. I mean,
there are Black West Indians just like there are Black Africans, Black Hispanics . . . hell, even
Black Germans. Black people don't get to be from different countries like white people? I don't
understand why Americans don't know . . . or don't want to know . . . that Black people can be
ethnic too.

These are the remarks of Gianna,[1] a twenty-nine-year-old second generation
Trinidadian woman living in Flatbush, Brooklyn.[2] Gianna received her bachelor's
degree from Brooklyn College,[3] works as a nurse in a prestigious Manhattan
hospital, is currently single with no children, and lives what she describes as "a
completely ethnic life" – with friends from a variety of ethnic backgrounds. And
she argues that her life typifies the lives of her other co-ethnics in New York City.

For individuals who live in one of the several major destination American
cities for Black immigrants such as New York, New Jersey, Miami, Boston, or
Washington D.C., Gianna's comments might seem to be pointing out the obvious.
She is stating the lived reality of many residents in these cities – that interacting
with Black people from regions of the world is the norm, rather than isolated
incidents. However, Gianna's remarks reflect her dissatisfaction with how Black
people, particularly Black ethnics, are treated and discussed, or not, in the national
discourse about race and ethnicity in the United States. Her life experiences have
been nothing but exposure to different immigrant groups, including her own, yet
Gianna has a heightened sense of "invisibility" to the larger American public that
often provides a context for how she views herself and others.

Like Gianna, the other sixty-four women and men discussed in this paper are the
children of West Indian immigrants and raised (almost) entirely in the boroughs
of New York City. The respondents all are currently employed, each have varying
levels of education, grew up in diverse New York City neighborhoods, and are from
different socioeconomic backgrounds. However, despite these sometimes stark

differences, they all share similar stories about growing up as second generation West Indians in an urban landscape which includes numerous people of various ethnicities. This paper argues that for these second generation immigrants, having a racial *and* an ethnic identity is a salient part of their lives. It is not an either/or proposition, but a situation in which being Black and West Indian in American society greatly informs how the adult second generation come to conceive of themselves and others.

The incorporation of West Indian immigrants into the American social and economic structure has long been considered a crucial test of the deterministic power of race in our society. Many researchers have commented on the roles of race and racism in shaping the social and economic plight of West Indians in relation to African Americans, with a substantial body of literature focusing on their social assimilation (Foner, 1979, 1985, 1987, 1998, 2001; Kasinitz, 1992; Kasinitz et al., 2001; Vickerman, 1994, 1999, 2001; Waters, 1994, 1999, 2001) and their socioeconomic success relative to African Americans (Butcher, 1994; Farley & Allen, 1987; Kalmijn, 1996; Model, 1995; Model & Ladipo, 1996; Sowell, 1978) with conclusions often posed in terms of the relative roles of culture, ethnic responses, and racial attributes in shaping these outcomes.

Receiving relatively little attention until recently (Vickerman, 1999, 2001; Waters, 1994, 1999) has been the experiences and assimilation processes (or not) of the children of West Indian immigrants. Previous studies have debated as to whether second generation West Indians will adopt the ethnic identity of their parents as "West Indians" or the racial identity of "Black" similar to that of their African American peers. However, the lack of attention paid to the contexts in which second generation West Indians' racial and ethnic identities act interdependently is particularly interesting in light of the presence of significant numbers of immigrant groups in New York City. This study is intended to address the gaps in immigration literature concerning the intricate nature of having a racial *and* ethnic identity for Black immigrants in general, and West Indians specifically. The primary analytic thrust of this chapter is to uncover the mechanisms that shape ethnic identity formation for second generation West Indians, while emphasizing the complexity of these identities and the contexts and circumstances that produce them. The goal of this research is to examine the following questions: Are the existing categories of identity in extant literature fully capturing the experience of second generation West Indian immigrants in New York City? Or, is ethnic identity construction unique and in fact more complex especially where boundaries are both flexible and open for contestation? The former assumes that individuals of the second generation adopt a primary identity which reflects either parents culture/ethnic enclave or a hyphenated American one and therefore resembling more of an assimilated identity. In contrast, the latter assumes that identity is more fluid in nature and that structures are themselves transient and changing in especially in a place like New York City.

In this perspective, second generation West Indians utilize various parts of their ethnic background and experience at different stages of their life and, I would argue, even at different points within the same day, in attempts to piece together identities germane to their larger social environment. What are the circumstances and contexts in which second generation West Indians emphasize their ethnicity? The research presented here attempts to illuminate how ethnic identity is constructed in relation to the social phenomena of class and gender for second generation West Indians.

Moreover, the shifting demographics of New York City communities, as well as the intense degree to which different racial and ethnic groups share public space, provide a landscape in which the process of identity formation can be problematized. Specifically, the presence of a large African American community in New York City (and surrounding areas) strongly influences second generation identity formation. It is simply not a matter of choosing between a racial and ethnic identity, but a process in which the concept of "Blackness" is given new meaning. Similar to the racial classification of "white" which encompasses Italians, Russians, and the Irish, we must acknowledge that the term "Black" also incorporates multiple ethnic groups. As such, I argue that the broadening definition of "Blackness" is being played out in New York culture where it is just as common to hear reggae and Latin music on street corners as it is to hear rap and pop music. Quite simply, New York City provides individuals with more options and more space for creativity when constructing their own identities. In essence, this research seeks to illuminate how racial and ethnic identity are constructed in particular contexts and within an urban landscape for second generation immigrant adults.

This chapter then, will do five things: (1) provide an overview of earlier theoretical approaches to assimilation; (2) outline the various contexts in which identity choices are made; (3) discuss the importance of New York City as a site for identity development; (4) identify the ways in which class and gender impact racial and ethnic identity construction; and (5) point to some of the implications of a diasporic understanding of race.

THE RESEARCH CONTEXT: THEORETICAL AND EMPIRICAL

The Straight Line Assimilation Model

The term "assimilation" has had various meanings within the discipline of sociology and American popular discourse (Gordon, 1961). Early 20th century sociologists often disagreed on the degree to which (mainly European) immigrants would come to share American values and norms, or in fact change American society, and tended to assume (and the continued use of "assimilation" within current American society still assumes) that incorporation into the dominant society means adopting the *culture* of the dominant society, and that that culture was correlated with upward mobility.

This model is highly problematic for the children of contemporary immigrants as it suggests that each succeeding generation will become more similar to the general native-born population in the United States.[4] Generation has thus been a key term in assessing the assimilation of different ethnic groups in American society (Gordon, 1964; Hirschman, 1983; Lieberson, 1980; Lieberson & Waters, 1988; Perlmann, 1988; Waters, 1990). While this depiction of socioeconomic mobility was generally true of the various European immigrant groups, it is important to note that there were differences in the pace of assimilation across the groups. For instance, authors such as Richard Alba (1985) and Stanley Lieberson (1980) both suggest that East European Jews achieved social mobility by the second generation, while it took Italian immigrants and their descendants several generations to reach parity with native-born whites of American parentage.

One of the earliest and detailed discussions of identity and the experience of the second generation is Warner and Srole's (1945) study of ethnic groups in New Haven. Warner and Srole describe a generational march of ethnic groups from initial residential and occupational segregation and poverty to residential, occupational and identity integration and Americanization (Mollenkopf et al., 1997). The authors put forth a model suggests that the second generation first learns an immigrant culture in the home and then encounters the more highly valued American native culture in the schools, their peer groups, and the mass media. They then internalize American culture and identity and reject their parents' culture and identity as foreigners.

This model's central assumptions may have been true for generational change among white ethnic groups, however, these assumptions most certainly do not hold for the children of contemporary immigrants. Warner and Srole, and other early twentieth century immigration scholars, assumed that immigrant children would absorb a self-reliant, individualistic, middle class "American culture," that by adopting, would lead to upward mobility. This model ignores the possibility that *retaining* immigrant culture might provide access to networks that facilitate upward mobility (see Light, 1972; Portes & Zhou, 1993; Waters, 1994; Zhou & Bankston, 1998). Additionally, the concept of straight line assimilation mistakenly assumes that American culture remains untouched or unaffected by the presence of large numbers of immigrants. For example, it is important to recognize that while the Irish and the Jews are often considered as having "assimilated" to American culture, they vastly changed the culture and social structures of numerous American cities at the turn of the century, particularly Boston and New York.

It is the misassumption that immigrants do not impact the societies they enter that this chapter is most concerned with. For many of today's second generation, and I would argue, even for those at the turn of the twentieth century, they are not entering a monolithic American society which over time comes to define their "Americanness." Rather, the children of contemporary immigrants impact, and are impacted by, the cities and contexts in which they live their daily lives. Particularly in a place like New York City which has always prided itself on its ethnic diversity, how can the second generation help but to redefine New York City culture while at the same time seeking to define themselves?

In addition, Warner and Srole assume that being "American" has higher status than immigrant culture. While this may be the case for some immigrant groups, for many of today's second generation, this model is antithetical to their experiences and belief systems. For the second generation, experiences with racism, prejudice, and discrimination teach them that they are the "unmeltable" Americans – people who by definition of their phenotype get defined out of what it means to be "American."[5]

In other words, for immigrants of color, the idea of assimilation gets turned on its head – they can only assimilate into a racialized American society which may facilitate downward mobility rather than upward. For example, if West Indian immigrants lose their ethnic distinctiveness, they become indistinguishable from African-Americans, thereby making their American experience not necessarily higher than their home country experiences. They are coming from societies where, for the most part, they constitute the racial majority, where Blacks are in positions of leadership and authority, and the ascription of a minority status is perceived as at step down (Bryce-Laporte, 1972; Laguerre, 1984).

In fact, it is the severe racial discrimination and inequality experienced by African-Americans that has led some first generation West Indians to resist assimilation by engaging in a distancing of themselves from native-born Blacks, even though they are constrained from doing so by virtue of their phenotype (Foner, 1987, 1994; Halter, 1995; Kasinitz, 1992; Vickerman, 1994, 1999; Waters, 1994, 1999; Woldemikael, 1989). However, for second generation West Indians who are raised primarily with (and treated as) African Americans as their peer group, what assimilation choices do they have, if any?

Contemporary Theories of Immigrant Adaptation

Several speculative theories describing the experiences of becoming American emerged after numerous scholars realized that the straight line assimilation model was not necessarily applicable to the post-1965 immigrants and their children (Gans, 1992; Perlmann & Waldinger, 1996; Portes & Zhou, 1993). These works stress the multiple and contradictory paths which can be followed by second-generation children. Some may achieve socioeconomic success while retaining strong ethnic attachments and identities, while others assimilate to American subcultures with limited socioeconomic mobility.

Herbert Gans (1992) speculates that the youth who do not "become American" and adopt the negative attitudes toward school, opportunity, hard work and "the American Dream" that their American peers have adopted, but rather stay tied to their parents' ethnic community and values, will end up doing better. Portes and Zhou (1993) make a similar argument in their conception of the model of "segmented assimilation" in explaining the outcomes of the different groups of second-generation youth. The authors argue that the mode of incorporation of the first generation creates differential opportunities and cultural and social capital in the form of ethnic jobs, networks and values that create differential pulls on the allegiances of the second generation. For those immigrant groups who face extreme discrimination, reactive ethnicity emerges in the first generation. The model asserts that those in the second generation whose parental generation lacks the degree of social capital to provide opportunities and protection for them are likely to develop an "adversarial stance" that American minorities such as poor African Americans and Latinos hold toward the dominant white society. This adversarial stance stresses that discrimination in the United States is very strong and devalues education as a vehicle of advancement. Portes and Zhou emphasize that the adversarial stance of this peer culture directly contradicts the immigrant parents' their expectations of upward mobility and educational success for their offspring. The second generation that ally themselves with America's racial minority groups will most likely be at risk of downward social mobility.

These ideas greatly inform the work of Mary Waters (1994, 1999) who seeks to explain and understand the experiences of second-generation West Indian youths in New York City. Waters specifically explores the racial and ethnic identities adopted by these youths. In her study, Waters (1994) found three types of identities among the second-generation – a Black American identity, an ethnic or hyphenated national origin identity, and an immigrant identity. "These different identities are related to different perceptions and understandings of race relations and of opportunities in the United States" (Waters, 1994). She found that those in the second generation who identify as West Indians tend to see more opportunities and rewards for individual effort and initiative, while those who identify as Black Americans tend to see more racial discrimination and limits to opportunities for Blacks in the United States. Thus, Waters suggests that assimilation to America for the second-generation Black immigrant is complicated by race and class and their interaction, with upwardly mobile second-generation youths maintaining ethnic ties to their parents' national origins and with poor inner city youths assimilating to the Black American peer culture that surrounds them.

Given these findings, the identities of the adult children of West Indians become a theoretically and empirically fascinating case study. Do these three categories of racial/ethnic identity hold for adult West Indians? How does the race/class/gender interaction impact racial/ethnic identity? Is West Indian ethnicity still used as a distancing tool among the adult second generation from African Americans? Additionally, what role has the changing demographics and culture of New York City played in identity formation among this population?

This chapter aims to contribute to, and problematize previous research by not only examining the racial and ethnic identity of adults rather than youth, but also by suggesting that the adult second generation do not view themselves as having to choose one identity over the other, but as a hybridization of both their racial and ethnic selves. For the second generation West Indian adults in this study, New York City provides a context in which they can embrace their multiple identities while maintaining close ties to other racial and ethnic groups, particularly African Americans and Latinos.

DESIGN AND METHOD OF THE STUDY

The findings of this paper emerged from an analysis of semi-structured, open-ended interviews with sixty-five second generation West Indians between the ages of twenty and thirty-two. This age category was chosen because this was the oldest children born of post-1965 immigrants could be in 1998. The lower age limit was chosen as the research was trying to tap the second generation that may have some work experience.[6] Thus, the men and women in this age bracket have come into full adulthood and experiencing socioeconomic advantages and disadvantages, as they are now primarily responsible for their own lives. In addition, "in the wake of dramatic changes to family form, women's labor force participation, the economy, and the labor market, this crucial cohort in now making the transition from home and school to work and forming their own families" (Mollenkopf et al., 1995, p. 3).

I defined *West Indian* to include all people not of Asian ancestry descended from those born in the Anglophone Caribbean: the thirteen Caricom member nations, the mainland countries of Guyana and Belize, the Caribbean British colonies, and English speaking Panamanians.[7] *Second generation West Indians* were identified as those for whom at least one parent was born in the West Indies.[8]

Respondents were recruited via a snowball sampling approach, which began with my own personal network of second generation West Indians, and moved into the larger New York West Indian network through word-of-mouth. My sample was selected based on some basic demographics – age, gender, education level, socioeconomic status, with my sampling strategy shifting as I tried to ensure that no relevant categories were missed.[9]

In addition the in-depth interviews, I also conducted ethnographies at two different sites from December 1998 until May 1999. After observing the goings-on in several neighborhoods in Brooklyn and Queens, I selected two service industry stores as my sites of study: a farmer's market in central Brooklyn and a unisex hair salon in southeast Queens. In both cases I used a small business in the neighborhood as a way of meeting and talking to people. In addition, these locations were selected because they have both been documented as being home to the majority of the West Indian community in New York City (Foner, 1979, 1985, 1987; Kasinitz, 1992; Vickerman, 1994, 1999; Waters, 1991, 1994, 1999). I spent approximately three days a week at each site, which not only allowed me to become familiar with the people frequenting the businesses at both sites, but also with the people who simply hung out in both neighborhoods.

The Brooklyn store, Plaintain Market,[10] is located on the corner of two major streets in the neighborhood and is patronized primarily by West Indians. In fact, the entire time that I was there, I did not see any non-Black patrons, even though the store was owned by Korean grocers.[11] The store was next door to a West Indian bakery, so many people shopped at the store while they were waiting for their orders from the bakery.[12] Plaintain Market is a rather large corner store, and carries specialty foods from the Caribbean that are used in traditional dishes,[13] as well as fruits and vegetables that can be found at regular markets. Plaintain Market obviously did well as it was often full of customers, regardless of day or time.

The Queens store, Hairstyling, is located on major street, situated between a pharmacy/drug store and a dine-in/take-out restaurant. While it is a unisex hiar salon, the majority of the clients are women. Hairstyling is relatively small, by salon standards, but has a rather large clientele.[14] Clients usually go the salon every week to two weeks, with a standing appointment. Many people have formed and sustained friendships based on seeing each other every week for several hours at a time. As in the case of Plaintain market, Hairstyling's clientele is predominantly West Indian.[15] However, the clientele often interact with the ethnically mixed clientele from the drug store and the restaurant.[16]

While both sites catered to a predominantly West Indian clientele, the neighborhoods differed in various ways; the Brooklyn neighborhood has a predominance of West Indians living in the area, with the Queens area being home to a more ethnically diverse population.[17] The working-class Brooklyn neighborhood contains many small store fronts, high-rise apartment complexes next to each other, with a subway station located nearby. The working- to middle-class

Queens area is almost the direct opposite of the Brooklyn one as it has a few stores located on the main streets, is mainly comprised of private homes, and there is only a bus line that runs down the main street.

Concepts and Measures Employed

The major analytic thrust of this research is to demonstrate the complexity of ethnic identity formation. As such, this research treats *race* and *ethnicity* as two distinct concepts. *Race* is defined as socially constructed distinctions drawn from physical appearance, while *ethnicity* is operationalized in terms of distinctions based on national origin, language, religion, food, and other cultural markers.

In addition, most of the scholarship on ethnic adaptation employs a bimodal framework that engages one of two opposing outcomes – either complete abandonment of ethnic identity for an American one or a complete rejection of an American identity. This research seeks to illuminate the fact that the experiences of second generation West Indian immigrants, and even the general Black immigrant population, does not conform to such rigid and simplistic notions of ethnic identity. Like Alba (1985), Barth (1989), and Waters (1990) I argue that the meanings of ethnic identity are shaped through the nature of interpersonal and intergroup relations and the social context. In this study, ethnic identity is treated as a dynamic process that is negotiated and renegotiated in different social contexts and at different stages of the life course (Nagel, 1994).

The examination of ethnic identity and its significance for second generation West Indian immigrants entails looking at the ways in which they define themselves; how these identities influence their social behavior, networks, and attitudes; and how they define the membership boundaries of their group (Barth, 1969; Nagel, 1994; Patterson, 1976; Waters, 1990). The salience of ethnic identity will be evaluated with measures used in other studies such as: preferences for and use of home country language/style of speech, patronage with co-ethnics, church membership or religious affiliation, participation in voluntary organizations, and participation in events and activities sponsored by such organizations (see Alba, 1990; Bakalian, 1993; Nagel, 1994; Waters, 1990). In addition to traditional measures, I also considered the degree to wich the respondents listen to West Indian music, read West Indian books and/or newspapers, and participate/attend in city-wide West Indian activities (e.g. the annual Eastern Parkway celebration in Brooklyn on Labor Day – see Kasinitz, 1992). I also inquired as to how often they or their parents return to their home country, whether or not they send remittances to family members there, or if they make contributions to West Indian causes.

WHAT DID YOU CALL ME? HAVING A RACIAL AND ETHNIC IDENTITY IN NYC

Based on the in-depth interviews and the ethnographies in Hairstyling and Plantain Market, it became readily apparent that the racial and ethnic identity construction among second generation West Indians was an extremely complex matter. Before I could begin any interview or conversation in either store, the person whom I was talking to would ask, where are you from? When I replied Queens, I would frequently receive looks of disbelief or rolling eyes, and a response of, No, you know what I mean. Where are you REALLY from? It was not until I explained my own West Indian background that respondents seemed open and willing to talk with me. When I asked why they *had* to know, one respondent stated, *who you know who is actually FROM New York? We're all immigrants in one form or another. You know, now that I think about it, the question shouldn't be "where you from?", but "how long you been here?"* Jason commented,

> I don't talk to people that I don't know. Knowing that you from a yard [from Jamaica] tells me something about you. I know how you were raised, I probably know your family, and know that you understand patois. The most important reason I need to know where you're from is so that I know that you will understand what I am saying to you as bredren [fellow Jamaican] in this country. You know the best and worst parts about growing up Black and West Indian in New York City, same as me. If you said that you were from somewhere else, I would stop and explain more things to you, but now I don't have to . . . cause we have a common understanding.

Jason's comment was more the norm than the exception in response to my question. Many respondents stated that their response to my question of *how do you identify?* was intricately tied to their question of where I was from, in that their identity is based on who is asking and in what context is someone asking about. Another respondent asked to be more specific about in what context I was referring to:

> What do you mean by how do I identify? You mean to you, at work, at home with my immediate family, with my aunts and uncles and cousins, with my friends, with my acquaintances, with my teammates . . . Let me tell you something . . . I am the same person in each situation, a Black Trinidadian man. But how I choose to express that to other people is done in multiple ways . . . What are you, by the way? (Michael).

In every case, both interviews and conversations, respondents reported that they were prepared to talk to me, but how they identified may have changed depending on what I reported my identity to be. In many cases they had already speculated that I was West Indian, Jamaican even, but their unsurety would have led them to simply identify as "Black."[18] When I asked about why they would have identified as "just" Black, Joyce replied,

> You act like I am not Black. Just because I would have talked to you as a Black person, does not
> mean that I'm not Guyanese. I mean . . . I'm a Black Guyanese, I listen to calypso and eat roti,
> but Lord knows that the people in this country are not going to let me forget that I am Black.

Joyce's comments reflected the fact that I fell prey to the same missteps that I was critiquing in other scholars – the question posed assumed that one's racial/ethnic identity was an either/or proposition. However, several other respondents talked about feeling at different points of their life when they still have to choose whether to be "Black" or "West Indian":

> You know, I used to think that when I grew up, I would stop having to say whether I was Black
> or West Indian, but every once in a while it comes back up. For instance, I was a some friend's
> party . . . white guy of course, and he introduces me as his "Jamaican friend" . . . now mind you,
> this was not relevant to the conversation in any way, but he just said it. I was like what the fu . . .,
> oops, sorry won't curse . . . but damn, does me being Jamaican make me somehow different to
> these people? Does it make me any more or less Black? Of course people started asking me
> whether I listened to Bob Marley, with other people telling how they had been to Jamaica and
> they got some really good weed . . . I was tempted to tell everybody that I also listen to hip-hop
> and jazz and had gotten some good Ecstasy from a white guy in college. But I knew better than
> that. Then they would all be thinking that's what all Black people do, and that somehow I was
> not a *real* Jamaican. Cause you know I represent either all West Indians or all Black people. To
> them I can't be part of both cultures . . . (Winston).

When I specifically asked whether respondents identified as African American, West Indian, their national identity such as Jamaican or Trinidadian, or simply as American, many continued to respond that they identify with all the terms depending on who they are talking to, where they are, how they are feeling that day, etc. For example,

> I can be all of those at the same time, and often am. I mean . . . uh . . . we are all African Americans
> because we all come from Africa and now we are here in America. I don't think of myself as
> American, but my cousins in Barbados call me "the American", so I guess I am. I don't use
> "West Indian" unless I am talking to a white person or Blacks not from New York. And when
> I say West Indian, everyone usually assumes that I am Jamaican, so I just let them. I know that
> they don't know the difference one way or another anyway. But I prefer Black. Cause while I
> might look like some of the African immigrants who live here, I definitely didn't grow up like
> them or Black Americans for that matter (Justin).

Similar to Justin, none of the respondents referred to themselves as "American" until they left the United States and went to their parents' home country or some other country:

> I used to go to Guyana every summer from the age of 5 until I was 15. And I spent the entire
> summer . . . all 3 months . . . that's one-fourth of the year. And do you know my cousins still had
> the nerve to call me an American?! I used to get so mad! I mean, now I sort of understand it,
> but they could never understand why I would get so angry. They meant that I lived here, and
> did and said things that were American . . . which was technically true, I am an American. I

tell them now that I got mad because somehow I always knew that the word American did not apply to me. I knew that my parents weren't American because they were not from here, but I was born here and still feel like I didn't belong. "American" was for the kids we used to see on TV . . . the little blond haired, blue-eyed white girls playing with their Barbie and their Barbie playhouse in their big houses . . . not the little dark-skinned girl playing with some old doll in a small house while her parents are struggling to make it . . . (Sharon).

Sharon speaks to the fact that all of the respondents felt that by definition, the term "American" does not refer to them. And not just because they are immigrant children, but because they are Black:

For our whole lives, America has told us that American is everything that Black people are not. It is not dark-skinned, it not having kinky hair, it is not struggling to survive, and it definitely is not having to ask for help. And you know as Black people who have been historically enslaved almost everywhere in the world, we still have to ask for stuff for equality. It is no surprise why many African Americans feel that we should demand and take what is due to us as opposed to asking for it . . . (Sharon).

In a very interesting way, Sharon talks of African Americans as a group of which she is not a part. And as far as the second generation I spoke with were concerned, they all saw themselves as separate from the African American community. The West Indians had specific ideas about what constituted being "African American", and they most often did not see themselves as fitting into that identity. Sheila stated,

Being African American means that you have a specific cultural background, just as being Basian [Barbadian] has a particular culture to it. African Americans have a general understanding of their migrant experiences the same way that we generally know of ours. . . . I mean, we can all trace our slave history to Africa, but African Americans can also trace their family history to down South somewhere, and I can trace mine back to the Caribbean. They know grits, hamhocks, and pigs feet, and we know about cornmeal porridge, tripe, and oxtail . . . I mean, we all Black, but we're not all the same . . . cause everybody different from the straight-up Africans.

Like Sheila, many of the respondents regarded African Americans as an ethnic group as opposed to a racial group, so most people stated that they would not identify as both African American and West Indian. They did not see this as a method of "distancing" themselves from African Americans, but acknowledging the different histories of the Black groups in the United States. Winston commented,

When I got to high school and learned about the Civil Rights Movement, I was very self-conscious that I didn't know much about it before I started the class. All my African Americans friends had some knowledge about it, and some of their parents had participated in the marches. I remember being impressed by that fact and them just sort of brushing it off as normal. They would want to know why I didn't know anything and I would tell them it was because my parents missed most of it by coming to this country in 1972. I always felt like I missed something really important to my history as a Black person in this country. My parents always reminded that we

had our own history too, it was just different . . . So when my African American friends say that
they do not have an ethnicity, I tell them that yeah, they do, we just don't talk about it right.
We are all Black, but we are *not* all African American with everything that goes along with
it . . . There is still a Southern culture that I am still trying to learn about in the same way that
they are learning about the history of the Caribbean . . .

Contrary to the social science identity categories of West Indian and African
American, the second generation does not see themselves as one identity or the
other, but rather something in between the West Indian and Black American:

My family tells me that I am not Guyanese because I did not grow up there. But I am not
African American either. I mean . . . I grew up differently than my African American friends.
Their parents were not as strict as mine, I had to work harder in school because my parents
were not accepting less than an A . . . not that my African American friends' parents didn't
care about their grades, but there was this sense of . . . I don't know urgency with my parents?
. . . after leaving everything that they had even known, we could not let them down? . . . I don't
know, its still hard to explain. I just know that my life has been different from my parents *and*
my African American friends. No one knows what its like having to decide everyday when and
where I can be West Indian, Guyanese, or Black. Well, I shouldn't say that . . . because I am
Black everyday, I don't really have a choice . . . (Precious).

Precious and many other West Indians detailed their struggle of trying to exist in
between two cultural experiences while retaining a commitment to both their racial
and ethnic identities. Their phenotype frequently defined how they were treated in
society, however, when West Indians spoke of their experiences between the two
worlds, they often used African Americans as a reference point:

Come on man, I know that white people just see me as another nigga on the street . . . ready
to shoot you in the front, back, upside down and all around, and then get away with it like
nothing.[19] When you ask me about how I identify, I think about if you mean when I am hanging
with my West Indian family and friends, or my African American friends . . . cause I think about
them first. I mean, I don't hang out with white people, so I don't give a rat's ass what they think.
But I do care what my African American brothers think about me. They are the ones that I roll
with on a daily basis . . . But sometimes it is hard being with them. They don't understand why
I saw or do certain stuff because they are not from the islands. And I don't know . . . I don't call
myself an African American . . . not because I don't like them or because I think that I'm better
than them . . . it's just . . . that's not what I am . . . and what I am is a Jamaican from Maypen.[20]

It is particularly interesting to note that while first generation West Indians (and
some scholars) perceived better treatment from whites as a result of their ethnicity,
the second generation have a sense of that "the tide is starting to turn." Winston
commented,

Maybe the older white people thought that West Indians were better than African Americans,
but not the ones I know now. In fact, I think that we might be considered worse than them in
some circles . . . (laughs) My mother would be pissed if she knew . . .

As a direct result of drug trafficking, the rising criminality in the West Indies, and the vast increase in tourism, West Indians are no longer seen as hard-working, industrious people, but drug-dealing violent criminals:[21]

> Don't get me wrong, I know that for white people, *all* Black people are dangerous, and they don't care where you come from. But . . . people going on with some things down there [the West Indies] . . . now they think all Jamaicans sit around all day smoking weed and robbing people of their hard-earned money. African Americans are the crack-heads and we the weed-heads . . . (laughs) . . . I wonder what they going to be saying about the Africans them next . . . cause you know its going to be something bad. They can't be Black people and not have evil things thought about them . . . (Steve).

NEW YORK CITY AS CONTEXT FOR IDENTITY DEVELOPMENT

The city of New York presents a particular context for second generation West Indians that is unique when compared to other major immigrant cities such Miami and Los Angeles. The physical proximity of racial and ethnic groups in the five boroughs of New York City lends itself to a co-mingling of individuals from a variety of backgrounds. The West Indians whom I spoke with frequently mentioned the physical structure of New York City as being conducive to their contact with co-ethnics and with other groups, which in turn impacted the way they saw themselves in the larger NYC social world (see also Butterfield & Trillo, 1999). The second generation often talked of how the 24 hour NYC transportation system (trains and buses) provided easy access to any cultural centers that they wished to observe which were described as: parades, parks, concerts, dance clubs, restaurants, and even neighborhoods in general. For example, Steve greatly appreciated his ability to be several different ethnicities all in the same day if he wanted,

> Alright, I can start off in Flatbush with the Jamaicans, jump on a train to Besonhurst and hang with the Italians . . . I might not *want* to, but I could . . . then get on a train to Flushing, hang with the Asians and get some food, take another train to Harlem and hang with the African Americans on 125th Street, keep taking the train uptown to the Heights and hang out with the Dominicans and dance some salsa real quick, and then go to the Bronx and get some good pasteles from the Boricuas up there . . . you can't get that anywhere else. And I ain't really done a good job . . . I forgot all about the Jews . . .

For the West Indians who resided in Brooklyn, their identity development was mainly impacted by the presence of other West Indians in the neighborhood:

> Of course I am West Indian. I mean, what else would I be? All the people that live around here are from some part of the Caribbean. Have you seen some of the people walking down the street around here? . . . multi-colored clothes, loud reggae music coming from double-parked

cars, and flags flying from any and every country in the West Indies. Even if I wasn't from the
Caribbean, I would be now, living all around these crazy people (laughs) (Sharon, 21 year old
Jamaican).

Look ere missus, I am Guyanese and will be to the day I die. Even though me grow up
in America, I know what I am. New York has too many Guyanese people for me to try to be
anything else, my family would kill me. You know how many of dem live right here on this
block? My God, you can't away from them . . . unless you leave Brooklyn . . . (Nadine, 26 year
old Guyanese).

Brooklyn also presents an interesting case in that it is such an insular community
that West Indians could, and some do, function entirely in a West Indian world –
they work with other West Indians, they shop at West Indians stores, and frequent
West Indian social events. The high-rise apartment complexes that typify central
Brooklyn facilitates a transference of culture from national origins such as Jamaica,
Barbados, or Guyana, to a larger understanding of the West Indies in general. In
other words, while many West Indians in Brooklyn socialize with their fellow
countrymen, the majority of them are at least exposed to the cultural dialects,
traditions, and foods of different West Indian countries:

For years my parents would talk about why they didn't like Trinidadians, but they never said
why. Now, our neighbors are Trinis, and they make my mother try to remember why she did
not like them in the first place. And of course she can't remember, so now they just argue
back and forth about why the Federation of West Indian countries never happened back in the
60s . . . their cool with each other, sorta. But I hang out with the neighbors' children all the time.
We don't give a damn about the Federation cause we weren't alive then, and we couldn't care
less anyway . . . we like the food and music . . . (Pearl, 29 year old Jamaican).

Those from Queens had more contact with racial and ethnic groups other than
West Indians, yet also strongly identified with their ethnic identity. They often
maintained regular contact with their Brooklyn relatives via phone calls or by
visiting at least once a week:

I was mad when my mom moved us to Queens . . . there wasn't anything to do out here, and
all my friends and family are back in Brooklyn. I know that she wanted a house and all that,
by why did we have to come to boring-ass Queens? You need a car to get around everywhere
since we live in a two-fare zone, so no one wants to come to visit me[22] . . . I mean, this whole
thing makes no sense to me since we still go to church in Brooklyn and visit my family
every week. . . . Though now I hear that some of my aunts, uncles, and cousins are thinking
about moving out of Brooklyn too. I guess that it is getting too dangerous for everybody over
there . . . (Donna, 24 year old Trinidadian).

However, as neighborhood composition in Queens is more ethnically diverse,
respondents there often had social networks that extended beyond the West Indian
community:

[W]ith some of my other friends . . . um like the Boricuas, we all just hang out knowing that
none of us are from here and that we are all from the Caribbean. I mean, we know that we're

from different countries, but that don't matter to us. [Interviewer: what is the ethnic identity of your friends?] Girl, they are everything and from everywhere . . . you know how they say that New York is a melting pot, well that is how me and my friends are . . . most of us are from different islands of the Caribbean and some of from South America. We all live around here somewhere, or went to school together, so that's how we hooked up. We learn lots things from each other, so it works out great. The Boricuas teach me how to speak Spanish, and I teach them how to make roti (Nadia, 23 year old Trinidadian).

Another respondent commented:

At first, when I was about ten, I hated living in Queens. Everything was so quiet, nothing was ever going on. After living in the Bronx for 6 years, I thought that I was going to go crazy from boredom. But after we moved out here, my parents bought me a bike and I was allowed to go out in the streets and ride it . . . safety had its privileges . . . (laughs) . . . I also remember thinking that we would not be able to eat the same stuff, or would have to go back to the Bronx for food, since I didn't think any other West Indians lived near us. But, I was mad wrong . . . I realized that there was a gang [a lot] of West Indians around, I just had to find them. . . . I just knew that meant there were places to get West Indian foods. It surprised me to see that the market where my mother got groceries did not just have West Indian goods, but from everywhere in the Caribbean . . . the Spanish people too. You want to know who lives in the neighborhood? Find the nearest market and see who shops in there, then you know . . . For example, if you go to *Key Foods* on Jamaica Avenue today, they have flags on the top of the building that represents every country in the Caribbean, Central and South America, and a bunch of African countries . . . That shows you the different kinds of people that live around here, if everybody got their own flag. In fact, they got a bunch of flags from white countries too . . . (Donovan, 25 year old Jamaican).

Overall, for those who reside in concentrated West Indian neighborhoods, the similarity in background among the second generations' neighborhood peer group succeeds in fostering an intense West Indian identity, while residence in more ethnically heterogeneous areas seems to be leading to a pan Caribbean identity. However, it is evident that these ethnic identity choices did not come without a clear understanding of what it meant to be Black in their respective neighborhoods over their life course.[23] There is a sense that the presence of other immigrants is leading to an immigrant-identified, or ethnic-identified community where the different generations can and do celebrate their ethnicities in ways that are not dependent on or based out of distancing mechanisms.

CLASS(IFYING) RACE AND ETHNICITY

Scholars of West Indian immigration had discussed at great length of the socioeconomic successes of the first generation (Bryce-Laporte, 1972, 1987; Foner, 1979, 1985, 1987; Kasinitz, 1992; Laguerre, 1984; Sowell, 1981; Vickerman, 1999; Waters, 1991, 1994, 1997, 1999).[24] What is missing from this research is a discussion of the Black middle class, and how similar their values and behaviors are to that of middle class second generation West Indian immigrants.[25] While the first generation may engage in distancing behavior from African Americans at all class levels, can the same be said for their adult children?

In the previous section of this chapter we saw that the second generation is not "distancing" themselves based on the rationale of their parents. I would argue that distancing does occur, but between class lines, and not just along ethnic lines. Second generation West Indians distance themselves from poor African Americans *and* poor West Indians.

The majority of my respondents qualify as middle class because they meet many of the standards criteria for such a designation. As put forth by Mary Pattillo-McCoy (1999),

> Economists use a measure called the *income-to-needs ratio* to identify class categories. The income-to-needs ratio divides total family income by the federal poverty level based on the family's size. The lower bound of the income-to-needs ratio for middle-class status is frequently set at two; that is, if a family earns two times a poverty-level income, they are middle class (1999, pp. 14–15).

Over half of my sample, 66% have an income-to-needs ratio of two or greater, qualifying them as middle class. In addition, sociological conceptions of class include occupation and education along with measures of income (Blau & Duncan, 1967). Studies of the Black middle class in particular have used white-collar employment as the marker of middle class position (Landry, 1987; Oliver & Shapiro, 1995; Wilson, 1978, 1996). In this sense, my respondents do not qualify because less than half of the working residents are employed in white collar jobs. However, the most strict definition of middle class includes only those with a college degree. Over 44% of the sample has a college degree, which is a much larger proportion than the 12% (in 1990) of African American adults overall with a college degree.

The high level of education among the sample can be attributed to the City University of New York (CUNY) educational system.[26] With relatively easy access to the schools in the CUNY system, it is not unusual for New Yorkers to make use of them.[27] What is particularly interesting about this sample is the high numbers of skilled labor. While they may not be engaged in white collar work, the respondents work as technicians for various electronic companies, mechanics, sanitation workers and truck drivers, all which pay relatively well. Some of the people in the sample have thus taken their education and in various ways transferred it into actual income that does not necessarily reflect their educational attainment.

In addition to the class divisions based on income within the various occupations, many of the respondents made frequent distinctions between the "haves" and the "have-nots" that seemed rooted in "culture" arguments similar to those of social scientists. In fact, among the middle-class respondents, there was a general disdain, if not outright disgust for those people who were perceived as "not doing anything with themselves":

> You know, sometimes white people know what they are talking about. There are some serious shiftless people around here these days, and damn it if they all not Black. They don't work, they don't know how to act, and they are not even trying to better themselves. Just chilling on the corner drinking and playing dominoes . . . and I'm talking about men and women. I'm always wondering where they get money for the drinks if they broke, but I can't be bothered to care . . . I just need to get up out of here, away from these people. They just bring the neighborhood down . . . (Carmen).
>
> I remember when this was not the ghetto neighborhood that it is now. My parents like to say that the neighborhood started going down when the Black Americans moved in . . . I don't know whether they are right or wrong about that. But I do know that is was these damn West Indians that *brought it down*! Kids running loose all the time . . . what people don't believe in sending their kids to school anymore? . . . And would cutting the grass really be that bad? I am about to offer this guy down the street my lawn mower cause his grass reaches the top of his stoop, and I know that he cannot like it like that. My next door neighbor said that he is going to sneak over there one night and cut it himself cause he can't stand to look at it anymore . . . Why these people got to come here and ruin our neighborhood? We're looking for somewhere to move where people like that can't follow up . . . maybe out on Long Island . . . (Sharon).

In talking to the respondents, there was a definite sense of "us" and "them" when referring to people in the lower classes. "Us" was typified by having manners, education (at least through high school), taking care of property – personal and public, being well spoken, attending church, and knowing how to dress appropriately for different occasions. "Them" was automatically relegated to whatever the middle class was *not*. Even the younger second generation respondents who came from middle class backgrounds, yet were much more products of a New York youth culture, made distinctions between themselves and others:

> I hate that they don't know how to speak right. I mean, everybody uses slang and that's fine, but you got to know when you can't be talking like that. In high school I used to hate hearing Black people talk, West Indians and African Americans, cause most of them didn't know how to speak properly. I would always be so ashamed to be Black cause I knew that everybody probably thought that I spoke that way too . . . (Tania).

It is important to note that the respondents did not always situate themselves in opposition to people from other classes in order to establish their own class identity:

> You know, I heard that there is this group in New Jersey for children in West Indian families who aren't raised in a West Indian neighborhood. These parents come together and have their kids hang out together so that they have a sense of West Indian culture . . . they go to museums, plays, musicals, and do some sort of community service. At first I thought that it was a little strange . . . but, you don't want those kids to end up hating themselves and not knowing their history because they grew up around all those dysfunctional white suburban kids. I told my

sister that she needs to start thinking about something like that for her kids. She lives way out there on the island [Long Island], and I worry about my nieces' thinking that there is something wrong with them just because they are Black (Sheila).

Talking to Sheila about this West Indian parent/child network in Jersey, I was struck by how similar the mission of the group sounded to that of the national Jack & Jill organization for African Americans.[28]

When I asked Sheila what she hoped that her nieces would take away from an organization like that, she responded:

They need to know who they are. They need to know their Black history and they need to know their Caribbean history. They won't be able to go anywhere if they do not know where they are from. Even if my sister decides not to do this, I am going to start taking those girls on field trips to the Schomberg and places like that, get them subscriptions to the West Indian magazines that we have around here, and probably take them with me to Trinidad next year . . . they need to know where they come from . . .

While scholars have argued that ethnic identity may facilitate social mobility among the second generation because they engage in distancing behavior from African Americans, my respondents indicated that the opposite may also be true. The selectivity process of post-1965 enabled many middle class immigrants to gain entry to the United States, along with working class immigrants who possessed skills that would facilitate mobility. For the most part, the adult children in this sample grew up middle class, so their class position cannot be viewed as a result of their own ethnic identity. However, it is apparent that their class position, and the things associated with it, (access to higher education, cultural events, museums, etc.) is facilitating a maintenance of their ethnic identity.

Sexism, Independence, and The Endangered Black Man

While there was no overall difference between women and men in the choice of identity they adopted, the meaning of "being American" varied by gender. The two main differences were that the women talked of having been under greater restrictions and control from their parents than their male counterparts during adolescence. The men discussed Blackness in terms of racial solidarity in the face of societal exclusion and disapproval. Women also faced exclusion based on race, but they discussed being American in terms of the freedom they received after leaving their families, which seems to be equally salient in their lives along with their racial and ethnic identities.[29]

Consistent with the literature on societal gender roles, there were different expectations for the women than the men of the sample, and this had implications for how the West Indians saw themselves individually, and as a group. West Indian women reported having more domestic responsibilities at home when they were growing up than their brothers or male family members, such as washing dishes, cooking, cleaning, and serving food to the family. West Indian women also felt that they had stricter rules than their male counterparts in that they had an earlier curfew, had to constantly be accountable for their whereabouts, and were told by their parents that they could not date until they were of legal age.

> My parents were so strict about me going out with friends and stuff like that, I just stopped asking. I mean some of my other friends were West Indian, and their parents weren't that bad. I just started making up stories about why I couldn't go to parties and bowling because I knew that my parents would have said no and I didn't want to hear it. And don't even ask me about dating because you know that that didn't even happen. I mean, I had a couple of boyfriends, but we only saw each other at school and they could not call me at home or my father would go off! That's when I swore I wanted to be anything but Jamaican. Who else would be so damn strict! (Carol).

In contrast, West Indian men rarely had household chores, with the exception of taking out the trash and shoveling snow, and had a more flexible curfew than the women in their families. However, the men described how they had the additional burden of being responsible for their sisters and/or mother. They saw their identity as "West Indian men" dependent on how they treated their female relatives:

> My sister complained growing up that I got to do whatever I wanted to do while she had to sit at home. She don't know how I had to make sure that she was okay, whether I wanted to or not. Even though she was older, I had to make that she got home safely, that nobody tried to mess with her, and that brothers knew to stay away from my sister. What kind of Guyanese man would I be if I could not even take of my sister? A real man always takes of his family . . . (Leon).

However, in addition to gender inequalities, West Indian women often spoke of having "submissive" roles at home, but that they were raised to be independent individuals as they got older. They were encouraged, if not expected, to finish their education, get a good job, and then get married and have children. In most cases, West Indian mothers insisted that their daughters be able to "take care of themselves without a man."[30] As a result of this pressure, second generation West Indian women saw themselves as redefining what it meant to be a "West Indian woman":

> When I was younger, I used to see all the women in my family running around serving their husbands and it used to make me sick! The men would just sit their waiting for their wives to make them a plate, and then complain about it when they got it. I always said that I was not doing that when I got older. I could never understand when I said that to my mother . . . she would look at me and tell me that she didn't want me serving some man either. Then . . . I don't know, why was she doing it? She would just say that's how things were, but she wanted me to be better than her. She told me not to get married until after I finished school, so I could be sure of what I wanted. . . . [M]e and my friends are the "new" women of the Caribbean. After

> growing up the way we did, none of us are trying to take shit from men the way our mothers did. We want men who are going to pull their own weight . . . have their own money and degrees. If not, we're just better off by ourselves (Carla).

Interestingly, the roles from adolescence had a direct impact on the second generation's adult lives. Many second generation women quickly realized that being independent meant that they would not be able to date and/or marry what they saw as "old school" West Indian men. While they initially want someone from their country of origin, they are not willing to deal with the blatant sexist attitudes that they feel "traditional" second generation West Indian men hold. Rather, they want, "*someone whose mama raised them right.*" West Indian women of the second generation spoke of wanting other second generation West Indians as their potential mates – because they would have been raised with the same values and culture as themselves, yet they would have been "Americanized enough" to expect that the relationship will be an equal partnership. One woman in particular said that she is waiting for the "*new and improved West Indian man. A man who can be sensitive to my needs, but not be arrogant, sexist, and possessive.*"

Whereas second generation West Indian women are looking for someone who does not fit the traditional characteristics of a West Indian man, second generation men talked at great length about how they are looking for someone just like their mother. Familiar and comfortable with the gender roles of their adolescence, for the men, their mothers epitomized the kind of woman that they wanted their spouse to be – someone who takes care of them. Robert stated, "*a good West Indian woman knows how to take care of her man and her family . . . dinner is on the table when I get home, the kids are fed and doing well in school, and the house is clean.*" In addition, the male respondents also expected their mates to work a full-time job.

> Oh no, she got to work. Plus, we're going to be trying to have kids . . . I ain't trying to pay for all the bills myself. I got to be able to buy the stuff for myself that I buy now. If I work, she has to work . . . maybe she can find a job that gets her home before me so that dinner will be ready by the time I get there. I mean, my mom worked and she still did everything around the house, why can't these other women? But these Americanized girls are all too independent . . . as far as they are concerned, they don't even need a man. What I want with a woman like that? If I am going to still have to take care of myself, I might as well stay single . . . (Michael).

In fact, several of the men stated that they wanted to go back to their home country to find a wife because they were not finding what they wanted in New York City.

Independent of potential mates, second generation West Indian men often identified more strongly with African American men due to their experiences with racism and discrimination in their daily interactions, and specifically with the police:

I am so tired of riding the train, walking down the street, or just standing still, and if cops are around, they will always ask me what I'm doing . . . like I'm bothering them. I would ask them why they are harassing me, but I know that they need very little motivation to shoot me. Guliani has showed us over and over again, that police have the right to shoot Black men in open daylight for no reason and that they can get away with it[31] (Leon).

Chile, I can't even think about getting married these yet. I am still waiting to see if I will make it to my thirtieth birthday . . . I got two years to go. Not because I am doing anything illegal, but because they are just killing us for breathing these days. I mean, I drive the Jersey Turnpike for work all the time, and I have been pulled over three times in the past year. I am just waiting for the time when they don't feel like wasting the time writing the ticket and would rather shoot me.[32]

Among the men I interviewed, there is a definite sense of the what one respondent coined, *"that the Black man's life is at stake, and the cops don't care where you come from"* among all Blacks in New York City, regardless of ethnicity and class.

CONCLUSION

Contradictory to the literature on second generation Black immigrants, the second generation West Indians in this study convey the saliency of their racial *and* ethnic identities in their everyday lives. While one identity often gets played up more than the other, this contextually based, with racial and ethnic identity choices dependent on the audience. Identity choices are not made based on what the second generation perceive they can gain economically or socially from whites, but in an attempt to relate with their immediate social world. For example, non-New Yorkers may not be familiar with West Indians, so the second generation will identify as Black. However, if someone identifies themself as a New Yorker, there is an assumption that they are familiar with West Indians generally, and the respondent will identify as such. Surrounded by West Indians, the respondent will instead identify with their national origin. This process indicates that there are various levels of identification for the West Indian second generation. The culture of West Indianness in New York City also fosters an ease of identification that might not otherwise be present in another American city.

The prevalence of West Indians and other Black immigrants such as Africans, Black Latinos, etc. in New York City indicate that we need to acknowledge the ways ethnicity operates for Blacks in this country. Race and ethnicity are not interchangeable concepts; we need a reconceptualization of "Blackness" that allows for different meanings in various American contexts, and not just international ones.

Class status impacts ethnic identity in a way that is understudied in the literature on second generation Black immigrants. Scholars have argued that upwardly mobile West Indians use their ethnicity as a distancing tool from African Americans. However, for this sample, there is a co-mingling of ethnicity and class status that is used to distance themselves from all Black people in the lower classes, African American and West Indian. In addition, class position appears to facilitate the maintenance of a stronger identity due to one's greater access to their ethnic cultural and historical knowledge.

Gender complicates racial and ethnic identity even further as men seem to be more racially conscious while the women were more ethnically conscious. The men revealed that the combination of their racial and ethnic background put them at a dangerous disadvantage in terms of dealing with law enforcement. However, the women spend a good deal of time trying to renegotiate what it means to be a West Indian female, as they strive to move out of the subservient role. This is a clear indication of the way race and discrimination impact Black women and men differently.

Up until this point, researchers have not adequately addressed the fluidity of identity and that the *meaning* that people place on their ethnic identifications can also change over time and space. The data also indicates that the physical and social environment of New York City plays a critical role in identity formation, as the residential segregation of some NYC neighborhoods and residential integration of others places native born and immigrant communities of color together. The proximity and integration of various immigrant communities is fostering a new identity among the second generation. The complex identity construction of West Indians shown here problematizes how immigration researchers think of the process of assimilation. When referring to "assimilation", social scientists often think of immigrants assimilating into mainstream culture. What happens if there is no clear dominant culture, or if the immigrant culture has been adopted into what is thought of as mainstream as is what has happened to West Indian culture in New York? New York presents a case in which new models thus need to be developed. If New York City was not the cultural center for the country as well as home to millions of immigrants, how would this impact identity development among the second generation? In-depth research must continue to be conducted in order to evaluate how the particular nature of NYC in its politics, roles, culture change, and personality types influence identity development.

NOTES

1. Names and any identifying characteristics have been changed to protect the anonymity of the respondents.

2. Most of the fieldwork for the project that produced this data was conducted in September 1998 through June 1999. Thus, all references to age pertain to that time period.

3. Brooklyn College is one of the schools contained within the City University of New York (CUNY) educational system. CUNY is the largest urban university in the United States and its third-largest public university system. There are 19 campuses all within the five boroughs of New York City – 10 senior colleges, 6 community colleges, a 4-year technical college, a doctoral-granting graduate school, a law school, an accelerated medical program and a medical school. Similar to the immigrants at the turn of the last century, CUNY has (and continues to) welcome waves of recent immigrants and their children. CUNY now enrolls students from 145 countries who speak 115 native languages. Its student body also reflects the city's ethnic diversity: 32% of students are black, 31% white, 25% Hispanic and 12% Asian.

4. "Contemporary immigrants" refers to those arriving in the United States post-1965.

5. Michael Novak (1972) first coined the term "unmeltable ethnics" in his discussion of the plight of lower-middle-class whites and white southern European ethnics within American society. I, however, am using the same term to convey the idea that by continuing to engage in racist and discriminatory behavior, American society treats immigrant groups of color as the "unmeltable ethnics."

6. I set the lower age limit also hoping to avoid those who still may have been still attending high school full-time.

7. Almost half of the Panamanian immigrants to the United States are of Jamaican descent (Waters, 1999).

8. I also included those respondents who immigrated to the United States before the age of 12 – the 1.5 generation as defined by Rumbaut (1991).

9. For instance, I began targeting West Indian male respondents when I realized that my sample was becoming skewed to females. The sample is almost evenly split with thirty-five female respondents and thirty males).

10. The names of the stores have been changed, with all other detail remaining factual.

11. While the owners were Korean, all of the six employees were West Indian.

12. The people running the bakery would often come to Plaintain Market for ingredients for their dishes.

13. Some of the specialty foods that Plaintain Market sells is plaintains, oxtails, goat meat, curry powder, jerk seasoning, salted (cod)fish, ackees. While these ingredients are not all unique to the Caribbean, they are used for such West Indian dishes as: curry chicken, curry goat, jerk chicken, roti, and saltfish and ackees.

14. Many of the patrons have been going to Hairstyling for five or more years and have referred the salon to others. In fact, many members of the same family frequent the salon.

15. The owner of Hairstyling is an African-American woman from South Carolina, yet all her employees are West Indian – Jamaican, Haitian, St. Lucian, and Grenedian.

16. Both the drug store and the restaurant have an ethnically mixed clientele: African Americans, West Indians, whites, Puerto Ricans, and Dominicans. Often times the patrons from Hairstyling get something to eat while waiting to have their done, or after they're finished. The drug store also provides a convenient service to the patrons as they are able to pick up last minute items before entering or after leaving the salon.

17. Some of the groups represented in the Queens neighborhood: African Americans, West Indians, Puerto Ricans, Dominicans, and native whites.

18. Several people commented that they thought that I "looked" Jamaican. When I asked what features or characteristics that used to make that decision, no one could give me a definitive answer. Many said that they could tell I was Jamaican in the same way they call

tell just by looking who is Haitian. Again, when I probed this, no one could provide a concrete answer; they just "knew."

19. This interview took place after the an African immigrant Amadou Diallo was fatally shot 41 times by New York City police officers. Though the verdict in the trial had not been decided at this time, the respondent correctly predicted the outcome.

20. Maypen is a province in the country of Jamaica.

21. As New York City is home to thousands of West Indian immigrants, and that millions of tourists fly to the Caribbean from New York City airports, there are frequent news updates about any potentially dangerous situations occurring in the West Indies. During the period of my data collection, Jamaica was undergoing some major uprisings between the police and the local residents over a mandated curfew. For a time all flights to Jamaica were cancelled until the situation had calmed down. During this week period, there were broadcasts daily about Jamaica during the evening news. When flights resumed, there were still broadcasts about what areas remained too dangerous for tourists – basically encouraging tourists to stay in their resorts. The news depicted such a bleak picture, that many West Indians themselves were afraid to "return home" for fear of the violence.

22. "Two-fare zone" refers to places in which it is necessary to take a bus to the train station in order to travel to other parts of the city. This was always seen as a burden since it makes travelling much longer than those who lived near the actual train stations.

23. It is also important to note that the constant in-migration of other West Indians in these neighborhoods serves to maintain these particular ethnic enclaves.

24. Others such as Suzanne Model (1991) and Richard Alba et al. (1997) have determined that these successes are not that significant when compared to the socioeconomic attainment of African Americans.

25. The exception to this is Waters' 1999 work.

26. The CUNY system currently includes: 3 professional and graduate schools, 12 four-year colleges, and 6 community colleges.

27. In fact, the CUNY system student body predominantly consists of immigrants and their children (Mollenkopf et al., 1995).

28. Jack & Jill is an organization for middle- and upper-class African American children that facilitates exposure to other African Americans through a variety of social and service activities. Admission is based on parental income and there is a fee to become a member. Interestingly, this organization has come under fire within the larger African American community for elitist and separatist.

29. Women also reported feeling a greater sense of responsibility for their families (parents, siblings, extended kin network), than their male counterparts even after leaving the home.

30. Several women in the sample were raised by single mothers, while others had fathers whom they described as extremely domineering.

31. Leon is referring to the fact that in all the fatal shootings that have occurred between the New York City Police and innocent Black victims, New York City Mayor Rudolph Guliani has excused the officers' behavior, and in one case, actually opened the victim's juvenile records to demonstrate that the man had previously been a juvenile offender, attempting to justify the shooting.

32. The New Jersey Turnpike is a major New York Metropolitan thruway that in the past two years been exposed for engaging in high levels of racial profiling.

ACKNOWLEDGMENTS

I thank Sara Lee and Alex Trillo for their comments and suggestions.

REFERENCES

Alba, R. (Ed.) (1985). *Ethnicity and race in the U.S.A.: Toward the twenty-first century.* Boston: Routledge & Kegan Paul.

Bakalian, A. (1993). *Armenian-Americans: From being to feeling Armenian.* New Brunswick, NJ: Transaction Books.

Barth, F. (Ed.) (1969). *Ethnic groups and boundaries: The social organization of culture difference.* Boston: Little, Brown, & Co.

Bryce-Laporte, R. S. (1987). New York City and the new Caribbean immigration: A contextual statement. In: C. Sutton & E. Chaney (Eds), *Caribbean Life in New York City: Sociocultural Dimensions.* New York: Center for Migration Studies.

Bryce-Laporte, R. S. (1972). Black immigrants: The experience of invisibility and inequality. *Journal of Black Studies, 3,* 29–56.

Butcher, K. F. (1994). Black immigrants in the United States: A comparison with native blacks and other immigrants. *Industrial and Labor Relations Review, 47*(2), 265–283.

Butterfield, S., & Trillo, A. (1999). The effects of multi-ethnic neighborhoods on the construction of racial and ethnic identities among second-generation immigrants. Working Paper at the Center for Urban Research, CUNY Graduate Center.

Foner, N. (1979). West Indians in New York City and London: A comparative analysis. *International Migration Review, 13,* 284–313.

Foner, N. (1985). Race and color: Jamaican migrants in London and New York City. *International Migration Review, 19,* 708–727.

Foner, N. (1987). The Jamaicans: Race and ethnicity among migrants in New York City. In: N. Foner (Ed.), *New Immigrants in New York.* New York: Columbia University Press.

Halter, M. (1995). Immigration. In: J. Salzman, D. Smith & C. West (Eds), *Encyclopedia of African American Culture and History.* New York: Macmillan Press.

Kasinitz, P. (1992). *Caribbean New York: Black immigrants and the politics of race.* Ithaca, NY: Cornell University Press.

Landry, B. (1987). *The new black middle class.* Berkeley: University of California Press.

Model, S. (1991). Caribbean immigrants: A black success story? *International Migration Review, 25,* 248–276.

Model, S. (1995). West Indian prosperity: Fact or fiction? *Social Problems, 42*(4), 535–553.

Mollenkopf, J., Kasinitz, P., & Waters, M. (1995). The immigrant second generation in metropolitan New York. Research Proposal to the Russell Sage.

Nagel, J. (1994). Constructing ethnicity: Creating and recreating ethnic identity and culture. *Social Problems, 41,* 152–176.

Oliver, M. L., & Shapiro, T. M. (1995). *Black wealth/white wealth: A new perspective on racial inequality.* New York: Routledge.

Pattillo-McCoy, M. (1999). *Black picket fences: Privilege and peril among the black middle class.* Chicago: University of Chicago Press.

Vickerman, M. (1994). The response of West Indians to African-Americans: Distancing and
    identification. In: R. Dennis (Ed.), *Research in Race and Ethnic Relations* (Vol. 7). Greenwich,
    CT: JAI Press.
Vickerman, M. (1999). *Crosscurrents: West Indian immigrants and race*. New York: Oxford University
    Press.
Waters, M. C. (1990). *Ethnic options: Choosing identities in America*. Berkeley, CA: University of
    California Press.
Waters, M. C. (1994). Ethnic and racial identities of second-generation black immigrants in New York
    City. *International Migration Review*, 28(4), 795–820.
Waters, M. C. (1997). Immigrant families at risk: Factors that undermine chances of success. In: A.
    Booth, A. Crouter & N. Landale (Eds), *Immigration and the Family: Research and Policy on
    U.S. Immigrants*. New Jersey: Lawrence Erlbaum.
Waters, M. C. (1999). *Black identities: West Indian immigrant dreams and American realities*. New
    York & Cambridge: Russell Sage and Harvard University Press.
Wilson, W. J. (1978). *The declining significance of race: Blacks and changing America institutions*.
    Chicago: Chicago University Press.
Wilson, W. J. (1996). *When work disappears: The world of the new urban poor*. New York: Knopf.
Woldemikael, T. (1989). *Becoming Black American: Haitians and American institutions in Evanston,
    Illinois*. New York: AMS Press.

APPENDIX

Demographics of Respondent Sample

	Number of Respondents	% of Sample
Racial groups represented		
Black	55	85
Bi-racial – Black/East Indian	6	9
Bi-racial – Black/White	3	5
Bi-racial – Black/Chinese	1	1
	65	100
West Indian Islands represented		
Jamaica	32	49
Trinidad and Tobago	12	18
Guyana	12	18
Barbados	4	6
Belize	2	3
Panama	1	1

APPENDIX *(Continued)*

	Number of Respondents	% of Sample
St. Kitts and Nevis	1	1
St. Lucia	1	1
	65	100
Gender of respondents		
Females	35	54
Males	30	46
	65	100
Age of respondents		
20–22	4	6
23–25	20	31
26–28	24	37
29–31	11	17
32–34	6	9
	65	100
Educational levels		
High School Diploma/GED	9	14
Some college	27	42
College degree	17	26
Advanced/Professional degree	12	18
	65	100
Income		
$0–$10,000	5	8
$11,000–$20,000	7	11
$21,000–$30,000	10	15
$31,000–$40,000	20	31
$41,000–$50,000	16	25
$51,000–$60,000	3	5
$61,000–$70,000	1	1
$71,000–$80,000	2	3
$81,000 and above	1	1
	65	100

APPENDIX (*Continued*)

	Number of Respondents	% of Sample
Family status		
Single	42	65
Married/Cohabitating	19	29
Separated	4	6
Divorced	0	0
	65	100
Residential location		
Bronx	4	6
Brooklyn	33	51
Queens	26	40
Manhattan	3	3
Staten Island	0	0
	65	100

TITI YEYA'S MEMORIES:
A MATRIARCH OF THE
PUERTO RICAN MIGRATION

David A. Badillo

Race and Ethnicity in New York City
Research in Urban Sociology, Volume 7, 137–158
Copyright © 2004 by Elsevier Ltd.
ISSN: 1047-0042/doi:10.1016/S1047-0042(04)07006-0

The women of Puerto Rican migrant families provided a broad range of options and accommodations for their relatives. They were family fundraisers who cemented internal networks, as well as those with community institutions. Their tenacity and resourcefulness often made them natural leaders. The focus on a single family that participated in the Puerto Rican migration and its integration into the history of the homeland – as well as destination points – offers rare glimpses on otherwise commonplace urban and social developments. It also provides a historical frame of reference spanning several generations that enhances understanding of migration patterns from the Hispanic Caribbean to New York City.[1]

Titi Yeya (Aunt Aurelia), the author's grand-aunt, was born on August 26, 1909 in Cayey, Puerto Rico, and raised in Caguas. She has lived a colorful, and ultimately fulfilling life despite a grueling childhood, adolescence and early adulthood. After leaving her homeland early in 1941 Yeya lived for a decade and a half in New York City, mostly in Spanish Harlem (El Barrio), before moving to southern California, where she stayed for another fifteen years. After returning briefly to Puerto Rico to care for an ailing relative she relocated to central Florida; she has spent the last several years at a senior center in the Melrose section of the Bronx. The story of this 95-year-old matriarch reveals much about the immigrant and ethnic dimensions of the Puerto Rican saga, interlaced with uniquely colonial elements. She refused to accept limitations imposed in her environment by hardship and death, and struggled long and hard for her own survival, as well as the regeneration of her family in a strange land.

At the age of eight, upon the tragic suicide of her mother, Yeya and her two sisters were separated into the homes of different extended relatives. Carmen – the oldest – moved in with a Baptist aunt; Dámaris (Mary) – the youngest – went with her godmother and had a Catholic upbringing. Aurelia moved in with her father, Eloy Rivera, a well-known practitioner of spiritism who ran a *centro*. An unstable childhood merged into an uncertain adolescence, as Yeya left high school in the third year to marry a local boy; the couple had two sons. When her husband divorced her in the mid-1920s, she entered the labor force, working in cigar production curing leaf tobacco.

In the early Depression years Yeya witnessed the devastating effects of a tuberculosis epidemic that took the lives of sister Carmen and brother-in-law Francisco (Paco) Badillo, leaving her to care for their infant son, as well as her own two children. Not long afterwards, she reluctantly relinquished her youngest son to sister Mary and her husband – a financially stable, childless couple. She then secured employment at the Puerto Rican Emergency Relief Agency (La PRERA), a colonial arm of the New Deal that provided U.S. government rations of food and clothing to desperately needy families on the former Spanish island. Within a few years Yeya found herself on a steamer bound for New York with two eleven-year-old boys – her eldest son José Luis and nephew Hermán, now her unofficially adopted *hijo de crianza*. Remarkably, her sister's boy would grow up to become a four-term U.S. Congressman (the first of Puerto Rican descent).

THE IMPORTANCE OF "PLACE" IN PUERTO RICO

The "change of sovereignty," the transfer of Puerto Rico to U.S. rule after Spain's loss in the Spanish-American War of 1898, could not easily erase centuries of Spanish misrule of its island colony. Nor could it reconstruct an economy based on monocultural agricultural crops. For centuries, ranching and subsistence farming had lured settlers from the coast. Highland towns, founded in the eighteenth century under royal auspices but increasingly isolated and removed from imperial control came to define the peasant, the *jíbaro*, who though generally slight in stature came to loom large as the cultural backbone of Puerto Rico. Run by ministers of the Spanish monarchy and corrupt and sometimes tyrannical military governors, the island during the 1800s ineptly staggered through sequential agricultural monocultures. Sugar crops tended by coastal workers of mixed African and European backgrounds (with slavery and peonage existing side by side) yielded prominence in mid-century to large-scale coffee plantations in the mountainous interior, attracting capital and labor from the coast as well as from the Spanish homeland. By the mid-1800s U.S. interests had begun to pull on this strategically located military outpost – first through trade and then by conquest and new guardianship.

Thereafter, monumental social and economic changes produced massive internal population shifts, culminating in external migration. Not even a signatory to the 1899 Treaty of Paris, Puerto Rico, a war prize, came into the twentieth century reconstructed, though not integrated. Sugar again became king, along with tobacco and, to a lesser extent coffee – these "after-dinner crops" soon became heavily capitalized and monopolized by absentee U.S. investors. Sugar trusts controlled the politics of the island legislature and the Bureau of Insular Affairs while new refineries gained prominence by vastly improving quality, marketability, and volume. A modern system of sugar cultivation on the island based on the *central*, using new technologies for grinding cane on increasingly larger agglomerations of land, became an important factor in the island's development. This occurred as both the Puerto Rican and the U.S. governments ignored the legislative reform passed soon after the change of sovereignty, known as the "500 Acre Law," that restricted the size of holdings. Within a short time, much of the sugar labor force became a "rural proletariat."[2] Subsistence plots increasingly disappeared and work increasingly came to be remunerated for piecework or compensated in the form of tokens exchangeable for goods at company stores. This was particularly difficult for women in the tobacco and garment trades, who were usually paid at a weekly rate, rather than the daily rate customary for men.

At the time of the American occupation, Puerto Rico's population was about 15% urban. Urbanization grew steadily, accelerating by mid-century to 60%. After 1910, migration from the interior increased urban congestion. The traditional "colonial atmosphere" of isolated mountain towns diminished and many of the artisans moved into industrial occupations. As rural flight accelerated, peasant farmers migrated into towns and cities, boosting their populations. Business districts spread out into the increasingly congested residence quarters, forcing the original occupants to move to the outlying areas. Tenement districts arose in Old San Juan, pushing migrants into squatter and land rent neighborhoods with their clusters of shacks, the *arrabales*. The capital bustled with growth in cigar manufacturing, fruit and sugar shipment, banking, and insurance. Displaced laborers in squalid slums, along with a small middle class, formed a surplus labor force subject to migration abroad.[3]

Even before 1900, migrants had left the island in small groups, to the Dominican Republic and other points in the Caribbean, to Hawaii to work sugar cane and pineapple fields, and to New York to work as *tabaqueros*, or hand rollers of cigars. There, along with Cuban and Spanish immigrants, they pioneered a Spanish-speaking *colonia*, leaving their small workshops to become ethnics in a vast metropolis. There they became caught up in another series of changes, exodus upon urban exodus, of Jews, Italians, and others. The years after 1917, when Puerto Ricans were collectively naturalized as U.S. citizens, sparked an important pioneer migration during the twenties. In the early 1930s widespread economic distress and several short-lived strikes in Puerto Rico persuaded labor leaders in New York to organize the island's "seasonal" unions of needle workers. North American labor activist Rose Pesotta even conducted a brief campaign on the island in the mid-1930s that consolidated the needle trades into a single local with several thousand members. Migrants had begun to leave the island, and many women from Mayaguez and other needlework centers who learned dressmaking at an early age entered the garment industry in New York City. Others went to work in the factories of the northern metropolis.[4]

San Juan was becoming a booming metropolis, although even counting its adjoining municipalities of Río Piedras and Bayamón it boasted a population of less than 177,000 inhabitants out of an island-wide total of just over 1,700,000 in 1935. Congested slums had arisen, yet the time-honored rural imprint was felt even in fairly large towns, where many had migrated after having grown up in the countryside, and where the perils of the one-crop economy might be mitigated through employment in some of the rising urban sectors. In the winter of 1928–1929

Caguas, then a town of just under 20,000 residents, housed some twenty tobacco factories employing almost 2500 women and 1000 men with an average per capita wage of $183. The town enjoyed a slower pace than the capital, where trade with the outside increased as boats entered San Juan harbor with food products and the raw materials of needlework for the roughly 40,000 women working in the island's garment industry. These included hundreds of cases of handkerchiefs, tablecloths, lingerie, and other items destined for embroidery.[5]

Yeya had gained a familiarity with the demands of urban life and its new possibilities. In this respect she differed significantly from most of those arriving in the so-called Great Migration of 1946–1965, the jíbaro families. She was also a product of the dramatic changes that had reached into all aspects of Puerto Rican culture and society and she had encountered a series of family tragedies throughout her childhood and early adult life. One major setback, and also a contributing factor to her eventual departure from the island, was the affliction of her studious brother-in-law Paco, who had graduated as a teacher trainee, a *normalista* in local parlance, from the newly established University of Puerto Rico. Paco was a scion of the respected Badillo family of Aguadilla, whose ancestors had in the mid-1800s first introduced Protestantism, a proscribed faith, to Puerto Rico. A Dutchman from the Virgin Islands brought Juan Antonio Badillo a Spanish Bible and he and other *bíblicos* (Bible believers) surreptitiously practiced their religion. His son Antonio Badillo Hernández launched humanitarian endeavors such as organizing schools and hospitals to provide for local residents during a smallpox outbreak. These Christians gained for their descendants a fair amount of respect from the incoming U.S. Presbyterian missionaries, as they had from local townsfolk of all faiths. Some of their ancestors by the early twentieth century also rose to prominence in law and politics, gaining positions as municipal officials in the west coast town of Aguadilla; later, a Badillo descendant served in the cabinet of Governor Luis Muñoz Marín's Popular Democratic Party as Attorney General.[6]

In the town of Caguas, to which he had been assigned to teach school, Paco also played violin at the Baptist church until contracting tuberculosis; thereafter he was no longer permitted either to teach or perform music. After Paco fell ill his wife, Carmen (Carmelita), Yeya's older sister, soon followed. Yeya believes, perhaps mistakenly, that Carmelita would have been better off going to see a specialist in San Juan – paid for by the government – but she refused and instead "cried and cried," believing that Christ would help her, if He wanted to. Although Carmelita survived for several years after her husband died, when she realized the end was near she requested that her sister take her son Hermán in, exclaiming, "God wants you to care for him, because no one else can raise him." Yeya complied, and remembers sadly her sister's painful deterioration: "She stayed in the house, had her own room, and no one, not even her son, could visit her." Yeya maintained separate plates for Carmelita's meals and, along with the other adults, she enforced her quarantine, especially from the children; they could see her from afar, but not close up. To Yeya fell the responsibility of ensuring that young Herman would avoid exposure to the dreaded disease from his mother.

Tuberculosis spread more readily in areas of malnutrition and cramped houses along crowded streets became breeding grounds for the bacilli. Yeya's family was not immune from prevailing conditions. They had a very poor diet, lacking even oatmeal, eggs, and meat. Like most municipalities, Caguas maintained a public hospital, but it offered inadequate facilities for treating tuberculosis patients. After the Organic Act of 1917 created a Department of Health it became possible to coordinate local services to some extent with the Commissioner's office, but this proved to be of limited utility in the face of the epidemic. The overwhelming majority of the afflicted had to live with their families. Unlike enteritis and other diseases, tuberculosis usually struck adults in the prime of life, especially in cities, where the contagion struck at rates almost four times as high as in rural areas. The large urban migration of the previously isolated mountain peasantry, especially after World War I, also increased the incidence and mortality of the plague. The family fit closely the model profiled by pathologists, as Yeya's mother came from Barranquitas, in the highlands, while she was born in the remote mountain village of Cayey and moved as a young girl to Caguas.[7]

Furthermore, the development of the Puerto Rican cigar industry throughout the Caguas region between the world wars spurred countryside-to-town movement and the town's population doubled during the 1920s. The rise was attributable mostly to an influx of tobacco workers from the nearby countryside. The slump of the island's cigar and tobacco industry in the early thirties caused a sharp reduction in the growth of Caguas. One report spotted a new trend, that of intensive outward movement among people whose families "had lived in the same neighborhoods for centuries [as they] suddenly began to move from their ancestral homes." Some migrants proceeded to San Juan and a few others went north, to New York. An economist warned in 1930 that the "export" of workers from the "supersaturated mountainlands" had prompted a pattern that "threatens to involve San Juan and New York in one of the largest slum developments in modern urban history." The forecast presciently described an important dimension of the migration of the immediate post-World War II decades.[8]

While still a teenager, Yeya went to work in a tobacco factory. Unlike her mother, who had worked as a cook at one such factory, Yeya's job was to gather and dry the crop's green leaves six days a week. The cured tobacco then went to the United States. This afforded enough for the family to eat, but soon the entire industry left the island – to Connecticut, according to Yeya. Bitter strikes in the principal island cigar factories, most recently in 1926, failed to gain concessions from the plants, whose absentee U.S. owners relocated their largest tobacco enterprises. Caguas workers lost out, though Yeya recalls that when the factory shut down permanently at the onset of the Depression, people promptly sought assorted jobs in town; even with the closings life went on "like always." Desperation wrought by the new hardships, however, drove many in Caguas, including some children, to the streets, trying to sell trinkets, and even begging for food.

During the 1920s, the labor force participation of Puerto Rican women had increased, and they became more actively engaged in personal and community betterment, in part due to the acquisition of the guarantee of suffrage and improved schooling in towns. Whereas most rural children only received three years of instruction, among town dwellers over half finished the seventh grade. Yeya, having attended high school (Caguas Central) up to the third year (surpassing most of her contemporaries) had even learned to speak a little English, which helped in landing her next job, for which "if you spoke a few words, you qualified." In search of employment, Yeya had written to Berta Badillo, a distant relative of her deceased brother-in-law in Aguadilla. Consequently, she managed to get an introduction and interview in San Juan for a position in the Puerto Rican Emergency Relief Agency (la PRERA, as it came to be known), a branch of the U.S. federal government that distributed New Deal relief funds to the island. Yeya acknowledged that having a sister who married a Badillo had helped her. Many years later, however, nephew Herman reminisced wryly of his hard, grueling years in poverty, "It would have been nice [for me] to have known [earlier] about the Badillos of Aguadilla."

The self-described "Señora de la PRERA" ("PRERA lady") found herself working in the Caguas countryside for the government, venturing into a field where at the time men held the majority of jobs. Her duties included asking people in rural barrios about their diet and giving them food and clothing vouchers redeemable for canned goods, medical supplies, and cash. Inexpensive coaches (*carros públicos*) took Yeya to various places on her appointed rounds, frequently waiving the fare. Other times she visited homes on horseback, the jíbaros' preferred mode of travel across the treacherous mountainsides, especially following rainstorms. Yeya would spend entire days in outlying settlements such as San Salvador and Turabo before returning to the home office and supply store in Las Cruces, located between Caguas and Cayey. The people were poor, without shoes and the Americans, through the PRERA, had helped them considerably. What did the jíbaros think of the *yanquis* back then? A great deal, but "they had their prejudices," Yeya chuckled, "since the Americans provided them with money." Governor Muñoz Marín later said of the PRERA that it did little more than illuminate and reflect the failings of the existing social system; it did, however, ameliorate harsh conditions. In 1935 the Puerto Rico Recovery Administration, a successor agency, adopted additional stopgap measures to help impoverished farmers, assist rural families, and expand the traditional three-crop agricultural system beyond a reliance on limited foreign markets.[9]

In the Caguas that Yeya left in 1941 wages were low, but so were costs. Few foreigners passed through the valley other than teachers and clergy (mostly American or Spanish), and the average person's perspective remained local and self-contained. Nor did very much news arrive from outside, though the capital broadcast music from a large radio transmitter. After World War II, however, the city rapidly grew through annexation of outlying *barrios* and neighboring lands. Fed by internal migration and industrial development stemming from the island-wide economic plan known as Operation Bootstrap, Caguas kept pace behind San Juan, Ponce, and Mayaguez, to remain the island's fourth largest city, a position it had held since 1900. Having gained a broader perspective after many years on the continent, however, Yeya would always view the Caguas of old as a little town (*un pueblo chiquito*).

As a child and young adult, Yeya had visited San Juan occasionally to see relatives and friends. There she saw neighborhoods with elegant houses and new cars, as well as busy streets and large factories – evidence of much more wealth than had existed in Caguas. In the Puerto Rico of her youth Yeya had detected outlines of "three societies" – rich people, poor people, and *medianos* (the middle class). Remarkably, despite her family's poverty, she considered herself part of the medianos, more for her aspirations for mobility than because of any realistic assessment of earnings or property: "I belonged to the middle not the lower class, because I [always] believed in progressing, getting ahead, going forward" ("*yo me movía*").

Caguas progressed politically, as well as economically, though Puerto Rican society hardly offered the complexity of the U.S. electoral system. Nevertheless, institutions of representative government, including an executive branch (appointed by continental colonial officials until the late 1940s) and, after 1917, a bicameral legislature, encouraged the rise of political parties with branches in most municipalities. In Caguas the *republicanos*, *unionistas*, and *socialistas* were most active. By the mid-1930s, a few supporters of the *partido independentista* – the independence party, led by the fiery orator Pedro Albizu Campos – could also be found. This group was bitterly opposed to United States rule and had begun to rally for complete separation. Yeya was not among them. She worked for the unionistas and was an admirer of one of its founders, Luis Muñoz Rivera, a respected journalist, politician, and father of the future Puerto Rican governor, "a man who did much for Puerto Rico." Her activism abruptly ended after one incident at the plaza following a meeting, when a socialist threw a stone that grazed her head. "They're going to kill me," she remembered thinking, and thereafter withdrew from the public arena.

During the 1930s, Yeya learned that some of her extended family members had gone to the continent to work, and their monthly remittances had helped pay household expenses and sustained several households during hard times. Two of sister Carmelita's brothers-in-law, Tomás and Hermán, had, through contact with U.S. tobacco merchants in Caguas, learned of possible opportunities in Chicago, for which they boldly took aim. Upon their arrival to the Windy City, they began earning good money as chefs in downtown hotels. Relatives shared some of these earnings with Yeya and the boys. The remuneration from abroad certainly broadened her horizons, but Yeya hardly imagined making such a trip herself. In a culture where women customarily stayed home it would take extraordinary circumstances to propel her to an unknown land fraught with unknown dangers.

Meanwhile her sister Mary, who had married Blas Sorrentini, a restaurateur of Italian ancestry, had moved to San Juan. The childless couple, sensing Yeya's plight and seeking to raise a child as they had always wanted, arranged to take her youngest son, Manolín, and at the age of six the lad went off to live with his adopted kin. Hermán and José Luis stayed in Caguas, mostly with Yeya but sometimes with their grandfather. The two boys spent much time together, living like brothers (*como dos hermanos*). Mary took care of Manolín for several years, raising him as a Catholic and affording him ample material benefits. As everyone was coming to learn, "the Sorrentinis had money." Anchored in the family's hotel and restaurant business and anxious to keep her newfound domesticity, yet concerned by Yeya's lack of resources, Mary contributed half of the cost of the ticket for her sister and the boys to go to New York City. Yeya paid the other half, with help from the Badillo migrants in Chicago. She recalled somewhat bitterly, "[I] had three children and no father [and was being] sent out to work." In early 1941 she, José Luis, and Hermán left San Juan harbor on the U.S.S. *Coamo*, bound for New York City.

Yeya had not prepared much for the trip ahead of time, but quickly responded to the exigencies of the moment. She remembers the five-day voyage as "fine, [at least] the food was good." The boat docked and passengers disembarked in Brooklyn. Yeya and the boys went to stay with a friend in Manhattan, on 105th Street in El Barrio, Spanish Harlem. Fortunately, at that time rents were relatively inexpensive. She discovered, moreover, that due to a temporary glut in the market, apartments were available rent-free for two months, so she was able to save a little on expenses at the start.

YEYA IN EL BARRIO

Yeya was part of the tail end of the pre-1945 wave of migration from Puerto Rico to New York City. Since the early 1900s, regularly scheduled steamship lines ran between New York, Puerto Rico, Curacao and Venezuela, regularly calling at ports before returning to Ponce. In the 1890s the Cuban-Puerto Rican "Spanish-American" colony concentrated in the east nineties and cigar makers and separatists were heavily represented among the original settlers. Cigar makers, having converged mostly from Havana, Key West, Tampa, as well as from Puerto Rico, had formed a tradition of being among the most literate and educated groups of workers. After the Spanish-American War, most returned to the Hispanic Caribbean; among the remaining, status continually diminished with the industry's decline.

Passenger travel increased after the collective naturalization of all Puerto Ricans in 1917 and throughout the 1920s New York City received an influx of Puerto Rican migrants. The newcomers bolstered the city's economy, which had suffered with restrictions on the entry of European laborers. During these years, meanwhile, thousands of migrants from Jamaica and the British Caribbean, as well as Cuba and elsewhere in Latin America also entered the metropolis. Ship travel remained the favored mode of transportation for all comers, with commercial aviation still in its infancy. From Puerto Rico air travel involved boarding a seaplane from San Juan to Miami for ten hours – including a refueling stop in Haiti – and then undertaking an arduous four-day bus journey to New York. Few Puerto Rican migrants came in the years immediately after the U.S. entrance into World War II, as German U-Boats began patrolling the Caribbean waters and endangering the San Juan to New York City run. Within a year of Yeya's arrival, wartime mobilization shut off migration from the island, temporarily freezing existing neighborhood patterns.

Puerto Ricans came from a variety of backgrounds. One individual from a wealthy family arrived in New York City in 1922 from Rio Grande, a small coastal town, at the age of twenty, having previously attended the University of Puerto Rico. His father had owned a small sugar-cane plantation, but a drop in sugar prices in the world market put an end to the family enterprise, forcing him to migrate to New York, where he found a job at a candy factory.[10] In the mid-1930s one man from Caguas interviewed in Manhattan recalled working in island tobacco factories as a youth, traveling all over Puerto Rico "always looking for a better job." After first leaving home he went to a labor camp in the South building barracks and digging ditches, before finding his way to New York, where he worked for a while as a cigar maker. He adapted to life in the United States, becoming "so used to this country and the people here that this is my home."[11]

In far greater percentages than the general population, early migrants were urban dwellers and largely literate. In the early 1920s, Brooklyn became the birthplace of the modern day Puerto Rican community of New York City, its piers became disembarkation points of the steamships, and ferries as well as bridges connected with Manhattan. Gradually the fledgling East Harlem *colonia* soon exceeded its Brooklyn counterpart in numbers as well as in prestige. Throughout the 1920s and

1930s, for example, Brooklyn Puerto Ricans had to go to Spanish Harlem, also known as El Barrio, for legal, medical or other professional care. Migrants arriving there in the thirties and early forties tended to have some urban skills, though they also came from among the growing pool of common laborers. From only about 500 persons of Puerto Rican birth scattered throughout the city in 1910, the figure climbed to 7000, by 1920, and to some 60,000 by 1930 (with considerably higher unofficial estimates), making them the largest of the Spanish-speaking groups. Migrants lived in cross-class ethnic neighborhoods, sharing their institutions with Cubans, Spaniards, and others in the Pan-American immigrant mosaic. They often benefited socially, politically, and economically from contact with those of similar cultural backgrounds.

Puerto Ricans clustered in Brooklyn and Manhattan buildings in some of the worst cold-water flats – the only housing they could afford. In 1924 the idea of a council of federated organizations became a rallying point within the migrant community, and the Puerto Rican Brotherhood of America, a Manhattan-based organization, was founded; within a few years it enumerated twenty-seven Manhattan and twelve Brooklyn based community organizations. Meanwhile, the newer Puerto Rican settlers of East Harlem began to open and patronize their own stores. During the summer of 1926, after two weeks of interethnic fighting, a meeting was called by the Puerto Rican Brotherhood with other local groups at the Harlem Casino on Lenox Avenue and 116th Street. Out of this emergency session came a new organization, *La Liga Puertorriqueña y Hispana*, which promoted "civic defense and the welfare of United States citizens from Puerto Rico and others of Latin American or Spanish origin." It helped smooth over the violent outbreak between Jewish and Puerto Rican merchants by calling for the intervention of Cardinal Patrick J. Hayes, who successfully appealed to Mayor James J. Walker for police protection. The Resident Commissioner of Puerto Rico to the U.S. House of Representatives, stationed in Washington, D.C., was also called upon, but he proved too distant and inaccessible to effectively engage in local matters. The Migration Office of the Puerto Rican Department of Labor, which came into being in the immediate postwar era, later had greater success in assisting migrants in their adjustment to life in New York City.[12]

By the late 1920s, Spanish Harlem had clearly become "the most typical Puerto Rican spot in all New York." Along upper Fifth Avenue, drug stores, restaurants, barber shops, bars, candy stores and dress shops replicated in an urban environment the habits and customs of the homeland. Migrants were attracted to the liveliness and camaraderie of other Spanish-speakers. Various civic groups, home town clubs, brotherhoods, and similar organizations arose in the 1920s and 1930s for a variety of purposes, including sponsoring dances, helping to raise funds for hurricane relief on the island, and assisting the unemployed in New York's neighborhoods.

Puerto Rican migration to the United States halted between 1930 and 1934, when almost 10,000 migrants returned home.[13]

The early "pioneer" Puerto Rican migrants to New York City entered a wide range of ethnic communities that included European ethnics, blacks, and a conglomeration of Spanish-speaking peoples as well as others from throughout the globe. Especially close ties in the city had developed between Puerto Ricans and Cubans, who owned many barrios music and record shops, as well as vaudeville and motion picture theaters such the *Teatro Cervantes* and the *Teatro de Variedades* along upper Fifth Avenue. These institutions helped foment Spanish-speaking cultural unity, and the "picturesque row of cafes, billiard parlors, restaurants, and dance halls, brightly decorated and with captions in Spanish" advertised "a great number of articles, opportunities and amusements." One Cuban man in the late 1930s noted that he felt at home living in Harlem among Cubans and Puerto Ricans; his family ate "strictly tropical food the whole year around," although his children were fed mostly American-style. He found that his neighborhood, including the blocks on Eighth Avenue from 110th to 116th Street was becoming the "most prosperous of the whole Spanish speaking community" as thousands of Puerto Ricans moved into the area. Cuban "satellite" colonies emerged downtown in Chelsea and in Brooklyn as well as uptown in East Harlem.[14]

Spaniards, whose population stood at only 23,000 by 1930 (well under half that of Puerto Ricans), had always constituted a diverse group. With their own cafes, groceries, tailors, and barbers, the primary institution that brought them into contact with others was the school. The Spanish tended to base their immigration societies on regional and provincial origins, celebrating their fiestas in the *Centro Galicia*, the *Centro Asturiano*, and the *Centro Andaluz*, among others. The Spanish community of Greenwich Village contained a floating population, varying in size and composition as boatloads of sailors came and went. There they kept very strictly to themselves, the women never going out except to church and the men associating closely within their own group, largely avoiding external conflict and contact. Spaniards residing in New York celebrated their own version of Columbus Day, or *Día de la Raza* – also observed by the Cubans, Puerto Ricans and South Americans – as well as other national holidays. Despite their reputed clannishness, the Spaniards were particularly militant trade unionists and were more often found as skilled help than the more recent Caribbean arrivals. In 1918 José Camprubí, an engineer and buyer for the Spanish railways, Puerto Rican-born but raised in Barcelona (the sign of an "elite" upbringing), purchased the newspaper, *La Prensa*, and transformed it into one of the several weeklies read by the New York colonia. During the 1920s, however, Puerto Ricans concerned themselves less with local affairs than with island politics, which was reflected in the pages of contemporary periodicals.[15]

Yeya liked El Barrio for its familiar sights and sounds. She soon discovered the vast open market under the train tracks on Park Avenue, spanning several books around 116th Street. *La marqueta* not only had a wide selection of many Caribbean items like *plátanos* and *yautía*, but they were affordable. There were many inexpensive Latin American restaurants on 110th Street, and on Fifth Avenue. "There were Cubans, Dominicans, *de todo*." There were also "Italians and Puerto Ricans fighting with each other." Yeya was always gregarious, but she didn't have any Italian friends; all of them were Latino. The many ethnic groups each had their own turf, with the Italians located east of Third Avenue. Few Jews, who had once dominated the area, remained, though many retained businesses in El Barrio. Mostly their families had moved to the Bronx or Brooklyn; others remained downtown on the Lower East Side. Puerto Ricans and Latinos stood squarely in the center of East Harlem, mainly between Third and Fifth avenues and 105th and 116th Streets.

The growing Puerto Rican presence in East Harlem had facilitated the subsequent entry of African Americans from the neighborhood's northern and western boundaries. Harlem Renaissance writer Claude McKay noted this role in transitional areas: "When white Puerto Ricans moved into a house, the brown ones followed." Puerto Rican grocery stores, record shops, and other businesses along upper Fifth Avenue catered to a sizable Spanish-speaking community as well as to West Indian immigrants. McKay saw Puerto Ricans as comprising part of a section of the "Negro Quarter" of Harlem, roughly from 116th to 110th streets, between Lenox and Lexington avenues. With access to less expensive quarters they "wedged themselves into every available space, in basements and front rooms of first floor apartments" and paved the way for blacks as they moved south. Puerto Ricans met with a color line unknown in either urban or rural Puerto Rico; their fine-tuned perceptions and classifications of color clashed with the existing binary black/white categories accepted by New Yorkers.[16]

Throughout their history, and especially in the urban shantytowns that developed in the island's largest cities after the mid-1920s, Puerto Ricans learned to navigate within a multiracial society. Racial distinctions became informally accepted and it had become virtually impossible to impose a strict color line on the island given the history and extent of intermarriage. According to the 1935 Census of Puerto Rico, under the ambiguous category of race, enumerators found that residents in Caguas were 71% "white" and 29% "colored," compared with the island-wide total, 76% and 24%, respectively. When asked about her racial ancestry, Yeya reacted with surprise, but eventually responded, "We were Italian. My grandfather was an Italian immigrant. . . . There was [also] another relative from Panama." She described the racial composition of Caguas as "of all kinds, colored, mixed." Being Puerto Rican also meant having close relatives with different skin complexions, and this was certainly evident in Yeya's family – her sister Mary was noticeably more *trigueña* (darker-complexioned, the "color of wheat"); Carmen, her other sister, a redhead, had the fairest skin, while Yeya was somewhere in between. In New York City, however, one was defined by nationality or ethnicity – West Indians, Jews, Italians, southern African Americans – more than appearance. Though she could pass for Italian or vaguely "Euroamerican," her identity within El Barrio remained unmistakably Puerto Rican, and she retained a strong affinity with other Spanish-speakers.[17]

Italians, mostly from the south of Italy, had gained control over many of East Harlem's neighborhood institutions since their arrival several generations earlier. Since the late nineteenth century the Church of Mount Carmel had held a yearly festival, or *festa*, celebrating the Madonna extravagantly and vividly, while asserting a sense of community. The July celebration reinforced Italian street life, with parties, food, and dancing, as the church on 115th Street became transformed increasingly into an Italian-American parish during the 1940s and 1950s. It remained inaccessible and impenetrable to the Puerto Rican newcomers, though both groups were predominantly Catholic. According to one social historian, when the Puerto Ricans began arriving in the 1940s and 1950s, the Italian procession and the devotion served as a means of reclaiming the blurred margins of El Barrio from the newcomers.[18]

Religion had never been a strong suit in Yeya's upbringing. She remembers that sister Carmelita was a devout Baptist. Yeya was baptized a Protestant (*evangélica*), learned to read the Bible, and was married at the Caguas Baptist church by a Puerto Rican minister. She sometimes went to the Catholic Church with her younger sister, Mary, but "never understood much about Catholicism [and I] didn't learn how to pray Catholic style, [to recite] *el Padre Nuestro* (the Our Father) and all that." Yeya's father taught spiritism and ran an active center, but she never understood those practices either, nor did she become much involved with the centro's activities, exclaiming, "How can you speak with the dead?" She remembered, "They didn't want me [involved] either." That whole episode in her life, as she tells it, remains shrouded in mystery, and some embarrassment, especially in the eyes of her sisters, who feared she had become a *bruja* (witch). In those days Yeya liked church for the opportunity it afforded to "read the Bible and sing hymns," but in New York City she no longer attended regularly, although El Barrio had churches of all denominations – including Baptist and Catholic ones, as in Caguas. Catholicism, in particular, was extremely popular, but not for Yeya, although her son Manolín attended East Harlem parishes soon after he migrated.

From its founding in the early 1500s until 1898, the Catholic Church in Puerto Rico monopolized educational as well as religious life. Parish structures deteriorated after U.S. takeover and the return of Spanish clergy. Consolidations of several churches under a single priest, often under temporary assignment, further alienated Catholics, while many pueblos were left virtually unattended. With the departure of Spanish clergy after 1898, U.S. Catholic missionary clergy entered the arena. Catholic churches attracted parishioners from miles away. In turn, priests visited their homes to attend to both spiritual and temporal concerns. There were few rural chapels at first, but priests, especially religious order clergy, the Redemptorists increasingly conducted circuits, or missions, from San Juan. By 1930, ten American priests worked in Caguas' nine rural chapels. They held mass in four barrios every Sunday and conducted Sunday school classes in the afternoon. One barrio, San Salvador, had about 500 church members.[19]

The Redemptorist Fathers had a large number of fine schools in urban centers and they helped in the educational work on the island. Part of this involved overcoming the perceived over-involvement of the locals with spiritism. Meetings occurred regularly in some barrios, with participants gathering in a house and sitting at a table "meditating," as the president opened the sessions designed to evoke the spirits. Spiritism was also a path for healing; though never visibly acknowledged, it became very much a part of Puerto Rican culture. Many persons who considered themselves Catholics attended spiritist meetings. The clergy considered the jíbaros backward in religious matters when compared with their urban counterparts in Puerto Rico and, especially, in the continental U.S.[20]

Protestant activities, though prohibited under Spain, had been introduced and practiced surreptitiously in the late 1800s. The arrival of U.S. missionaries in the early twentieth century took place in an orderly fashion, based on a Comity Agreement whereby, with the exception of San Juan and Ponce, specific regions of the island were assigned to specific denominations. In some towns, by the 1930s, Protestants claimed more active adherents than did the Catholic Church (usually located in the town square). The congregations rapidly spread, led by a native clergy that introduced new approaches to sermons and Sunday school lessons, even singing and music. They considered themselves spearheads of a new faith that would advance the people beyond the religious negligence perpetuated under the Catholic regime. Ministers also officiated at baptisms, marriages, and burials, putting them in direct competition with the Church and threatening ingrained patterns of Catholicism. Protestants offered an alternative for those wanting to break with the Church for a variety of social, religious, and political reasons. Many evangelicals perceived Puerto Rican Catholicism in a negative light, as superstitious and lax – as did the Redemptorist clergy. They urged prospective converts to relinquish religious rituals and activities centering on the saints as intermediaries, as well as religious festivals. During the twenties and thirties, Pentecostals branched out throughout Puerto Rico, though at first they had no permanent ministers or church buildings. Their converts in those days generally came from among the poor, at first in small towns and later in the countryside as well.[21]

After widespread Jewish departure from Harlem began in 1919, new areas had opened for Puerto Rican settlement as it expanded. During the fifties many more Puerto Ricans had moved to New York, pouring into El Barrio and the older colonias, which were bursting at the seams. Yeya moved to the West Side, around 110th Street and Amsterdam Avenue, a burgeoning Puerto Rican neighborhood. She avoided the many housing projects going up in New York City, and never apparently took home relief, always working, though she occasionally was forced to turn to unemployment insurance, which was different, "like what the PRERA gave." She had remained single for many years, working in small businesses, or factories – including an aluminum factory, run by Greeks. There was not that much work in New York, and jobs were moving to New Jersey, to the Campbell's Soup factory. She worked in a candy factory, a hospital, and a toy company.

Access to better apartments at higher rents encouraged the time-honored immigrant practice of taking in lodgers. Yeya had many boarders, which distracted her boys. There were also tough economic times and, for a spell, soon after arriving, Hermán was sent to live with relatives in Chicago and California before returning to New York City. Upon his return he applied himself assiduously to his studies, graduating Haaren High School then gaining entrance to prestigious City College and, finally, completing evening classes at Brooklyn Law School while working as an accountant by day. As a young adult he and his wife lived with Yeya for a time in the mid-1950s. Within a few years, however, Yeya had remarried and moved to North Hollywood, California, where she lived for fifteen years and worked as a cook in a hospital. From there, she and her husband sent money back occasionally to help Hermán with expenses for books. Yeya's new life involved little contact with Puerto Ricans (besides a few members of her extended family, which was what prompted to move there in the first place). She now lived and worked among mostly Americans (and some "Germans"), with few Latinos ("Mexicans were on the other side, in Los Angeles"). Her second husband, Ricardo, worked in the merchant marine, and the couple was able to afford a mortgage for the house. Ricardo, however, died at a relatively young age, leaving Yeya on her own again. She moved back to Puerto Rico to live with her sister when Mary fell gravely ill, and helped care for her. After a few years in San Juan, Yeya moved to Florida to live in a house that had belonged to Mary. Located in a small town with a growing Puerto Rican enclave about an hour east of Orlando, the climate and lifestyle was in some ways "a lot like California," though she preferred the latter. Weary with age and unable to maintain a household alone, Yeya reluctantly relocated to a senior center in the Bronx during the 1990s. She always kept moving as long as she could, mentally as well as geographically, and even into her nineties retains a sharp mind with vivid recall, usually laced with humor and a sense of irony. Yeya has been a matriarch of the family, though she would never think of making such a claim.

NOTES FROM ANA

The prevalence of family leadership and strength under duress is seen also in the experience of Ana Badillo, born in 1923 in Esperanza, a rural barrio outside Caguas, where her father Gregorio worked in a tobacco storehouse. The family moved to town when she was very small. Her mother died when she was five and soon after her father took ill. Ana's brother (Paco) had been married Yeya's sister Carmelita. Soon after Paco marrried, she went to live next door to him with some of her siblings; he died about two years later. At the age of eleven, Ana left for Santurce, near the capital, with her aunt, a strict Baptist who worked in a textile workshop and "didn't want [me] to dance, and things like that." There, she enrolled as a boarding student at the Blanche Kellogg Institute, a secondary school for girls sponsored by the Presbyterian Church. Her goal in life at that time was to be a nurse, since times were so hard and "there was so much sickness in the family." Her father, who had enlisted in the U.S. Army in 1899, drew a veteran's pension, part of which Ana received for a few years after he died in the mid-1930s.

Whereas her mother and other siblings were raised Catholics, Ana was baptized in Santurce at the age of thirteen by a Puerto Rican Protestant minister from Caguas, who had taken charge of a congregation in the capital. She attributes much of her interest in religion to her older brother Paco. Ana was always one of the most religious of the family and raised her children accordingly. One of her sons became a Protestant minister and she now belongs to the local Lutheran church. She was always able to integrate religion into her life, and found her church contacts helpful, both in Puerto Rico and on the continent, where she was "always able to find a church." Originally a Baptist, she became a Lutheran, and she found the practices and beliefs of the two denominations to be similar, "except for baptisms, [where] instead of immersion [Lutherans] throw water on your forehead." Early on, she came to understand that "you could be just as happy being a Catholic as a Baptist. Believing in God, that's the main thing." Growing up in Puerto Rico, however, she remembered feeling uncomfortable as a Protestant, as "the children used to make fun of me because I wasn't baptized in the Catholic Church," and they teased her, saying that when she died she was going to remain "in limbo."

At the age of seventeen, in July, 1941, after graduating high school, Ana left Puerto Rico, less than a year after Yeya. At the time jobs were scarce, especially in tobacco, and she needed money and a home. Soon one of her brothers in Chicago sent her $100, and she headed north with her sister-in-law. After arriving in New York the pair spent the day in New York at Yeya's house, then departed by rail the next day to Chicago; there Ana stayed with her older sister at a boarding house. After about a month, her brothers moved to the town of Burbank in southern California, seizing the opportunity to change occupations from hotel chefs to machine shop workers in defense contracting; Ana soon followed them. There her twelve-year-old nephew, Hermán, had joined the family after first having stayed with her sister Carmen in Chicago (who, like Yeya in New York City, could not care for him at the time). After a year or so in California he was returned by bus to New York to live with Yeya again. An extra mouth to feed during a trying, transitional period, it had become impossible for relatives to give young Hermán a stable home as the family spread across the continent. When asked why the family faced so much separation, Ana noted, "For one thing, [my brothers] wanted to better themselves, [though] all of us took care of the others, especially the little ones."

Ana made some efforts to continue her nursing studies in southern California but, lacking tuition money, she instead went to work at Lockheed Vega Aircraft, where she became a "Rosie the Riveter," helping to install gang channels for fuel tank doors on B-17 bomber wings. At Lockheed she met and soon married Gordon English. The couple has lived in a small town in southwest Oregon since 1964, where Ana stayed home and raised four children. When the youngest entered high school, she returned to work as a school aide in a bilingual program; she has also tutored Latino immigrants. Her husband of almost sixty years notes poignantly, "It was a tough [and stressful] life growing up in Puerto Rico. I am not saying that she would not have enjoyed her life in Puerto Rico fully had she stayed there [but] she has experienced things that she would not [otherwise have, and] has appreciated the opportunity to come to the states."

FAMILY LEGACIES

Yeya, not merely a catalyst for inexorable developments, played a vital role in her family's survival, taking decisive steps at crucial junctures. At times, her actions seemed counterproductive, such as sending her nephew to relatives in California for a spell when she could not adequately care for him. But that was a measured response to unavoidable circumstances. Her loyalty to family was genuine and has persisted to the present. She contributed to Hermán's success in many ways, large and small.

Her familiarity with politicians in El Barrio, in fact, helped him gain access to important political contacts. Yeya knew Tony Méndez, an activist in a local Democratic club on 116th Street. He also ran a jewelry store where Yeya bought a ring and then got to know his wife Olga (who herself later entered the electoral arena, and who is now a long-time State Senator). When Hermán graduated law school, he strongly hinted to his aunt at his interest in politics, saying, "*Tía*, you know politicians." She then told him about Tony Méndez and arranged an introduction. Recalled Yeya, "He said he wanted to be a politician and Tony helped him [since] he knew Kennedy and all the political types." Yeya was ever resourceful, and never reluctant to use the political acumen forged in Puerto Rico when she worked for the Unionist Party.

Nephew Hermán fully recognizes his aunt's decency, gregariousness – even glamour – and persistence. "She had to scrap, she always worked . . . and she took care of us," he recollects. This is not to suggest that the matriarch was soft and fuzzy. On the contrary, she was tough and "not particularly warm." She sometimes even discouraged Hermán's studiousness, sending him to dance class instead (where, incidentally, he met his first wife). Not surprisingly, Hermán and José Luis both left Yeya's house early, and continued to face trials and tribulations: José Luis in the military service and merchant marine, Hermán in the political arena.

After a few years of lawyering while gaining contacts in the clubhouse, Hermán rose within the appointed ranks of city government, as a Commissioner of Relocation under Mayor Robert Wagner, Jr., and then successfully ran for Bronx Borough President. In 1970 he won a tough congressional election and went to Washington, DC, representing an area with a modest plurality of Puerto Rican voters, freshly redistricted to include large barrios in upper Manhattan and the Bronx. Yeya could hardly contain her awe at that improbable outcome, saying that she never would have believed back in Caguas "that Hermán would rise to serve in the Congress of the United States." For someone of Yeya's generation that prospect was almost unimaginable for any Puerto Rican. Despite their U.S. citizenship, island residents were not then, nor are they today, eligible to vote for the President or for members of Congress unless they relocate and register in one of the states.

Hermán concedes that despite the poverty and the difficulties for Puerto Ricans, "New immigrants have it tougher since they're undocumented." Yeya, no doubt, greatly influenced her famous nephew. Not surprisingly, perhaps, because of his unstable family upbringing and his own successes in public life as a "self-made" man, Hermán, like Yeya, is not a religious person, having lost whatever nominal affiliation he might have assimilated from his paternal Protestant ancestry. He also shares Yeya's tenacity, resolve, and survival instincts, which is evident in both public and private life. Yeya, for her part, shies away from any conclusions about her role, either in the family or in the migration writ large. When asked about the role of women she deflects any praise, citing instead public Figures such as her old friend, Olga Méndez, "who knew everyone in the El Barrio."

Yeya returned many times to Puerto Rico, but always gravitated back to her adopted land. Her life story and reflections illuminate several core issues and dilemmas of Puerto Ricans in the twentieth century, a time that saw tremendous material progress for the island, yet brought on continued political, social, and psychological ambiguity, both on the island and on the continent. Indeed, by 1930 Puerto Ricans had dispersed to all the 48 continental states. Sociologists cite the pre-1945 wave of pioneer migrants as more comparable to the European experience of immigration. This is true, but their circumstances nevertheless were extraordinary, with a harsh reception that more closely resembled that of African Americans. The postwar airborne (and transnational) migration more closely linked the island with the mainland, though the devastating out-migration of jobs hurt economic prospects for the migrants and, along with social differences, further weakened the likelihood that Puerto Ricans would develop a purely "ethnic" identity in New York City.

The newest migrants faced dislocations caused by urban renewal and other aspects of neighborhood dispersal, casting them too as pioneers of sorts. Taken as a whole, the Puerto Rican experience paved the way for the city's subsequent "Latinization," through the adaptation of new technologies of transportation and communication, as well as through increasingly complex neocolonial relations, involving the premiere metropolis with communities of mixed race people, often with dual national allegiances. The 1940s and 1950s migration, however, proved more reflexive, with individuals exerting choice and control over different (and fewer) areas of their lives than the earlier migrants. In the larger context, the Puerto Rican diaspora has been anything but predictable. Puerto Rico became a model for addressing, if not resolving, the many economic – and to a lesser extent social and cultural – problems emerging in developing societies. Currently, the trend seems to be away from the city and the metropolis – to suburban locales throughout the Northeast and to Florida, as well as back to the island. One commentator noted that the Puerto Rican migrant has brought with him "his own peculiar brand of drama."[22] This has included a pronounced, persistent matriarchal dimension to family leadership.

NOTES

1. The author gratefully acknowledges the support of the faculty of Brooklyn College's Department of Puerto Rican and Latino Studies and, in particular, Professor Virginia Sanchez Korrol. Several relatives generously contributed their time and their thoughts, particularly Aurelia Rivera, Ana and Gordon English, and Hermán Badillo. Sections of this chapter appear in Vicki Ruiz and Virginia Sanchez Korrol, eds, *Latinas in the U.S.:*

An Historical Encyclopedia (Bloomington: Indiana University Press, forthcoming 2005). Portions of this chapter also appear in David A. Badillo, *Latinos and the New Immigrant Church* (Baltimore: John Hopkins University Press, forthcomig).

2. José L. Vázquez Calzada, "La distribución geográfica de la población de Puerto Rico," *Revista de Ciencias Sociales, 23* (March–June 1981), 291–296; History Task Force, Centro de Estudios Puertorriqueños, *Labor Migration Under Capitalism: The Puerto Rican Experience* (New York: Monthly Review Press, 1979), 72–75; Fernando Picó, *Libertad y servidumbre en el Puerto Rico del siglo XIX (Los jornaleros utuadeños en vísperas del auge del café)* (Río Piedras, PR: Ediciones Huracán, 1979), 161–163.

3. Porto Rico Bureau of Labor, *Report on the Housing Conditions of Laborers in Porto Rico* (San Juan: Bureau of Supplies, Printing, and Transportation, 1914), 40–48, 55, 110.

4. "Case of J. J." February 14, 1939, *Spanish Book*, New York Municipal Archives and Records Center (hereafter *SB*); James L. Dietz, *Economic History of Puerto Rico: Institutional Change and Capitalist Development* (Princeton, NJ: Princeton University Press, 1986), 154; Elaine Leeder, *The Gentle General: Rose Pesotta, Anarchist and Labor Organizer* (Albany: State University of New York Press, 1993), 65, 66.

5. Puerto Rico Reconstruction Administration, *Census of Puerto Rico: 1935; Population and Agriculture* (Washington, DC: Government Printing Office, 1938), 52.

6. See Samuel Silva Gotay, *Protestantismo y política en Puerto Rico: 1898–1930* (Río Piedras: Editorial de la Universidad de Puerto Rico).

7. See Victor Clark, *Porto Rico and its Problems* (Washington, DC: The Brookings Institution, 1930).

8. John P. Augelli, "San Lorenzo, a Case Study of Recent Migrations in Interior Puerto Rico," (1952) in Eugenio Fernández Méndez, ed., *Portrait of a Society: Readings on Puerto Rican Sociology* (Río Piedras: University of Puerto Rico Press, 1972), 203, 204.

9. Rafael Picó, *Puerto Rico: planificación y acción* (San Juan: Banco Gubernamental de Fomento para Puerto Rico, 1962), 42, 44, 210. The governor, typically, won Yeya's full admiration: "His party gave out land (*parcelas*) to people to build houses on and to plant, and they gave them bread." She remembers, however, that the "people were ungrateful [and] they sold the lands without even having planted on them."

10. Case History #7, March 13, 1939, *SB*.

11. Case History #5, February 15, 1939, *SB*.

12. For background see Virginia Sanchez-Korrol, *From Colonia to Community: The History of the Puerto Ricans in New York City, 1917–1948* (Berkeley: University of California Press, 1994, 1983); Luis A. Cardona, *The Sojourner from Puerto Rico: An Account of Their Heritage, Sojourn, Agony and Aspiration* (Bethesda, MD: Carreta Press, 1987); and Luis A. Cardona, *The Chronicles of the Puerto Ricans in the United States of America: Volume I (1492–1920): Before the Twentieth Century Through World War I* (Rockville, MD: Carreta Press, 1991).

13. César Andreu Iglesias, ed., *Memoirs of Bernardo Vega: A Contribution to the History of the Puerto Rican Community in New York* (New York: Monthly Review Press, 1984), 187.

14. Spanish Speaking Migrants in New York, Life Histories, 1939, *SB*; Individual Case #2, February 21, 1939, *SB*; Leo Lancier, "Spanish Colony" December 16, 1935, *SB*; Caroline F. Ware, *Greenwich Village 1920–1930: A Comment on American Civilization in the Post-War Years* (Boston: Houghton Mifflin, 1935), 16.

15. Ronald H. Bayor, "The Neighborhood Invasion Pattern," in Ronald H. Bayor, ed., *Neighborhoods in Urban America* (Port Washington, NY: Kennikat Press, 1982), 34; Gerald Fitzgerald, "Spanish Fiestas, Songs and Dances in New York," August 6, 1936, *SB*; Louis Masin, "Spaniards in New York," Jose Camprubí, Nov. 27, 1936, *SB*.

16. Claude McKay, *Harlem: Negro Metropolis* (New York: E.P. Dutton and Co., 1940), 41, 69, 112. See also Charles L. Franklin, *The Negro Labor Unionist of New York* (New York: AMS Press, 1968, 1936) and Lawrence R. Chenault, *The Puerto Rican Migrant in New York City* (New York: Columbia University Press, 1970, 1938).

17. On race and identity among Puerto Ricans, see Eduardo Seda Bonilla, "Social Structure and Race Relations," *Social Forces, 40* (December 1961); Samuel Betances, "The Prejudice of Having No Prejudice in Puerto Rico," Part II, *The Rican, 2* (Spring 1973); and Jaime R. Vidal, "Citizens Yet Strangers: The Puerto Rican Experience," in Jay P. Dolan and Jaime R. Vidal, eds., *Puerto Rican and Cuban Catholics in the U.S., 1900–1965* (Notre Dame, IN: University of Notre Dame Press, 1995). On subtle yet pervasive manifestations of racial discrimination in Puerto Rico, see Eduardo Seda Bonilla, *Los derechos civiles en la cultura puertorriqueña* (Río Piedras, PR: Editorial Universitaria, 1963) and Eric Williams, "Race Relations in Puerto Rico and the Virgin Islands," *Foreign Affairs, 23* (January 1945). On contemporary Puerto Rican racial identity see, for example, Clara E. Rodriguez, *Puerto Ricans: Born in the U.S.A.* (Boulder: Westview Press, 1991).

18. Robert A. Orsi, *The Madonna of 115th Street: Faith and Community in Italian Harlem, 1880–1950* (New Haven: Yale University Press, 2002, 1985), 102, 182, 183.

19. See Estéban Santaella Rivera, *Historia de los Hermanos Cheos: Recopilación de Escritos y Relatos* (Santo Domingo: Editora Alfa y Omega, 1979).

20. See Joseph Bram, "Spirits, Mediums, and Believers in Contemporary Puerto Rico" (1958) in Fernández Méndez, ed., *Portrait of a Society*, 374–375.

21. Charles C. Rogler, *Comerio: A Study of a Puerto Rican Town* (Lawrence: University of Kansas, 1940), 130, 137, 139.

22. Gordon K. Lewis, *Puerto Rico: Freedom and Power in the Caribbean* (New York: Monthly Review Press, 1963), 1.

THE DECLINE OF THE PUBLIC SPHERE: A SEMIOTIC ANALYSIS OF THE RHETORIC OF RACE IN NEW YORK CITY

Timothy Shortell

Race and Ethnicity in New York City
Research in Urban Sociology, Volume 7, 159–177
Copyright © 2004 by Elsevier Ltd.
ISSN: 1047-0042/doi:10.1016/S1047-0042(04)07007-2

ABSTRACT

*Habermas' theory of the structural transformation of the public sphere has
been a point of departure for theoretical debate for more than forty years.
Habermas' explains the decline of a discursive space for public discussion
of collective interests as resulting from the emergence of consumer culture
in post-industrial capitalism. Whereas the public sphere was originally a
location of rational-critical activity, public life today is a spectator sport.
The dominance of media corporations has undermined the potential for
critical debate of pressing social issues, including race. This study seeks
to illuminate the change in public discussions of race in New York City.
A comparison is made between nineteenth-century and contemporary
discourse. The nineteenth-century discourse is represented by texts from*
The Weekly Advocate *and* The Colored American, *two important black
Abolitionist newspapers published in New York City between 1837 and 1841;
this discourse has a two-sided focus: an attack on slavery and a call for
civil rights, and as such, combines analysis of the violence of racism and the
nature of racial inequality. To find a parallel in the contemporary discourse,
news articles from* New York Times, *from 1998, were collected. An innovative
semiotic content coding strategy is used to describe the conceptual network
and ideology of public discussions of race in New York City.*

It is common today to encounter well-intentioned, thoughtful people who express
a weariness about public discussions of race. Both black and white, there are
many who feel that the nation has overcome or should move past its troubled
history of racism and racial violence. This is an understandable sentiment. Public
discussions of race do seem ubiquitous. Urban political discourse is, one might
say, saturated by the discussion of race and ethnicity. And yet, there is something
profoundly dissatisfying about the way that race and ethnicity issues are presented
in contemporary public discourse. The terms are there, the formulaic expressions
are familiar, but the discussion avoids critical engagement at the same time as it
appears to express pressing issues of public policy and urban life.

The paradox of contemporary public discourse can be understood only in a
historical context. Public discussions of race have not always been like they appear
today. At earlier points in American history, the discussion of race was sharper,
more to the point. The modern Civil Rights movement brought discussions of
race into the mainstream public discourse in the twentieth century, where they
have remained, but serious consideration of conflicting notions and disturbing
consequences has disappeared in recent decades. Our first substantial engagement
with "the problem of race" occurred in the nineteenth century with the debate

over slavery. Indeed, Abolitionism remains our most insightful public discussion of key race issues.

In this work, I would like to use a historical comparison to highlight the features of contemporary public discussion of race. An innovative semiotic content coding strategy is used to describe the conceptual network and ideology of public discussions of race in New York City. The nineteenth-century discourse is represented by texts from *The Weekly Advocate* and *The Colored American*, two important black Abolitionist newspapers published in New York City between 1837 and 1841; this discourse has a two-sided focus: an attack on slavery and a call for civil rights, and as such, combines analysis of the violence of racism and the nature of racial inequality. To find a parallel in the contemporary discourse, news articles from the leading daily New York newspaper, *New York Times*, from 1998, were collected.

THE PUBLIC SPHERE

To understand the changing nature of public discourse, I have borrowed from the Habermas' theory of the structural transformation of the public sphere. Habermas (1992, p. 455) asks the question

> whether, and to what extent, a public sphere dominated by mass media provides a realistic chance for the members of civil society, in their competition with the political and economic invaders' media power, to bring about changes in the spectrum of values, topics, and reasons channeled by external influences, to open it up in an innovative way, and to screen it critically.

To answer such an important question, we need to know the characteristics of public discourse in urban settings. To begin, we need to know the extent to which the meaning of race in urban public life is constrained in the mass media as a result of the emergence of consumer capitalism. How have arguments about race in public discourse changed since the nineteenth century?

Habermas (1989) defines the "public sphere" as an ideal type of social activity associated with politics in the modern era. He notes:

> The bourgeois public sphere may be conceived above all as the sphere of private people come together as a public; they soon claimed the public sphere regulated from above against the public authorities themselves, to engage them in a debate over the general rules governing relations in the basically privatized but publicly relevant sphere of commodity exchange and social labor (Habermas, 1989, p. 27).

It emerged only when authority became depersonalized and a civil society developed as distinct from the state. It is the place where individuals, as private citizens, converged to discuss political principles that bear on their interests (Calhoun, 1992; Habermas, 1989).

The public sphere is not simply the context of politics in modern societies. Rather, it is a kind of communicative practice. The spread of news, which accompanied the spread of commerce, made possible a sense of common interests. The connection between private economic interactions and political discourse is of vital importance for the developing meaning of "public." Calhoun (1992, p. 8) notes, "the same processes helped to engender both a more widespread literacy and an approach to the printed word as a source of currently significant 'public' information." The meaning of "public" shifts from the physical representation of the ruler to the abstract bond of common purpose which resulted from increased experience with labor and commodity markets. This sense of the concept could materialize only with rational discussion. Because of its rational basis, the bourgeois public sphere, Habermas (1992) argues, contained universalistic discourses that, at least potentially, could be adapted as new groups were incorporated into the cultural elite. It was potentially inclusive as a result of the spread of public texts, such as books, newspapers and pamphlets. What mattered was the quality of the idea, not the status of the speaker (Calhoun, 1992).

Habermas' important study documents not only how the bourgeois public sphere came into being, but also how it deteriorated. The public sphere was founded on the practical and ideological separation of private productive activity and the administration of the state. It collapsed, in part, when that distinction broke down. Habermas (1989, p. 142) notes,

> that society was essentially a private sphere became questionable only when the powers of 'society' themselves assumed functions of public authority . . . Likewise, the opposite process of a substitution of state authority by the power of society was connected to the extension of public authority over sectors of the private realm.

Perhaps as importantly, the role of public text changed. The expanded state needed a more elaborate communication network, and as the media grew, the larger size and greater capitalization of publishing led to a new form of power. Public discourse could no longer be just the exchange of ideas. Consumer capitalism made culture production a matter of consumption, rather than participation (Habermas, 1992). The increase in the administrative activities of the welfare state also shifted the focus of public discourse from rational-critical debate to negotiation of status and entitlements (Calhoun, 1992).

The idea of a bourgeois public sphere has been roundly criticized on many different grounds. Habermas intended it as an ideal type, rather than an empirical entity, though he used research on Britain, France and Germany to substantiate his main ideas. Schudson (1992) has argued that nineteenth-century American public discourse was not an exemplar of rational-critical communicative action. Instead, he finds evidence of rough and rude partisanship. Avery (1995, p. 25) concurs, calling the party press period (1783–1833) "a time of back-stabbing, name-calling, lies and liars." On the other hand, it was also a time of public discussion of political issues. Interests were debated; policies were justified or criticized. Avery (1995, p. 36) concludes, "despite the admitted rancor of the party press era, the media response to politics was often to help define political factions, issues and personalities."

PUBLIC DISCOURSE IN NINETEENTH CENTURY NEW YORK

At mid-century, the most significant issue being debated in America's newspapers was slavery. The public discussions about slavery and Abolitionism helped push the press away from a strictly partisan role toward a more complex and far-reaching function in the shaping of public opinion (Tripp, 1995). Indeed, anti-slavery newspapers played a key role in the establishment of Americans' commitment to a free press. Because the supporters of slavery feared anti-slavery discussions would threaten the security of Southern society, they often advocated restrictive measures to control the public debate. Abolitionists were the vanguard of pro-First Amendment forces (Nye, 1945, quoted in Tripp, 1995). Public debate resulting from the conflict over slavery would revisit the issue of press freedom during the Civil War (Reynolds, 1995).

Black newspapers were more than party platforms in the antebellum period. They tended to present a broad-based reform perspective. They were concerned with collective identity as well as social justice (Tripp, 1995). Hutton (1993) has demonstrated the socialization function of the black press. Black editors "continually prompted readers about the virtues of frugality, good deportment, temperance, industriousness, and so on. Messages in these categories were intended not only for the middle class but also for those with middle-class aspirations" (Hutton, 1993, p. 103).

Newspapers were central to life in nineteenth-century New York City in many ways. They circulated, often hand-to-hand, among immigrant communities. The city was home to Irish, German, English, French, Spanish and Italian journals, among others (Ernst, 1994). Newspapers promoted the new urban sociability, based on the emerging market-oriented public space. They were both a source of information about the city and an important form of social interaction among strangers (Henkin, 1998).

Rhetoric in public discourse is necessarily connected to power; that is, it is ideological. As the work of Foucault (1970, 1980) has made clear, in any particular historical and social context, not just anything can be said. Some potential arguments are silenced (as blasphemous, irrational, unpatriotic, etc.) or simply unimaginable. Nineteenth-century public discourse is situated in the republican worldview, just as the meaning of contemporary public urban life is marked off by the ideology of consumer capitalism.

CONTEMPORARY PUBLIC DISCOURSE

Large American cities are often described as multicultural centers because of the numerous racial and ethnic backgrounds of urban dwellers. As the residential segregation literature demonstrates, however, our neighborhoods tend to be islands of sameness in a sea of diversity (see Massey & Denton, 1993). This means that our sense of others comes not so much from direct interactions, but rather, from media representations (Bobo, 1997). This can happen even when stories do not address explicitly the issue of racial or ethnic identity. Krase (2001) has documented the ways in which meanings of ethnicity get encoded visually in our public spaces, both for the community itself as well as for outsiders. Images or descriptions of place speak of identity through many layers of signs and symbols. References to urban spaces – especially neighborhoods – almost always implies group identities. For this reason, the meaning of race in urban public discourse cannot be separated from the complexity of identity construction.

Cities are both sites of social problems and centers of discursive production about them. Cities are stages for the political spectacle (Edelman, 1988). Rhetoric plays a role in the social construction of some particular aspect of urban life as a problem, and not as merely an unpleasant or damaging condition. Recent work on the public sphere has demonstrated that public discourse in the welfare state is a form of claims-making (Calhoun, 1992; Habermas, 1992). Negotiations over social policy often play a critical role in the rhetorical construction of problems (Edelman, 1988).

CONCEPTUAL NETWORK ANALYSIS

It is not my intention to examine directly questions of mass communication, public opinion formation, or persuasion. It is enough to note that messages in circulation in our public discourse do influence, to some extent, the way that people think about issues. Jacoby's (2000) work on framing, for example, demonstrates this. Our collective understanding of the urban milieu is constructed from the familiar material of the news. Formulaic news presentations can have substantial effects (Gilliam & Iyengar, 2000; see also Oliver & Myers, 1999).

I want, instead, to suggest a strategy for mapping the conceptual network of the urban public discourse about race. I believe that Habermas' analysis of the connection between rational-critical discourse and democratic practices justifies an endeavor such as this. If we hope to exert greater control over our public life, it is imperative that we examine the structure of our collective understanding of race and ethnicity.

Discourse analysis begins with the notion of speech as a form of mediated action. Text is produced as an interaction among actors in specific settings. Intelligibility does not adhere to words independently of their use, but rather, only through social interaction within a system of hierarchical relations. As a result, the concept of dialogue suggests contention, negotiation, and struggle, rather than merely transparent communication. Discourse reflects collectively constructed interpretations about the meaning and value of social objects and practices. Because power is unequally distributed in the community, not all participants have equivalent opportunities of expression.

Steinberg (1998) recommends that "discursive fields" be used to describe how meaning facilitates and constrains collective action. The field is the context for the planning, perception, and interpretation of collective action. It is partly limited by hegemony. The ways in which meaning-making promotes and inhibits action are not always fully intentional. But neither are they entirely outside the control of the actors involved.

Network analysis allows the researcher to categorize the kinds of relationships between the ideas, or concepts, that comprise the building blocks of a text. Carley (1997) argues that concepts have meaning only in relation to other concepts. Two concepts can be linked directly or indirectly, resulting in local and extended networks. Relationships may be measured along several dimensions and a semantic taxonomy of the network constructed.

In the present study, I have taken a somewhat different approach. Using probabilistic relationships between concepts as the basis for links in the conceptual network, I have borrowed some of the key ideas of the structural analysis of networks in order to bring a new vocabulary to the discussion of discursive fields. By studying the development of the conceptual network over time, this research can show how conceptual hubs develop and describe how network properties such as fitness (see Albert & Barabási, 2002) gave direction to that development. The discursive field emerges out of the social context interacting with the structure of the conceptual network.

By using the structure of networks as one of the explanatory factors, conceptual network analysis has the potential of offering more than simply a description of discursive change. The causal agent for change is not only, or primarily, the creative intentions of authors, but rather, is the result of opportunities within the discursive field, defined, in part, by the state of the conceptual network at any particular time. In other words, the play of meanings, as well as styles, in the discursive field is not unlimited. Concepts are tools whose utility is restricted by the pattern of links to other concepts. Arguments about collective identity and claims-making have to do with the situated perspectives of social agents and the pattern of their interactions.

To describe the conceptual basis of the discursive field, I have used probabilistic relations among key concepts as demonstrated by patterns of co-occurrence. Previous work has shown this to be an effective means of capturing the dynamic quality of public discourse (Shortell, 2004). A set of ten concepts (*race, public, urban, business, character, politics, law, money, poverty*, and *suffering*) was coded for on the basis of keyword searches.

IDEOLOGY

Examination of ideology requires the discourse be situated with regard to power (see Eagleton, 1991; Fairclough, 1992). This can have three distinct manifestations. First, the construction of meaning in hierarchical social relations involves contention. In order to measure the contentiousness of discourse, I have borrowed from Leech's (1983) theory of pragmatics. He defines "illocutionary action" as the interpersonal relational aspect of text. Messages can be thought of as adhering to particular kinds of social goals. Leech identifies five modes, but two are of immediate concern. The most common mode in written English is *assertive*, in which the intent is to state the facts about the subject matter at hand. In the *expressive* mode, messages function as evaluations. Rather than just stating the facts, as it were, these illocutions judge (e.g. praise/condemn) the facts. By comparing the number of instances of expressive illocutions to the number of assertive, it is possible to describe a text in terms of its degree of disputation.

Second, as the concept of hegemony suggests, power shapes the construction of values and norms. In the present study, Rokeach's theory of values was adapted to content coding. Rokeach (1973, p. 5) defines a value as "an enduring belief that a specific mode of conduct or end-state of existence is personally or socially preferable to an opposite or converse" one. Values are different from other kinds of beliefs and attitudes in that they are necessarily relatively enduring and relatively small in number. We regard them as more central to our sense of self and our sense of community; as a result, they have a normative character. I have employed only the terminal values (end-states) in the present study. Keyword lists were constructed for a list of 17 terminal values (*comfort, excitement, accomplishment, peace, beauty, equality, security, freedom, happiness, harmony, love, pleasure, salvation, self-respect, recognition, friendship*, and *wisdom*).

Finally, ideology can be manifest in the ways society justifies itself. Explanations are provided, in public discourse, about why things are the way they are, how they got that way, and why this is the best of all possible worlds. To code for ideology in this sense, I borrowed from Thompson's (1990) theory of mass communication. Thompson identifies the major dimensions of ideology in contemporary discourse. In his view, *legitimation* concerns arguments that justify current arrangements on the basis of their sensibility or familiarity. Weber's (1946) classic view is incorporated into this formulation; claims that social practices or institutional arrangements are rational, conventional, or traditional are considered instances of this ideological discourse. Challenges to such claims may properly be referred to as counter-ideological, but for the present study, were included in the coding as end-points of the same underlying dimension.

First, keywords for the domain were generated, including *power, status, rights, authority, government, economics, public,* and *inequality,* among others. Next, keywords for six aspects of ideological arguments were generated, including *legitimacy, sensibility, intelligence, tradition, popularity,* and *efficacy.* Since ideology concerns meaning in the service of domination, only arguments about power, relations of authority, etc., can be considered ideological. I included economics and government in this domain because they imply power relations, even if not explicitly mentioned. Paragraphs in which the any of the domain keywords were found were coded for the six aspects of legitimation. Because not all aspects are equally important as indicators of the ideological dimension, a weighting algorithm was used in the coding.

A COMPARISON OF DISCURSIVE FIELDS

Table 1 displays the prevalence of concepts in the discursive fields for the two samples. The concept of race occurs at about the same relative frequency in both samples, roughly 15% of the paragraphs studied. The conceptual profile of the two samples is significantly different in a number of ways. There are substantial decreases in the prevalence of some concepts, such as "public" and "character." At the same time, there were also large increases in prevalence for "urban" and "law." Other concepts, as with "race," occur at approximately the same relative frequency.

Table 2 reports the results of the contingency analysis for the concept of race. Odds ratios are used as the measure of contingency in the present analysis; instead of measuring the degree to which proportions of one variable vary by the other, as is the case with the standard Chi-square test often used with percentage tables, odds express the likelihood that a random case possesses one value of a variable rather than any other. Odds ratios show if the odds for a value of one variable are contingent on the value of the other variable (Knoke & Burke, 1980; Rudas, 1998).

Table 1.   Prevalence of Concepts by Time.

Concept	Time Period		
	19th C.	Contemporary	$p<$
Race	16.6	14.4	n.s.
Public	34.2	14.5	0.001
Urban	7.1	27.1	0.001
Business	5.8	3.2	0.05
Character	48.5	15.4	0.001
Politics	34.2	30.8	n.s.
Law	16.6	38.8	0.001
Money	4.6	5.0	n.s.
Poverty	5.5	5.1	n.s.
Suffering	19.1	14.5	0.05
Paragraphs	325	3,541	

Note: Prevalence is indicated by the percentage of paragraphs in which the concept occurs.

There are, generally, stronger contingencies for "race" in the nineteenth-century sample. The differences between the two samples are interesting. In the earlier texts, "race" is significantly related to "character," "politics," "law," and "suffering." Although the significant contingencies for "race" with "politics"

Table 2.   Contingency Analysis of Race by Time.

Race and	Time Period	
	19th C.	Contemporary
Public	1.28	1.11
Urban	2.37	1.73^{***}
Business	1.37	0.69
Character	2.18^{*}	0.91
Politics	2.67^{***}	1.35^{**}
Law	2.58^{**}	1.20
Money	1.89	0.70
Poverty	2.03	0.53^{*}
Suffering	2.58^{**}	1.67^{***}
Paragraphs	325	3,541

Note: Contingency is indicated by odds ratios. Odds ratios represent the likelihood that the concept will occur in paragraphs where "race" is also present. A dash indicates that the odds could not be calculated.

Chi-square:

$^{*}p < 0.05.$

$^{**}p < 0.01.$

$^{***}p < 0.001.$

and "suffering" remain, they are lower in the contemporary sample. "Race" is independent of "character" and "law" in the recent texts. The most marked contrast is the reversal between "race" and "poverty"; in the earlier sample, there is a positive relationship (that is, the occurrence of one is associated with the occurrence of the other), but in the recent sample, there is an inverse relationship (i.e. the occurrence is "race" is more likely in paragraphs in which "poverty" is absent).

In terms of contentiousness, there was a significant difference between the two samples. Evaluative illocutions occurred in 13.2% of the paragraphs in the nineteenth-century texts but only 6.7% of the paragraphs in the contemporary sample ($p < 0.001$). The ratio of evaluative to assertive illocutions can serve as an index of disputation. For the nineteenth-century sample, the value of the index is 0.173; previous work has shown that this is a typical figure for reform discourses in this period (Shortell, 2001). For the contemporary example, the index of disputation is 0.093. This is consistent with the Habermas' decline hypothesis.

These findings are, by themselves, not conclusive of the decline of the public sphere, but offer evidence of a transformation away from critical engagement with the meaning of race. The contrast between nineteenth-century and contemporary engagement can be seen in the following passages. In this passage, the author is describing the leader of the mutiny of the *Amistad*, a story that black communities in the North followed with great interest:

> This noble hero, by his defense of liberty, has placed himself side by side with Patrick Henry, John Hancock, Thomas Jefferson, and Samuel and John Adams – fathers of the Revolution. The justice of the nation has stood up in vindication of his deeds, in defense of his course, and decreed them right. How could they have done otherwise, with an example so illustrious as the American Revolution before them. Were he not an African, a black man, his fame would be emblazoned forever on the tide of time, and written in high eulogium by the historian's pen (*The Colored American*, March 27, 1841).

The use of the reference to the Patriots is common in black Abolitionist discourse. Such a feature is inherently critical, since the revolutionary rhetoric is turned on the people who still prided themselves on their recent historical accomplishment. No reader would have misunderstood the accusation of hypocrisy this passage contains. The argument here is that blacks have the same human rights that the American colonists claimed for themselves some sixty years earlier.

The link between race and politics is the subject of this letter published in the second issue of *The Weekly Advocate*:

> The colored people should all understand this: that the prejudice which exists against them arises not from the color of their skin, but from their condition. Hence they may see that, just in proportion as they elevate their condition, prejudice will wear away. There is a strong prejudice existing against the whites, of a degraded character; it is of course against their condition, and they can never be elevated or respected, until they become sober, industrious, intelligent, and

religious. Moral and intellectual attainments will raise any man from the gutter to the throne, and a man may attain to almost any degree of eminence, if lie makes his mark, and then goes to work intelligently and wisely to accomplish it (January 14, 1837).

The author is clearly contesting the widely accepted fact that blacks are "degraded" by nature. His remarks are as optimistic as they are critical. There is no mistaking the distinctive voice; the contentiousness and concern for self-improvement are telltale signs of black Abolitionism.

Two passages illustrate aspects of the prophetic rhetoric that was a major element of the early discourse (Shortell, 2002a):

To honoured mothers, we would particularly say, encourage the *Advocate* by admitting it into your families. Its columns will contain nothing but what is in perfect accordance with the principles of religion, and sound morality. Thus while you yourselves may be benefited by its perusal, your children too may receive impressions which will materially affect their character in after-life. Encourage then this journal! Females of colour, let not our hopes of its success be indulged in vain, for want of effort on your part to sustain it and we trust that we shall never be deficient in zeal; and energy to make the paper worthy of our approbation and an efficient instrument in the hand of Providence in hastening that glorious period when our unfortunate race shall no longer be the victims of galling slavery, or cruel prejudice (*The Weekly Advocate*, January 7, 1837).

Is the colored man degraded? Who degraded him? The white man – the church of Jesus Christ. Has she not organized all her institutions? does she not perform all her holy services? and arrange all her sanctuaries and seats, in obedience to the spirit of CASTE – PREJUDICE AGAINST COLOR? Does she not take from, and deny the colored man all the means of improvement, respectability, and education? Truly she does.

We know instances in which colored members in some of our white churches, are as wealthy, as moral, as intelligent, and as refined as any of the white members–as far removed from what is called the degraded mass, as any white man in the country, except in their complexion; and yet the ministers and people of the said churches, draw the strong cord of caste, and cherish the same paralyzing, unholy prejudice against them, which they do against the most degraded. Still the editors of the *Observer* tell us, "The condition of the colored people in this country is partly their own fault!" Shame on these intelligent brethren, to wish, in this way, to lull the consciences of the church and the community, to sleep in their sin against God, and cruel inhumanity to his image (*The Colored American*, July 8, 1837).

The rhetoric is energetic and caustic, but also hopeful. Since it is man-made, the degradation of the free black population might be undone. At the same time, this hope is not just political. It is eschatological. Using this rhetoric, the black Abolitionists claimed the subject position of suffering innocent on whose behalf divine justice is promised.

The discussion of race in the contemporary discourse is strikingly different. In this passage, the author is relating a long (9800 words) narrative of (the then) Mayor Giuliani's "last war" against welfare:

For a moment, the room fell silent. The city's new Welfare Commissioner – this Ivy League-educated, Republican white man – had just traveled to the heart of Harlem and proclaimed it

> morally instructive for the poor to face empty cupboards. Once upon a time, there might have been a riot. In the end-welfare age, the stunned silence leads to applause (*New York Times*, December 20, 1998).

The author tells of the episode with great interest, but without taking a position about the meaning of the change. This is typical of the contemporary discourse. Attention is called to daily life, but with only hints, at best, of a critical perspective.

Another passage conveys the lack of critical engagement. This article is about a defamation lawsuit against Rev. Al Sharpton, a controversial community activist. The author relates different points of view, but with studied neutrality.

> Mr. Sharpton cast the defamation lawsuit yesterday as a coordinated effort by his enemies to undermine his political influence. His allies, meanwhile, spoke passionately on his behalf, many representing a gallery of Mr. Sharpton's past causes.
>
> Moses Stewart, the father of Yusef Hawkins, the black youth killed during a 1989 racially charged incident in Bensonhurst, Brooklyn, called Mr. Sharpton "our fearless leader and my brother." Margarita Rosario, president of Parents Against Police Brutality, credited Mr. Sharpton with rushing to help crime victims. Iris Baez, whose son, Anthony, died in police custody after he hit a patrol car with a football, said Mr. Sharpton was guilty only of "confronting the truth" (*New York Times*, July 18, 1998).

The quotes in defense of Mr. Sharpton are presented one after the other, creating the effect that the story is about the variety of perspectives about the community leader. The truth, the author implies, depends on who you ask. The choice is left to the reader.

Table 3 shows the prevalence of values for the two samples. Overall, the nineteenth-century discourse is more likely to contain references to the terminal values. There are several substantial differences in the two samples. "Freedom" is about ten times more likely in the older texts (22.2% v. 2.5%). This is not unexpected, given that the nineteenth-century texts come from anti-slavery periodicals. The earlier texts also were more likely to express "friendship," "wisdom," and "excitement." There were smaller differences, favoring the earlier sample, in "equality," "happiness," and "love" and "recognition." Only for "security" did the contemporary sample yield a higher prevalence.

Comparison of the prevalence of legitimation also yields evidence of a shift in the discursive field. In the nineteenth-century texts, legitimation occurs in 38.5% of the paragraphs. For the contemporary texts, the figure is 31.6% ($p < 0.05$). This is not to suggest that the contemporary discourse is less ideological, but rather, that it is less directly engaged with the justification of race in public life. The nineteenth-century discourse is a platform for the expression of a critical examination of the meaning of race; the black Abolitionists disputed the taken-for-granted nature of racial differences. They argued that the degraded status of their community was not the result of nature, but instead, of systematic oppression by the majority.

Table 3. Prevalence of Terminal Values by Time.

Value	Time Period		
	19th C.	Contemporary	$p<$
Comfort	4.0	1.7	0.01
Excitement	8.9	2.5	0.001
Accomplishment	2.8	1.1	0.05
Peace	1.2	0.6	n.s.
Beauty	2.2	0.8	0.05
Equality	4.0	0.5	0.001
Security	2.5	4.0	n.s.
Freedom	22.2	2.5	0.001
Happiness	5.8	1.2	0.001
Harmony	1.5	0.5	0.05
Love	4.6	1.3	0.001
Pleasure	4.3	0.3	0.001
Salvation	1.5	0.1	0.001
Self-Respect	2.5	0.6	0.001
Recognition	6.2	1.9	0.001
Friendship	15.1	4.7	0.001
Wisdom	17.8	2.1	0.001
Paragraphs	325	3,541	

In the contemporary texts, the significance of race is acknowledged, but its position relative to other social forces is made ambiguous. Contemporary news reports are much more neutral in tone and value-free in orientation – this is partly a result of the change in journalistic norms, since the distinction between reporting and opinion-making is more rigid in contemporary news. But it also signals a shift from critical engagement to evocative description in the discursive field. Authors of twenty-first century news reports mention race, often in a deliberate "different-but-equal" perspective (much criticized as "political correctness"), but without a sense of what ought to be done about the unresolved issues. In place of the claims-making on behalf of the oppressed there is matter-of-fact observation.

This difference can be seen clearly in the following excerpts from the two samples. Commenting on an article that appeared in the *Baltimore Chronicle*, the author of this editorial from *The Colored American*, speaks of the hypocrisy of white attitudes about justice:

> So the *Chronicle* regrets that the scoundrels have been arrested in their career of infamy and crime! "Respectable gentlemen"–quotha! Where is their respectability? If acts of piracy and outrage against the laws of their country and humanity entitles them to the appelation of "gentlemen occupying respectable positions in society," why, then, society in Baltimore must take rank for respectability next to Sing Sing State Prison (November 23, 1839).

In contrast, a passage about an episode in which two fire department employees participated in an offensive display at a Labor Day parade in Queens, brings no sense of outrage:

> Mr. Walters and Mr. Steiner both contended that they did not mean to offend black people when they covered their faces in black lipstick, donned black wigs and joined friends who tossed pieces of watermelon to the crowd, posed next to fried chicken cartons and parodied break dancing while on a float called "Black to the Future: Broad Channel 2098" (*New York Times*, October 8, 1998).

This event had clearly racist connotations, but the author of the story is careful to present the incident as open to different interpretations. There is no deliberate critical consideration of the meaning of the men's behavior, or the community's response to it. It is clear that the article is not intended to speak on anyone's behalf.

RACE AND THE DECLINE OF THE PUBLIC SPHERE

Discourse about race has followed an uneven trajectory over the course of American history. During the nineteenth century, the conflict over slavery produced the pinnacle of critical engagement with the meaning of race in American society. The discursive field of black Abolitionist discourse yielded a variety of powerful arguments on the basis of creative combinations of concepts and artful deployment of rhetoric and familiar styles. Black Abolitionists had to confront, directly and continually, an ideology of racial hierarchy; they made significant contributions to American public discourse by inverting the meaning of several key republican ideas. They used the fiery speech-making of the Patriots to raise questions about the evolving meaning of liberty and citizenship. Their efforts called into question the legitimacy of existing beliefs about race.

As Habermas suggested, changes in the nature of the state and its relation to civil society undermined the foundation for rational-critical debate about public issues. The power of media corporations in the age of consumer capitalism shifted public discourse away from the exchange of ideas based on interested perspectives and toward an emphasis on the false equality of the market. As far as capitalist producers are concerned, all consumers are alike, and the liberty of contemporary society is manifest in the almost endless choice of consumer goods. A public discourse that highlighted differences as conflicting interests is incompatible with the consumerist mentality. In its place, media corporations produce news as another consumable.

The present analysis showed some of the features of the shift in the discursive field from the nineteenth century to the present. The disengagement of the concept of race from concepts such as character, politics, money and law, and the conspicuous absence of references to values (except for security) suggest the loss of a critical perspective. Modern journalism is much more matter-of-fact in general than it was in the nineteenth century. This shift, however, is more than just the development of a new journalistic practice. It represents a fundamental alteration of the status of public discourse.

Habermas worried that the new public sphere was incapable of sustaining a truly democratic politics. This is especially worrisome on the issue of race. Without public discussion of the meaning of race in contemporary society – one that permits a the free exchange of ideas based on competing interests – democratic resolution of pressing social issues will be unlikely. We will have lots of talk about race with little creative problem-solving. Over time, public interest in the meaning of race in a society defined by inequality will wane, until an explosive event (or events) forces us to reconsider familiar ideas and accepted notions.

As the present analysis showed, one of the most significant changes in the discursive field involves the obscuring of the ideological nature of the meaning of race. The black Abolitionist texts contested directly the taken-for-granted quality of American prejudice. It rendered problematic the collective republican identity by turning the critical ideas and rhetoric of the Patriots on the politics of Jacksonian America. Although contemporary public discourse is focussed on race to a similar extent – a remarkable observation, considering the relative social and political climates – the modern discursive field lacks the conceptual tools from which new insights into ongoing problems are likely to be produced.

Semiotic analysis of public discourse, such as the present study, can contribute to the re-establishment of critical engagement with the meaning of race in contemporary society. By showing the structural foundation for collective meaning-making, we can take notice of the gaps in our thinking about the present, and especially, how we got here. The nineteenth century discourse described in this work, and others (see Condit & Lucaites, 1993; Foner, 1980; Levesque, 1970), has the virtue of demonstrating the possibilities of rational-critical debate. Based on a recognition that race and ethnicity imply, among other things, competing interests, the kind of discursive field needed for democratic politics can provide the opportunity for creative problem-solving.

Scholarship on the meaning of race that examines the concept of "whiteness" can help reinvigorate public debate about inequality in contemporary society (see Roediger, 1991). By calling attention to the "unmarked" category of race, the notion of privilege is reinserted into the discussion. Nineteenth-century discourse did not use the term in this sense, but the seeds of the idea were planted in the fecund soil of the contest over slavery. The black Abolitionists mounted a sustained attack on the legitimacy of racial hierarchy in American society.

The present study can not hope to settle the question of Habermas' theory of the transformation of the public sphere. Still, interesting evidence has been brought to bear on the unfolding of public discourse from the nineteenth century to the present. Conceptual network analysis has great utility in the interrogation of public discourse. The elements of rational-critical understanding can be documented by examination of the conceptual network, in conjunction with analysis of rhetoric and ideology. If Habermas' hypothesis is to be supported empirically, it will require the kind of analysis outlined in this work.

ACKNOWLEDGMENTS

Thanks are due to Nancy Sánchez, Mary Howard, Chris Toulouse, and Jerry Krase.

REFERENCES

Albert, R., & Barabási, A.-L. (2002). Statistical mechanics of complex networks. *Reviews of Modern Physics, 74*, 47–97.

Avery, D. (1995). Battle without a rule book. In: L. Chiasson, Jr. (Ed.), *The Press in Times of Crisis* (pp. 23–40). Westport, CT: Praeger.

Bobo, L. (1997). Race, public opinion, and the social sphere. *Public Opinion Quarterly, 61*, 1–15.

Calhoun, C. (1992). Introduction: Habermas and the public sphere. In: C. Calhoun (Ed), *Habermas and the Public Sphere* (pp. 1–48). Cambridge, MA: Massachusetts Institute of Technology.

Carley, K. (1997). Network text analysis: The network position of concepts. In: C. W. Roberts (Ed.), *Text Analysis for the Social Sciences* (pp. 79–100). Mahwah, NJ: Lawrence Erlbaum.

Condit, C. M., & Lucaites, J. L. (1993). *Crafting equality: America's Anglo-African word*. Chicago: University of Chicago.

Douglass, F., & Blassingame, J. W. (1979). *The Frederick Douglass papers*. New Haven: Yale University Press.

Eagleton, T. (1991). *Ideology*. London: Routledge.

Edelman, M. (1988). *Constructing the political spectacle*. Chicago: University of Chicago.

Ernst, R. (1994). *Immigrant life in New York City, 1825–1863*. Syracuse, NY: Syracuse University.

Fairclough, N. (1992). *Discourse and social change*. Cambridge: Polity Press.

Foner, E. (1980). *Politics and ideology in the age of the Civil War*. Oxford: Oxford University.

Foucault, M. (1970). *The order of things: An archaeology of the human sciences*. A. Sheridan (Trans.). NY: Random House.

Foucault, M. (1980). *Power/knowledge: Selected writings, 1972–1977*. C. Gordon (Ed.) and C. Gordon et al. (Trans.). NY: Pantheon.

Gilliam, F. D., Jr., & Iyengar, S. (2000). Prime suspects: The influence of local television news on the viewing public. *American Journal of Political Science, 44*(3), 560–573.

Habermas, J. (1989). *The structural transformation of the public sphere: An inquiry into a category of Bourgeois society*. Cambridge, MA: Massachusetts Institute of Technology.

Habermas, J. (1992). Further reflections on the public sphere. In: C. Calhoun (Ed.), *Habermas and the Public Sphere* (pp. 421–460). Cambridge, MA: Massachusetts Institute of Technology.

Henkin, D. M. (1998). *City reading: Written words and public spaces in antebellum*. New York, NY: Columbia University.

Hutton, F. (1993). *The early black press in America, 1827 to 1860*. Westport, CT: Greenwood.

Jacoby, W. G. (2000). Issue framing and public opinion on government spending. *American Journal of Political Science, 44*(4), 750–767.

Knoke, D., & Burke, P. J. (1980). *Log-linear models*. Thousand Oaks, CA: Sage.

Krase, J. (2001). Ethnic theme parks: Images of social and cultural capital. Paper presented at the annual meeting of the American Sociological Association, Anaheim, CA.

Leech, G. (1983). *Principles of pragmatics*. London: Longman.

Levesque, G. A. (1970). Black abolitionists in the age of Jackson: Catalysts in the radicalization of American abolitionism. *Journal of Black Studies, 1*(2), 187–201.

Massey, D. S., & Denton, N. A. (1993). *American apartheid: Segregation and the making of the American underclass*. Cambridge, MA: Harvard University.

Nye, R. B. (1945). Freedom of the press and the antislavery controversy. *Journalism Quarterly, 22*, 1–11.

Oliver, P. E., & Myers, D. J. (1999). How events enter the public sphere: Conflict, location, and sponsorship in local newspaper coverage of public events. *American Journal of Sociology, 105*(1), 38–87.

Reynolds, D. (1995). Words for war. In: L. Chiasson, Jr. (Ed.), *The Press in Times of Crisis* (pp. 86–102). Westport, CT: Praeger.

Ripley, C. P. (1985). *The black abolitionist papers*. Chapel Hill: University of North Carolina Press.

Roediger, D. (1991). *The wages of whiteness: Race and the making of the American working class*. London: Verso.

Rokeach, M. (1973). *The nature of human values*. NY: Free Press.

Rudas, T. (1998). *Odds ratios in the analysis of contingency tables*. Thousand Oaks, CA: Sage.

Schudson, M. (1992). Was there ever a public sphere? If so, when? Reflections on the American case. In: C. Calhoun (Ed.), *Habermas and the Public Sphere* (pp. 143–163). Cambridge, MA: Massachusetts Institute of Technology.

Shortell, T. (2001). The black abolitionist jeremiad: An innovative analysis of anti-slavery newspapers in New York state. Paper presented at the annual meeting of the Social Science History Association, Chicago, IL.

Shortell, T. (2002a). Collective identity construction in black abolitionist discourse: A conceptual network analysis of the New York anti-slavery press. Paper presented at the annual meeting of the Social Science History Association, St. Louis, MO.

Shortell, T. (2002b). SemioCode: Complex semiotic content coding. BrooklynSoc.Org, Brooklyn, NY (www.shortell.org/semiocode).

Shortell, T. (2004). The rhetoric of black abolitionism: An exploratory analysis of anti-slavery newspapers in New York state. *Social Science History, 28*(1), 75–109.

Steinberg, M. W. (1998). Tilting the frame: Considerations on collective action framing from a discursive turn. *Theory and Society, 27*(6), 845–872.

Thompson, J. B. (1990). *Ideology and modern culture: Critical social theory in the era of mass communication*. Stanford, CA: Stanford University.

Tripp, B. (1995). Journalism for God and man. In: L. Chiasson, Jr. (Ed.), *The Press in Times of Crisis* (pp. 49–66). Westport, CT: Praeger.
Weber, M. (1946). *From Max Weber*. H. H. Gerth & C. W. Mills (Eds, Trans. and Intro.). NY: Oxford University.

APPENDIX
A NOTE ON METHODOLOGY

All coding in this study was conducted using *SemioCode*, a software tool for semiotic content analysis (Shortell, 2002b). The paragraph is used as coding unit in all analyses in *SemioCode*. In formal written English, the paragraph is the basic syntactic container for the argument. Researchers studying concepts generally use the sentence as the coding unit, since the sentence is the basic syntactic container for meaning. *SemioCode*, though, is for research on arguments; concepts are regarded as the building-blocks of arguments, and it is necessary to use a standard coding unit best suited for arguments rather than meanings. Content is coded as present or absent. Coding is done by keyword pattern matching. Algorithms for the different kinds of content combine the pattern matching in different ways to compare to a threshold; for value coding, for example, any instance of any keywords for each value codes the content as present. For ideology, in contrast, a certain breadth and density of content is required to trigger the coding switch.

The nineteenth-century texts (from *The Weekly Advocate* and *The Colored American*) drawn from available published collections (Douglass & Blassingame, 1979; Ripley, 1985) and available microfilm reels at the New York Public Library's Schomberg Center for Research in Black Culture. For the contemporary sample, I collected articles from the leading New York daily, *New York Times*, in which "race" and "poverty" or "violence" co-occur in the same paragraph at least once. Articles were selected from the news sections (or Sunday magazine) only. Texts were gathered from the newspaper from 1998 using the Nexis database.

The nineteenth-century sample contains 325 paragraphs and more than 34,500 words. The contemporary sample contains 3541 paragraphs and about 193,600 words.

EMERGENT AFRICAN IMMIGRANT PHILANTHROPY IN NEW YORK CITY

Mojúbàolú Olúfúnké Okome

Race and Ethnicity in New York City
Research in Urban Sociology, Volume 7, 179–191
Copyright © 2004 by Elsevier Ltd.
ISSN: 1047-0042/doi:10.1016/S1047-0042(04)07008-4

Philanthropy is one of the central ideals of African traditional mores. It is no wonder then that African philanthropy takes many forms within New York City's immigrant community. The key features of immigrant African philanthropy include the prominent role of informal institutions, lack of visibility to external observers and non-members of group, and small-scale philanthropic efforts by groups organized along ethnic, kinship, and national lines. The outlines of philanthropy are also determined by globalization, which shapes the decision to become an immigrant, the location chosen for settlement, and the challenges faced in both home country and country of settlement. Many African immigrant organizations are male dominated in leadership and decision making, with an emphasis on volunteerism and recognition of those with leadership skills. Professional associations tend to be national rather than continent-wide. Because the focus of these groups is derived from the historical experience of their members, there is high interest in foreign policy issues, and U.S. foreign policy toward Africa is subjected to much discussion, debate and thought. However, the power and voice of African immigrants is yet to be felt in policy advocacy circles.

The nature of African philanthropy is affected by other factors as well. Elders are privileged for positions of authority, and there may be underlying attempts to perpetuate structures that favor distinct interests. Old stereotypes die hard, thus, unity across divisive national and ethnic boundaries is elusive. Gender, class, religion, prestige, and ethnicity are some of the crosscutting variables that delineate lines of power. These interests are covered over by the attempts to persuade members that decision-making within the group understands and works actively to promote group interests. Dissenters are punished by something that amounts to excommunication from the group because philanthropic groups and institutions, whether they are African or otherwise, are not immune from relations of power. This does not mean that the groups and institutions in question are not well meaning, or that they do not perform socially meaningful acts.

FORMS OF PHILANTHROPY IN AFRICAN IMMIGRANT COMMUNITIES

Philanthropy takes many forms among African immigrant communities. It exists in the form of mutual aid for friends, extended family, lineage, and fictive kin. This last category includes, but is not limited to, those from an individual's ethnic group, or even from their country of origin. Philanthropy is also to be found in the form of kindness and generosity toward strangers. Above all, elements of philanthropy are to be found in the corporatization of community-based efforts to develop the human and material resources among many African ethnic groups. Many studies of the process of urbanization in Africa indicate the ubiquity of formation of hometown organizations that perform social functions including philanthropy among newly urbanized Africans. These organizations assist urbanized home folk from the villages and the towns of origin from which these urbanized groups originally emerged in various respects. The assistance offered include giving material and moral support in times of significant social celebration and mourning, for education as well as for home construction, construction of infrastructure for the home community, and for various other community-based development efforts. The efforts of African immigrants in the United States and elsewhere closely follow the patterns described above. The patterns are so ubiquitous as to warrant a claim of their emergence from a philosophical orientation toward philanthropy in African society.

Some groups of African immigrants have both welfare as well as broader sociopolitical and economic functions. All groups that are identified in this study, with the exception of the Yoruba Studies Association, have a presence in Nigerian politics. While it espouses a non-partisan philosophy, the Egbé Omo Yorùbá tends to be associated with the ruling People's Democratic Party. Afénifére tends to be associated with the Alliance for Democracy. Some factions of the Egbé Omo Yorùbá are part of a mass-based, anarchist and actively engaged group that is challenging all major bases of power within the political system, particularly in the Western states of Nigeria. Yoruba immigrants in these groups are actively engaged in Nigerian politics, with some individuals traveling to Nigeria to participate in party activities, management, or even running for office. If we bear in mind that Nigeria has more than 250 distinct languages spoken within it, we may begin to grasp some of the complexity that exists in these African immigrant communities. As a case in point, many assume that all Ibos would probably belong to a pan-Ibo group, but fail to realize that Onitsha Ibos, Mid-Western Ibos and those in central Iboland consider themselves to be quite distinct historically, culturally, and that they even have major differences in dialect. Many philanthropic groups are formed to cater to the social welfare needs of several immigrant communities. They provide avenues for informal socializing (parties, picnics, dances, and all manner of get-togethers) and mutual support in times of need, e.g. financial assistance for burial costs, for transporting a body back home for burial, child naming ceremonies, weddings, graduations, etc.). They are a source of informal counseling for the youth, and may be used to resolve marital conflicts, for job and professional advice, as well as for relationships, be they of friendship, or dating. And they provide an avenue for leadership of a group that validates the immigrant's gifts, expertise and skill. The associations may also provide development assistance to individuals and groups in home communities. Such assistance includes the provision of funds for scholarships for indigent students at all educational levels, for infrastructure such as roads, electricity and telephone access to rural villages, and for public health including the provision of access to potable water and the construction of health centers.

This paper focuses on African immigrants in New York City. Because many groups may be located outside New York City but have membership in New York, it will also include examples of African immigrant philanthropy in other parts of the United States. The information revolution that has been made possible by the development of the World Wide Web has caused the emergence of ties among widely dispersed groups of Africans in news groups, discussion groups, and chat rooms. This permits groups to agglomerate and communities form in the absence of propinquity (close proximity).

IMMIGRANTS

I define immigrants here as people that move from their country of origin to another and decide to settle in the new country either for the long term or for good. Immigrants may be documented or undocumented. Documented immigrants may have problems arising from their interactions with economic, social and political systems, including access to employment, problems with underemployment and fair wages, lack of adequate/appropriate benefits, or discrimination in employment.

Through their involvement in the economic system of their community of settlement, African immigrants experience first-hand, the stigmatization of people of color, and the implications of white skin privilege. Many are astounded because they come from countries where they were part of the privileged few. Some believe that the United States is a place that embodies spaces where equality, equity, and equal opportunity are norms that apply equally to everyone. Other immigrants believe that those who do not work hard cannot expect to be rewarded, and thus, associate the stigma suffered by minorities with the unwillingness to work, while still others believe negative media portrayals of many of America's minorities as accurate reflections of what people really are. In order to fit in better, they work very hard and want to be considered exceptions to the rule. There are also some who claim to be African, but not black. This group is not necessarily limited to the North Africans from Egypt, Morocco, Algeria, Tunisia, some Arab Sudanese, and white South Africans, Zimbabweans and Mozambicans, or Asian Africans. In these cases, the African immigrants distance themselves from those considered discreditable in hopes that the stigma and discrimination suffered by those groups would not be visited upon them, often to suffer the rude awakening that their color marks them too as equally discreditable.

Self help. Micro-credit is now recognized as an essential element of development. Many African immigrant communities have àjo, esusu, and other informal contribution groups that are organized on an informal basis. The groups tend to be small. Usually, approximately five to twenty people come together. A trusted individual is made the banker. A contribution and rotation cycle is determined either by lot or negotiated agreement. Each person takes the entire amount of money as a payoff at his or her pre-determined turn in the rotation. People have traditionally used these funds for either business or pleasure. This system is also used as the basis of ensuring that small-scale entrepreneurs have the capital required to establish a business.

Mutual Aid. Mutual aid takes place within the context of informal institutions that operate like an extended family. These institutions are usually mono-ethnic, although they could benefit from pan-ethnicity and philosophical revolutions that encourage collaboration beyond one's ethnicity and nationality. The groups stand essentially in the place of the extended family, refer to one another as family, and use familial terms to refer to one another. Many an African immigrant child's experiences of extended family relationships is within the context of the parents' membership in these groups.

REFUGEES

Some undocumented aliens among African immigrants are also refugees. For this population, there may be little awareness of the services that exist to support refugees. Most depend on networks of friends or family (broadly defined). Some religious institutions have risen to the challenge of serving this population. Notable in terms of outreach to African immigrant communities are the Coptic Church and its record of service to Egyptian Copts, the Lutheran Church and its growing record of service to refugees from Liberia and Sierra Leone in particular and many new Evangelical missions from various African countries. Mosques that are founded by African immigrants also perform the same functions. While the Catholic Church has a strong record of activism on immigration issues, demonstrated by lobbying for legislative change, increases in budget allocations, expansion of rights for all immigrants, and the like, its presence in serving African refugee populations is very limited. The Christ Apostolic Church, Methodist Church as well as several Pentecostal Churches and indigenous African churches like the Aladura and Celestial Church of Christ are examples of churches originating from Africa that have established missions in the United States. They do not, in the main, serve refugees exclusively.

Increasingly, African immigrants break away from African American mosques and establish their own independent mosques with Imams from the various African countries from which the immigrants originate. Necessarily, these institutions also serve a multi-purpose function. Many have become involved in refugee servicing by default, and ought to be supported in the institutionalization of their services. Many who are familiar with New York City are also aware of the wide reach of Yorùbá religion. While most of the visible believers in this indigenous West African religion are Africans from the Diaspora, there is a growing number of babaláwo (diviners) especially from Nigeria in the United States. Some non-religious organizations also serve the immigrant refugee population. In the New York City area, these include African Services and RAINBO. The services provided are crucial, but their reach is limited. However, extent to which the services offered are adequate, the extent to which the information on their availability is widely disseminated in the target population, and the extent to which these organizations are effective ought to be subjected to serious study and independent assessment.

The health care needs of the refugee population include not only access to physical care, but equally, if not more importantly, access to mental care. Many refugees are newly escaped from harrowing, devastating situations that have profound, lasting negative consequences on their psyche. Psychological counseling and psychiatric care is needed to ensure that this population makes an adjustment to normal life in their community of settlement. Groups of refugee children have been brought into the United States from the war-torn areas of Sudan as well as groups of amputated children and youth from Sierra Leone. Many are coming as a result of the successful advocacy of religious organizations. While these efforts are to be commended, there is cause for some concern. Are these children and youth provided with adequate orientation before and after their arrival? What services exist to support them? Under whose supervision are they? Are there any plans to help them determine if their parents or close relatives are alive and if so, to help them re-connect with their family? Is this a temporary solution or is it permanent?

The structure advocacy organizations may also raise some concerns. Why are so many organizations top-heavy with native-born Americans, excluding recent African immigrants, who would have been a logical interest group, upon whose expertise advocacy organizations can rely? Are recent African immigrants involved in any advocacy efforts? Are there any Africans with expert knowledge of issues concerning refugees? The answers to these questions would reveal what appears to be enduring bias against recent African immigrants. There seems to be an underlying belief that recent African immigrants could not possibly contribute anything to discourse, advocacy or outreach to refugee populations from their own continent. If one considers that African immigrants are also among the most educated immigrants in the United States, then, we are faced with the problem of explaining why the lacunae exists.

EXILES

African exiles who reside in the United States include some very prominent scholars, some of whom have become a fixture in the U.S. academy. Ngugi wa Thiong'o of Kenya is a Professor at New York University. Wole Soyinka, Nigeria's Nobel Prize Laureate, was also in exile during the period of the Abacha regime. During the apartheid era, many South African scholars and students were resident in the United States. Their activities in raising consciousness and developing public awareness of the plight of black South Africans contributed immensely to giving a human face to the anti-apartheid movement. It also contributed to the strengthening of the U.S. anti-apartheid movements and UN initiatives to bring the weight of the world's public opinion to bear on the apartheid regime. Many of the anti-apartheid groups established in the United States by South African exiles were philanthropic as well as political. Members provided one another with mutual support, information, and a variety of individual and collective assistance efforts. The documentation of such efforts is ongoing.

With the level of political upheaval in many African countries, it is to be expected that more exiles would increasingly seek political asylum in the United States. The most likely countries from which these population movements might come include Sudan, Liberia, Sierra Leone, the Democratic Republic of the Congo, Côte d'Ivoire, Zimbabwe, Ethiopia, Eritrea, Rwanda, Burundi, and Kenya. As these exiles settle in their new communities, it is to be expected that they will build networks and institutions that both support them and provide philanthropic services for the exiles, as well as to those left behind in the home countries.

NEGOTIATING ETHNICITY: TENSIONS AND PHILANTHROPY

In the workplace, it is not unusual for the recent African immigrant to face animosity from native-born African Americans who consider the immigrant as taking jobs that ought to belong to African Americans. Some schoolteachers and university professors are also faced with students who claim not to understand their accents and colleagues and supervisors that suggest accent-altering classes. Many such individuals use the organizations that they belong to within the African immigrant communities as a resource base from which they get informal counseling and support as well as advice on how to assess such issues and the consequent anger and or insecurity that is experienced. The counseling and support received is often within the context of conversations with others at weekly meetings, parties, religious worship, and social events. Much of it is informal, and depends on an individual asking for and receiving help from people that they are most familiar with.

Within the four categories of *immigrant, migrant, exile*, and *refugee*, one can further identify some groups based on gender, socioeconomic class, age, religion, linguistic differences, and interest groups. These categories are even more interesting when considered as crosscutting each other in multiple dialectical interactions. By this I mean that a refugee for instance may be male/female/other; child/adult/youth/elderly, poor/middle class/wealthy, belong to a pressure group/community-based organization of Africans from one of five different regions/Africans from one of fifty-four countries/Africans from one of thousands of ethnicities/Africans from one of several thousand kinship groups/lineages. Such a person may be Christian (Lutheran, Baptist, Catholic, Methodist, Presbyterian, Pentecostal, Aládùúra, Coptic, Ethiopian Orthodox), or Muslim (from one of several paths established to worship the prophet Muhammad) or the individual may well be a believer in any one of the multitude of African traditional religions. These dialectical interactions mean that a holistic perspective cannot be taken toward issues related to African immigrant analysis across the board. Matters are further complicated by the immigrant African's relative newness to the American sociopolitical and economic systems and they come into an environment where Pan-Africanism resonates more profoundly than nationalism. There is also the further complication of lacking a voice that is clearly identifiable because an African could well be an African American whose family has been in the United States since the 17th Century or someone who just landed yesterday, fresh from the African continent. This being said, what philanthropic issues are thrown up by an inquiry into the circumstances of African immigrant communities?

We must consider a further distinction between documented and undocumented aliens. The number of African immigrants is minuscule when compared with that of other immigrant communities but it is no exaggeration to claim that undocumented immigrants are grossly undercounted. Among undocumented Francophone immigrants interviewed in the New York City Area, one paramount issue is what most of them call "papers." Many are hard working and even entrepreneurial. Some have established a deep, profound, and wide-ranging presence in the economy. However, they lack legal authorization to live in the United States. For these immigrants, support for amnesty for all immigrants would be a number one priority issue.

The group most threatened by the presence of African immigrants, be they documented or undocumented aliens, are African Americans. Many African Americans believe documented African immigrants unjustifiably benefit from Affirmative Action policies for which they did not struggle, and the historical underpinnings of which they either choose or refuse to understand. Many Africans indeed take the negative media portrayal of African Americans as unbiased truth and fail to recognize the long-term negative repercussions of racism, bias, and institutionalized injustice. Since the historical construction of blackness is the very antithesis of the purity of whiteness, most Africans tend to instinctively distance themselves from the stigma by claiming to be African, and not black. This complicates matters immensely because African Americans also assert their African identity. This is a testament to the relevance of the concept of intra-racial ethnicity developed by Irma Watkins-Owens. Her conceptualization was applied specifically to the case of people of African descent from the Caribbean, South America, New York and other parts of the North, as well as the Southern region of the United States in the Harlem section of New York City from 1900 to 1930. Despite this, it describes the tensions and potential for cooperation that could, and sometimes do exist in such communities today.

Historically, immigration also caused a great degree of anxiety among African Americans. Such anxiety has not been without good reason, since the rise of immigration as a source of free labor was also tied to the emancipation of enslaved African Americans. Black leaders of the day, including Frederick Douglass and Booker T. Washington, held radically different views on the causes and effects of the United States government's push for recruiting immigrant labor from Europe. However, most agreed that immigration has negative consequences for African Americans in the workplace. Unfortunately, the situation persists today. Immigrant blacks may face bias in the workplace, but they are still relatively more privileged than African Americans, particularly when they assert their non-African American-ness. It stands to reason then that the various communities of black people remains extremely tense. At the base of such tension is the competition for upward mobility and, in some cases, the need to demonstrate that one or the other community is the "ideal" black one. Immigrants tend to hold the belief that by hard work, they can show that they are not the stereotypical African American, and thus will be rewarded and embraced. Most African immigrants take negative experiences of race-based stigma as exceptions to the rule. Therefore the Amadou Diallo case – where an undocumented Guinean young man was mowed down in a hail of 41 gunshots by the members of the Special Task Force of the New York City Police Department in the vestibule of his own apartment house – was especially disturbing for many African immigrants who naively and erroneously believed that such violence would never be experienced if one did not deserve it.

Other issues that are high on the priority list for most African immigrants is access to affordable and good quality health care, access to English language classes for the Francophone, Lusophone, Arabic speaking, and to the population that speaks only one or several languages indigenous to Africa. When African immigrants are new to the United States, they tend to depend on their networks of friends and family for advice on how to access these services. Most new immigrants also pay out of pocket for health care and tend to only avail themselves to it on an emergency basis. Informal networks provide advisory services in different communities where needed. Two Nigerian doctors have sought to establish a free medical clinic in the Far Rockaway section of New York City, an area that is a very popular first place of settlement for many immigrant groups, including Africans.

As more African immigrants become active in local, state, and national politics, another source of tension may develop. The lines of disagreement are already being drawn, as indicated by disagreements over who should be counted as black in the 2000 census. African American leaders argued that all people of African descent should join the "Black Box Campaign" by only identify themselves as "Black or African American," whether or not they have other ancestry. Most black immigrants tend to identify as a national of their country of origin. Thus, they claim to be "Jamaican" or "Senegalese" rather than "Black or African American." For Professor Bolaji Aluko of Howard University, who is the coordinator of the Washington, DC-based African Expatriate Caucus, (AEC) "The category 'African American, Negro or Black' was not sufficiently descriptive of all the people in the group." Statistical data that are provided by Census Bureau, will continue to be unreliable if African immigrants do not identify themselves as such. Doing so would not only give an accurate number of immigrants, it would also enable the immigrants to show their "potential collective political power." Aluko also states: "At the end of the day, when you are trying to lobby Congress for a cause, people will ask you about your electoral clout . . . The benefit is that if they have the numbers on our groups, we can use them to influence policy on foreign affairs and immigration."

This discussion has wider ranging implications for people of African descent who also have other points of origin. If they "Check Black Only" as they are encouraged to do by the campaign of that name, where does this leave them in terms of the strongly felt need that they are not part of a homogenous whole that is fully and accurately described by the categorization "Black." This issue was raised by Charles Michael Byrd, publisher and editor of the New York-based magazine *Interracial Voice*, who recognizes the historical basis of the need for the racial categories in the census. The categories may have been an essential factor when Jim Crow laws had to be overturned through positive policy initiatives. For him, this rationale is no longer a necessary one, and thus, the policy should be abandoned. Since the census Figures are used to determine the service needs of various communities, when people are undercounted, they will also be under-served. The fiscal and economic losses are tremendous. However, for Byrd, the economic and fiscal losses should not justify over-counting. "The black community has been artificially inflated for decades by the numbers of multiracial peoples, . . . If black numbers decrease, that is where they should be. All the constitution calls for is simple enumeration of all Americans, not a count based on the pseudo-science of race, which has no biological basis" (Tanu, 2000).

The implications of the census issue for philanthropy is that reliable statistics are needed for advocates, government bureaucracies and philanthropic institutions and organizations in order to plan, disseminate information effectively, and locate services where they are most needed. If indeed people are to be encouraged to "Check Black," cooperation and collaboration among the various communities of people of African descent must also be vigorously pursued, and some power sharing must be undertaken. One of the problems is that it is unlikely for this to happen. Gate keeping by old power centers within the Black communities would still persist until the cost of maintaining the status quo become unbearable.

There are numerous tensions that militate against successful cooperation and collaboration among people of African descent in the United States. These tensions are strengthened by economic concerns among more established diasporic communities that African immigrants are taking away jobs that ordinarily would go to them. There are also feelings that African immigrants lack an understanding of the deep-rooted and pervasive nature of discrimination in American society. Alternatively, African American and African Caribbean people may feel that Africans try to take advantage of divide and conquer tactics that are deployed by racists, or that they unfairly benefit from affirmative action programs and policies that were achieved at great cost by earlier generations.

The problems and tensions among the various communities of people of African descent must be confronted, addressed, and diffused. African immigrants ought to make an effort to study African American history. This is particularly important because many Africans claim not to have studied anything related to something as basic as the history of enslavement of African Americans in their home countries. Knowledge is also crucial in other respects. Access to information about fair wages, labor standards, sources of employment and adequate benefits are all crucial. Broadening one's social network beyond those from one's home country is essential to gain this knowledge. This is of course, easier said than done. Many African immigrants not only exclusively socialize with those from their home countries, they only socialize with those from their country that speak their language.

Many community-based organizations that have established an institutional presence in the African immigrant community are organized around ethnicity. Other organizing factors include, but are not limited to professional specialization, religion, and social status. A few examples from the African immigrant community include, but are not limited to those described briefly below.

The *Association of Nigerian Physicians Abroad* engages in fund-raising for outreach to medically needy areas in Africa. Services, equipment and medicines are donated. The organization was involved in the pro-democracy movement in Nigeria from 1995 until there was a democratically elected government in Nigeria. The organization donated funding that sponsored exiled pro-democracy activists like Wole Soyinka and provided assistance in lobbying Congress in conjunction with pro-democracy interests for United States diplomatic and other assistance for encouraging democracy in Nigeria (Sayo, 1999). *Afénifére* is another Yoruba political group that is actively involved in Nigerian politics. At least one of its members, Dr. Sikiru Fadairo participated in the 2001 New York City Council elections for a district in Queens County.

Africamix is a nonprofit organization of volunteers seeking to use touring multicultural arts and music festival to promote global awareness and prevention on child abuse and neglect." To this end, the organization planned a year-round festival held in eighteen countries. Its goal was to "raise global consciousness and funding for the prevention of child abuse and neglect in black communities as a way of encouraging and supporting the nonprofit and non-governmental organizations providing residential services and therapeutic foster care for abandoned, abused, and neglected children" (www.africamix.com). Other goals include reaching out to children living with HIV/AIDS, street children, and addressing the problems of child abuse, child trafficking, children in pornography, child soldiers.

Other representative organizations include the *Association of Nigerian Lawyers* (which provides immigration and other services *pro bono* and facilitates networking among professionals in this field), and the *Africa Women's Fund*, launched in New York City in the Winter of 1999. The goal of this organization, founded by Joanne Foster from Ghana and Bisi Adeleye Fayemi from Nigeria., is to build an endowment that makes grants for philanthropic outreach to women.

Finally, the *Yoruba Alliance* was established in November 1996 with eight independent U.S.-based activist and progressive organizations. The *Alliance* is a community-based umbrella organization whose individual organizational members send five delegates to represent them at the Alliance General Assembly meeting which meets monthly.

DIRECTIONS FOR THE FUTURE

African immigrants need to engage in vigorous interactions, collaboration and relationships with those beyond the familiar ethnic, national, and regional boundaries that limit the depth and breadth of past and contemporary philanthropy. Faith-based institutions have in many ways led the effort to organize outreach to

African refugees. These efforts ought to be strengthened. One way to do this would be to create a database of service providers for the target population to document the nature of services that they provide that can be made available to community based organizations, churches mosques, and other houses of worship within the African immigrant community. The larger institutional philanthropic community must develop deeper and more extensive coalitions be with African community based organizations, professional associations, and faith-based organizations to identify issues, develop strategies, and use the expertise of Africans in the service of their own people. They need to be intimately and intricately connected to the communities that they purport to serve. This could be accomplished by recognition that African immigrants have considerable leadership skills that would, if mobilized, transform the face of advocacy, relief, and philanthropy.

This is only the beginning of research to identify and document African immigrant philanthropy. The most important point to be made is that these efforts are deeply grounded in the philosophical traditions of African peoples. They also draw upon Western modes of institutionalization. The danger is that the more the groups become institutionalized, to the extent that they associate modernity and progress with Westernization, the more they would lose the philosophical traditions that ground them. Without the involvement of and the participation of members of the African immigrant community, over time they will come to resemble your run of the mill philanthropic efforts that bear the stamp of Western homogeneity.

REFERENCES

Sayo, I. (1999). ANPA at work: At Ado-Ekiti . . . from America, Succour comes to Ado-Ekiti patients. *The Guardian* (Tuesday, 26 October) (at http://www.anpa.org/guardian.htm).

Tanu, T. H. (2000). Counting blacks in U.S. census 2000. (http://www.africana.com/DailyArticles/index_20000530.htm).

RELATIONS BETWEEN THE JEWISH AND CARIBBEAN AMERICAN COMMUNITIES IN NEW YORK CITY: PERCEPTIONS, CONFLICT AND COOPERATION

Holger Henke and J. A. George Irish

Race and Ethnicity in New York City
Research in Urban Sociology, Volume 7, 193–220
Copyright © 2004 by Elsevier Ltd.
All rights of reproduction in any form reserved
ISSN: 1047-0042/doi:10.1016/S1047-0042(04)07009-6

ABSTRACT

This study explores the history of conflict and future options for cooperation between two distinct ethnic groups in New York City, Caribbean-Americans and Jews. The argues, however, that relations between both groups cannot be read through the crude lens of "Black/Jewish relations." The article is divided in two major parts. In the first part, the authors explore the historical trajectory of relations between the two groups largely by focusing on the Crown Heights district in Brooklyn, home to a variety of Caribbean nationals, and the Jewish Lubavitcher Hasidic community. As the survey of historical material will reveal, in the late 1960s/early 1970s, issues pertaining to contestation over space and resources increasingly affected relations between both groups. A low point was reached in 1991 with the "Crown Heights unrest," which threw this part of Brooklyn into several days of openly violent conflict. Although – as Part II will demonstrate – issues such as crime, cultural peculiarities, access to resources and political influence, remain on the agenda, both groups have since managed to restore less conflict-prone and productive relationships. Although conflicts have been often couched in terms of these relations, additional cultural factors suggest that the conflict has been shaped by other dynamics.

INTRODUCTION

Throughout the 20th century, relations between African-Americans and Afro-Caribbeans, on the one hand, and Jewish people in the United States, on the other, have had their ups and downs.[1] Indeed, as various writers (Diner, 1997; Williams, 1997) have argued, their contradictory relationship "underscored a long-standing discrepancy between the ways Blacks and Jews 'saw' each other on a metaphoric level and the ways they 'saw' each other in the flesh" (Diner, 1997, p. 88). The messages in both communities of the metaphoric images of the respective other were – important for the investigative scope of this pilot study – more often than not formulated and voiced by their elites. Generally for Jews, however, African-Americans and other Black people were a group of "noble victims" of an oppressive system they themselves suffered from and to whom they had to show solidarity. Vice versa, for Blacks, Jewish people in the United States were not simply another group of Whites, but a group through which they could reflect on their own aspirations, fears and concerns. By reflecting upon each other in such terms, both groups tended to create metaphorical stereotypes of each other (Diner, 1997).

In recent years, a widespread perception has emerged that painted relations between African-Americans and Jews in terms of mutual distrust, decline, and conflict. Again, a cognitive disparity between images and the multi-faceted reality of Black-Jewish encounters in the United States seems to be at the center of, or at least deeply involved in, the trajectory of the declining relationship.

It is precisely this kind of broad, simplistic characterization, in the context of infinitely more nuanced encounters, that is itself part of the cause of the breakdown (Williams, 1997, p. 371). While Williams does not raise the question of the source of mutual accusations, his observation that the public use of racial epithets and characterizations suggests both groups have bought into the racial taxonomy proffered by American mainstream society, leads to the question as to what role do leadership and rank and file of both communities play in the diffusion of stereotypical characterizations of the respective "other" (Williams, 1997, p. 372).

In New York City, since the early 1970s the closest encounter on a regular basis between Afro-Caribbeans and Jews occurs in the Crown Heights section of Brooklyn. There are about 15,000 people in Brooklyn's Crown Heights who belong to the highly visible Lubavitcher Hasidic faith. Crown Heights community is a majority Black community of about 200,000 people where African-Americans live alongside immigrants from many different Caribbean islands.[2] In recent years, however, open animosity and incidents of violence marred community relations in Brooklyn. In August 1991, the orthodox Jewish graduate student Yankel Rosenbaum was fatally stabbed by a group of Black youths as an act of revenge for a car accident earlier that day which killed a seven-year old Guyanese boy named Gavin Cato and critically injured his cousin. Three nights of rioting followed during which groups of Black and Hasidic residents clashed in the streets, Jewish families were attacked in their homes, and shops operated by Black, White, and Asian merchants were looted. Black youths marched to the world headquarters of the Lubavitchers on Eastern Parkway, where some threw stones and bottles and shouted anti-Semitic slogans. While most West Indians condemned the violence, some outside "leaders" seized the opportunity to put themselves into the limelight of the press.

Although many authors make fleeting reference to these conflicts, there have to this date been only very few in-depth studies of the motives, perceptions and economic realities underpinning them.[3] Without doubt, the particular markings of the conflicts (as well as the existing cooperation) in Crown Heights raise the question as to whether it can only be "read" in terms of the disintegration of a historic alliance. It is important to point out that African-Caribbeans and Lubavitch Hasidics differ in significant ways from the larger communities they are often identified with. While the Hasidic community by their dress and appearance do not blend with either Whites or Gentiles, which exposes and "marks" them in the eye of the larger public, many African-Caribbeans take a different view of American society and issues of race than their African-American brothers and sisters.[4] In fact, both Caribbean-Americans and Hasids are, to varying degrees, at odds with their respective "reference groups" (i.e. African-Americans and Jewish/White). To some extent, therefore, the issue here is precisely "whether unassimilated racial, ethnic, and immigrant groups can live in peace not just with another, but within a culture that resolutely denies their particularity as just too *unpleasant*" (Williams, 1997, p. 372). To put it differently, instead of simply interpreting conflicts and cooperation between Caribbean-Americans and Jewish communities (including Hasids) through a "Blacks vs. Jews" lens, the larger question in the background of this pilot study is to what extent the relations between both groups are informed by the earlier observed tendencies of immigrant groups to buy into the racial taxonomy of the host country.

Nevertheless, this study acknowledges that both (sub-) groups operate within the imposed discourses of their respective "reference group." That is probably even more true for African-Caribbeans than for Hasidic Jews because of the latter's strict life-style and religio-sectarian world-views which tend to shield them more from ideas and concepts they perceive as secular and/or Gentile.[5] By virtue of their everyday (imposed or chosen) identification with African-Americans, Caribbean-Americans are relatively more susceptible to discourses and concepts originating in that community.

OBJECTIVES, METHODOLOGY, AND THEORETICAL CONSIDERATIONS

Given the paucity of empirical data and analysis about perceptions, conflict, and cooperation between Jewish and Caribbean people in Brooklyn, the first objective of this research project was to collect pertinent information about this relationship, which allows us to draw conclusions about the dynamics involved. Several aspects are of importance:

(1) Given their historical relationships and current public information in the media and education system, a survey probing into the conflicts and possibilities for re-energized cooperation between both groups should first attempt to get a keen grasp of the perceptions both groups have of each other. In order to assess the distance between perceptions and the actual extent of cooperation and conflict, researchers need to have an objective yardstick by which to assess the character of mutual prejudice and misperceptions. These views were collected

from community leaders who in various ways represent or work in, or for, the respective communities.

(2) The leaders and organizers of both communities also were asked for an objective account of the current state of interaction between their particular institution/organization/church/synagogue and the respective other group. That is, the survey intended to arrive at an objective measure of the extent to which both sides interact not just in ephemeral and casual ways, but also in structured and organized settings.

(3) To the extent that this research report also intends to introduce greater levels of mutual understanding and suggest approaches to conflict resolution, an attempt was made to interpret and contextualize the perceptions both groups have of each other and to explain their deeper cultural significance. One measure to achieve this is to introduce a historical account of the community relations into the analysis. If both groups can recognize the extent of their historical relationship they are – perhaps – more likely to open up to each other. Of course, ultimately this depends on the degree to which media and community leaders will disseminate this information to their constituents and act upon this information.

Given the scope and objectives of this study, a two-pronged approach was taken:

First, a search of archives and libraries was undertaken in order to produce a historical overview of the relations between Jewish and Caribbean communities in the city. The researchers' interest was to find internal documents, position and policy papers, and accounts of events reported in the media that helped answer the questions outlined above. Since the amount of materials is limited and much of the collective memory of Caribbean-Americans is preserved by memory and tales, an oral history component was added to this approach. A series of interviews with elderly Caribbean-American residents in New York was conducted in order to gather a sufficient amount of primary source material to formulate an informed view.

Secondly, two sets of interviews were prepared which sought to elicit views of the respective other group. A series of open, or semi-structured interviews (where not available to be administered as questionnaires) were held with relevant leaders of the Hasidic Jewish and the Caribbean-American community.

The sample selection method was a combination of a systematic sample and a snowball-type sample. Respondents were drawn from community organizations, the media, and political activists based in or concerned with the community districts of Crown Heights, Flatbush, and East Flatbush in Brooklyn which were identified in collaboration with consultants, leaders, and activists in the Jewish and Caribbean communities. The sample units were individuals. All interviews were audiotaped with the consent of the interviewees, who had also been made aware of their rights under CUNY's standard agreements that apply for such research.

Since this pilot study confined itself to objective and self-appointed leaders in both communities, it is appropriate to consider the general position such individuals occupy within the hierarchy of any society. As indicated in the introduction, elite views may in significant ways differ from the views of the community they supposedly represent. In the past, systems theory and functionalism presupposed that society is held together by a common set of values, while conflict theory pitted different sociological groups against each other, emphasizing the unequal distribution of power and class-specific interests. In practice, however, representation of a community by community leaders, even by democratically elected officials, may represent a combination of the above. Thus, while there may be an actual sharing of values, leaders often tend to (re)interpret these if, when, and to the degree to which these values might threaten their position. To put it positively, community leaders are likely to support positions that are, at a minimum, not contrary to their position of relative privilege, and to emphasize positions that actually support their leadership position, even if this runs contrary to significant sentiments in the community they supposedly represent.

With regard to the communities investigated in this pilot study, the following can be said regarding the relative representation distance between leadership and community. In the Hasidic Jewish community, which constitutes the study's main sample of Jewish citizens in Brooklyn, the distance between community leaders and community is very small. Two reasons account for this: (1) the community is very closely knit, some would even say sectarian, which is internally guaranteed by the strict adherence to Talmudic doctrine, and externally demonstrated by its members' uniform appearance of dress; and (2) individualism and ambition for public recognition (for its own sake) are generally more discouraged than reinforced (as in American mainstream culture). With regard to the Caribbean-American focus group of this study, it is obvious that despite its relative open religiousness, it is largely a secular community. This alone accounts for a relatively greater distance between leadership and community. Indeed, there have been instances where the Caribbean community in Brooklyn did not elect members from its midst to public office because it perceived them as not representing their interests adequately or sufficiently (Holder, 1990, p. 24).[6] A contemporary example of this is former State Senator Marty Markowitz who comes from a district that has a majority of Caribbean and African-American residents.[7] In past surveys, over 60% of Caribbean-Americans indicated that their choice for a politician would not be determined by race (Riviere & Winborne, 1990, p. 63).

In addition, while African-Americans and African-Caribbeans share substantial concerns about (a history of) racial discrimination, the fact that a significant part of the leadership of the "Black community" of overwhelmingly Caribbean districts in Brooklyn actually consists of African-Americans, and not Afro-Caribbeans, also points to the fact that a certain cultural distance between the representatives and the represented might be lurking in some of the interpretations offered by some interviewees in this study. The obvious implication of these factors is that the voices of Afro-Caribbean representatives in the community will have to be read with much greater skepticism regarding their representativeness of the wider community, than the statements made by Jewish Hasidic community leaders as representatives of their own community. From the point of this study, however, it is also important to keep in mind that members (both "leaders" and other residents) of both communities utilize their commentary on the issues raised in the interviews to define, demarcate and locate the (unstable and contested) place and identity of their community (see also Goldschmidt, 2000, p. 42).

From a methodological point of view, it is important to note that the media consciously or unconsciously advance the identification of the Afro-Caribbean/Hasidic conflict with "Black-Jewish relations." Much of the media reports utilized in this study therefore promotes this doubly abridged interpretation of the conflict. In contrast to this, our point of departure – as already indicated – will attempt to stress that the Afro-Caribbean/Jewish relationship has been a dynamic one that has changed over the years, has had different dynamics, and has been framed in varying concepts applying different keywords and categories, symbolic tropes, and racial and ethnic signifiers. This study also acknowledges that the Afro-Caribbean/Hasidic conflicts of more recent years are only one aspect of the larger painting of Black-Jewish relationship. By inquiring into the nature and characteristics of Afro-Caribbean/Hasidic conflict and cooperation, this pilot study hopes to demonstrate the much more complex and often contradictory nature of the Black Atlantic world and its relations with other minorities.

BLACK-JEWISH RELATIONS IN BROOKLYN (NEW YORK) IN HISTORICAL PERSPECTIVE

Since the 1991 violence that erupted in the Crown Heights section of Brooklyn, it has become apparent in the mind of the media and much of the public that contemporary relations between Black people and Jews in the United States are being framed in terms of "race" and ethnic difference.[8] However, it remains an open question whether these categories really capture the variety and complexity of fundamental social contradictions and tensions between both groups in an appropriate manner. That there is sufficient reason to doubt this has been pointed out recently by an analyst who appropriately reminds us "the neighborhood is

caught in a tangled web of multiple, competing and intersecting axes of difference"
(Goldschmidt, 2000, p. 4). A historical analysis of the interface between both
groups might reveal that conflicts are not (or not always) about issues of "race"
and ethnic matters, even if these issues have always been lurking close beneath
the surface. In addition, taking a *longue durée* perspective will demonstrate that –
contrary to the filtered images of the media – cooperation between both groups is
another significant facet of the relationship.

Residents of Brooklyn and, in particular, of Crown Heights have been comprised
of different ethnicities and "races." In fact, parts of today's Crown Heights (or
Crow Hill, as it was known then) started out in the first half of the 19th century as
a sparsely populated, predominantly African-American, semi-rural settlement on
the outskirts of New York City. Following substantial development in the late 19th
century, the ethnic and "racial" composition of the area became significantly more
diversified – a process which in essence left the African-American settlements in
the area marginalized. By the same token, the Black population became a minority
while other parts of Crown Heights were developed into solidly middle class
areas populated by a broad range of European immigrants.[9] From the late 1910s
to the late 1950s, Crown Heights was an overwhelmingly White neighborhood,
predominantly and increasingly Jewish. According to New York City estimates,
in 1950 the neighborhood was some 89% White (50–60% thereof Jewish – see
Goldschmidt, 2000, p. 108) and 11% African-American. Nevertheless, in the 1940s
and 1950s an influx of African-Americans from the South and a small number of
Afro-Caribbeans led to a tripling of the Black population.

Lubavitch Hasidic Jews also started to move in greater numbers into the
area in and after 1940 in their escape from the Nazi Holocaust.[10] Although
the Lubavitchers were apparently also perceived as an "oddity" by secular Jews
living in the area, the subsequent and familiar "White flight" was more due to
the White fears of Black people and the possibility to move due to upward
mobility. With secular Jews and other Whites leaving the area, Crown Heights
and adjoining neighborhoods become more clearly defined by the presence of
African-Americans, Afro-Caribbeans and the Lubavitcher Hasidic Jews who had
– based on religious reasons – made a strategic decision not to join the White
exodus from the area. The steady, absolute and relative growth of the Black
population in Crown Heights flipped over the ethnic and "racial" composition
in the 1960s and 1970s; while in 1960 Crown Heights was still 70% White,
by 1970 it was 70% Black (City Planning Commission, 1973, Table 3.3). Rapid
growth in the Hasidic communities continued throughout the 1950s. Due to the
White flight process and the Lubavitcher distinct way of dressing, the Lubavitcher
Hasidic Jewish population in Crown Heights gained much greater visibility on the
streets of the neighborhood. In fact, while in the wider society the relationship is

reversed, White (Lubavitcher) Jews in a matter of a few years became an easily identified (White) minority in the midst of a community predominantly inhabited by people of color. Given the history and persistently widespread practice of "racial" discrimination in the United States, this inverted relationship between "majority" and "minority" in the narrow space of Crown Heights was quite likely bound to lead to tensions.[11] Certainly, from the early days of this heightened – and, arguably, externally imposed – contradiction, both communities were acutely aware of the respective "other."

There is not much, easily accessible, documented material available about the trajectory of this relationship from, say, the 1940s onward.[12] Some tantalizing information can be glanced from the creative writing and memoirs of this period. Thus, in Paule Marshall's (1981, pp. 11, 70) novel *Brown Girl, Brownstones* the protagonist's mother spends long days "scrubbing the Jew floor" to make a " 'few raw-mout' pennies at the end of one day which would eventually 'buy house' " and, in the process, picking up "old clothes which the Jews had given them." Without doubt, this points to the unequal social position and class difference between some members of both communities. Even more pronounced is this perceived relationship in the comment by a neighborhood storekeeper, which evokes similar post-Emancipation social relationships back in the Caribbean:

> They gone now to lick out their money in the bars and whiskey stores. I tell you, these people from down South does work for the Jew all week and give the money right back to he on Sat'day night like it does burn their hand to it (Marshall, 1981, p. 38).

However, neither was this social relationship a one-way street, nor was it entirely determined by socioeconomic class. Apart from these factors, elements of ethnic difference also played a role in the shaping of this relationship.[13] Although all elements of ethnic, "racial" and socio-economic differentiation clearly existed, it seems equally clear that neither of them had gained a clear ascendancy in defining the political and discursive dynamics of the relationship. Certainly, the issue of "race" had not yet started to poison (or, depending on one's perspective, enable) the relationship. Thus, it is not surprising to hear the voice of solidarity speaking loudly from Paule Marshall's (1981) book:

> But c'dear, these White people getting on too bad. They say that Hitler put all the Jews in a gas chamber. But you know, somebody oughta take up a gun so and shoot down that man so, 'cause he's nothing but the devil-incarnate (Marshall, 1981, p. 69).

And by way of a reply, this larger truth:

> It's these politicians. They're the ones always starting up all this lot of war. And what they care? It's the poor people got to suffer and mothers with their sons (Marshall, 1981, p. 69).

Does the apparent paucity of sources and (published) accounts mean that Blacks and Jews in Crown Heights simply got along better from the 1940s through the 1960s? The question is hard to answer without more systematic research on the early trajectories of "Black-Jewish" relations in Brooklyn. However, the above glimpses from the 1940s, 50s, and 60s would seem to suggest that the relationship was more fluid, less politicized and more open (and, perhaps, open-minded), than in the latter decades of the 20th and into the opening decade of the 21st century.

As the neighborhood continued to change – becoming the center of Caribbean life in the United States, while dwarfing the Lubavitcher community – the quest for territorial space also seemed to engender challenges for, and shifts in, the definition of identity, the cultural hegemony in, and the character of, Crown Heights.[14] Both communities, the Afro-Caribbean *and* the Lubavitcher, have over the years been growing persistently. While the Afro-Caribbean community has expanded readily into other neighborhoods, the Crown Heights Lubavitcher community has expanded both inwardly and outwardly, and in an effort to sustain its relative cultural homogeneity, attempted to acquire space both within and in the immediate vicinity of its core settlement and (international) religious center – the synagogue on 770 Eastern Parkway.

As we will proceed to describe below, issues of contest over limited space and the terms under which both communities interact and face each other increasingly became public concerns (read: media attention) during the 1960s and 1970s, but also persist until today. Hasidic Jews living in Crown Heights often framed their concerns about housing and economic development in the area in terms of class. Indeed, while they resisted the "White flight" out of Crown Heights, both Lubavitchers and middle class people of color became concerned about the influx of welfare residents into often decaying apartment houses. However, against the apparent expectation of some activists in either community, this was not to become the basis for a "natural alliance" (Lichtenstein, 1974). Rather, both communities continued to steadily drift apart. One particular contentious issue was the formation and presence of Hasidic patrols. It has been reported that these patrols often stopped Blacks running for a bus or to meet an appointment and would question them for their identity. In cases where there was a refusal to produce identity papers, this would sometimes result in attempts to arrest them or other forms of harassment. Rightly or wrongly, the Hasidic community perceived the need to protect itself against "outsiders" they accused of perpetrating criminal acts (e.g. street robbery, theft, burglary) within their community.[15] However, these vigilante groups over the years proved relatively resistant against joining forces with the Black community.[16] The fact that they repeatedly stopped Black citizens in the streets to harass them, (illegally) demanded identification papers or even tried to arrest them, clearly show that consciously or unconsciously, as well as gradually, parts of the Hasidic community have bought into the racial taxonomy of American mainstream society, which puts African-Americans and African-Caribbeans at the bottom of the social ladder and promotes subtle psychological fears of Black bodies and Black men in particular.[17]

Although these vigilante groups go back to the 1960s, they became a particular concern in the late 1970s when, in two unrelated incidents within three days, a Black Crown Heights community leader died in police custody, and a 16-year-old Black youth was beaten into a coma by a group of young Hasidic men (Krebs & Rubenstein, 1964; Raab, 1978). In subsequent community activism both issues were tied together to underscore the relative powerlessness of the Crown Heights Black community (Raab, 1978; Wilkins, 1978). There was a clear feeling at this juncture that – as one Jamaican community leader put it – "that the 1960s are over" and that outsiders (i.e. people not from Crown Heights) "looking for political openings" were no longer tolerated by both communities (Vecsey, 1978).

In late December 1976, the respective quests for space and (political) control over it became publicly visible when the Hasidic community lobbied against the proposed, inclusive, Community District H. Lobbying for greater voice in the affairs of their immediate neighborhood, Hasidic leaders and residents argued for a division of the proposed District H and the creation of a separate community district (Fowler, 1976a). As one Hasidic community leader put it back then, whether the additional community board (Community Planning District 9), which the community was eventually granted by the City of New York, was primarily meant to "improve the community for everyone" can be doubted (Collins, 1976).[18] Equally questionable was the proclaimed interest of some leaders in the Black community in implementing the City Charter's intention to draw planning-board boundaries along historical, geographical and traditional community lines, which – given the history of Crown Heights – was not an unambiguously objective claim grounded in the settlement history, geography or ethnic demographics of Crown Heights. Rather, behind both claims stood thinly veiled and quite clearly perceived interests of local power distribution. While the Hasidim in the newly created District 9 still remained a minority of about 40%, they undoubtedly stood to gain considerable influence, which many Black community activists and residents angrily denounced as, in the words of the Rev. Robert Hardman, the conferral of "a special place and privilege on one people at the expense of another" (Fowler, 1976b).

However, looking back on this and other incidents, it would appear as if it could also be interpreted as an attempt by some politicians or community organizers to seek control over a less tightly organized community (the Afro-Caribbean) and to assert itself over a better organized, if numerically smaller, community (the Lubavitchers). This was done by mobilization behind public appeals to "racial" identity.[19] Obviously there was a measure of representational disjunction involved, reflected in the criticism by a Black resident who remarked that the whole dispute reflected the "connivance of politicians" over issues that could perhaps also be seen as somewhat removed from the real seats of power in the city (Browne & Todd, 1978; Clines, 1976; Jetter, 1989; Vecsey, 1978).

From yet another perspective the question arises whether issues of minorities can be resolved by simply juggling with numbers. Indeed, ultimately the issue is rather whether the rationality of numbers is by itself sufficient to establish democratic legitimacy and just representation.[20] After the dust had settled in late 1976, some community leaders pointed to this larger question. Thus, the Rev. Clarence Norman voiced his view: "I really feel the point is in Genesis – where Cain asks God, 'Am I my brother's keeper?' – and I definitely feel the answer is 'yes' " (Clines, 1976). And, echoing this more sophisticated approach to the question of community and representation, Rabbi Arnold Wolf cautioned: "What is the difference, I ask, where the lines are drawn if you truly believe in living together." Indeed, then, the more pertinent questions may be of a moral or ethical nature, such as one of good vs. bad representation, or – better yet – good vs. bad politicians.

To be sure, as hinted at already, over the years a number of initiatives and community organizations emerged that sought to address and redress conflicts between both communities. Mostly these efforts centered on specific and tightly circumscribed issues, on which both communities sought alleviation of tensions. These included community/vigilante policing, rent issues, etc. Only relatively few institutions emerged that sought to improve community relationship by sharing spaces and events for common activities that were not of an immediately utilitarian nature. Some of these groups include the *Crown Heights Clergy Council, Mothers to Mothers, Project CARE (Community Alliance Revitalization Effort), Dr. Laz & The CURE/Project CURE*, the *Crown Heights Youth Collective*, the *Crown Heights Community Mediation Center*,[21] and the *Crown Heights Coalition*. All of these have been laudable initiatives that deserve full support by all communities involved. However, several of these projects have had a relatively short life span and were mostly active in times of crisis. This unsteadiness in institutional community relations speaks to a lack of resources dedicated to this important aspect of ethnic relations in Crown Heights. Greater levels of financial commitment from City and State Administrations, which would allow for the establishment of a permanent center for Jewish/Hasidic and Caribbean- and African-American communities, are therefore highly recommended. Probably most likely to succeed are approaches that include or are built around interfaith initiatives which aim to celebrate biblical stories (e.g. the Exodus story) dear to both communities, or that attempt to alleviate tangible socio-economic problems.

The gap between both communities, however, remains large and would appear to require a structured and permanent approach to improve perceptions and mutual understanding (Beiles, 1998; Safer, 1997). Given this situation, it was – certainly from a perspective of liberal political theory and (Christian) communitarianism – surprising to read statements by several Lubavitcher Hasidic leaders closely related to some of the above mentioned community relations improvement efforts to the effect that there should be no interaction between Hasidic and Caribbean-American children. Thus, one rabbi was quoted as saying, "Jewish children should be playing games with Jewish children. Black children should be playing with Black children. Just leave each other alone"; another leader added, "All [Hasidic children] should have their minds on is education. Being that that is their primary goal, neighborhood relations and community relations is only a hindrance to their progress" (Pogrebin, 1992/1993). While not premised on racial or other prejudice, in this case a narrowly defined approach to education would appear to exclude the most promising place to start improving understanding and tolerance – that is, among the youth – from any and all efforts of bringing both communities together.

The issue clearly speaks to the fact that on some issues both groups will only be able to agree to disagree. It also poses a profound epistemological challenge to Caribbean-Americans (and, indeed, the wider society) to increasingly think "understanding" in terms of including the *impossibility* of fully understanding others and to conceive of community not as a result of sameness, but as encompassing various degrees of autonomously defined, unassimilated "otherness." As followers of Christian and/or liberal political theory, Caribbean-Americans – as all of mainstream America – need to learn to accept that there are groups that simply wish to be left alone in certain aspects of sharing urban public spaces. The worldviews of both Caribbean-Americans and Hasidim are in many respects just too contrary to allow for standard liberal democratic initiatives. It will require permanent initiatives aimed at allowing both communities to create the mechanisms and approaches which will, if only temporarily, help to bring both sides closer together in shared activities.

Nevertheless, living together in a very confined and densely populated urban space, Caribbean-Americans and the Lubavitcher Hasidim would both seem to have respective obligations that make human and good neighborly relations a possibility and, hopefully, a permanent reality. John Rawls, one of the most widely quoted liberal philosophers and author of the seminal work *A Theory of Justice*, recently staked the field that has to be negotiated by both communities and their respective leadership the following way:

> We recognize that a liberal society is to respect its citizens' comprehensive doctrines – religious, philosophical, and moral – provided that these doctrines are pursued in ways compatible with a reasonable political conception of justice and its public reason. Similarly, we say that, provided a nonliberal society's basic institutions meet certain specified conditions of political right and

justice and lead its people to honor a reasonable and just law for the Society of Peoples, a liberal
people is to tolerate and accept that society (Rawls, 1999, pp. 59–60).

The second sentence of this quotation would seem to speak to Caribbean-
Americans and other peoples in their attempts to come to grips with Hasidic cultural
worldviews and customs. In Rawls' conceptualization, liberalism requires the
toleration of peoples with differently defined concepts of justice, and he suggests
that a liberal people should "suppose that a decent society, when offered due respect
by liberal peoples, may be more likely, over time, to recognize the advantages of
liberal institutions and take steps toward becoming more liberal on its own" (Rawls,
1999, p. 62).[22] Equally, now presumably speaking to communities such as the
Lubavitcher Hasidim, Rawls stipulates an obligation for "decent peoples" that
includes recognition of the laws of peace, a system of law that follows "a common
good idea of justice that takes into account what it sees as the fundamental interests
of everyone in society," and a sincere adherence of officials to the belief that the
law is guided by this idea (Rawls, 1999, p. 67).

Rawls's work has been justly criticized for relying too much on decontextualized
and abstract procedural rules which are premised on liberal notions of
individualism and the alleged existence of a separated, autonomous, atomistic
self (Sandel, 1982). With its critics among the communitarianist schools, liberal
political theory shares a logic of identity as the meta-theoretical basis on which
its prescriptions rest. In other words, both schools are conceiving a community of
implicitly or explicitly shared values, which unfortunately leaves little room for
perceived "others." As Young (1990, p. 235) argues, "The ideal of community [. . .]
validates and reinforces the fear and aversion some social groups exhibit toward
others." What Rawls and much of political liberalism fail to grasp is that societies
and communities fundamentally different from Western traditions (also) have to
be understood on their own terms, rather than from the vantage point of the West.[23]

In the light of these positions, it seems apparent that both communities could
improve relations by promoting adjustments in their attitudes toward the other
community. From this vantage point, therefore, both communities would seem to
be called upon to make a considerable inward stretch and outward reach.[24] The
direction of this "reaching stretch" has to be the search for what Martin Buber
(1965, p. 19, emphasis added) called "genuine dialogue," that is, dialogue "where
each of the participants really has in mind the other or others *in their present
and particular being* and turns to them with the intention of establishing a living
mutual relation between himself and them."[25] In a colloquy as such, both sides,
as individuals and as collectives, are likely to discover that "to be human is to be
intended toward the other" (Spivak, 1999, p. 46).

INTERVIEWING COMMUNITY LEADERS
IN BROOKLYN

Two main findings emerged from the interviews conducted with leaders in the Caribbean-American and the Jewish community in Brooklyn.[26] Most obvious is that the cadre of leaders on both sides has become more aware of the other side's idiosyncrasies. This does not necessarily mean an endorsement, but has helped to evolve a working consensus in certain specific areas of common interest. The new awareness has also translated into higher levels of understanding and tolerance in public statements about the other group. Clearly much ground still has to be covered, and the increased sophistication of many community leaders does not necessarily translate to the rank-and-file or throughout all leadership circles, but progress certainly has been made in the past ten or so years.

The second major finding is that there is a profound gap in perception between both communities that will be hard or impossible to ever close. We are referring here to what is often called a person's or a group's *Weltanschauung* or world-view. However, this gap in perception really goes further and deeper than just a divergence of interests or differences of value-systems and customs. What is in many ways at the root of misunderstandings are different epistemologies. That is to say, the ways that both communities extract and construct knowledge from the natural and social phenomena impacting on their lives, adhere to different belief systems about their role in the larger scheme of things. Consequently, the logics according to which they live their lives as individuals and as a group among other groups are fundamentally different from each other and just as susceptible to disruption from another logic (or way of life, if you prefer) as mathematical logic has been proven brittle by Russell's paradox. Thus, Caribbean-Americans raised in the Christian tradition believe (whether they are Christians or not) that ideally all people should "come together and live as one," the fraternity of all humanity. On the other hand, Lubavitcher Hasids regard themselves as the elect, a chosen group of God, and extend the title of "brother" only to fellow-Jews. While this certainly does not rule out respect for all human life and the pursuit of good, neighborly relations – as prescribed by basic Jewish law of the Talmud, it nevertheless draws a line between Hasidic-Jewish communitarianism and Hasidic relations with non-Jews.[27] From a perspective of Christian values, however, it is enormously difficult to draw a strict distinction between a fraternity imbued with Jacobin notions of egalitarianism and a communion steeped in separatism and religious mysticism. It is this incisive epistemological chasm which lies at the very root of many other misunderstandings and misperceptions in both communities.

Despite the observed improvements in mutual awareness of each other's idiosyncrasies, the interviews also revealed pockets of latent stereotypes on both sides. Indeed, while both groups tried to carefully differentiate when making statements about the other group, in many interviewees a lingering "we-they" dichotomy was never far away from the surface of these answers. One respondent, Dr. Polly McLean,[28] a part-time management consultant in Congressman Major Owens' office, made the following comment about the need to give the relations between both communities an economic basis (as opposed to symbolic bridge-building): "Build me some economic bridges. Get me in the diamond industry. That's building bridges. Those are sustaining; the others are temporary." While it is acknowledged that economic empowerment is an important issue for the Black community, the obvious stereotypical assumption expressed in this statement is that many (most?) Jews in the United States are linked to wealth and in the position to provide bridges for economic empowerment of the African- and Caribbean-American community.

Dr. McLean also pointed out that in office meetings with orthodox/Hasidic community leaders she has become "very conscious of . . . not being in there," since "being a woman and being black was not something that they would have accepted." Her statement, however, may well reflect a self-imposed restriction resulting from her or Major Owens' office's perceptions about Hasidic "set characteristics about women's roles or where women should be." Certainly she did not say that Hasidic leaders requested that she not attend meetings, and it appears unlikely that this would have occurred.[29] Caribbean-Americans' (mis)perceptions about the particularly suppressed role of women in Hasidic communities are also easily put into perspective by reading, for example, St. Paul's statements in the New Testament about women (I Corinthians 11: 3–10). In marked contrast to McLean's views, New York City Jamaican-American Council member Una Clarke opined that as a woman she has learned to appreciate and "give deference" to the different customs of ethnic groups other than her own, because "I want people to give deference to me for my culture, my upbringing, my own religion and the way in which I practice it." In her view, special treatment of women by the Hasidic community is to be regarded as an aspect of the traditions and customs that "make you who you are."

Another interviewee, Michael Behrman, project director of Operation Survival, a Crown Heights community organization for the prevention of substance abuse, pointed out that the Hasidic community is a separatist culture and as such "we're not looking for unity, but for harmony" – a theme that reverberated through several interviews with Jewish and Hasidic leaders. As Behrman explains the rationale behind this separatism: "We're priests and as a priesthood we have to be separate [. . .] we're not supposed to play basketball with black kids," not so much because it is a distraction, but rather because it is regarded as undermining Jewish values; and – somewhat in the mystic register of Hasidic philosophy – "We'll be in the world when the Messiah comes."[30] This stance reverberates the opinions of the Lubavitcher Grand Rebbe Menachem Schneerson, expressed some 30 years ago. Thus, Dr. Heron Sam, a Guyanese immigrant, remarked that when he reached out in the early 1970s to the spiritual leader of the Hasidic community to improve relations between both groups, he received a one-liner answer saying: "The Hasidic community has no dealings with the Black community in Crown Heights and there can be no relation between us. – Signed Menachem Schneerson."

There is also an interesting gap in the perception of the oppression suffered in the United States. To the question whether Jews and Blacks in the United States have suffered similar oppression, much greater efforts to differentiate were made by Jewish leaders. Caribbean-American community leaders were generally much more inclined to see the parallels while Jewish leaders generally went to greater lengths to explain differences between patterns of oppression suffered by both groups.[31] Thus, for example, Assemblyman Clarence Norman, an African-American political representative of Crown Heights, points out that because both groups suffered comparable oppression there should actually be a "natural alliance – Blacks and Jews – because we are people who have been oppressed." A more differentiated view expressed by several Jewish leaders was perhaps articulated best by Rabbi Bob Kaplan,[32] who pointed out that Jews on the whole have become an "empowered minority," while "African-Americans on the whole are still not as empowered, they're more disenfranchised on many different levels." In Kaplan's view "the color line has a lot do with it, Jews have the ability to pass . . . while African-Americans don't." Bentzion Meltzer, a Hasidic community leader and project director of the inter-ethnic Project CARE, makes the following distinction:

> Every people who are oppressed, are oppressed in a different manner by those who oppress them, and that changes throughout history . . . [. . .] The oppression that happens in Georgia or Alabama is not the same oppression that happens in New York or Montana.

While none of these views is "wrong," they, again, seem to reflect different historical experiences, and distinct epistemological or religio-ideological *vistas*, and reflect not so much each community's level of preparedness to engage with others, but rather their different modes of this engagement and the results expected from it. An interesting difference of perception also emerged between both communities with regard to the 1991 unrest in Crown Heights. While Jewish and Hasidic interviewees did not object to the term "riots," which was used in our questionnaire, several Caribbean-American community leaders rejected this term.

Despite obvious differences in views between both communities, one has to be careful not to lend too much weight to these gaps in perception. All of the above does not mean that there is no genuine desire on the part of the Hasidic community to live in peace and in a relationship of mutual respect with African-Caribbeans (and, indeed, all other non-Jews), but the rigid religious prescriptions imposed on the Hasidic "priesthood" put the onus of understanding and pro-active accommodation squarely on the shoulders of the Caribbean-American population. At the same time, however, this separatist stance tends to obstruct attempts in the Hasidic community to gain a better grasp of the special experience Caribbean-Americans have historically had in their contacts with (non-Jewish) Whites and how difficult, therefore, it can be for Black Caribbeans to make the required outward reach to a group that they primarily perceive as "White."[33] Thus, while Caribbean-Americans do not regard themselves as a "priesthood," there are definitely tacit and sometimes unacknowledged separatist ideas (i.e. vis-à-vis Whites) permeating their community as well. To the extent, then, that the Hasidic worldview prevents a better grasp of the specific needs of Black Caribbeans and Americans, the responsibility for improving relations is reflected back on the Lubavitcher community as well. This would seem to be a consequence of the liberal notion of reciprocity.[34] In this context it is also interesting to note that, in general, our Caribbean-American interviewees appeared to be more aware and knowledgeable of the existence and social situation of Jewish communities in the West Indies, than the Jewish/Hasidic interviewees themselves.[35]

There are encouraging signs of attempts to perform exactly such epistemological splits. There can be little doubt that at the leadership level of the Caribbean community in Crown Heights, great efforts have been and continue to be made to reach out and to promote a greater understanding and acceptance of their Hasidic-Jewish neighbors' idiosyncrasies. At a certain level there is indeed a genuinely felt respect for their achievements and strengths as a community. Thus, Sam Palmer, a community activist who came to the United States from Jamaica, pointing out that "some of them treat me better than my own people," emphasizes the need for the Caribbean and Black communities to come together and work on their own projects, rather than, as he perceives it, focus too much energies on decrying the efforts made by others. Assemblyman Norman points to the fact that there is more even-handed sharing of public resources in Crown Heights than there used to be twenty years ago and that his attempts to represent the Hasidic community have actually led him to keeping a yarmulke in his car. Despite the distinction noted earlier, there were a few voices in the Jewish community as well who saw parallels between the Jewish and Caribbean/African-American experience of oppression in the United States.

The absoluteness of Hasidic "separatism" may also have become more contested within the Hasidic community itself than in the past. This is probably true in particular for some members of the younger generation, for example, young men like Yudi Simon,[36] who became a media-featured basketball sparring partner in games between Jewish and Black youth in Crown Heights arranged by community activist Richard Green and held at Medgar Evers College. As Simon points out, his involvement in the racial harmony group Project CURE has greatly benefited the development of his persona. He is currently active as a musician in a band that is influenced by a multiplicity of musical directions and has no problem associating himself with different cultures and peoples.[37] However, voices of the older generation who are battling on the frontlines of Hasidic/Caribbean-American community relations have also stated: "If the Jewish parent is afraid that their child is going to be swayed out of the path [*inaudible*] because of playing basketball with somebody else, the child isn't so firmly on its path" (Bentzion Meltzer).

At the far end of the continuum of persons interviewed for this pilot study are the Crown Heights political representatives for whom involvement with and engagement of all different communities they are representing translates into votes and, therefore, makes the difference between political success or survival and the fall into disrepute and rejection at the ballot box. At times, despite their probable forthrightness, some statements border close on the comic. Consider, for example, Senator Marty Markowitz's struggle with concepts of minority and majority culture:

> Brooklyn no longer has majorities, uh, minorities. There is no minorities, we're all majorities in Brooklyn. The White population is not the majority in Brooklyn, by the way. It isn't. It's one minority. Blacks are a minority, Latins, uh, and if you add it all up, we're a majority. So everyone's a majority. That's it. There are no more minorities.

While there certainly is a point to the senator's (convoluted) description of the ethnic composition of Brooklyn, his statement also tends to gloss over the real existing "race"-power lines in American society that penetrate Brooklyn's multi-cultural cosmos and can rupture the everyday appearances in cataclysmic upheavals such as the Crown Heights unrest/riots in the summer of 1991. Despite the progress, a note of caution was appropriately issued recently by Columbia University's Samuel Freedman, who pointed out that the 1991 violence "wasn't the nadir of black-Jewish relations but perhaps its last significant flare-up" (Mark, 2001). Our interviewee Yudi Simon also uttered similar skepticism about a general improvement of relations.

SUGGESTIONS AND PERSPECTIVES ON COOPERATION

While the leadership of both groups has considerably improved its practical and theoretical conduct with regard to relations with the respective other groups, all parties concerned would be well advised to remember that leadership perceptions are not necessarily shared widely throughout all segments of both communities. As Abraham Foxman, national director of the Anti-Defamation League points out, while anti-Semitism is 12% in the general population, it runs at about 35–40% in the African-American community (Mark, 2001). Similarly, the Crown Heights Hasidic community, as an international crossroads of Hasidim experiences, a steady influx of new members coming from Israel or Russia, who are importing some of the worst stereotypes about Black people (particularly young male Blacks, as crack addicts, drug dealers, and generally violent criminals of all sort), which are likely to compound with already existing stereotypes perpetuated both in some quarters of the Hasidic community and in American mainstream society.

In this regard, practically all representatives in both communities expressed the need to be constantly involved with each other, in order to learn more about each other and the concerns each community has for itself, as well as about those it shares with the other. Words such as "dialogue," "cooperation," etc., constantly reverberated through the answers to the question how conflicts can be ameliorated. This important recognition has to be read as a challenge to outside groups and political decision-makers to support (including financially) such efforts to create formal and informal mechanisms, where such coming together can be initialized and developed. It is a challenge not just for the good of Hasidic/Caribbean-American relations alone, but one for the wider community, which consciously or unconsciously follows what goes on in Crown Heights, in Brooklyn, in New York City.

And yet, the demand for dialogue and contact is in and by itself not a sufficient condition for the resolution of conflict between both communities. A successful neighborly relationship between two culturally and/or ethnically different groups or individuals requires the deliberate and careful creation and cultivation of common points of reference. Although the mere process of talking with each other and explaining oneself to the other is a necessary precondition for the detection of common ground and an increasing understanding and appreciation of each other's differences, a relationship that transcends this ephemeral and evanescent moment of sitting together and exchanging views is necessary in order to elevate two completely different worlds such as the Afro-Caribbean and Hasidic to the status of a well functioning neighborhood. In this context, it is important to note that several Jewish leaders interviewed for this study made claims for common ground that are based on issues relating to socio-economic class.[38] Indeed, these economic interests may very well be the most promising route to follow with regard to the above-mentioned creation of common points of reference. As one of our interviewees (Bob Kaplan), speaking for the organization he is representing, put it:

> Although I am a believer in intergroup dialogue, I think that that is merely a starting point. What we have developed as a paradigm that we have now around the city, where we create opportunities for groups to work together on quality of life issues. One of the main issues we work together is on health care. There [are] many other issues as well, whether it be census, or voting, or education, or just fixing a pothole out in the street, so that the relationship goes beyond just the dialogue – I like you, you like me, and we both like the same food or we don't like the same food – to something where people form concrete relationships and they seek concrete results from communities working together in a positive fashion.

To link groups around such concrete issues would indeed appear to be a more promising approach, which can indeed yield the very common points of reference (e.g. autonomous institutions promoting local empowerment, investments, infrastructure, and social benefits, etc.) that are needed to concatenate the Lubavitcher Hasidic and Caribbean-American communities.[39] The impression from the interviews with African-Caribbean and African-American leaders is that often an implicit yearning for recognition is foregrounded to such pragmatic perspectives. It appears that there is ample room for greater integration of these perspectives in Caribbean-American initiatives and thought about relations with the orthodox Jewish, particularly the Lubavitcher Hasidic, communities. At the same time, a cultural convergence should not (immediately) be expected from this work towards a socio-economic convergence.

Ultimately, however, the responsibility for a peaceful and good neighborly relationship between both communities rests at the level of each and every individual member of both. Apparently with the stereotypes mentioned at the beginning of this section in mind, it is therefore important to heed Council member Una Clarke's advice about our shared responsibilities regarding the words spoken in the privacy of the family home:

> We have to watch what we say about other people, whether they be Jews whether they be Muslims, and whether they be of your own ethnic group. I think our human relations have to be . . . such that we demonstrate both in what we do and how we live respect for each other.

The challenge posed by the Lubavitcher community to mainstream notions of community based on either liberal political theory (e.g. Rawls, Habermas) or communitarian ideals is encapsulated in the question why Caribbean-Americans (and, by extension, much of the rest of mainstream America) find it so hard to provide space for peaceful sectarian communities who insist on defining and living their difference "on their own terms." Only when liberal society begins in earnest to ask itself this question, will we begin to see the growth of a "genuine dialogue" and the beginning of the "living mutual relation" Martin Buber called for.[40] As Iris Young (1990, p. 241) points out correctly, it ought to be kept in mind that in order to make peaceful life in a multi-ethnic city possible, the "public cannot be conceived as a unity transcending groups' differences, nor as entailing complete mutual understanding. In public life the differences remain unassimilated, but each participating group acknowledges and is open to listening to others. The public is heterogenous, plural, and playful, a place where people witness and appreciate diverse cultural expressions that they do not share and do not fully understand."

NOTES

1. This is not to argue, of course, that at any given point they were clearly just one or the other. Jewish-Black relations in the United States have been a multi-layered and very complex affair.

2. About 85% of the population in New York's 42nd A.D. (i.e. East Flatbush and a tip of Crown Heights) are black with the remaining population composed mainly of Jewish and Italian families (see, for example, Green & Wilson, 1989).

3. For a brief account of the Crown Heights incident and the subsequent disturbances, see, for example, Philip Kasinitz (1992, pp. xii–xiii); for a very thorough and well balanced analysis of the more fundamental issues of identity and conflict in both communities, see Goldschmidt's (2000) dissertation.

4. For some of the literature on these issues see, for example, Henke (2001), Goldschmidt (2000), Waters (2000), Foner (2000, pp. 150–155), Vickerman (1999), and Harris (1995).

5. With regard to the impact of non-religious holidays on the Lubavitch Hasidic community, Harris (1995, p. 213) graphically noted that "they would no more think of adopting the customs associated with them than they would think of donning feathered headdresses and performing a rain dance."

6. With regard to elected officials (as opposed to grass roots community leaders), it has to be pointed out, however, that the Lubavitchers are almost as likely to vote for non-Jews as African-Caribbean electorates are to vote for Whites. While this may or may not be because of lack of opportunity, the fact is that Lubavitcher support for Clarence Norman, Jr. and Mary Pinkett mirrors Caribbean-American support for Marty Markowitz and others.

7. In summer 2001 Markowitz ran for and was elected to the office of Brooklyn Borough President.

8. We emphasize that "race" (like "religion") is a socially constructed category. Nevertheless, as a lived everyday reality it circumscribes in substantial and concrete ways the perceptions and world-views of all "racial" groups. For ethnic groups discriminated on this basis, the category "race" has an immediate impact and reality to it, despite its constructed character. It is our view that, to a considerable extent, the Caribbean-American/Jewish tensions in Crown Heights, as well as the larger contemporary latent Black/Jewish antagonism in the U.S. is embedded in or a byproduct of the larger (historical) complex of White claims for supremacy.

9. It has to be noted that there were significant shifts and expansion of the area that was considered "Crown Heights." For some historical accounts see Manbeck (1998) and Ment and Donovan (1980).

10. A handful of Lubavitchers lived in Crown Heights as early as 1925 (Mintz, 1968, p. 40).

11. We are, of course, mindful of the history of ethnic discrimination against Jews in America, which in fact renders the relationship a "doubly inverted" one.

12. Such materials may exist, however. There was, no doubt, a broad range of complex and ambivalent relationships between Blacks and Jews in Crown Heights prior to White flight. The unfortunate – but telling – fact, however, is that this earlier period of "Black-Jewish relations" is simply not widely documented in the published or archival sources examined for this pilot study. A more thorough perusal of some of the "ethnic" presses (including the un-catalogued *New Amsterdam News* and the currently inaccessible files of the Brooklyn Historical Society) would likely reveal interesting and relevant information.

13. Thus, in her memoir, Shirley Chisholm (1970, p. 12) recalls her own mother's rather different relationship with the much poorer, Yiddish-speaking Jews of Brownsville, to whom she was "a kind of neighborhood oracle and leader."

14. Although there are a few blocks likely to have Jewish populations of 60 or 70%, it is hard to speak of a predominantly Hasidic area in Crown Heights. Thus, there is no census (1990 Census) tract with higher than 40% Jews. Given the income diversity in Crown Heights and adjoining communities, and despite external appearances caused by a core area around which Jews in Crown Heights are clustered, there is a broad comparability of socio-economic status between Black and Jewish neighborhoods in this area of Brooklyn; in fact, according to Goldschmidt (2000, pp. 125–126, emphasis added), ". . . in 1990 the per capita income of Jews in Crown Heights was about 20% *lower* than that of their immediate Black neighbors in the area to the south of Eastern Parkway, and 15% *lower* than that of Blacks in Crown Heights as a whole." Therefore, we do not consider socio-economic factors as the objective primary determinant of conflicts between both groups (for an in-depth discussion and data see Goldschmidt (2000, Chap. 2).

15. For an unsystematic and certainly incomplete history of random acts of violence committed against Lubavitcher Hasidics, see "Jew carrying (1975)," Todd (1979), and Goldman (1992).

16. Conversely, the Hasidic claim that Black Crown Heights residents have been welcomed to join patrols is certainly true, but often lost interest soon after joining (Vecsey, 1978). As Richard Green, director of the Crown Heights Youth Collective, points out, there are still efforts under way to form such joint patrols.

17. Given that much of the more serious crimes experienced by this community are committed by "outsiders," who in this case often happen to be Black, it becomes obvious how easily such a valorization of racial stereotypes can occur. In fact, as one Lubavitcher woman commented in 1994: "The hardest thing for me as a mother in Crown Heights is to raise children who are not racists. [. . .] . . . here they are surrounded by incidents that could influence them against black people, and I am always trying to say, 'But it's not all black people.' " (Rule, 1994). As Rev. Dr. Heron Sam pointed out in his interview, the vigilante forces inflicted a lot of hurt on Caribbeans living in the area by their indiscriminate ways of stopping and arresting Blacks that – as in the case of his own son – were "guilty" only of running to catch the subway train.

18. The reason for this doubt are the practices of the Hasidic organization Chevra Machazikei Hashchuna. In 1978 it was investigated by the FBI for fiscal irregularities and accused by then City Council President Carol Bellamy of harassment and discrimination against Black tenants in buildings that Chevra hoped to renovate – with federal subsidies – for Hasidic Jews (Bellamy, 1978; Robbins, 1981).

19. This is not to argue that "racial" discrimination against people of color and favoritism of Whites (including Hasidic Jews) does not play a role in the relationship between both groups. It clearly does, as could, for example, be clearly seen in an incident in which a 27-year-old male Hasid punched a 15-year-old Black girl, herself an Orthodox Jew and

honor student in a special high school program at Yeshiva University. According to the newspaper report, the police at the 71st Precinct did not proceed to arrest the perpetrator (Browne, 1988; Day-care center, 1972; Kihss, 1978).

20. This, of course, reflects John Stuart Mills and Alexis de Tocqueville's concerns about the implications of the logic of majoritarianism for individual liberties. For a more recent discussion of these issues see, for example, Scott's (1999, pp. 159–189) chapter on community, number and the ethos of democracy.

21. While the *Crown Heights Community Mediation Center* is a highly welcome long-term institution, its mandate is not explicitly to promote Black-Jewish harmony in Crown Heights.

22. Rawls offers a number of definitions for "decent peoples" and "decent society" and further differentiates these categories, which makes his treatise rather complex. However, in the beginning of his book he defines the term " 'decent' to describe nonliberal societies whose basic institutions meet certain specified conditions of political right and justice (including the right of citizens to play a substantial role, say through associations or groups, in making political decisions) and lead their citizens to honor a reasonably just law . . ." roughly understood as human rights (Rawls, 1999, p. 3).

23. This discrepancy is also an obvious factor operative in the current conflict with militant Islamic fundamentalists following the September 11, 2001, attacks on New York City and Washington, DC. Thus, for Islamic fundamentalists the *umma*, the global community of Islamic believers, is the central organizing principle. Therefore, the mere existence of (secular) states in the Islamic world is already perceived as a Western imposition (Tibi, 2000).

24. I am referring here to Rex Nettleford's book title *Inward Stretch, Outward Reach* (1993).

25. It is important to note that Buber points out that "genuine dialogue" is not equal to love. This may indeed be the common expectation among proponents of liberal political theory and many Christians. However, he also notes that "love without dialogic, without real outgoing to the other, reaching to the other, and companying with the other, the love remaining with itself— this is called Lucifer" (Buber, 1965, p. 21). Buber's "genuine dialogue" and his appropriately implicit critique of liberal political theory is, however, premised on the idea that universalism and particularity are merely two sides of the same coin.

26. We remind the reader that, while we also interviewed non-orthodox Jews, the overwhelming majority of interviewees in that group were either orthodox or a member of the Lubavitcher Hasidic community. Similarly, we also interviewed several African-Americans who happen to work as representatives or on behalf of Caribbean-Americans.

27. It is noted that, in practice, both Hasidic and Christian brotherliness are problematic. Neither has Christianity lived up to its universal promises, nor is the Hasidic community free from internal tensions, rivalries and violence.

28. Dr. McLean is originally from Trinidad and Tobago, and is also a professor of media studies at a university in Colorado.

29. At this point it might be interesting to point out that historically, Hasids have conferred leadership roles to their women. Thus, Adel (born ca. 1720), the daughter of the Baal Shem Tov, and Hannah Rahel (1805–1892), known as the Virgin of Ludomir, actually led Hasidic communities. For the influence of American society on the role of Jewish women, see Foner (2000, pp. 144–120).

30. Similar views were expressed, for example, by Batia Barachaim of the inter-ethnic community group Mother-to-Mothers. Indeed, the Bishop Dr. Heron Sam reported that in

a meeting with the late Israeli Prime Minister Golda Meir, she confided to him that the Hasidim in Israel "are a pain in my [. . .] here as well" and "when tourists walk past their . . . synagogues in short pants they stone them."

31. Some of the subtle differences of discrimination experienced by both groups are explored by Beck (1998), Waters (1998), Dyson (1998), Gould (1998), and Wright (1998), to mention only a few of the plethora of interventions on these issues.

32. Rabbi Kaplan describes himself as "modern orthodox." Thus, he is not a member of the Lubavitcher community. He is director of intergroup relations and community concerns for the Jewish Community Relations Council in New York City. Rabbi Kaplan's acknowledgment of Jewish Whiteness and privilege quoted here is significantly more progressive than anything most Lubavitchers would say.

33. Whether the Hasidic community is aware of it or not, a significant adjustment is expected from Caribbean-Americans who, as Councilmember Clarke points out, are themselves, like the Hasidim, prepared to buy into (racialized) aspects of American mainstream society. Coming from homogenous societies, Caribbean-Americans are "independent, determined, . . . there are very few of us with low self-esteem . . . and so we will go head to head with anybody, be they Black or White, be they Jew or Gentile, be they Irish or Italians . . . [. . .] It is about feeling that you are equal to others and that therefore you are not going to give and you will not be subservient, and I think that they have come to understand that and to recognize that." To the extent that Caribbean-Americans are indeed marked by this trace of resilience and resistance against (perceived) oppression and to the extent that some quarters of the Jewish/Hasidic community may have bought into White mainstream expectations of "black subservience," the profile of the required adjustments on both sides becomes more defined.

34. This also seems to be the general position of Rawls (1999, p. 168), who argues that "if, when stand-offs occur, citizens simply invoke grounding reasons of their comprehensive views, the principle of reciprocity is violated. From the point of view of public reason, citizens must vote for the ordering of political values they sincerely think the most reasonable. Otherwise they fail to exercise political power in ways that satisfy the criterion of reciprocity."

35. It is interesting to note that the oldest synagogue in the Western Hemisphere stands in Curaçao. There are substantial numbers of mostly Sephardim and Ashkenazim in various countries of the region (Levine, 1993).

36. It has to be pointed out, however, that Mr. Simon is by no means a typical Lubavitch youth. In fact, with his pierced tongue, participation in Manhattan night-life and a more flexible ritual observance, he is probably regarded by most Lubavitcher parents as the worst example of what interacting too much with Gentiles or Blacks can do to their kids.

37. As Richard Green points out, there are also cultural efforts under way that seek unity under the theme "Blacks, Blues and Jews."

38. This emphasis on practical and pragmatic issues pertaining to the improvement of the neighborhood can also be observed in many statements made by representatives of the orthodox Jewish and Hasidic communities reported in earlier cited newspaper articles.

39. For suggestions on the specific character of such local empowerment agencies, see Barber (1984) and Young (1990, pp. 248ff.). Interesting information can also be gleaned from Cuba's practical experience with local direct democracy (Roman, 1999).

40. Buber's thoughts have been further elaborated in the little known *oeuvre* of the Swiss philosopher Hermann Levin Goldschmidt (see, for example, his 1964 book entitled

Dialogik). Much of the spirit of these philosophers can also be found in the writings of novelist Hermann Hesse.

ACKNOWLEDGMENTS

We would like to acknowledge the assistance of Henry Goldschmidt, Brian Purnell, and Elizabeth Gold in this research. This study was funded by a grant from the CUNY Dispute Resolution Consortium which was supported by the William and Flora Hewlett Foundation.

REFERENCES

Barber, B. (1984). *Strong democracy*. Berkeley and Los Angeles: University of California Press.
Beck, E. T. (1998). From 'Kike' to 'JAP': How misogyny, anti-semitism, and racism construct the 'Jewish American Princess.' In: M. L. Andersen & P. H. Collins (Eds), *Race, Class, and Gender* (pp. 430–436). Belmont: Wadsworth.
Beiles, N. (1998, April 17). The Crown Heights laboratory. *The Brooklyn Jewish Week*, 22–23.
Bellamy, C. (1978). A Report on Chevra Machazikei Hashchuna, Inc. (mimeo).
Browne, J. Z. (1988, June 11). Are police afraid to arrest Hasidic Jews in Brooklyn? *New York Amsterdam News, 3*, 35.
Browne, J. Z., & Todd, G. (1978, July 22). B'klyn Blacks warn Jews. *New York Amsterdam News*, A1, B1, and B6.
Buber, M. (1965). *Between man and man*. New York: Macmillan.
Chisholm, S. (1970). *Unbought and unbossed*. Boston: Houghton Mifflin.
City Planning Commission (1973). *City planning handbook: Brooklyn community district 8*. New York: City Planning Commission.
Clines, F. X. (1976, December 28). About New York. A Christmas sermon: Brooklyn redistricting. *The New York Times*.
Collins, T. (1976, December 25). Crown Hts.: White flight stopped? *Daily News*, 7.
Day-care center scene of protest (1972, November 18). *The New York Times*.
Diner, H. (1997). Between words and deeds: Jews and Blacks in America. In: J. Salzman & C. West (Eds), *Struggles in the Promised Land. A History of Black-Jewish Relations in the United States* (pp. 87–106). New York: Oxford University Press.
Dyson, M. (1998). The plight of black men. In: M. L. Andersen & P. H. Collins (Eds), *Race, Class, and Gender* (pp. 136–146). Belmont: Wadsworth.
Foner, N. (2000). *From Ellis Island to JFK. New York's two great waves of immigration*. New Haven and New York: Yale University Press and Russell Sage Foundation.
Fowler, G. (1976a, December 23). Hasidim and Blacks are disputing new community lines in Brooklyn. *The New York Times*, 27.
Fowler, G. (1976b, December 24). Hasidic Jews in Crown Heights get separate community district. *The New York Times*, B3.
Goldman, A. L. (1992, February 7). Angry protests follow killing in Brooklyn. *The New York Times*, B1.

Goldschmidt, H. (2000). *Peoples apart: Race, religion, and other Jewish differences in Crown Heights.* Ph.D. dissertation, UC Santa Cruz, Santa Cruz.

Goldschmidt, H. L. (1964). *Dialogik.* Frankfurt a. M.: Europäische Verlags-Anstalt.

Gould, S. J. (1998). Science and Jewish immigration. In: J. Ferrante & P. Brown, Jr. (Eds), *The Social Construction of Race and Ethnicity in the United States* (pp. 301–308). New York: Longman.

Green, C., & Wilson, B. (1989). *The struggle for Black empowerment in New York City. Beyond the politics of pigmentation.* New York: Praeger.

Harris, L. (1995). *Holy days. The world of a Hasidic family.* New York: Simon & Schuster.

Henke, H. (2001). *The West Indian Americans.* Westport, CT: Greenwood Press.

Holder, C. (1990). The Rise and Fall of West Indian Politicians in New York (1900–1987). In: J. A. G. Irish & E. W. Riviere (Eds), *Political Behavior and Social Interaction Among Caribbean & African American Residents in New York* (pp. 5–34). Brooklyn: Caribbean Research Center, Medgar Evers College, CUNY.

Kasinitz, P. (1992). *Caribbean New York. Black immigrants and the politics of race.* Ithaca: Cornell University Press (3rd printing).

Kihss, P. (1978, July 17). 2,000 assail police at Black rally as off-duty officers meet nearby. *The New York Times*, p. B2.

Krebs, A., & Rubenstein, S. (1964, May 29). Brooklyn vigilantes against crime. *Herald Tribune.*

Jetter, A. (1989, May 11). Ethnic makeup of building's tenants sparks controversy. *NY Newsday*, 23.2 NY-B.

Jew carrying no funds on Sabbath slain in holdup (1975, September 25). *The New York Times.*

Levine, R. M. (1993). *Tropical diaspora. The Jewish experience in Cuba.* Gainesville: University Press of Florida.

Lichtenstein, G. (1974, August 1, 31). "Transitional" Crown Heights now in midst of comeback. *The New York Times.*

Manbeck, J. (Ed.) (1998). *The neighborhoods of Brooklyn.* New Haven: Yale University Press.

Mark, J. (2001, August 10). Apocalypse then, healing now. *The Jewish Week.* http://www.thejewishweek.com/news/newscontent.php3?artid=4919.

Marshall, P. (1981). *Brown girl, brownstones.* New York: Feminist Press.

Ment, D., & Donovan, M. (1980). *The people of Brooklyn. A history of two neighborhoods.* Brooklyn: Brooklyn Educational and Cultural Alliance.

Mintz, J. R. (1968). *Legends of the Hasidim.* Chicago: University of Chicago Press.

Nettleford, R. (1993). *Inward stretch. Outward reach. A voice from the Caribbean.* London: Macmillan.

Pogrebin, R. (1992/93, December 28, January 4, 1 and 18). Rabbis resisting a project's cure for Crown Heights. *New York Observer.*

Raab, S. (1978, June 23). Past police incidents moved Blacks to coordinate protests. *The New York Times*, A13.

Rawls, J. (1999). *The law of peoples.* Cambridge: Harvard University Press.

Riviere, E. W., & Winborne, W. (1990). Political behavior patterns of Caribbean immigrants in the nineteen eighties: An exploratory inquiry. In: J. A. G. Irish & E. W. Riviere (Eds), *Political Behavior and Social Interaction Among Caribbean & African American Residents in New York* (pp. 35–98). Brooklyn: Caribbean Research Center, Medgar Evers College, CUNY.

Robbins, T. (1981). Tales of Crown Heights: The fruits of harassment. *City Limits*, *12*(10).

Roman, P. (1999). *People's power. Cuba's experience with representative government.* Boulder: Westview Press.

Rule, S. (1994, April 15). The voices and faces of Crown Heights. *The New York Times*, C1.

Safer, S. (1997). Mothers reshuffle the race card in Crown Heights. *Lilith*, *22*(1).

Sandel, M. (1982). *Liberalism and the limits of justice.* Cambridge: Cambridge University Press.

Scott, D. (1999). *Refashioning futures. Criticism after postcoloniality*. Princeton: Princeton University Press.

Spivak, G. C. (1999). *Imperative zur neuerfindung des planeten/Imperatives to re-imagine the planet*. Wien: Passagen Verlag.

Tibi, B. (2000). *Fundamentalismus im Islam. Eine Gefahr für den Weltfrieden*. Darmstadt: Primus.

Todd, G. (1979, November 3). Racial tension in Crown Heights. *New York Amsterdam News*, 54.

Vecsey, G. (1978, July 24). In Crown Heights, an uncertain alliance is put to the test. *The New York Times*, B1

Vickerman, M. (1999). *Crosscurrents. West Indian immigrants and race*. New York: Oxford University Press.

Waters, M. (1998). Optional ethnicities: For Whites only? In: M. L. Andersen & P. H. Collins (Eds), *Race, Class, and Gender* (pp. 403–412). Belmont, CA: Wadsworth.

Waters, M. (2000). *Black identities: West Indian immigrant dreams and American realities*. Cambridge and New York: Harvard University Press and Russell Sage Foundation.

Wilkins, R. (1978, July 25). There are voices that talk for Blacks in Crown Heights. *The New York Times*, B8.

Williams, P. J. (1997). On imagining foes, imagining friendship. In: J. Salzman & C. West (Eds), *Struggles in the Promised Land. A History of Black-Jewish Relations in the United States* (pp. 371–383). New York: Oxford University Press.

Wright, L. (1998). One drop of blood. In: J. Ferrante & P. Brown, Jr. (Eds), *The Social Construction of Race and Ethnicity in the United States* (pp. 422–426). New York: Longman.

Young, I. M. (1990). *Justice and the politics of difference*. Princeton: Princeton University Press.

THE CARIBBEAN NATION-STATE IN BROOKLYN POLITICS: AN EXAMINATION OF THE UNA CLARKE MAJOR OWENS CONGRESSIONAL RACE

Evrick Brown

Race and Ethnicity in New York City
Research in Urban Sociology, Volume 7, 221–244
© 2004 Published by Elsevier Ltd.
ISSN: 1047-0042/doi:10.1016/S1047-0042(04)07010-2

ABSTRACT

The political campaigns of Una Clarke and Major Owens show an interesting display of ethnic politics. In this paper, I argue that the presence of a Caribbean population in Brooklyn New York presents itself as a challenge to the already present African-American structure. The Caribbean politicians do not subscribe nor fully ally with the African-American politicians, and instead, seek to carve out a niche for themselves and utilize their ties to home in an effort to cajole the Caribbean populace for support. Through the purview of a political campaign in Brooklyn between an African-American incumbent and a Caribbean insurgent, I attempt to contribute to the transnationalist literature through illustrating the concept of the nation—state, which can be explained as an immigrant's continual bond to their home country while living abroad.

INTRODUCTION

New York is a city of immigrants and ethnic neighborhoods which is evident during any political campaign. Immigrants who become ethnic groups once they comprehend and begin to demand their rights as naturalized citizens of the United States enter into the political foray and challenge others for scant resources. Portes and Rumbaut (1996) observe the trend and strength of ethnicity and ethnic identification in politics:

> Ethnicity . . . was to provide the fundamental matrix of American based politics for subsequent generations. Ironically the class consciousness of the more literate immigrants faded away while ethnic consciousness forced on the peasant by native discrimination endured.[1]

An immigrant city such as New York is likely to have its mixture of competing interests based on ethnic lines.

In Brooklyn, against the backdrop of this enduring competition for control, there are changes in the political consciousness of the new arrivals. At a previous point in history the variation among the populous was primarily among white ethnics with blacks receiving minor patronage and holding political posts under the watchful eye of the former. Eventually, as with any population change, the demographic profile of the central Brooklyn landscape saw increases in the black population and with that the potential to gain an independent foothold, which took place in the form of the Empowerment Coalition. With the advent of the West Indian[2] population shortly afterwards it became the African-American's turn to defend, although by this time there exist West Indian public officials some of whom entered with aid from members of the Kings County Democratic organization, there are insurgents who question the African-American's right to maintain power. The latter phenomenon is occurring in the midst of a resentful southern white population who desires to regain their stronghold and possibly take advantage of the disconnection between the two black groups.

In this paper, I note the establishment of the African-American political machine to hopefully highlight a trend of succession. The West Indian population in Brooklyn represents an attempt of a group to establish their claim to political efficacy often referred to as ethnicity or ethnic identity. However, this claim in itself represents a challenge to the notion of a supra ethnicity as argued by Portes and Rumbaut. The authors, using Hispanics as an example, document that the usage of a common labeling which overestimates the tenuous bond that groups share before immigrating to the United States. Hispanic politics in Miami Florida is different from the politics of California which has different historical roots. In ethnic identity among Asian Americans, a collection of essays shows different ideas behind the meaning of "Asian American" between Koreans and Chinese Americans.[3] Each group has distinct experiences with their own notion of a nation-state. Indeed, for the Battle for Brooklyn the labels "West Indian" or "Afro-Caribbean" do not encompass all groups as will be shown in the Una Clarke Major Owens political campaign.

Furthermore, in this paper I document some of the properties which are characteristic of this arena of politics from the vantage point of an individual starting from the ground-up. A portion of the information has been gained through engaging in field research which involved interviews, field notes, flyers, periodicals and other various forms of literature. Being in the field accorded me the opportunity to gain information that would otherwise be difficult to obtain.

I argue by presenting the example of the Una Clarke Major Owens Congressional race as evidence that ethnicity or ties to home were utilized by Clarke to present a viable threat to the incumbent. It's this ethnic sentiment which provides evidence of the transnationalist concept of the nation-state or affinity that West Indians have for their home countries.

TRANSNATIONALISM

One great contribution to immigration studies of Transnationalist thinking lies within its questioning of immigrants' loyalty to a single locale. There is now serious consideration to the dominant thought of immigration leading to the eventual waning of home country cultures. Transnationalism, at present, is described as a linking of social, economic and kinship bonds beyond a single national boarder fueled by the economic interests of global capital. Yet, unlike the global cities approach, which focuses more on the super structural processes and how culture and human agency falls victim to this macro tide, Transnationalism notes, and gives credence, to how migrants make adjustments through their establishment and maintenance of immigrant networks beyond national borders.[4]

Human volition is often referred as Transnationalism "from below" or the day-to-day interactions of those who utilize ethnic-based social ties and kin networks to seek not only basic needs such as employment and shelter but to gain information and utilize a network bridge to find a feasible host country. It is because of the maintenance of the immigrant networks to the home countries that the term transmigrant is used intermittently with immigrant.

Researchers may oscillate between the two in an effort to question and clarify the notion of transnational space, what I will refer here as an ethnic based nation-state, hence the Caribbean prefix. The nation-state is an obvious amalgam of two concepts which combines the idea of the state, as a political/geographical boundary and the nation, as represented by an affinity for one's country or patriotism to further illustrate the hyphenated conflation. Although, in the transnationalist literature there's an emphasis on a social boundary or space which involves kin-networks, national ties and emotional attachment or affinity for home countries, all of the actions of the "transmigrants" are rooted in place. A prime example was presented by researchers Glick Schiller and Fouron (1998) who noted that Haitian president Jean-Paul Aristide institutionalized the idea of a nation-state through his tenth department which represented a political and "geographical" boundary of Haitians living abroad.[5] Through Aristide's tenth department Haitians could obtain dual citizenship status and hold public office. A question concerning the strength of the host nation becomes an issue. If these immigrants, sometimes referred to now as transmigrants, can occupy a state are they still subjected to the juridical laws of that political apparatus. Smith points out that they are subjected to the laws of the locale since they are affected by changes in immigration legislation which can affect their status as immigrants and have an impact of where they stay and where further immigrants will travel.

Another main point of contention has been the longevity of the immigrant ties, it is believed that the immigrant's affinity for their home country will fade as successive generations replace preceding ones in the home country. Smith and Goldring (1998) address this question by discussing "transnational communities" which are created by Mexican migrant workers. Such communities are not haphazard, unorganized processes but are maintained by hometown associations. Host country community organizations with a goal of transmitting and socializing youth with ancestral ties to a home country also play a role in creating a social bond or transnational tie.

For the purposes of this study, I will point out the distinction between the actual transnational social relations and the effect these relations have on pre-existing social organization.[6] The social ties which Afro-Caribbeans have with their home countries aid in the fortification of their ethnicity which they utilize as a resource in their interpersonal interaction with whites and in their Caribbean labeled community organizations. This tie to their homeland and alteration of the communal and political landscape has caused a clash with African-Americans. In the subsequent Congressional race for the 11th district such ties were utilized by West Indian immigrant Una Clarke in her attempt to topple the African-American incumbent Major Owens.

Battle for Brooklyn

Historically there have always been groups competing for political control over the borough.[7] In previous decades starting from the early 1900s until the present time, the majority of control has been between white ethnics, from the days of Irish "boss" McCoey to the Steinguts. The Irish dominated politics in Brooklyn and then oscillated between the Italians and Jews who later made an apparent alliance during the time of Meade Esposito's rise to power in 1969.

Meade Esposito was credited as the last of the "old-line" bosses of Brooklyn. He was the son of Italian Immigrant and became acquainted with Brooklyn democratic district leader Hymie Schorenstein whose tactics apprized Esposito of the workings of the Democratic party. The process of "making rounds" throughout the community and helping individuals with their various requests was one of the mechanisms which impressed Esposito to become involved with the Democratic Party, even though most Italians at the time were Republicans. Subsequently, Esposito started the Progressive Democratic club at age 18 which eventually became incorporated into the larger Democratic organization. Through his training he pushed for greater Italian American participation in the community and politics. Eventually, Esposito became one of the more influential players as a District Leader of the immense Thomas Jefferson Club in the Canarsie section of Brooklyn under the guise of the county leader Stanley Steingut, whom Esposito helped to acquire that position. When Steingut later resigned, the State Committee Members of the Brooklyn Democrats voted Meade Esposito in on January 10, of 1969. As a county leader and head of a political club with 2000 members, Esposito entered the 1970s with a firm political hand on Kings County.

What was often cited as the end of political clubs was the involvement of good government reformers who weakened the power of political organizations such as the Kings County Democrats through welfare reform and civil service jobs.[8]

It can be argued that government involvement, primarily through programs which vaguely fall under the War On Poverty, played a role in altering the Political Machine's actions in Brooklyn's politics through patronage and certain political appointments.

Newfield and Dubrul (1977) document changes that were taking place within Brooklyn through the election of non-machine candidates to political office. One of the main participants in the Kings County organization was African-American City Councilman Sam Wright, boss of central Brooklyn, who entered the community through the school board in district 23 which includes the Brownsville section of Brooklyn. Through his control, he also headed the Brownsville Community Development Corporation, Wright was in command of more than 25 million dollars through the school board budget, and other publicly funded programs. One assembly district with a predominantly black population within Councilman Sam Wright' school district became available. Immediately Wright choose an Elmer Hamilton to run for the district, but came across his first snafu as his choice was ineligible because he failed to meet residency requirements, Elmer Hamilton lived in the state of Georgia. Afterwards, Wright chose Charles Hamilton, a former president of school board district 23, who was defeated by Thomas Boyland who was allied with then State Senator Major Owens, a librarian from the south who entered the community through the New York City Community Development Agency and entered politics in 1974, and recent Assemblyman Albert Vann, who was a school teacher and union representative, two members of a future alliance involving African American empowerment.[9] Within the next decade as a result of the initial entrance into politics while skirting the guise of the machine, other African American politicians were able to gain political office.

When redistricting was taking place during the 1980s the New York State reapportionment committee set up new lines that would weaken the African-American voting block. Noticing this attempt State Senator Owens accused the County organization of stripping independent Black Leadership through punishment for non compliance.[10] The Justice department disapproved the plan because of its violation of Section 2 of the 1965 Voting rights Act which required equity in representation of minority neighborhoods.[11] In response the State's redistricting lines were amended to include two Congressional Districts, one of which Owens ran for. Meanwhile, challenges took place in other State Senatorial Districts. Clarence Norman Jr., an assistant district attorney and son of well known Reverend Clarence Norman, challenged incumbent and County favored Assemblyman Woodrow Lewis, a former ally. Citing an informal breach of contract and coining himself as a part of "a new generation of leadership," Norman decided to challenge his former ally who initially told him that he was no longer going to run for reelection but later changed his decision. In that same election year, another member of the future new empowerment team, Roger Greene who was then director of a neighborhood improvement association challenged Assemblyman Harvey L. Strezlin. Both Greene and Norman Jr. lost in the ensuing primary with Clarence Norman losing by 14 votes requiring a runoff election.[12] Two years later, both candidates were able to defeat the incumbents and add to the growing presence of non-county African American ascendancy in Brooklyn.

In its continued effort to gain control over central Brooklyn, county candidate State Senator Vander Beatty, former sociology professor and Chairman of the New York State Black and Puerto Rican Caucus entered the fray to challenge Major Owens for the new 12th Congressional District. What was perhaps an ironic twist to this race, although not too surprising when considering the vagaries of politics, Congresswoman Chisolm, the first Caribbean woman from central Brooklyn who entered elective politics against the county's wishes, supported Vander Beatty. Furthermore, Vander Beatty supported City Councilman Sam Wright against her in 1976 while Owens supported Ms.Chisolm. Another source of controversy stemmed from what was perceived as Beatty's attack on the empowerment team by attempting to remove one of its leaders.

Both Assemblymen Al Vann and Vander Beatty both clashed as members of the Black and Puerto Rican Caucus threatening the caucus' strength in voting power in both the State Senate and Assembly. The discontent between the two public officials went beyond professional differences. Al Vann envisioned a germinating African-American political bloc and perhaps a county takeover. Vander Beatty represented the present county leadership and was perceived as counter productive. Evidence of the dissension and Vann's opinion had to do with Vander Beatty's refusal to support Al Vann's candidacy for a fourth term in the Assembly. Instead, Vander Beatty supported Carl Butler and was able to force Vann off of the Democratic primary ballot due to petition irregularities. Vann ran as a liberal in the general election and won back his seat through a recount.[13] Another strand of evidence came from Vander Beatty's support for white, county approved, candidates within central Brooklyn while not pushing possible black candidates.[14] Thus, Vann and the other members of the independent black leadership supported Major Owens for the Congressional race. The campaigning was fierce as both candidates were equally familiar to the public with Vander Beatty having an advantage because his state senatorial district covered more of the 12th than Owens.

After the primary, Major Owens was declared the winner of the new 12th Congressional District; however, this did not take place without challenges. There were charges of fraud and forgery. Owens charged that many of the registration cards contained signatures without any election number or inspection signatures on them. Owens believed that these forgeries were created after the election and allowed by the County influenced local election board which permitted irregularities in order to force another vote. Vander Beatty charged that non-registered voters participated in the election and inflated Owens' numbers and created a false victory. Irregularities were found and the acting supreme court justice had invalidated the primaries after finding 1500 fraudulent voter signatures and a little over 1300 votes cast by voters with no political party affiliation who were ineligible to vote in a primary. However the New York State Court of Appeals canceled the decision of the State Supreme Court as it found no evidence that Major Owens was responsible for voter fraud.[15] The extent of the county organization's desire to maintain control can also be shown in the period after the primary. In February of 1983, Vander Beatty faced his first series of charges, he was indicted on forgery, conspiracy and election law violation. While the Brooklyn District Attorney initiated its investigation, the State Commission of Investigation began its probe of former Senator Vander Beatty's questionable involvement with the Bedford-Stuyvesant Urban Development Corporation.[16] In the ensuing trials, the disclosure of the voter scheme revealed a cloak and dagger plan, Beatty's supporters hid in a crawlspace over a bathroom in the New York City Board of Election Office and emerged when the office was closed and fabricated voter registration cards. The aid of a handwriting expert lead investigators to Vander Beatty's election aide Betty Edwards who cooperated with investigators by taping conversations.[17] The State Commission's Investigation alerted the United State's Attorney's office where it was discovered that between the years 1979 and 1983 Beatty had siphoned off more than 200,000 dollars in funding through various schemes such as having the director of the Development Corporation write checks addressed to nonexistent employees and consultants only to give the money to the ex-State Senator.[18] Subsequently Vander Beatty was found guilty for election fraud, racketeering and tax evasion in 1984.[19] Six years later when he emerged from prison, he was shot and killed allegedly by long term friend Arthur E. Flournoy who was acquitted and maintained his innocence.[20]

Newfield and Dubrul often note the action of dishonest "graft" and money laundering as normal practices of any political machine. The trial of ex-State Senator Vander Beatty revealed tactics and practices ordinarily executed by a County organization which provides evidence suggesting Beatty's tie to the Brooklyn Democratic Machine, County Leader Meade Esposito and the Thomas Jefferson Club in the Canarsie section of Brooklyn, the area in the path of the growing black population. The discovery of the ex-Senators illegal activity also illustrated the county's desire to maintain control over the growing black populace although that was about to change.

New "Boss" County Leader

A change in the county organization took place, Meade Esposito "retired" his position as Chair of the Brooklyn Democratic Committee. The "new" county leader/boss was Borough President Harold Golden until a City Charter Provision barred major party leaders from holding top municipal jobs. Golden decided to retain his Borough Presidency of Brooklyn and vacate the County leadership position. In November of 1990, Clarence Norman Jr. of the 43rd Assembly District became the first African American County Leader of Brooklyn and ran the Thurgood Marshall Club in the Prospect-Lefferts Gardens section of Brooklyn. This occurred despite Asseblyman Anthony Genovese's, a member of the Thomas Jefferson Club – the political Club of the now late Meade Esposito, desire to become the new county boss and once again place the Jefferson club in its once powerful position.[21] Four years later Norman Jr. attempted to make amends by supporting Genovese for speaker of the Assembly but Sheldon Silver from Manhattan was able to acquire the position.

Often with any political machine once a new "boss" has been elected, there is often a period of adjustment which can be synonymous with a struggle, members and "generals" of previous political machines may and often try to topple and undermine the present leadership in order to establish its own. The threat doesn't necessarily have to come from one specific group, it may come from any side. In the 2000 state wide election for Assembly James Davis, a well-known police officer with his "Stop The Violence" movement, decided to run again for Assemblyman of the 43rd Assembly District against county leader Clarence Norman Jr. In the previous election of 1998 James Davis ran for the same seat against Norman Jr. and lost by 581 votes. Because the votes were lost by such a close margin between an iconoclast insurgent and an established incumbent heading the entire County democratic organization, it revealed a weakness in the Norman political machine. It was later discovered that Davis could not be nominated while holding a job as a police officer and Police Commissioner Howard Safir ordered Davis to retire. Although Davis claimed that he was not nominated by the Liberal Party his name appeared on the ballot.[22] Adding to the suspicious nature of his firing, years later when Davis ran again against Clarence Norman and his District Leader William Boone, Davis claimed that no such requirement was impressed upon him when he ran for a City council seat against African American Mary Pinkett.[23] In the 2000 election Davis defeated Boone. A possible substance to the Davis-Norman Jr. feud would emanate from James Davis' apparent ties to Assemblyman Anthony Genovese, an error which he openly admitted to a reporter in the Daily News was that Genovese was a consultant to his campaign against Clarence Norman jr. Davis would later run for City council leaving his District Leadership post while Norman supported Letitia James for the 35th City council district. In the Primary James Davis won the election by 945 (6691 to 5746) adding insult to injury by receiving more votes from the 43rd assembly district, Clarence Norman's district, than Letitia James.

Also ever present in this arena are the "less" threatening insurgents who are overwhelmingly Afro-Caribbean. Their occupations differ but share a common thread. Their desire is to constantly challenge the political incumbents at various levels. At a particular meeting of an insurgent's political campaign, there was a list of candidates running from various districts for a variety of political offices, Judicial Court Judge, State Assembly, City Council and House of Representatives. These insurgents represent the ever present groundswell borne of the growth in the Caribbean population. They are not directly supported by the anti-county machine although they would represent threats to the county. They claim that there is a lack of a Caribbean candidate who has not been incorporated in the established political structure truly representing Caribbean interests which primarily revolve around immigration and a positive Afro-Caribbean presentation which involves pushing for a stronger tie between the United States and the Caribbean Economic Community. Not a single insurgent has been a viable threat to the established structure, they seem to lack the networking skills to obtain a staunch system of human and monetary resources. Instead, they appear to be challenging positions to vie for economic improvements similar to the tactics of the late Wesley MacDonald Holder but have largely been ignored in their efforts. However, they are persistent and if they do acquire a political position it would indeed suggest an extremely tenuous position for the County Leader.

Despite the continual challenges to the African-American county leadership, it has managed to retain its hold on the various political seats. The various disputes are often thwarted or brushed aside as most insurgents do have neither the resources nor the organizational skills to thrive against knowledgeable incumbents, James Davis notwithstanding. Davis' style of campaigning is similar in scope to Una Clarke's epic challenge to Major Owen's political seat. Both insurgents had charismatic affable styles which entreated the public through their images of humble servants going against political corruption and preferential treatment, although Davis didn't initiate an onslaught against one of the most powerful African-American incumbents in central Brooklyn his move did chip the armor in the county's organization. Other differences are clear in terms of gender and ethnicity. It was not the African-American political structure that Una Clarke was challenging alone, she grossly offended male West Indian elected officials who apparently desired to advance through a more traditional advancement by going through the county structure something which Clarke decided was unacceptable.

Una Clarke Major Owens Political Race

Jamaican born Una Clarke migrated to the United States in the 1950s where she obtained a bachelor's degree in Business Management and eventually earned a Master's degree in Early Childhood Education which she used to operate day care centers in Brooklyn. When a city council district with a sizable Afro-Caribbean population became available during the early 1990s, Representative Major Owens, who had developed a rapport with Clarke decided to endorse her campaign against Carl Andrews, the candidate who was endorsed by the county boss Clarence Norman Jr. Clarke was a consultant for the city's Agency of Child Development and served both on the New York State's Task Force on Children and the Congressional Black Caucus Educational Brain Trust. She appeared to have some knowledge of the community but with little familiarity with the public. Thus, Clarke's race against the county proved difficult. She was virtually new to the area and many of the Caribbean population were not registered voters. Clarke's supporters often had to remind her to refrain from using "Caribbean Empowerment" or "Caribbean" in her public speeches for fear that she would disillusion the much needed African-American vote. In such a tight election, Carl Andrews was initially declared the winner, beating Clarke by 49 votes (2117 to 2068). Subsequently, Clarke filed for a recount in which the voting machines, affidavits and absentee ballots were examined, it was later discovered that Clarke had an actual majority of the votes.[24] During her tenure in office, what the papers (Caribbean and otherwise) often focused on was her stance on legalizing the notorious Caribbean-based "dollar" vans which were more available than public transportation, and the development of an open market similar to Mart 125 in Harlem New York where street merchants could sell their items within a shelter along with a myriad of requests for immigration aid.[25] In effect, her functioning resembled that of the "old style" bosses who performed favors for immigrants who were not familiar with the city's structure or process for obtaining social services. Clarke's office was often teeming with West Indian immigrants seeking aid. One particular issue which was constantly recurring was women's health which subsequently resulted in the establishment of a "satellite" hospital geared toward Caribbean Families on Church Avenue and eventually opened up a clinic at 123 Linden Boulevard, Clarke's Office.[26] The Church Avenue building which houses this satellite center has a marquee painted in tropical green with a slightly prostrate palm tree, representing a cue of familiarity and warmth to the Caribbean clientele.

In an effort to expand leadership capabilities and because of Term Limits there was a constant belief that Clarke would run for Major Owens' office. Often because of her flamboyant and charismatic style Caribbean-Americans identified with Clarke whose West Indian accent contained an aristocratic flair reminiscent of their home countries. What helped her early in the race in addition to her belief for a West Indian Empowerment was the negative "Middle Finger" politics article carried by the *CaribNews* which noted that Major Owens was one of the Representatives who voted against adding the Carribean economic union (Caricom) to the North American Free Trade Agreement. To add salt to the wound, the next feature of that particular issue focused on the World Trade Organization's desire to force the European Union from giving preferential treatment to the Caribbean Banana producers.[27]

On March 11, 1999, Una Clarke filed a declaration to run against Major Owens in the 11th Congressional District. Partially because of Clarke's discussion and aggressive talk of Afro-Caribbean rights and the failure of the current leadership, in October 1999 the County Organization under the Coalition for Community Empowerment and the leadership of boss Norman Jr., dispatched a team headed by Assemblyman Al Vann to persuade Clarke not to run citing the need to retain the 18 years of experience and seniority Major Owens acquired. The Coalition for Community Empowerment also feared that if Clarke maintained her desire to run it would cleave divisions among blacks along ethnic lines. At the meeting Clarke brought an entourage of her own much to the dismay of the Empowerment group, they wanted a "friendly" chat in which to dissuade her, but the presence of "others" altered that possibility. By the time the meeting took place, Clarke and her supporters had already established a Clarke 2000 committee and had their first fund raising event thereby committing her to Congressional race.[28] The Empowerment team made another attempt to dissuade Clarke in January 2000 this time they tried by a written request pleading for her not to run, in response a set of community activists including radio personality Bob Law wrote her a letter to ignore the wishes of the establishment and run against Owens. In a cable television interview Major Owens, apparently exasperated by Clarke's refusal, erred and stated that appealing to ethnic loyalties was the worst way to acquire power and likened Clark's act to Hitler.[29]

Throughout the year, the *CaribNews* and *Caribbean Life* published articles featuring the campaign of both candidates. The majority of the articles, particularly from the *CaribNews*, favored Clarke and cited Owens' as a failure to the Caribbean Community. However the publications rated the candidates, it appeared that the majority of constituents acquired their news either through the papers from their respective islands or by, what they noted most, word of mouth by "talking to people." It appeared that the "village" or small town characteristic was what made Clarke the favored candidate. Clarke would often meet her constituents and Caribbean immigrants from other districts with openness and a warm disposition which resembled the types of interactions characteristic neighbors of the islands. When asked about the communal environment at home most residents referred to a similar scenario:

> I remember . . . an elderly person maybe 80 years sitting on a sidewalk with maybe 200 dollars on a stack of each paper and not a police in sight and that money is safe there. You would never see a police officer with a nightstick and there is that interaction where people respected the police because they were like their brother, you were a family you were a relative not that you had to know the individual but from top down you had to respect the citizen and the citizen had to respect you that was an ongoing relationship an unwritten contractual relationship.[30]

Not surprisingly then, most news, which is covered in the Caribbean-based Newspapers, is not acquired by them but through the warm communal discourse between compatriot or kin:

> I call my brother at home and of course I have friends who reads those papers anything that comes up they call me and say Jim did you know that such and such happened my friends also keep me up to date, but I don't read the CaribNews.[31]

Additionally, political figures from the Caribbean are sometimes referred to as arrogant and unwilling to meet the commoners:

> I know on the Islands, ya' cant meet with them, ya' never see them on the street like I see them here. That's important we have to see who we voting for. If we don't how can we vote for them. Kendall Stewart [District Leader] sees us he talks to us.[32]

Thus it appears that Clarke had somewhat of an inherent advantage with residents even within Major Owens' Congressional District. Therefore, Owens' first initiative to improve his relations with the Caribbean community was to hire the Consul General to Barbados, Clyde Griffith, as the chief of staff of his Brooklyn Office. As a distinguished gentleman with a discernable Caribbean accent Griffith would smooth relations between Owens' office and the Caribbean electorate. As the summer approached, campaigning increased, for the first time in years since the brutal run with Vander Beatty, Owens opened up a campaign office on Eastern Parkway and Utica Avenue, meanwhile the Clarke 2000 team was functioning one mile west at Montgomery and Nostrand Avenues.

An interesting difference between the two campaigns had to do with their human resources. Clarke 2000 consisted of community people who treated residents with a "country" familiarity analogous to her years as a member of the city council. At the numerous block party festivals which take place Brooklyn where residents are out grilling dinners, or socializing to blaring music members of Clarke 2000 were circulating with petitions or simply chatting with residents about various topics. In effect, the Clarke 2000 team was "making rounds" which also extended to casual street meetings since people on the street can lead to votes and other resources.

In mid-June of 2000, the Friends Of Major Owens had a recruiting session at his campaign office which contained staff members from out of town who

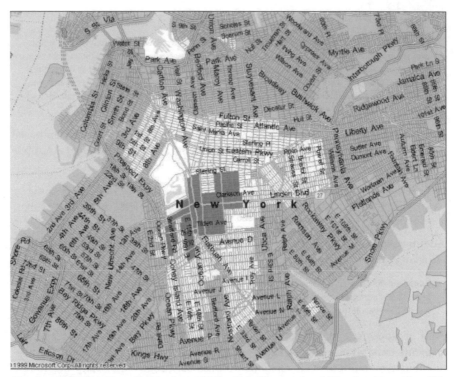

Fig. 1. 40th City Council District and The 11th Congressional District. *Note*: The 40th
City Council District is the darkened area within the 11th Congressional District.

communicated a desire to contact members of the community for aid in contacting
church organizations and volunteers. A few members of the "100 Women for Major
Owens" and "Martin Luther King Commission," both organizations established
by Congressman Owens as a base of human and monetary resources were present
but their aid was not directly solicited. In such a situation as the subtleties of
political etiquette suggest, this appeared as an insult as no members of either
organization participated until later in the summer and with minimal help. Owen's
strategy involved heavy campaigning within the congressional district shared
by the 40th city council district (see Fig. 1). This was done in the hopes of
weakening Una Clarke's stronghold with less emphasis on the other areas since they
would be covered by the District Leaders and their political Clubs. The situation
with the latter was similar to the end of Madison Club reported by Krase and
LaCerra (1991). The campaigning performed by Madison Club members was
traditionally done by direct contact with constituents. Club operatives often knew

their voters and engaged in their day to day activities. However, this changed as there were decreasing interests by local clubs in the community to a focus on campaign contributions and germinating ties with municipal unions. One of the most pernicious challenges to an established club is the rampant activism of an alternative political club or neighborhood group. What such a phenomena display is not only an apparent disjuncture within the democratic organization but a chasm between the later and populous. In this congressional race there was evidence of such a gap. In one case around the corner of a club, residents did not know who their District Leader was nor were they familiar with the title of District Leader or State Committeeman. Neither was they familiar with the concept of a political club nor were they in contact with any member of any, this did not fare well for the Owens' team. As Krase and LaCerra documented, the development of alternative clubs and unfamiliarity with the populous marked the end of the Madison Club as a major political organization. In this case, it would not necessarily end the clubs just perhaps weaken the African-American influence which could be replaced by Afro-Caribbeans or other groups. It appeared that Owens' political team had underestimated the strength of the ethnic identity and resources used by the Clarke 2000 team while also overestimating the power and influence of the African American machine over its constituents. Furthermore, the Owens campaign team initiated a fatal flaw. Ironically, when Owens ran against Vander Beatty in 1982, he charged Beatty of engaging in political maneuvering to gain office in this case the Owens team tried to challenge Una Clarke's eligibility to run stating that the ex-councilwoman wasn't a citizen when she registered to vote. The Election board unanimously and quickly dismissed the complaint and the subsequent backlash was ferocious. Although it may be seen as a standard tactic, similar to challenging signatures on a petition, given the fragile nature of this particular election these actions appeared insensitive. Owens was accused of playing "Dirty Tricks" and of committing acts disparaging to "all immigrant Americans" bringing further doubt about his "fitness to serve Congress."[33]

The challenges and calls of foul play alone indicate a strenuous and hotly contested race. If members of both campaigns were not entirely aware of the intense degree of this particular race at this point, they would soon become aware at the first debate.

Face to Face Debate

The Prospect-Lefferts Gardens Neighborhood Association decided to sponsor a debate between the two Congressional candidates. The event took place in a un air conditioned hall on a humid day in August. A few minutes after 6 p.m. Major

Owens' supporters began to file in accompanied by a few members of his Brooklyn district office moments afterwards members of Clarke's team entered and began to seat themselves on the opposing pews of the church. Aside from the proxemics, there were other distinctive differences in hairstyles and clothing worn by the two groups. It was apparent that before the debate began, the choices were made by the majority of those present. Within moments people were standing in all but the center aisle. By 6:30 the debate had not started and the flow of individuals stemmed to a trickle until they could no longer maintain the physical division and had to mingle within the foyer. If there were any undecided voters or other indicators of neutrality it was rather difficult to tell as the debate began.

Major Owens entered the church from the left aisle facing the front of the church and tensed as Una Clarke approached from the opposing aisle with her supporters cheering while others complained and questioned why the Clarke committee was informed of the debate so late. The moderator, one of the co-pastors of the church read the edict of the Prospect Lefferts Gardens Association and gave the rules of the debate, stating that each candidate was to be given five minutes for opening statements, and one minute to respond to questions and rebuttal.

During the early moments of the debate a man wearing dread locks stood up and held a placard created from a flyer which said "Una Clarke for Congress" moments later a woman did a similar act with a "Major Owens" flyer. Up at the front, Owens shook his head either in disbelief or disapproval. The heat, crowd and poor performance of a lone fan located at a corner of a church increased the tension and tempers of those present, what substantially exacerbated the social atmosphere was the disparity in sound systems. At times Clarke's voice crackled and faded under her microphone to which she often stood up from her seat and shouted, which made her appear nervous as she struggled from being muted by the growing hecklers. Clarke's supporters increased their complaints of favoritism as members shouted why Owen's mike was in better quality than Clarke's.

The few issues that made were audible included education, cultural differences and police brutality. Both candidates stated their contribution to education through the various amounts they have funneled into their respective districts and what they could do at the federal level. As the immigration issue came to the fore, Clarke made reference to Major Owens challenge of her citizenship which appeared as a divisive tactic counterproductive to the appreciation of cultural differences. In turn Owens made reference to the Commission put forth to investigate police brutality by Mayor Giuliani in light of shooting of Amadou Diallo, the sodomy of Abner Louima and the subsequent dismissal of the findings of the commission, which Clarke was a member, by Giuliani. Clarke didn't challenge Giuliani's decision, a move that would haunt her in the primary. Owens noted that the ties between Clark and Giuliani would cripple the unity brought forth by years of investment in the community from the Coalition for Community Empowerment and ended the debate with the words of Jamaican immigrant Marcus Garvey, "Unite! Unite! We Must Remain United." Owens words brought a thunderous applause from his supporters as Clarke's patrons' sang "Go Una Clarke!" as both groups marched out of the church thus ending the debate as they came close to blows outside but dissipated.

After the dramatic display of sharp divisions, an individual who worked in the Friends Of Major Owens campaign during 1982 against Vander Beatty commented:

> In '82 there were more people, it was a time when African American empowerment was taking place in New York City. It was a change of guard and when Major moved in to power it was to undercut Meade Esposito who was the County Leader at the time. Unfortunately the people who were around then working with us either gotten old or died out. There was a youthful energy in the front. Now we have young but naive people. I really didn't notice the politics of Jamaicans until the August debate. Outside many of Una's supporters were in Owen's face and confrontational, I noticed.[34]

In terms of electoral politics West Indians, are particularly known to be fierce. One Caribbean community activist commented: "We Jamaicans take our politics very seriously ya know. There's no joking about that we can get violent." This is apparently correct, in Jamaica the violence stemming from political discord has been fatal. Members of the two opposing political parties, the People's National Party (PNP) and the Jamaican Labor Party (JLP) often exchanged violence during elections. A particular series of incidents were catalyzed by allegations that high ranking members of one party tried to bribe members from the other side for support. Jamaica's violence during elections is so notorious that representatives from the International Monetary Fund warned that such activity would be damaging to the economy certainly in tourism.[35] The problem extends to other areas of the Caribbean as well, in Guyana racially motivated violence takes place between the Indo-Guyanese based People's Progressive Party(PPP) and the Afro-Guyanese People's National Congress Reform (PNCR). In one instance individuals associated with the PNCR were accused of robbing and murdering three Indo-Guyanese.[36]

It appeared that after the heated debate in August the Clarke2000 committee intensified their campaigning efforts. Clarke's office was opened well after the times of normal business operation until the wee hours of the morning with supporters and volunteers milling in and outside the constantly crowded office. It was very difficult to avoid the Clarke bumper stickers posted on the "dollar vans" throughout the city and the campaign vehicles blaring "Go Una . . . knock out Major" to a distinctive Caribbean beat. Supporters increased their circulation of the eastern portion of the Congressional District as evident through the heavy circulation Una Clarke flyers in store windows including those one block away from the "Friends of Major Owens" campaign office. A mile away Owen's campaign office was closed.

Foreseeing a possible victory for Una Clarke, incumbent Afro-Caribbean politicians organized an offensive. First, one political figure who was born in Brooklyn with West Indian roots organized a Pro-Major Owens rally at a catering hall, a local business whose owners frequently travel to their native home Guyana and provide huge scholarships to students seeking higher education there. With an audience of well over 100 people, a mix of West Indian and African Americans, a series of West Indian born political representatives spoke. In an eloquent plea to the potential volunteers and voters, one dominant figure responded to the constantly reprimands for not supporting a "Caribbean sister" and responded that Major Owens took time to meet with the then Caribbean insurgents which enabled them to acquire elective political posts. Summing the sentiments of all the public figures, another official ended by declaring that "ingratitude is not a Caribbean trait."

Second, Clyde Griffith organized a rally at a Soca Arena on Empire Boulevard, a social club known for its mix of not only Soca but other form of West Indian music and entertainment. The event represented a repetition of the previous rally at the small catering hall, there was a similar roster of speakers this one including the County Leader "boss" Clarence Norman Jr. who was defending his assembly seat from the recurrent insurgent James Davis. What set this event a part from the previous one was the presentation of a multi page flyer boarded by Caribbean flags with a smiling Major Owens on the cover. On the inside cover, four West Indian politicians are featured, term limited city councilman Lloyd Henry, Assemblyman Nick Perry and State Senator John Sampson are lined on one side while a sole photo of Una Clarke is on the opposing side facing away from the other three, the above caption reads "Congressman Major Owens Helped Elect 4 Members of the Caribbean Community to Office." That Una Clarke was placed on the opposing side of the flyer may be obvious to some and subliminal to others with the hopeful effect of steering voters away from Clarke to Owens.

Afterwards, Owens hired the aid of the "old timers" from his 1982 election. The campaign office remained open and active for the remainder of the race, a stark contrast to a month before. The icing on the cake was the engagement of the "old fashioned" canvassing done by the political bosses of long ago. Due to attrition, many of the Owens supporters' of the past were no longer present and there was a need to garner new support with the primary just weeks away. "Contracts" were made between the "Friends of Major Owens" committee and community activists in the various assembly districts fortified by Clarke 2000. The agreement involved "lit drops" to private homes days before the primary featuring a flyer of a smiling Una Clarke standing next to a grinning Rudolph Giuliani. In light of the political maneuvering the Mayor performed to get the

Table 1. Results Primary Election for 11th Congressional District.

Assembly District	Una ST Clarke	Percent Clarke	Major Owens	Percent Owens	Official Total Vote
39	1	33.3	2	66.7	3
40	349	37.8	575	62.2	924
41	911	46.5	1,050	53.5	1,961
42	3,487	49.2	3,596	50.8	7,083
43	5,732	54.5	4,782	45.5	10,514
44	1,842	34.8	3,448	65.2	5,290
45	530	46.3	615	53.7	1,145
48	249	51.4	235	48.6	484
51	44	30.6	100	69.4	144
52	115	39.9	173	60.1	288
55	1,248	39.7	1,894	60.3	3,142
56	684	45.4	824	54.6	1,508
57	2,372	41.2	3,383	58.8	5,755
58	3,275	48.0	3,545	52.0	6,820
Total	20,839	46.2	24,222	53.8	45,061

Source: New York City Board of Elections.

Amadou Diallo case tried in Albany New York leading to the subsequent release of police officers and his treatment of Patrick Dorismond, a Haitian immigrant who was shot as a result of struggling with an undercover Police Officer who solicited drugs, the picture became Una Clarke's Achilles heel. This last minute offensive, particularly the latter which also included a monthly political publication called "footnotes" which included a blistering article of the political relationship between Una Clarke and Mayor Giuliani produced a somewhat narrow victory for Owens winning 24,222 (54%) votes while Clarke received 20,839 or 46% out of the 45,061 voters in the September 12, 2000, primary representing 21% of all registered democrats in the 11th Congressional District (see Table 1). The highest voter turnout took place in the 42, 43, 44, 57 and 58th Assembly Districts. The 43rd represents a portion of Crown Heights in which a large Jewish Hasidic community resides, there, Una Clarke received the majority of the vote (5732 (54%) to Owens' 4782 or (46%)). In the remaining districts such as the 42, 44 and 58th in which a portion of Una Clarke's 40th city council district covers and where residents' opinions were pro-Clarke before the Owens offensive there was a surprising turnaround. Owens received the majority of votes in those districts by deceptively large margins considering the efforts of the Clarke 2000 committee. In fact, Owens dominated in all but two of the assembly districts within the congressional district.

The verbal backlash in the *CaribNews* all but convicted Owens' supporters of engaging in intimidation tactics and voter fraud. Cries of foul play perhaps from either side are not unwarranted, in the field many witnessed workers at the polls "helping" voters when they were going to pull levers. There were also reported incidents of verbal scuffles coming close to fisticuffs as one of the county machine who handing out Major Owens palm cards was shoved and leaflets were knocked out of his hand. Members of the Clarke team reported seeing a black van circulating the polls with its passengers warning voters and workers handing out leaflets to vote for the "correct" candidate. The acts of Jamaican Assemblyman Nick Perry through his seemingly aggressive Pro-Owens tactics at the polls and his alleged violation of election law were cited in the papers although no legal restitution was sought. [37] It appeared that the worst was over as Owens retained his Congressional Seat in one of the most intense political battles of his career. In the November general election, Clarke decided to run on the liberal line. In a heavy democratic borough such as Brooklyn attempts to defeat the winner of the primary is often futile. Clarke, in believing that she had 46% of the loyal democrats, thought she could carry that percentage plus the addition of any other party voters. The general election proved otherwise, Major Owens received an overwhelming majority of the votes as 88% (101,338) while Clarke received 6% (6689) and fell behind a Susan Cleary (7200) a white republican candidate who did very little campaigning in the district.

In the ensuing months Una Clarke's daughter, Yvette Clarke, would prepare and eventually win the city council district vacated by her mother and Una Clarke would go to "support" Pataki's race for governor of New York by garnering Caribbean Support. Out of all the Caribbean groups featured in the Clarke-Owens race, Clarke has been accused of primarily focusing on one specific immigrant group, certain immigrant voters claimed that they voted against Una Clarke "because she is from Jamaica and Jamaicans want to control everything." One local newspaper had cited that roughly 85% of the individuals who attended Clarke's concession speech were from Jamaica which suggests that the majority of the workers in her campaign were representing one specific Caribbean group. Additionally, Clarke had a disagreement with the Haitian community over funding to a Haitian Health Program. Haitian community members cite Clarke's British West Indian bias claiming she desired their portion of the funding to be spent on English speaking Caribbeans.[38]

Owens, in response to the increasing complaints of neglecting immigrants' needs, fired his entire staff, except Clyde Griffith, which consisted mainly of African-Americans, replaced them with West Indians and then started publishing a newsletter throughout his congressional district. The newsletter titled "District Observer" being conspicuously close in its appearance to the "Haiti Observer," a periodical geared to the Haitian community.

CONCLUSION

Battles between ethnic groups were taking place in other parts of New York City. For example, in the El Barrio section of Manhattan, the upper west side there has been a growing Dominican community in the midst of an already established Puerto Rican political organization. Similarly to the Caribbeans, the Dominicans claim to have established themselves economically better than their Hispanic counterparts and believe that their time for political advancement has arrived. In contrast, Puerto Ricans believe that the Dominican immigrants are essentially "green" and need to evolve into a political force which can join the already present Hispanic community in time.[39] If the African-American and West Indian situation can be a predictor what will soon occur is a clash between Dominican and Puerto Rican candidates.

Una Clarke's appeals to the supra ethnic idea of a nation state appeared as a viable threat. Her campaign illuminated the desires and fears of West Indians in Brooklyn by addressing issues of immigration and being available. Her traditional machine style of politicking which resembled "making rounds" and appealed to the general Afro-Caribbean sense of community nearly toppled the African American political power base which took several decades to be established. In her appeals to West Indian identity were her statements rejecting the title of African-American and the endorsement of her home country and the wider Caribbean economic community. Thus, her constant entreaty to a common ethnicity represented ethnic retention. However, her claim to a supra ethnicity would be misguided, the Haitian community's quandary represented an underlying intra-Caribbean conflict between English speaking and French speaking West Indians. It was that particular gap and racial strife which cost her. With her tie to Giuliani, through her picture standing next to a mayor, the latter being associated with the sanctioning of harm not only blacks regardless of ethnicity perhaps informed the West Indian public that sooner or later West Indians will eventually ally with African-Americans and place the ethnic divisions on the back burner.

Recently, an interesting phenomenon representing an attempt at intergroup consensus and compromise occurred. In the spring of 2002, 15 elected officials from central Brooklyn ranging from congressional representatives to district leaders attended a meeting to decide on a single candidate who would receive the full support of the Kings County Organization. The representatives present were a mix of Afro-Caribbean and African-American officials including Una Clarke's daughter Yvette Clarke, Major Owens and the County Leader Norman Jr. According to the selection process, the fifteen officials present selected three candidates through a process of elimination. The finalists were to speak in front of members of the community, this caused a certain amount of debate. First, certain members wanted only to keep the selection in front of the politicians but the county leader didn't want to decision to appear as unfair and wanted members of the community involved. There were different perceptions of who were members of the community which, after further debate on what constituted a member of the community, eventually included virtually anyone the three candidates knew since it was decided that they would pick the community people. In the ensuing "presentation" one of the candidates, a perpetual insurgent, conceded and supported Omar Boucher. With two-thirds of the community supporting him, Boucher easily won the presentation and the support of the County.

It appears not only through the campaign of the Owens Clarke race but also through the process of choosing a consensus candidate that the African American leadership recognized the importance of a West Indian identity and hence a nation-state. If African Americans want to maintain power they would have to acknowledge the growing West Indian constituency and ethnicity.

NOTES

1. Alejandro Portes and Ruben G. Rumbaut, *Immigrant America* (2nd ed.). (Berkeley: University of California Press, 1996), 102.

2. I use the two terms Afro-Caribbean or African-Caribbean interchangeably with black immigrant and West Indian, which I will define as immigrants from the Caribbean whose ancestry can be traced to African continent. In New York City this group has primarily settled in the East Flatbush, Flatbush and Crown Heights sections of Brooklyn and is largely comprised of Jamaicans, those from Trinidad & Tobago, Haiti, Guyana, and the smaller islands of the Caribbean economic community (CARICOM) such as St. Kitts & Nevis.

3. Nazil Kibria (2002). College and Notions of "Asian Americans": Second-Generation Chinese Americans and Korean Americans. In: *Second Generation: Ethnic Identity Among Asian Americans*, ed., Pyong Gap Min. New York: Altamira Press.

4. Blanc, Christina S, Linda Basch and Nina G. Schiller, Transnationalism, Nation-States and Culture, *Current Anthropology, 36*, 683–686, (1995).

Kearney, M. (1995). The Local and The Global: The Anthropology of Globalization and Transnationalism, *Annual Review of Anthropology, 24*, 547–565.

Guarnizo, L. Eduardo and Michael P. Smith. The Locations of Transnationalism. In: *Transnationalism From Below*, ed. Michael P. Smith and Luis E, Guarnizo.

(New Jersey: Transaction Publishers, 1998).

Smith, Michael Peter, Transnationalism and The City. In: *The Urban Moment*,(Ed.) Robert A. Beauregard and Sophy Body-Gendrot, (London: Sage Publications Inc, 1995).

5. Schiller Nina Glick and Georges Fouron, Transnational Lives and National Identities: The Identity Politics of Haitian Immigrants. In: *Transnationalism From Below*, (Ed.), Michael P. Smith and Luis E, Guarnizo,(New Jersey: Transaction Publishers, 1998)

6. Guarnizo and Smith, 1998, p. 27.

7. Krase, Jerome and Charles LaCerra, *Ethnicity and Machine Politics*, (Lanham, Md: University Press of America, 1991).

8. Newfield, Jack and Paul Dubrul, *The Abuse Of Power*, (New York: Viking Press, 1977).

Vincent J. Cannato, *The Ungovernable City*, (New York: Basic Books, 2001).

9. Both Owens and Vann entered politics through the good government reforms of liberal Mayor Lindsay who decided to undercut the traditional political forms in New York City. For a detailed discussion of the Lindsay era read, *The Ungovernable City John Lindsay and His Struggle To Save New York* by Vincent J. Cannato, (New York: Basic Books, 2001).

10. Simon Anakwe, Owens Attacks New Redistrictng Lines, *New York Amsterdam News*, (July 17, 1982): 9.

11. Simon Anakwe, Court To Meet On Voting Lines July 6, *New York Amsterdam News*. (July 3, 1982): 23.

12. Maurice Carroll, 3 in Assembly Face New Vote In City, *New York Times*, Oct. 19, 1980, Section 1 p. 37.

13. Richard J. Meislin, Brooklyn Assemblyman Is Ruled Off Primary Ballot, *New York Times*, August 23, 1980, Section 2 p. 27.

Staff Writer, The City; Assembly "Loser" Wins On Recount, *New York Times*, November 15, 1980, Section 2, p. 27.

14. E Dionne Jr, 46 New York Legislators Opposed in Primaries, *New York Times*, September 19, 1982, Section 1 p. 39.

15. Frank Lynn, Five Nominees From Brooklyn Still Challenged, *New York Times*, October 16, 1982, Section 2, p. 30.

Frank Lynn, Order Is Affirmed For New Primaries, *New York Times*, October 23, 1982, Section 1, p. 32.

Josh Barbanel, Court Cancels Rerun of Vote In Brooklyn In Race For Congress, *New York Times*, October 26, 1982. Section A, p. 1.

Sydney A. Schanberg, New York: Mississippi For A While, *New York Times*, October 26, 1982, Section A, p. 29.

16. Joseph P. Fried, Ex-State Senator Faces Vote Charge, *New York Times*, February 15, 1983, Section A. p. 1.

17. Joseph P. Fried, Ex-Beatty Aide Made Recordings As Evidence, *New York Times*, May 22, 1983, Section 1, p. 38.

18. Selwyn Raab, State Panel Accuses Beatty o Wrongly Taking $76,000. *New York Times*, February 16, 1983, Section B, p. 2.

19. Joseph P. Fried, Beatty Trial On Racketeering Begins, *New York Times*, July 19, 1984, Section B, p. 4.

Joseph P. Fried, Beatty is Guilty on Four Counts Of Tax Evasion, *New York Times*, September 18, 1984, Section B, p. 4.

20. Joseph P. Fried, Jury In Brooklyn Acquits Man In Death Of Former State Senator, *New York Times*, Jan 14, 1993, Section B, p. 3.

21. Frank Lynn, In Brooklyn, Party Leader sees New Era, *New York Times*, November 18, 1990, Section 1, p. 31.

22. Graham Rayman, Cop Forced to Quit In Election Breach, But Party Denies he was Nominated, *Newsday*, November 9, 1998, p. A18.

Bob Liff, Brass Can't Arrest Cop's Election Goal, *Daily News*, November 16, 1998, p. 4.

23. Derek Rose, Judge: Cop Who Runs For Office Can Sue For Job, *Daily News*, January 2, 2001, p. 15.

24. Merle English, Division Hurt Minority Campaigns, *Newsday*, September 12, 1991, p. 2.

Maurice Carroll, 2 Primary Night Losers Appear To Be Winners, *Newsday*, September 26, 1991, p. 22.

25. Edwin Ali, Una Clarke: Empowering Caribbean Immigrants, *Caribbean Today*, August 31, 1998, p. J18.

Paul H.B. Shin, Flatbush Marketplace Slated For Renaissance, *Daily News*, February 23, 1999, p. 1.

26. Joyce Shelby, Carib Group Opens Clinic Affordable Health Care Is Its Mission, *Daily News*, June 3, 1998, p. 1.

27. Staff Writer, Middle finger politics, *CaribNews*, Nov 8–21, 1998, p. 1.

Staff Writer, Banana bite hurting caribbean, *CaribNews*, Nov 8–21, p. 1.

28. Staff writer, Bronx Honors Susan Taylor, Brooklyn Honors Una Clarke, *The New York Beacon*, April 21, 1999, p. 22.

29. Peter Noel, Steal This Election, *Village Voice*, August 15, 2000, p. 21.

30. Interview July, 15, 2000.

31. Interview April 14, 2000.

32. Interview July 23, 2000.

33. Nelson King, Congressman Owens loses battle to Knock opponent off the Democratic Ballot, *Caribbean Life*, Aug 8, 2000, p. 6.

34. Interview. September 5, 2000.

35. Staff writer, One More Shot Dead In East Kingston, *CaribNews*, Vol. 19, No. 998, p. 4.

Tony Best, Avoid Election Violence Which Would Hurt Economy, *CaribNews*, 19, No. 1029, p. 6.

36. Staff Writer, Three Killed In Rose hall Bandit Rampage, *CaribNews*, Vol. 19, No 1030, p. 3.

37. Peter Noel, Brooklyn Rats, *The Village Voice*, September 26, 2000, p. 46.

38. J. Zamga Browne, Owens Defeats Clarke, *New York Amsterdam News*, Sept. 14-20, 2000, p. 1.

39. David Gonzalez, Dominican Immigration Alters Hispanic New York, *New York Times*, Sept 1, 1992, Section A, p. 1.

LITTLE ITALY: RESISTING THE ASIAN INVASION, 1965–1995

Philip F. Napoli

Race and Ethnicity in New York City
Research in Urban Sociology, Volume 7, 245–263
© 2004 Published by Elsevier Ltd.
ISSN: 1047-0042/doi:10.1016/S1047-0042(04)07011-4

In a description of New York's Little Italy district published in 1970, Pietro Di Donato, the Italian-American author best know for his novel *Christ in Concrete*, wrote:

> What keeps Little Italy there? Cheap rent? Choice of any superlative food? Family ties? National pride? Social life of the tenement? Or the personal patron saints? In my heart of hearts I belong there too and not among chilling other races and in a mixed neo-community that my soul disdains to digest. I remember what the pigeon fancier on the Mulberry Street roof said, 'Sure I like it here. Why should I leave, I'm with my own people. Is there any place better?[1]

The answer for many Italians and Italian-Americans of the district was simple: yes. Almost any place was indeed better. A community that numbered 20,000 in 1920 had dwindled by the time Di Donato wrote to roughly 14,000.[2] Today, it is virtually gone.

Whereas once it had been an ethnic enclave, by the mid-1990s, Little Italy had become a tourist destination, an Asian community, a wholesale and industrial district, a shopping area for the well-to-do, and an example of urban rebirth. In short, Manhattan's Little Italy is many things at present, but it is not an ethnic Italian community.

The transition from one type of community to another between 1965 and 1995 was not a smooth process, nor was it an easy one. In the 1970s Italians struggled to retain a presence in the district and along the way were forced to articulate and redefine what constitutes an Italian community. Those endeavors, I believe, allow for insight into the shifting and complicated nature of Italian ethnic identity in the late 20th century. While this early effort was motivated by fear and ethnic competition, as time has passed, conflict in the neighborhood has become somewhat less racially charged, and more a struggle among competing groups for the right to determine the "proper" use of public space. Still, at its core, consciously or unconsciously, with malice or without, the white residents of Little Italy have been resisting and attempting to control the Asian "invasion" for over 30 years.

This paper will trace that history. By way of introduction, I first outline the demographic shifts that have taken place within the neighborhood over the past century. Second, I tell the story of the Italian reaction to that change, and suggest what the Italian response to the "Asian invasion" may tell us about the nature of Italian ethnic identity in the late 20th century. Finally I will briefly remark upon the continuing transformation of the area.

DEMOGRAPHY

The boundaries of Little Italy are not precise, and have shifted over time. In the 19th century, the district extended south of Canal Street into the area identified by Jacob Riis as the "Mulberry Bend," and described as "the foul core of New York's slums."[3] By the 1960s, Little Italy had retreated across Canal Street, as the Italian population began to leave the neighborhood for other areas in the city. For the purposes of this paper, Little Italy shall be understood as comprising three census tracts in New York City's Manhattan county, numbers 41, 43, and 45. This area, lying within a short walking distance of City Hall, is roughly bounded by Canal Street on the south, Bowery on the East, Broadway on the west, and East Houston street to the north. Nicknamed the Mulberry District, it became the first and largest Italian enclave in the United States between 1870s and 1924. While there had been an Italian community in New York for generations, historian George Pozetta has argued that the winter of 1872–1873 was pivotal in the development of this community, when more than 2000 poor Italian immigrants, arrived at Castle Garden, the immigrant reception center, unable to care for themselves.[4] These immigrants were quickly fitted in to the preexisting Italian community, taking advantage of the contacts provided by the *bossi*, typically northern Italian men who had arrived earlier, to find jobs in such local enterprises as groceries and saloons, and with American employers. Once the new comers settled, a process of chain-migration began. By the later 1870s, the *bossi* were acting as agents for gangs of labor sent out from New York to work in other areas across North American. As a result, the Mulberry district became a sort of transshipment point for Italian labor.

In 1879, *Harpers Magazine* reported that there were over 20,000 Italians in New York, and this population was growing quickly, fueled by large waves of Italian immigration.[5] Between 1880 and 1920, over four million Italians would come to the United States. While substantial numbers of these people would head home again to Italy, as many as 2 million may have stayed, and not a few of them in New York City.[6] Professor Gabaccia has estimated that by 1890 two-thirds of the 14th ward, the area which in large measure comprises modern Little Italy, was made up of Italians, and by 1900 Italians "had completely taken over the ward."[7] The Italian population of the district peaked in 1910, and began declining soon after.[8]

If immigration filled the Mulberry District and sustained the Italian population there, a combination of factors served to empty it. Once large-scale immigration flows from Italy were ended by the Immigration Act of 1924, there would be, of course, virtually no new immigrants replacing those who left.[9] The development of other districts that offered better housing choices, including the opportunity of home-ownership, combined with the relocation of jobs to other areas, the demolition of older structures to make way for municipal projects, and the growth of mass transit, made logical the choice to move out.[10] The effects were quickly seen in the Mulberry District. In 1922, the neighborhood had been relatively full, with an only 3.3% of all dwelling units remaining empty. By 1932, 24.5% of the units were empty, though the neighborhood remained overwhelmingly Italian.[11]

In years after World War II, New York experienced extensive white flight as perhaps as many as a 2,240,000 white New Yorkers left the city and made their way to the suburbs. Italian-Americans participated in this movement in large numbers.[12] Indeed, Richard Alba has found that by 1970, second-generation Italians in the New York-New Jersey had "significantly dispersed to the suburbs," as 47% of this generation were living in communities with under 100,000 residents.[13] While during the 1950s, the Italian population of the districts of Lower Manhattan actually rose slightly, perhaps giving evidence of the nationwide post-war baby boom and a small rise in Italian immigration in the years following the war, the 1960s and 1970s saw the final exodus of Italian-Americans for other neighborhoods including Bensonhurst in Brooklyn, Arthur Avenue in the Bronx, and the suburbs of Long Island and New Jersey.[14] By 1990, the number of census respondents claiming "Italian" as their single ancestry represented only 10% of the population of the Little Italy area. (Although if those reporting multiple ancestry are included, the figure rises to 23%, perhaps reflecting the much-discussed practice of Italian intermarriage with other ethnic groups.[15]) If we use the numbers of people using Italian at home as an index of the degree of "Italianness" of the district, the numbers are even starker. Only 4.6% of the residents of Little Italy speak Italian at home. Some have suggested that in the years since the last census that number of Italian residents in the old neighborhood has dwindled more dramatically still.[16] The number of Italians living in the community by the time of the next census may be in the low hundreds, or it could well vanish altogether.[17]

Why would people want to leave? Ever since the 1940s, the neighborhood had been living under the threat that a Lower Manhattan Expressway would be built right through their neighborhood, crossing Broom Street and connecting the Holland tunnel with the Williamsburg and Manhattan bridges, essentially bisecting the neighborhood with cars and tons of concrete.[18] According to Tony Dapolito, a long-time area resident and the unofficial "Mayor of Greenwich Village," the threat of the expressway represented a significant factors in encouraging neighborhood residents that their futures should lie in other parts of the city.[19]

Furthermore, figures from the Census of 1960 provide clues to the reasons for the Italian exodus. In 1960, 7% of the residential structures in census tract 41, the most populous of the tracts in Little Italy, had absolutely no heating equipment whatsoever. Approximately 46% of the residential units in this tract were declared, for the purpose of the census, to be "dilapidated." 14% of the residential buildings either required residents to share toilet facilities with their neighbors, or had none at all. This was an improvement over the figures for 1950, at which time almost 36% of the residential units in the district had either no private bath, or one that was considered dilapidated.[20] Of the 4843 residential buildings in Little Italy in

1960, exactly 5 had been built since 1939.[21] The vast majority of the buildings in 1960, as is still true today, were built during the district's boom times during the turn of the century. The neighborhood had then, and has to this day, exactly one playground, the size of two standard New York City building lots; it is 200 feet wide and 100 feet deep. At the same time, New York City was particularly affected by post industrial revolution and fundamental shifts in the nature of global capitalism, including rapid technological changes, the increasing importance of finance relative to manufacturing, and the formation of a new international division of labor. While it is hard to say precisely how many Italian Americans in the Mulberry district were directly affected, the city lost manufacturing and industrial jobs at a rapid rate in these years, while federal policies encouraged the rapid growth of the suburbs and the exodus of whites from central cities. It is easy to understand how Italian-Americans could decide to leave the congested Mulberry District for what Kenneth T. Jackson has termed the "crabgrass frontier."

At same time, Chinatown had been expanding since 1965, when the Congress passed comprehensive changes to the 1952 McCarran-Walter Immigration and Nationality Act. The alterations ended the discriminatory features of the national origins system in place since the 1920s.[22] Under the new law, immigration into the United States of persons born either in China or Hong Kong expanded, running at a rate of approximately 20,900 per year between 1966 and 1976.[23] According to sociologist Min Zhou, New York City's Chinese population of Chinatown expanded by 73% in the 1960s, 111% in the 1970s, and 79% in the 1980s.[24] Whereas in 1980, the population of Chinatown was estimated at 70,000, by 1990, the figure stood at somewhere between 100,000 and 150,000.[25]

The old Chinese neighborhood quickly moved into territory once occupied by Italians, driven by pressure for new living and working space. Sociologist Roger Waldinger has observed that as New York's manufacturing sector crumbled in the late 1960s and early 1970s, loft spaces on the borders of the old Chinatown, including those in Little Italy, emptied out, rents tumbled, and immigrant entrepreneurs moved in.[26] As Chinese businesses moved in, coupled with an influx of Taiwanese money, Chinese and Chinese American businessmen began to purchase property in Little Italy.[27] Zhou's statistics indicate that by 1988, 33.6% of the total number of property lots in Little Italy were owned by people of Chinese origin, and that the Chinese had purchased over 40% of the lots sold since 1975.[28] The 1990 census revealed that almost exactly 50% of the 14,423 Asian residents living in census tracts 41, 43 and 45, the central districts of modern Little Italy, had come to the United States since 1965, and that Asians made up 58% of the population of the reduced area that had come to be known as Little Italy.[29]

ITALIAN REACTION

The reaction of neighborhood residents to this Asian "invasion" was conditioned by the ethnic "revival" of the 1960s and 1970s. Growing out of the movement for Civil Rights for African Americans, this so-called "new ethnicity" had its Italian-American component.[30] It can be most easily identified by the organizations established in the 1960s and 1970s to operationalize Italian-American discontent; to claim for the Italian community some measure of popular and political recognition. The Congress of Italian-American Organizations, founded in 1965, concentrated on issues related to the social-service needs of Italian-Americans.[31] The American Italian Historical Association was founded in 1966, and declared in its constitution its devotion to the "collection, preservation, development and popularization" of materials related to the Italian-American experience in the United States and Canada.[32] The Italian American Civil Rights League was founded in 1970 to combat discrimination against Italian-Americans, and concentrated on negative media portrayals of the group.[33] It drew an estimated 100,000 people to listen to speeches at its June 29, 1970 rally at Columbus Circle, in New York City.[34] The American Italian Coalition of Organizations (AMICO) also founded in 1970, was an alliance of 25 fraternal, civic, labor, professional and social organizations is another example, that fought discrimination against Italian-Americans.[35] The organized effort of Italian-Americans to "save" New York's Mulberry District grew, in part, out of this Italian-American ethnic ferment.

Responding to the both the decline of the area and the expansion of Chinatown, in early 1974 Little Italy residents joined together to form LIRA, the Little Italy Restoration Association. A remarkable 350 people attended the organization's first meeting, March 28, 1974.[36] From the first, ethnic tension pervaded the effort. Vincent Vitale, one of the organization's founders, explained to the *New York Times* that in his opinion, the Chinese were buying up buildings in Little Italy, and forcing the Italians out. At the same time, he asserted that "we don't want to keep the Chinese out, but we want to keep what we have and make it possible for our people to continue to live here."[37] LIRA's newsletter gave voice to blunter comments: "The more Italian people in the area, the better," said one contributor. "For the first time in many years Little Italy is showing a unity that we need in the area to combat growing infiltration of other nationalities," said another.[38]

Italians began to make known their intention to stop that Asian invasion in June of that year, when LIRA pickets prevented trucks from clearing a lot for the construction of a new public school in the neighborhood. LIRA, led by area resident Theodore Tarantini, told the *New York Times* that while the organization did not oppose schools in general, what the neighborhood really needed was middle-income housing.[39] Opposition to the school also focused on the obvious implication that new school space would bring in new school children, the majority of which, given the declining and aging population-base of Italians, would be Chinese.[40]

Over the summer, LIRA found important political support in John Zuccotti, chair of the New York City Planning Commission, Borough President Percy Sutton, and even Mayor Abe Beame. Zuccotti recognized from the first the novelty of attempting to rescue the ethnic character of an area. "This isn't just preserving a street or a building," he said. "It's an attempt to preserve an atmosphere, to give an area a cultural and spiritual flavor." Sutton exclaimed his enthusiasm for the project, saying "This is one of the best things to come along in years. I'm simply delighted at the response of the people in the community . . . and I'm going all the way with them."[41] Beame proudly announced a plan for a "risorgimento" or resurgence of Little Italy in September, just before the start of the festa of San Gennaro, the area's largest and most important street festival.[42]

According to John Zuccotti, the objective of the plans for Little Italy were to "identify, preserve and enhance Little Italy's special qualities so it can remain vital and viable."[43] However, Zuccotti warned against using the plan as a weapon in ethnic conflict. "Preservation is a two-edged sword," he said. "It can cut against destructive change, but it can be used also to ward off unwanted newcomers. Preserving neighborhoods must not become a veiled attempt by some to exclude others. One of the uses of the past must not be to sanctify private enclaves."[44] His warning seems to have fallen on deaf ears.

LIRA worked with Zuccotti and Raquelle Ramati of the City Planning Department's Urban Design group in creating a proposal that would transform the neighborhood. Ramati remembers that the effort began in a period of financial crisis for New York City, and the goal was to use as little City money as possible, while attempting to rehabilitate the neighborhood through private funds and development.[45] At the same time, the files of the Planning Commission reveal that ethnic preservation was the primary reason for the drafting of plans for the District. An unsigned note in the City Planning Commission files acknowledges that the area of Little Italy "is now reaching a point in its history where is own survival appears to be in jeopardy . . . the goals of this project are to stabilize and enhance a socially heterogeneous low-income neighborhood and to preserve and enhance, by specific measures, the Italian-American traditions in the City."[46] Costing about $50,000, the plan for Little Italy was viewed by Zucotti, Ramati, and others within the City Planning Department as a potential prototype for similar efforts that might be undertaken elsewhere in the city.[47]

The proposal for the creation of a Special District, announced in by Beame in September, 1974, seemed to recognize the nostalgic and symbolic significance of the area, arguing that "Little Italy is neither midway nor museum, though it has aspects of both."[48] "For all New Yorkers," the report stated, "Little Italy is a traditional symbol of the ethnic and cultural diversity which enriches the City."[49] Indeed, the proposal quite explicitly sought to strengthen those symbolic aspects of the neighborhood. The plan called for the conversion of the old Police Building at 240 Centre Street into an Italo-American cultural center. The original vision for this center was that it would "provide a showcase for art works," and that "Italian film festivals, opera workshops, shows of modern Italian art and industrial design could draw on a Citywide audience."[50]

At the same time, it called for the restoration and preservation of those elements that created a neighborhood ambiance. The 1974 plan called for the moderate rehabilitation of a number of the older buildings in the area, which, it was speculated "could make them highly attractive." A list of buildings with historic significance was provided. The plan further called for the preservation of historic store fronts, and the "pedestrianization" of certain streets to improve pedestrian flow through the neighborhood. Street improvements were planned, such as the widening of sidewalks, the addition of trees and shrubs, kiosks for the posting of notices, and "attractive new street decorations." Ramati recalls that in creating their designs, the group "used the San Gennaro festival as a hint or a concept of what could work well there."[51] As a result, the Urban Design group asserted that the delights of the Little Italy's famous religious festival "should be the rule, not the exception."[52]

Housing in the neighborhood was a major problem, given the aging and run-down state of the buildings. Members of the community argued that "a small number of Italian immigrants take up residence annually," and that "if additional housing were provided, the neighborhood would attract many more of the 22,000 Italian immigrants who come to the United States each year."[53] Further, because there had been little or no new construction in the neighborhood for roughly 60 years, housing "would offer an alternative to families who must now leave because they must find suitable accommodations – and to those who would return, if attractive apartment were available."[54] As a consequence, the plan called for the construction of some 700 units of new moderate-income housing on seven locations in the area, including the construction of a joint combined housing and school project at the corner of Spring and Elizabeth streets. Further if the neighborhood was to attract new residents, then the needs of families with children would have to be met. As a way of compromising over the tensions created by the construction of a new public school in the district, the plan called for a the construction of a school with space for 600–800 students, and 180 apartments above.[55] Community Board Number 2 supported this change.[56] The proposal also identified seven other sites as potential locations for the construction of additional housing.[57]

The new school was designed to provide something that might attract new residents, but so was the call for an increase in the amount of park space in the neighborhood, and the renovation of the one park that did exist. The plan advocated the acquisition of a number of vacant lots in the area, and the construction of vest-pocket parks in them. On the issue of parks, the Ramati and the Urban Design Group gave in to their dreams. The report proposed that an interior park be constructed between Mott, Broom, Mulberry and Grand Street, "if agreement of all the property owners could be obtained . . . these backyards could be pooled, creating a semi-private green oasis, free of all vehicular traffic." According to Doris Deither, a member of the zoning committee in Community Board 2, this was indicative of a fundamental problem in the Ramati's design plans. They looked good on paper, but "I don't think she really understood the area."[58]

The final element of the plan called for the strengthening of the commercial nature of what was dubbed the Mulberry Street Spine: the business heart of Little Italy. Lou DiPalo, an area businessman whose family participated in the LIRA movement, recalls that it was widely recognized as in everyone best interest to preserve Mulberry Street. For this reason, all local business participated either actively or as financial contributors.[59] The plan envisioned a local development corporation that would encourage business activity and job development, and hope to "attract businesses that would benefit from an association with the neighborhood's regional and ethnic shopping attractions." It is at this moment and place when the ethnic assumptions of LIRA, Ramati, and the Urban Design Group become visible. "Such businesses would not necessarily have to be Italian-owned," the plan asserted, "but might depend on workers with traditional Italian skills." It is easy to understand how and why Asians in the neighborhood understood the plan to be a threat.[60] Concretely, the Design Group called for the opening of sidewalk cafes, the installation of banners as decorative and visually unifying objects, and increased parking, all of which would make the area more attractive to visitors.[61]

As an experiment, in the fall of 1974 three blocks of Mulberry Street were converted into a pedestrian mall.[62] Success at the temporary mall, and another short-term closing of Mulberry Street in 1975, led to intensification of planning for permanent zoning changes.[63] Announced in September 1976, by the City Planning Commission, the new plan asserted that the proposed zoning would "strengthen the area's existing fabric by encouraging convenience-type stores on the ground floor and in inner-court yards, landscaped open space for residents, storefront renovation and sidewalk and park improvements."[64] Victor Marrerro, Chair of the City Planning Commission, clearly understood that the proposed district would help construct an island of Italian permanence in a Chinese sea. "To many New Yorkers, Little Italy is a home-away-from-home. To thousands of visitors from miles around, it is a place to sample special flavors . . . It is a magnetic regional asset and one of the City's most vital neighborhoods. Shaped by generations of New Yorkers, it is a critical part of our urban heritage."[65] In this new version of the plan, the significance of the Mulberry Street spine was emphasized, asserting, "it is the Old World flavor inherent in the physical and cultural characteristics of Little Italy, especially along Mulberry Street, that the special district legislation aims at preserving . . ."[66]

Partly as a result, ethnic feelings ran high in 1976 and 1977, as the proposal to create a Little Italy Special District made its way through the city bureaucracy toward approval by the Board of Estimate. Doris Deither, then chair of the zoning committee of Community Board 2, remembers that the Board insisted on the involvement of both the Chinese and Italian members of the community, much to the displeasure of Ramati and the Urban Design Group. Deither and the Community Board invited representatives of the Chinese community to Board meetings, but found that the Chinese did not like to speak in front of the Italians. So, Deither held separate meeting with both groups.[67] With exaggeration that underscores the depth of Chinese suspicions, John Wang, a journalist and urban planner complained in 1980 that the Risorgiomento plans were drawn up in an "unusually secretive manner . . . without ever consulting or seeking input from . . . Chinese residents in the area, who made up 70% of the district's population." According to Wang, Chinese businessmen and property owners felt threatened by the Special District legislation, worrying that it could hamper business development and other uses of local property.[68]

Chinese suspicions were publically aired in October 1976, at a public hearing on the City Planning Commission's plans. A representative of the National Chinese-American Civic Association asserted that the Risorgiomento plan was an effort "to get rid of the Chinese north of Canal Street." An Italian resident retorted that the Chinese were forcing the Italians out. "Our building is for sale and whenever Chinese people come to look at it we're afraid, she said. "We know if it's sold we'll be evicted."[69] In February, Mr. Paul J. Q. Lee of the Chinese-American voter's league asked "How can you propose what no longer exists?"[70]

When passed by the New York Board of Estimate in 1977, over the vehement opposition of the Chinese community, the legislation included language indicating that the general purpose of the Special Little Italy was designed to "preserve and strengthen the historical and cultural character of the community."[71] According to Deither, the plans were sold to the Italian community on the basis that the establishment of the district would keep the Chinese out.[72] Even those involved with the project recognized its symbolic significance. Salvatore Esposa told the *Times*, "We want to set an example that every area can do this. To restore the old. The old can sometimes be better then the new."[73]

The plans, provoked by the movement of Asian immigrants into the area, had forced the city and neighborhood residents to articulate the elements that they believed made Little Italy and Italian district. Housing, schools, and most importantly, a thriving business district were at the core of the plan. And, the

Risorgimento did work, at least as far as area businesses were concerned. According to one report, 15 new restaurants had opened in the Little Italy area between 1975 and 1981, and a dozen others repaired or renovated. By the early 1980s, business was booming on Mulberry Street.[74]

In the 1990s the most contentious symbol of Italian ethnicity has been the Feast of San Gennaro. Held annually along Mulberry Street, the feast honors St. Januarius, a Neopolitan bishop of the third century who died a religious martyr. Mayor Giuliani turned his spotlight on the festival in 1995, and threaten to close the festival because of its alleged ties to organized crime.[75] Just before the festival opened, organizers reached an agreement with the Mayor to allow outside overseers of the event's books.[76] In June 1996, Federal prosecutors indicted 19 members of the Genovese crime family in June, contending that they had turned the festival into a racket, deciding who could participate and skimming money from rents.[77] Then in August, the city denied a festival permit to the Society of San Gennaro, which had run the feast for the previous 68 years, arguing it was not a genuine not-for-profit agency. In its place, the Mayor appointed the Figli di San Gennaro Inc., and asked the Roman Catholic Archdiocese of New York to oversee the feast's proceeds.[78] According to Mayor Giuliani, before the city stepped in, organizers would take in as much as $324,000 and donate as little as $7,7600 to actual charities, the majority of the remainder lining the pockets of the organized criminals who ran the event.[79] In 1997, the Government earned a conviction of Louis Zacchia. Described by Government attorney as an associated of the Genovese crime family, Zacchia, was convicted of defrauding the city of $230,000 per year. Zacchia apparently collected more money from the San Gennaro vendors than was actually reported to the city.

Despite the controversy, the festa brings enormous recognition to the area, and perhaps as many as a 3 million visitors a year, according to festival organizers.[80] While observers noted in 1993 that large numbers of the visitors to the festival, and even some of the vendors, were Asian, John Fratta, whose great-grandfather helped organize the Society of San Gennaro some 70 years ago, believes that the festa's continued presence in the community helps stake a symbolic claim to that section of New York as an Italian *neighborhood*.[81]

As a result of the festa and LIRA's efforts to preserve an Italian presence on Mulberry Street, tourism and the commercial activity have become the principle means by which the neighborhood earns its income and maintains it public recognition as an Italian district. In New York's Little Italy, ethnicity has become tied inextricably to commerce. Indeed those activities have forced a renegotiation of the meaning of Italian ethnicity. No longer a matter of churches and social clubs, school and bacci games, Italian ethnicity is now largely a matter of food. This essentialization of the Italian ethnic experience may well by emblematic of the assimilation of Italians into the mainstream.

LITTLE ITALY WITHOUT ITALIANS

Still, the neighborhood has continued to change. Roma Furniture, a fixture on Grand Street for nearly 50 years, closed its doors in 1993, and opened a new store in Rockville Centre.[82] With no family member ready or willing to take over the business, John Fretta closed his shop at the corner of Hester and Mott, in the early 1990s.[83] Indeed, Mott Street, once the central market street in Little Italy, has very few very few Italian stores left at all, outside of DiPalo's on Grand and Mott.[84] These closings are indicative of the fact that with their third and fourth generation children becoming increasingly Americanized, and unwilling to take over family businesses in the old ethnic enclave, Italian businessmen in the neighborhood have, one by one, closed up and gone into retirement. In the past decade or so, the remnants of Little Italy have receded so that Italian-oriented business occupy just a few blocks along Mulberry Street, with scattered outposts, like the Paresi Bakery on Elizabeth Street, in other locations in the old Mulberry District. Sociologist Donald Tricarico said in 1990, "It just isn't an Italian-American community. There's an ethnic economy with nothing underneath."[85]

Now a neighborhood largely without Italians, contests between Chinese and newer residents have continued, but at least on the surface, the older ethnic tensions have dissipated. At present, conflicts center around zoning and the proper and legal use of public space. In 1995 the neighborhood fought unsuccessfully against the construction of a 12 story building on the northern edge of Little Italy, at the corner of Elizabeth and Houston Streets. The community, with the support of New York Council member Kathryn E. Freed, asserted that the building violated the zoning regulations established by the passage of the Little Italy Special District legislation in 1977.[86] Fights have erupted over the emergence of wholesale businesses in the Special District, which was clearly not zoned for such businesses.[87] In November, 1998, Freed held hearings before the Housing and Buildings Committee concerning her proposed legislation designed to give the Department of Buildings "padlock" power on those businesses engaged in illegal manufacturing in the Little Italy and Chinatown districts, areas that have been zoned for commercial and mixed-use, but not manufacturing. Freed asserts that these businesses, which are largely Chinese-owned and operated, "are noxious and hazardous and pose an increased public health, safety, and quality of life problem for our communities."[88]

Despite the altered nature of the contests between Asians and the white European residents, remnants of ethnic tension exist to this day. Anthony Luna, owner of Luna's restaurant on Mulberry Street told the New York Times in 1990 that a Chinese buyer had made an offer of several million dollars on property he owned in the area, but he elected to sell it to someone else, someone he knew.

"We stick together," he said. "We Italians don't want to sell anymore to the Chinese. We want to keep it Little Italy."[89] Anne Compoccia, leader of the Little Italy Chamber of Commerce, insists that Little Italy's Old World charm, and its residents' determination to stay put, will ensure the survival of this neighborhood—turned—tourist attraction. "We're stemming the tide," she says. "Even if it's down to just 10 blocks, we're going to preserve it."[90]

These attitudes, however, an not universally held by area Italians. DiPalo argues that the growth of Chinatown has prolonged and strengthened the life of the Little Italy community, by bringing in new economic life into a depressed area. "If the stores were empty, the buildings were losing large amounts of money, because the tenants were paying only a fraction of the cost of maintaining the building." By taking up vacant store fronts and filling abandoned buildings, the in-migration of Asians made the area safer and strengthened the fabric of the community. As for his shop, DiPalo wants to stay as long as customers, of whatever ethnicity, continue to come to his store.[91]

And even Chinatown changes. Once a boom town, Chinatown's growth may be losing steam. Frank Vardi, a city demographer, indicated to the *Christian Science Monitor* in 1994 that Chinatown was running out of room for further expansion. As a result, he indicated, Asian immigrants were beginning to by-pass the old ethnic gateways like Manhattan's Chinatown, and move directly into suburban communities, or growing Chinatowns in Flushing and Brooklyn.[92] Anecdotal evidence and personal observation indicates this may be so. Where once wholesale businesses occupied space along Mulberry Street now stands a shop with a for rent sign. Spaces on Elizabeth Street, vacated by Chinese business people, are being occupied by trendy clothing boutiques and expensive restaurants.[93] Indeed it might not be too much to say that the area could be about to undergo transition once again. Evidence can be seen in the recent attempts by some to have the areas north of Kenmare Street, once known simply at little Italy, as a brand new and separate entity, called "Nolita" or northern Little Italy. As Asians move out, it seems quite possible that SoHo will move in, one again altering the ethnic and social mix of this most contested urban landscape.

CONCLUSION

Remarking on a television documentary about Italian-Americans, Will Parrinello told the *New York Daily News* in 1996 that "Little Italy doesn't necessarily have to be that place, that physical place. . . . But it is more a place of mind. It is more a frame of mind."[94] Mr. Parinello is right, the old Little Italy is gone, replaced by a new one, a symbol of what was. And if sociologists Herbert Gans, Richard Alba, and

Mary Waters are right, that for white European Americans in general, and Italian Americas in particular, ethnic identity is being recast by intermarriage and other demographic forces into a voluntary, symbolic activity, then the transformation of Little Italy from 1965–1996 is a case study of this process. The attempt by LIRA and its collaborators to reconstruct the neighborhood as a "bulwark of Gemeinschaft against mass society Gesellschaft," redrew the public image of the neighborhood. By working successfully to strengthen the commercial nature of the Mulberry Spine, LIRA helped convert Little Italy in to a sort of ethnic strip mall, catering to white Europeans of all backgrounds who wish to sample Italian ethnic foods and play games of chance at ethnic festivals. In the "new" Little Italy that has emerged over the past 30 years, "Italianness" is something that can be sampled along the streets of an old ethnic neighborhood, and then put aside as necessary or desired. The history of Little Italy thus mirrors the changes in Italian identity itself.

The symbolic significance of the neighborhood, however, only achieved its meaning by virtue of having been constructed in the context of an influx of Asian residents and other neighborhood changes. It is that ethnic transition which forced the essentialization of the Italian-American experience: forced the movement to redefine and reconstitute the Italian-American experience in terms of its most basic constituent parts. The commercial enterprises of the festa and the neighborhood restaurants thus became the quintessential expressions of what it meant to be Italian. For Americans concerned about the continued existence of an Italian-American identity, this ought to represent a profoundly troubling development. For if Italian-Americans ethnic identity can best be represented by commerce, then perhaps it is true, as Richard Alba suggested over a decade ago, Italian-Americans are slipping into the twilight of their ethnicity, and Little Italy has become what Jerome Krase has termed an "Ethnic Theme Park." [95]

NOTES

1. Pietro Di Donato, *Naked Author* (New York: Phaedra Inc., 1970), p. 149.
2. *Little Italy Risorgimento*: Proposals for the Restoration of an Historic Community (New York: City Planning Commission, 1974), p. 5.
3. Riis, Chapter 6, p. 1.
4. Howard R. Marraro, "Italians in New York in the Eighteen Fifties, Part I," *New York History* (April 1945): 181–203; Howard R. Marraro, "Italians in New York in the Eighteen Fifties, Part II" New York History June 1945): 181–203; Howard R. Marraro, "Italians in New York During the First Half of the Nineteenth Century," *New York History* (July 1945): 278–306; Howard R. Marraro, "Italo-Americans in Eighteenth Century New York," *New York History* (July 1940): 316–323; George E. Pozzetta, "The Mulberry District of New York City: The Years Before World War One," in Robert F. Harney and J. Vincent

Scarpaci eds, *Little Italies in North America* (Toronto: The Multicultural History Society of Ontario, 1981), p. 14. See also "Swindling Immigrants," *New York Times*, 10 Dec. 1872; "The Swindled Italians," *New York Times*, 12 Dec. 1872; "Immigration an Emigration" *New York Times*, 3 Jan. 1873; "The Arrival of Italian Immigrants: Accommodations of the Commissioners of Emigration," *New York Times*, 4 Jan. 1873

5. "Italian Life in New York," *Harpers Magazine* 62 (April 1881), 676.

6. Luciano J. Iorizzo and Salvatore Mondello, *The Italian Americans* (Boston: Twayne Publishers, 1980), p. 285; Roger Daniels, *Coming to America: A History of Immigration and Ethnicity in American Life* (New York: HarperCollins, 1990), pp. 188–189.

7. Donna Gabaccia, *From Sicily to Elizabeth Street: Housing and Social Change Among Italian Immigrants, 1880–1930* (Albany: State University of New York Press, 1984), p. 67.

8. Donna Gabaccia, "Little Italy's Decline: Immigrant Renters and Investors in a Changing City," in David Ward and Oliver Zuns eds., *The Landscape of Modernity: New York City, 1900-1940* (Baltimore: Johns Hopkins University Press, 1992), p. 244.

9. Daniels, Coming to America, p. 189; Jerre Mangione & Ben Morreaale, *La Storia: Five Centuries of the Italian American Experience* (New York; Harper Perennial, 1993), p. 316.

10. Gabaccia, "Little Italy's Decline," passim.

11. Gwendolyn Hughes Berry, "Idleness and the Health of a Neighborhood," (New York: New York Association for Improving the Condition of the Poor, 1933), pp. 3, 4; Donna Gabaccia, "Little Italy's Decline: Immigrant Renters and Investors in a Changing City," in David Ward and Oliver Zuns eds., *The Landscape of Modernity: New York City, 1900-1940* (Baltimore: Johns Hopkins University Press, 1992), pp. 235-251.

12. Rosenwaike, *Population History of New York City*, p. 135; Oliver E. Allen, *New York: New York* (New York: Atheneum, 1990), p. 300. Binder and Reimers offer somewhat smaller number in their recent book. See: Frederick M. Binder and David Reimers, *"All the Nations Under Heaven: An Ethnic and Racial History of New York City* (New York: Columbia University Press, 1995), p. 206.

13. Alba, *Twilight of Ethnicity*, p. 88.

14. Compare US Census Bureau, "Characteristics of the Population by Census Tracts: 1950," p. 87, U.S. Census Bureau, General Characteristics of the Population by Census Tracts, 1960," p. 115. Bowser, Benjamin P. Census data with maps for small areas of New York City, 1910–1960: a guide to the microfilm. 1981; Iorizzo and Mondello, *The Italian Americans*, p. 285.

15. Alba, *Twilight of Ethnicity*, pp. 89–92; Crispino, *The Assimilation of Ethnic Groups*, pp. 104–106.

16. U.S. Census Bureau, "1990 Census of Population and Housing, Database: C90STF3A," generated by Philip Napoli, using 1990 Census Lookup, http://venus.census.gov/cdrom/lookup 1 Dec. 1990. In constructing this data, I included all those that listed Italian as their first or second Conversation with John Fratta, local area politician.

17. Use of census data to estimate the number of Italians in New York or any city is complicated. After 1930 it is very likely that a significant number of the additions to the Italian community are third and fourth generation members. However, these are not included in the census tabulations. According to Mary C. Waters:

> The decennial censuses through 1970 asked questions about the individual's birthplace and his or her parents' birthplaces. This made it possible to identify the first generation-immigrants themselves- and the second generation-the children of immigrants. (Together these two

generations were known as the "foreign stock.") Yet the grandchildren and later descendants
of immigrants were not identifiable in these censuses and were classified simply as "native
white of native parentage." As the population of European origin progressed generationally, a
smaller proportion of it consisted of "foreign stock" and a greater proportion disappeared into
the category "native white of native parentage."

"In the late 1970s leaders of organizations of white ethnic groups such as Irish-Americans,
Italian-Americans, and Slavic-Americans pressured the government to change the census
form by adding a question that would allow them to identify their potential members- the
third and later generations. This move was resisted by the Bureau of the Census on the
grounds that it would not produce "hard" enough data. In earlier tests of questions on ethnic
identity, the Census Bureau's monthly Current Population Survey had found that ethnic
identity was not very reliable-people changed their minds about it from survey to survey.
However, at the last minute, responding to pressure from these ethnic organizations, the
Census Bureau did add a question on ethnic ancestry." Mary C. Waters, *Ethnic Options:
Choosing Identities in America* (Berkeley, CA: University of California Press, 1990),
p. 9. See also, Ira Rosenwaike, Population History of New York (Syracuse, NY: Syracuse
University Press, 1972), p. 165.

18. Caro, pp. 769–770.

19. Tony Dapolitio, interview with the author.

20. Characteristics of Dwelling Units by Census Tracts, 1950 p. 507.

21. "Occupancy and Structural Characteristics of Housing By Census Tract," 1960,
p. 844.

22. Thomas J. Archdeacon, *Becoming American: An Ethnic History* (New York: Free
Press, 1983), p. 207; Ellen Percy Kraly, "U.S. Immigration Policy and the Immigrant
populations of New York," pp. 37–38, in Nancy Foner ed., *New Immigrants in New York*
(New York: Columbia University Press, 1987).

23. Emmanuel Tobier, "The New Face of Chinatown," *New York Affairs* 5 (Spring
1979), 68.

24. Min Zhou, *Chinatown: The Socioeconomic Potential of an Urban Enclave*
(Philadelphia: Temple University Press, 1992), p. 186.

25. Zhou, Chinatown estimates the number at 100,000. Rachelle Garbarine, "New York's
Changing Neighborhoods: "An Expanding Chinatown is Now Getting Condos," *New York
Times*, 16 Nov. 1990.

26. Roger Waldinger, "Immigrants Rescue the Rag Trade," *NY: The City Journal, 1*
(Winter 1991), 47.

27. Fred Ferretti, "Chinatown Leaps the Wall and Moves into Little Italy," 13 July 1980,
New York Times.

28. Zhou, Chinatown, p. 190. Zhou uses a definition of Little Italy that is somewhat
smaller than that created by using the Census Tracts. His Little Italy does not extend west
of Lafayette Street. While Zhou's definition more accurately corresponds to the boundaries
of present-day Little Italy, it does not take in to consideration the traditional boundaries of
the district, which included that western area.

29. 1990 U.S. Census Data, Database: *C90STF3A*, http://venus.census.gov/cdrom/
lookup 1 Dec. 1990.

30. Humbert S. Nelli, *From Immigrants to Ethics: The Italian Americans* (New York:
Oxford University Press, 1983), p. 174; Alfred Aversa, Jr., "Italian Neo-Ethnicity: The

Search for Self-Identity," *Journal of Ethnic Studies* (6 (Summer 1978), pp. 50, 51; Kathleen Neils Conzen, David A. Gerber, Ewa Morawska, George E. Pozzetta, and Rudolph J. Vecoli, "The Invention of Ethnicity: A Perspective from the U.S.A.," *Journal of American Ethnic History*, 12 (Fall 1992), p. 29.

31. Barbaro, p. 47.

32. Quoted in Frank J. Cavaioli, "Group Politics, Ethnicity, and Italian-American," in Michael D'Innocenzo and Joseph P. Sirefman, eds., *Immigration and Ethnicity: American Society: Melting Pot or Salad Bowl*, (Westport, CT: Greenwood Press, 1992), p. 71.

33. Donald Tricarico, "The 'New' Italian American Ethnicity," *Journal of Ethnic Studies* 12 (Fall 1984), p. 79.

34. Find more. Jay Maeder, "Stairway to Heaven: Joe Colombo's Great Civil Rights Crusade, 1971," *Daily News* 27 Oct. 1998.

35. Fred Barbaro, "Ethnic Affirmation, Affirmative Action, and the Italian-American," *Italian Americana* 1 (Autumn 1974), pp. 41–58.

36. Raquel Ramati, *How To Save Your Own Street* (Garden City: Doubleday and Co., 1981), p. 55.

37. Frank Prial, "Little Italy Is Restive as Chinatown Expands," *New York Times*, 26 April 1974.

38. Quoted in Peter Jackson, "Ethnic Turf: Competition on the Canal Street Divide," *New York Affairs*, Vol. 7, No. 4, 1983, 152.

39. "Pickets Block School Project Saying Housing is Needed First," *New York Times*, 18 June 1974.

40. "Court Stays Little Italy School," *New York Times*, 8 Aug. 1974.

41. *Ibid.*

42. Glenn Fowler, "City to Revive and Refurbish Little Italy," *New York Times*, 19 Sept. 1974.

43. John Zuccotti, "Planning with Neighborhoods: An Approach to Reality," *City Almanac*, Vol. 9, (December 1994), p. 8.

44. *Ibid.*

45. Ramati, interview with the author.

46. No author, Little Italy Restoration Project, File: Little Italy Background and Old Reports, 6th Fl., City Planning Commission. See Vivian Awner.

47. Ada Louise Huxtable, "Recession-Proof Plan To Rescue Little Italy," *New York Times*, 4 May 1975.

48. *Little Italy Risorgimento: Proposals for the Restoration of an Historic Community* (New York: Department of City Planning, 1974), p. 6.

49. *Little Italy Risorgimento*, Sept 1974, p. 5.

50. *Little Italy Risorgimento*, p. 33

51. Raquel Ramati, interview with the author, 21 Oct. 1998.

52. *Little Italy Risorgimento*, pp. 21, 7–9, 23; Raquel Ramati, interview with the author, 21 Oct. 1998.

53. *Little Italy Risorgimento*, p. 16.

54. *Ibid*, p. 17.

55. *Little Italy Risorgimento*, p. 17.

56. Manhattan Community Planning Board Minutes, 20 Feb. 1975. New York City Reference Library.

57. *Little Italy Risorgimento*, pp. 17–19.

58. Doris Deither, interview with the author, 24 Nov. 1998.

59. Lou DiPalo, interview with the author 26 Aug. 1998.

60. Little Italy Risorgimento, p. 45.

61. Raquel Ramati, interview with the author, 21 Oct. 1998.

62. "A Pedestrian Mall Along Mulberry St. Is Opening Today," *New York Times*, 30 Nov. 1974; " 'Little Italy Is Love' and Mulberry Street Becomes a Mall for the Weekend," *New York Times*, 1 Dec. 1974.

63. New York City Planning Commission, *Little Italy Special District* (New York: City Planning Commission, 1976), p. 8.

64. Press Release, City Planning News, 22 Dec. 1976. Columbia University Avery Library; Glenn Fowler, Preservation of Little Italy Urged, *New York Times*, 3 Sept. 1976.

65. Victor Marrero, "Proposed Little Italy Special District," City Planning News, 2 Sept. 1976, file: Little Italy – Background and Old Reports, City Planning Commission Files.

66. New York Planning Commission, *Little Italy Special District*, p. 13.

67. Doris Deither, interview with the author, 24 Nov. 1998.

68. John Wang, "Plans and Promises: Like Letters to Santa Claus," *New York Affairs*, Vol. 6, No. 3, 1980, pp. 74–75.

69. Glenn Fowler, "Italians and Chinese Clash on Zoning," *New York Times*, 15 Oct. 1976.

70. Beverly Solochek, "In Little Italy, the Word is Risorgimento," *New York Times*, 1 May 1997, Sec. 8.

71. Wang, "Like Letters to Santa Claus," p. 76; Zoning Resolution Web Version/Text, City of New York, Article X, Special Purpose districts, http://www.ci.nyc.ny.us/html/dcp/html/zonetext.html 11 December, 1998.

72. Deither, telephone interview with the author, 24 November 1998.

73. Beverly Solochek, "In Little Italy, the Word is Risorgimento," *New York Times*, 1 May 1997, Sec. 8.

74. Wold von Eckardt, "Little Italy Lives!" *Washington Post*, 4 April 1981.

75. David Seifman, "May Take Miracle to Save San Gennaro," *New York Post*, 9 Sept. 1995.

76. Rob Polner, "Blesses San Gennaro; Mayor, Organizers Reach Accord on Monitor for Mob—linked Fest," *Newsday*, 11 Sept. 1995

77. Don Van Natta, Jr., "19 Indicted in Blow to Genovese Mob," *New York Times*, 12 June 1996; Randy Kennedy, "Feast of San Gennaro Returns, a Lot Saintlier, Officials Say," *New York Times*, 13 Sept. 1996.

78. Vivian S. Toy, "Giuliani Installs Managers for Little Italy Fair in New Move on Mob," *New York Times*, 21 Aug. 1996.

79. Frank Lombardi, "San Gennaro Feast Kicks off Tonight," *New York Daily News*, 10 Sept. 1998.

80. William Banstone, "Porkstock '94, Eleven days of Meat, Merriment, and the Mob," *Village Voice*, 27 Sept. 1994.

81. Bruce Lambert, "Neighborhood Report: Lower Manhattan; A Little Italy Festival Marco Polo Would Love," *New York Times*, 19 Sept. 1993; John Fratta, interview with the author, 14 Oct. 1998.

82. David Herndon, "Arrivederci, Roma Furniture," *Newsday*, 29 July 1993.

83. Lou DiPalo, interview with the author, 26 Aug. 1998.

84. DiPalo, interview with the author, 26 Aug. 1998.

85. Quoted in Rick Hampson, "Little Italy: Smaller and Smaller," *Associated Press*, 23 July 1990.

86. Kathryn E. Freed to Commissioner Joel Miele, Department of Buildings, 31 Aug. 1995, Papers of Charle Caffiero; Michael Haberman, "C.B. 2 Opposes 12-Story little Italy Building," *The Villager*, 2 Aug. 1995.

87. Andrew Jacobs, "Neighborhood Report: Chinatown: Living With the Fishes on Mott Street," *New York Times*, 14 April 1996; Andrew Jacobs, "Neighborhood Report: Soho: As Vegetables Irk Residents, Dealers Unite, *New York Times*, 29 September 1996.

88. Kathryn E. Freed, "Community Board #2 Update," 19 November 1998, p. 2.

89. Constance L. Hays, The Talk of Little Italy: A changing Little Italy Says no to a Hotel, *New York Times*, 5 May1990.

90. Rick Hampson, "Little Italy: Smaller and Smaller," *The Associated Press*, 17 July 17, 1990.

91. Lou DiPalo, interview with the author, 26 Aug. 1998.

92. Sam Walker, "A Chinatown of Contradictions," *Christian Science Monitor*, 8 Aug. 1994., Sec. 1, p. 9.

93. Joyce Cohen, "If You're Thinking of Living In Nolita; A Slice of Little Italy Moving Upscale," *New York Times*, 17 May 1998.

94. Ellis Henican, "Seeking Italian Identity," *New York Newsday* 11 March 1996.

95. Jerome Krase, "Italian American Urban Landscapes: Images of Social and Cultural Capital." *Italian Americana*, Vol. XXII, No. 1, Winter 2003, pp. 17–44. See also in this volume "Visualizing Ethnic Vernacular Landscapes."

CHANGING RACIAL CONCEPTUALIZATIONS: GREEK AMERICANS IN NEW YORK CITY

Anna Karpathakis and Victor Roudometof

Race and Ethnicity in New York City
Research in Urban Sociology, Volume 7, 265–289
© 2004 Published by Elsevier Ltd.
ISSN: 1047-0042/doi:10.1016/S1047-0042(04)07012-6

Globalization entails the increasing economic, political, military and social interrelations between societies. While much has been written on core countries' exports of their cultural products to the semi-peripheral and peripheral economies, this exportation of cultural products and populations also occurs from the semi-peripheral to the core societies (see for example, Castells, 1998, 1996; Featherstone & Lash, 1999; Kennedy & Roudometof, 2002), thereby bringing immigrants and the host society into frequent contact.

Research on immigrant incorporation into American society in many ways assumes away the history of the immigrants in their home society. Immigrants are in many ways seen as arriving carte blanche, erasing their home society's political, economic and social histories. As the case of Greek immigrants discussed in this chapter shows, this is clearly not the case. The Greek immigrants' home society politics and its history is an important component affecting the immigrants' acculturation into American society and their interpretation of uniquely American cultural constructions relating to race.

In this chapter, we discuss Greek immigrants' incorporation of American racial ideologies into the racial repertoires they acquire in the home society. Greek Americans create a unique national/racial framework blending elements of both home and host society institutions and ideologies. Greek immigrants arrive in the United States with pre-existing national and racial identities and narratives about themselves and other groups. These have their sources in Greek national and political life of the past few centuries. In the U.S., Greek immigrants construct a new set of group narratives. This set is borne out of: (1) the complex interactions of the immigrants being citizens and members of two distinctive "imagined communities" (Anderson, 1991); (2) the interactions between Greece and the U.S. and their cultural and political markets; and (3) the immigrants' attempts to remain faithful to their motherland while maximizing their group interests in the U.S. These group narratives and identities occur through both formal and informal institutions. It is in this most current form of a "transnational cultural/political" space that Greek immigrants combine elements of home society political and national narratives along with American racial conceptualizations to create a "pot pouri" of group identities.

METHODS

The chapter relies on a variety of methods to trace the development of changing racial ideologies among Greeks. The methodologies used include: (1) historical secondary sources; (2) one hundred and ten interviews (of both immigrants and Greeks in Greece, with interviewees varying in age from 19 to 74); and (3) content analysis of poems, popular songs and electronic discussion groups. The primary aim of selecting the data was to understand the changing nature of racial classifications themselves rather than to measure rates and pervasiveness.

FROM "GENOS" TO "ETHNOS" AS A LINGUISTIC AND RELIGIOUS GROUP

The Ottoman armies overthrew the remnants of the Eastern Roman Empire in the 15th century and replaced it with a new regime for the Balkans and the Eastern Mediterranean region. In accordance both to Islamic religious guidelines as well as state interest, the Ottomans organized Eastern Orthodox Christians within their domain into a single political entity, referred to as the *Rum Millet* or the *Genos ton Romaion* ("Progeny of the Romans"). The *Genos* included all Eastern Orthodox people who were the former subjects of the Eastern Roman (or "Byzantine") Empire. Hence, the label "Roman" was a political and religious marker, not a racial or ethnic designation in the contemporary sense of these terms. The *Rum Millet* included Eastern Orthodox Christians of diverse linguistic and ethnic backgrounds (Greeks, Albanians, Vlachs, Bulgarians, Serbs, Arabs, and so on) (for a brief review, see Roudometof, 2001, pp. 51–55; and for further details, Clogg, 1982).

The Ottoman regime did not foster the development of identity constructions claiming biologically based differences between the rulers and their subjects. There was considerable acculturation of the Balkan peoples into the Ottoman elite and population. This was achieved through the "child levy" (*devshirme*), whereby Christian children were taken from their parents and trained by the Ottomans to become Muslim "slaves" (*janissaries*) to the Sultan (Sarres, 1990, I, pp. 226–240). Hence, it was possible for Eastern Orthodox Christians to "become Turks" – a linguistic expression denoting conversion to Islam. But this did not imply abandonment of family or ethnic ties (see Barber, 1973; Sarres, 1990; Sugar, 1977). The subjugated group turned the Ottoman policy of *devshirme* on its head, enabling those who left the group to maintain their ties with family and return to the group; furthermore, their children and even grandchildren could conceivably return to the group.

The contemporary Greek conceptualizations of nationhood and the relationship between language, religion and nation have their origins precisely in the *Rum Millet*. Eighteenth century Orthodox Balkan intellectuals used Enlightenment philosophies to proclaim and demand the rights of freedom and self-determination on behalf of the Sultan's subjects (Kitromilides, 1978). The initial idea of Greece and Greeks as a nation (*ethnos*) was borne out of this cross-cultural interaction, but it was further modified in the 19th century, when European romantic philosophies were exported to Greece.

For Greeks, the most influential racialist figure is Jacob Philip Fallmerayer, a German scholar who argued that there was no direct lineage between modern and Ancient Greeks, and modern Greeks are an inferior "mongrel race" since Ancient Greeks intermixed with the lower races of Africa and Asia thereby leading to the destruction of the civilization that was once Ancient Greece. In response, Greek scholars of the 19th century claimed the unbroken historical continuity of the Greek nation from Antiquity to the present (Roudometof, 2001, pp. 107–113), by blending cultural and biological Northern European racial elements into their theories.

In his *Memoirs*, Makrygiannis (1947) a popular military leader in the Greek War of Independence (1821–1828), uses the terms "Romioi," "Christians" and "Grekoi" to refer to the group that is currently self-identified as Hellenes. He conversely uses the terms "Turks," "Muslims" and "Ottomans" to refer to the occupying armies that Greeks were warring against. Makrygiannis writes that the "Greek blood" is distinguished from the Turkish blood by *language* and *religion*. While Christianity and the Greek language run through the Greek blood, Islam and the Turkish language run through the Ottoman/Turkish blood.

This intertwining of religion and language provided the basic blocs for the construction of Modern Greek national identity. At the turn of the 19th-20th centuries, Greek immigrants brought with them to the United States this type of national identity. There are no reliable estimates for the pre-1925 Greek immigration wave because many of the Greek immigrants arrived in the U.S. from countries other than Greece, thereby leading to considerable ambiguities regarding the accuracy of the recorded national or ethnic affiliation. Moreover, like other European immigrants, Greek immigrants also repatriated over the first three decades of the 20th century. Despite this, Zotos (1976) estimates that as many as 800,000 Greeks settled in the U.S. by the mid-1920s.

For this early Greek immigrant group, the relevant markers of a national identity were linguistic and religious in nature. Both criteria are blood-related, but more in the sense of kinship (e.g. family ties are blood ties) than of sheer biology. Races were synonymous with nations so that there were as many human races as there were nations or ethnic groups (such as the Irish, Chinese, Italians, Americans, and so on). As such, the first task of these early Greek immigrants to the United States was the creation of the Greek Orthodox Church in the United States. The fact that the Russian Orthodox had already established a church in the United States was irrelevant for Greek immigrants for whom language and religion were inseparable. Many arriving from lands still conquered by Ottoman forces viewed the idea of their joining non-Greek Orthodox religious institutions as a betrayal to their *ethnos*. This is precisely also the reason that the earlier (and more recent immigrants) were (and remain) opposed to their children's marrying outside the group. The first Greek Orthodox Church in NYC was created in 1881 in downtown Manhattan; by 1996, there were 500 Greek Orthodox parishes throughout the country and the Greek Orthodox Church of America still maintains its own Archdiocese, headquartered in NYC.

RACIAL IDEOLOGIES IN THE 20TH CENTURY

Because of changing national-territorial concerns of the Greek nation-state, immigrants arriving in the U.S. during the second half of the 20th century had been introduced to western and more consistent racial interpretations of the continuity thesis. The issues that provided the backdrop against which Greeks in Greece and Greek immigrants have been creating their national/racial identities include: (1) territorial rivalries between the expanding Greek nation state of the late 19th and early 20th centuries and the northern Slavo-Macedonian and Bulgarian ethnic groups; (2) Hitler's and Mussolini's invasions of Greece during World War II; (3) recurring rivalries with Turkey over Cyprus from the 1950s forward (including Turkey's invasion of Cyprus in 1974); and (4) renewed identity clashes with Slavo-Macedonians and Turkey in the 1990s (see for example, Karakasidou, 1997; Kyriakidies, 1955).

Greek Fascist ideologies of the 1930s to the early 1970s were a direct response to their Northern European counterparts. Greek Fascists rejected Hitler's and Mussolini's understandings of racial purity for Germans and Italians and the charge that Greeks were a "mongrel" and inferior race. Koumaris, an anthropologist, for example (quoted by Montague, 1945, p. 47) writes that the Greek race has

> almost uniform physical characteristics, physical and psychical, inherited in its descendants . . . Races exist and will continue to exist and each one defends itself. Because every infusion of new "blood" is something different and because children of mixed parents belong to no race, the Greek race, as all others, has to preserve its own fluid constancy by avoiding mixture with foreign elements. The Greek race was formed under the Acropolis Rock, and it is impossible for any other to keep the keys of the sacred rock, to which the Greek soul is indissolubly linked.[1]

In the post-World War II period, national holidays – such as the "Ohi Day" (October 28th) – became a vehicle for fostering the Right's version of history, whereby the Right-wing forces saved Greece from the double-headed evil of "Slavo-communism" (see Karakasidou, 2000) and Nazism. These celebrations offered a particularly prominent position to the Greek Church, a position enshrined in the military dictatorship's slogan of crafting a "Greece of Christian Creeks."

The fascist military regime of the late 1960s–1970s revised the continuity theses by introducing western concepts of biological race into their educational curriculum and the state controlled mass media. By the 1970s, commemorations of secular national holidays in the immigrant communities changed in their emphases. The fall of the fascist military junta and Turkey's invasion of Cyprus in the mid-1970s were the background against which these celebrations began focusing around resistance to Mussolini's and Hitler's invading armies as well as resistance to the Ottoman Occupiers. These celebratory events among immigrant communities still intertwine the religious and national elements into one identity and define language and religion as markers distinguishing Greeks from all other national/cultural/"racial" groups (*files*) (see Karpathakis & Roudometof, 2002).

NATIONAL/ETHNIC GROUPS WITHIN A GLOBAL CAPITALIST ECONOMY

Nearly 180,000 Greek immigrants arrived in the United States between 1966 and 1975, most of them settling in the Northeast U.S. The immigration numbers declined significantly in the post-1980 period: Only 29,100 new immigrants were recorded in 1981–1990 and 11,900 in 1991–1998 (U.S. Census Bureau, 2002). According to the U.S. Census Bureau (1998, 2002), in 2000 there were 1,153,307 persons of Greek ancestry in the U.S. (versus a total of 921,782 in 1990). Immigrant associations claim that these Figures grossly underestimate the actual number of U.S. Greeks, which, according to their estimates is closer to three million (for a discussion, see Roudometof, 2000). New York City received the largest numbers and Astoria became the center of Greek American life. According to the U.S. Census Bureau (2003) report of the 2000 U.S. Census there are 159,763 people of Greek ancestry in the New York state. There are no reliable data on the number of Greek immigrants and Greek Americans in Astoria, NYC in the post-1965 period, but social workers in the area gave estimates that range between 40,000 and 50,000.

According to the U.S. Census (1998), the majority of Greek Americans (77%) are private wage earners and salaried employees, earning a mean of $48,318 per household (in 1989 USD). Most of them worked either in managerial and professional positions (34.7%) or in sales and technical and administrative positions (32.2%). These figures are more representative of the earlier pre-1965 immigrant cohorts, which also make up the majority of the Greek American population.

Greek immigrant politics in NYC in the post-1965 period have been overwhelmingly about Greek politics (see Karpathakis, 1999). The military *junta*'s 1974 failed *coup* in Cyprus sparked Turkey's invasion and partition of the island which in turn led to the junta's downfall. Junta personnel fled Greece, some of whom were given "honorary visas" by the U.S., and settled in immigrant communities throughout the country. These "Ethnikophrones" (Nationalists) set up headquarters in Astoria and began grassroots educational campaigns. The exiled Left, no longer fearful to enter the public light in the immigrant communities, enjoyed the support of the post-1965 immigrants and the youth who had been radicalized by the politics in Greece. Beginning in the 1970s, and continuing to this day, every major Greek political party has a "Friends of . . ." organization in NYC so that Greece's political parties are represented in the immigrant community. Even though the conservatives won elections in Greece in 1975, it was the Left that became the country's and the immigrant community's definitive creator of a new national identity throughout the decades of the 1970s and 1980s. One activist informant described the period as a time of "freedom" and "euphoria." It was the first time in Greek history that Left intellectuals could participate in formal and state sponsored institutions and voice their interpretations of Greek national identity and history.

Theodorakis, Hatzidakis, Markopoulos and countless other exiled musicians returned to Greece and held a number of concerts for Greek immigrants and Greek Americans in the States. Poets and artists sympathetic to the Left – such as Yannis Ritsos – became national heroes. Their works were printed and disseminated throughout the Greek immigrant communities. Cafes sponsoring the works of Greek musicians and artists (till then declared illegal in Greece) became successful businesses in NYC. The "rebetes" and their music, making their way into Greece by the Greeks fleeing western Turkey in the 1920s had been staunchly anti-monarchist and thus considered anti-Greek. The Left resurrected this underground music, researched the "rebetes" and redefined them as part of the oppressed "people's history." The film "Rebetes," depicting the life of a woman "rebetissa" musician and which won the best film prize in the Cannes Film Festival in the early 1980s had cast local NYC Greek immigrant musicians.

In the 1970s and 1980s, both in Greece and the U.S., popular cultural creations (art, music, poetry, scholarly works and journalistic accounts) created empathy and affinity for people and nations in the developing world, in countries also with a history of imperialist exploitation. Thus, Greeks came to identify with people from Africa, Latin America and the Philippines. Costas Cavadias' poetry went to press and Left musicians turned some of his popular pieces into lyrics. Cavadias, a sailor, traveled the globe and wrote about and in his poetry celebrated sailors from Africa and the Philippines, men who like Greeks, left home to risk high seas to earn a living. His heroes found solace in the less than clean company of alcohol, hashish and men and women in bordellos of port cities. Furthermore, it was either stated explicitly or assumed in the lyrics that these men were from countries, which, like Greece, were poor and exploited by imperialist nations.

Images and reflections of American society made their way into the work
of journalists and artists traveling between the home society and immigrant
communities. One particular song "Ameriki Ameriki" by Yiorgos Kinnousis,
became a hit both in the community here and in Greece. The song describes
America as a land of magic, of immense contradictions, a country of wealth and
poverty, a land of abundance and yet a land of homeless and oppressed peoples. The
American poor and in particular, American Blacks and Native Americans are in the
popular cultural products of this period, a group who are economically, politically
and socially oppressed by the elite of American society. Poetry and music with
"black" characters enter the popular imagination, with Blacks or Africans being
portrayed as "men" without a country they themselves can determine and define.
From the perspective of the artists, this oppression pretty much parallels the
experiences of the Greek working class and poor.

The Left's construction of a new national identity was set in opposition to
the conservative or semi-Fascist regimes that ruled Greece between 1944 and
1974. Theirs was an attempt at an anti-racialist "left populist" national identity.
The elements used in their construction of Greek national identity included class,
exploitation and oppression by national and international elites and national elites'
acting in the interests of and supported by Western powers (specifically the U.S.
and England, given these two countries' history in Greece). The Left redefined
national history to include the working masses and bring to the fore the role that
it played and its repression from the 1930s until the 1970s. After fighting off the
Nazis, the Greek left was outlawed, its leaders imprisoned or exiled, and the leftist
sympathizers repressed (see Tsoukalas, 1981).

The Greek Socialists who came to power in 1981 espoused this "political
economy" in the 1970s. Andreas Papandreou, an American educated economist
teaching at Berkeley, and the leader of P.A.S.O.K. (Panhellenic Socialist
Movement) framed the party's original platform within the left-wing Latin
American *depentistas* approach of the 1960s. Within the Left's political-economic
framework, core economies (the United States and England, specifically,) had
reduced Greece to a largely peripheral economy and society in the global capitalist
system. Greece's troubles with Turkey were seen as products of the Greek right's
refusal to "confront the U.S. and its economic interests in the region," as one
P.A.S.O.K. activist in Astoria argued in the mid-1980s.

Despite the Greek Left's introduction to American society and Greece's own
"racialized" twentieth century history, the Left throughout this period failed to
confront racist theories on their own terms. Rather than looking at the role
that racialism played in nationalist and economic frameworks, the Left instead
interpreted racialism within the "global political economy" framework (Allen,
1994; Balibar & Wallerstein, 1991; Ignatiev, 1995). The Greek and Greek

American Left defined American minorities as national/cultural groups exploited and oppressed within economic, not racial, frameworks. In other words, the Left interpreted American minority groups' histories and experiences within a framework of national politics rather than racial politics. When, during a group reading, the work of Franz Fanon was discussed by Left intellectuals in the community in the 1980s, it was understood strictly within the realm of global economic politics and the racialist nature of this global system was simply ignored. When in the early 1980s a group of undergraduate college students read and discussed DuBois' work, they were unable to see and understand American race history precisely because it was completely unlike their own histories and experiences. The Greek American Left of the time did not create contacts with the American Left or grassroots organizations advocating for social justice issues. Their frame of reference was and remains, Greek politics.

The Left tried to construct an alternative to racialist theories without critiquing these theories. Greeks had already been introduced to western ideas of race in the second half of the 20th century, and turned new eyes unto pictures and images of Africans. For most of the 20th century, Africans were known in Greek popular culture as "arapides," a derogatory term derivative of the Turkish term "arap" to refer to Africans. Modern Greeks had learned of "arapides" or Africans through Ottoman slavery practices. Textbooks used in Greece and in Greek language programs in the U.S. well into the decades of the 1980s, with paintings of the Ottoman Empire, depicted African slaves serving the Turkish pashas, sultans and other *beys*. Interviews with elderly immigrants and Greeks in Greece pointed to an ambivalent and contradictory image of "Arapides." These images were an amalgamation of images and "historical memories" from the Ottoman days blended with the new images of Africans picked up by and articulated by Greek fascists. On the one hand, "Arapides" when discussed as Africans, were seen as one of the many groups enslaved and oppressed by Ottomans/Turks. On the other hand, the men were to be feared. As one 72-year old immigrant woman from the island of Chios said, "my mother would tell me they were fierce warriors. One killed the bey, another killed Greeks for the pasha. They were fierce. But they were slaves, like us. They were taken as children to fight in the sultan's armies, like our children." By the 1960s and 1970s, music and films produced under the military dictatorship added a new layer to the pre-existing understandings of "Africans" and "Arapides." Popular songs of the 1960s and 1970s sung of "dark beautiful" women in the ports of Africa with "flexible" bodies. By the 1960s and 1970s, films produced under the Right wing military regime depicted African women as exotic and beautiful dancers, i.e. their beauty and sexuality were prominent. The men received little treatment in these films, and most portrayed as wealthy businessmen (most likely oil men).

Greek immigrants had in other words, been exposed to biologically based race theories prior to their arrival in the U.S. In the meantime, by the mid-1980s they had begun entering the lower middle classes, and their children entered the public colleges of NYC. That is, Greek immigrants, had overcome the initial immigrant hardships, and turned these immigrant lenses on American racial minority groups and could not understand why these groups were still at an economic disadvantage. The only explanation offered was the American racist explanations of the "work ethic." From the perspective of the immigrants, they worked hard and succeeded in the long run. Lacking an understanding of racial politics and history, immigrants turned to racist explanations of American minority groups' economic hardships. As Ryan (1971) points out, the uniquely American ideology of the "work ethic" legitimates the victimization of individuals and groups in the U.S.

"POTPOURRI" OF IDENTITIES: ARE WE "WHITE" HELLENES?

The 1980s and 1990s bring new and old concerns to the forefront of Greek national politics. The Fall of the Berlin Wall, the dissolution of the Balkan nation-states in the 1990s, identity clashes with Slavo-Macedonians and Turkish irredentist claims to Greek lands and history, become the background against which Greeks in Greece and Greek immigrants in the United States try to define themselves as a national group. On a more micro-level, Greek immigrant and Greek American inter-marriage rates are increasing, and as Constantelos (1999) points out, mixed marriages accounted for over 60% of all Church marriages in the first half of the decade of the 1990s. The intermarriage rates are higher for the later American born cohorts and these numbers do not include those who marry outside the Church.

Greeks in Greece, Greek Americans and other Diaspora Greeks with access to the Internet, are contributing to the construction of the Hellenic identity in electronic discussion groups. Writers to these groups create an umbrella Hellenic identity connecting the numerous context-specific diasporic experiences, as they try to make sense of what it means to be Greek. While these diverse experiences are important in the construction of this transnational Hellenic identity, the primary frame of reference for these Internet-based intellectual groups is the Greek nation state and the contemporary challenges it confronts on both the international as well as the national level.

In the 1990s, the political and diplomatic conflict between the Greek nation-state and the former Yugoslav Republic of Macedonia (FYROM), as well as renewed challenges by Albanian and Turk activists, provided the context for a renewed discussions about race and Greek cultural and biological continuity (for details, see Danforth, 1995; Roudometof, 2002). These discussions often confuse issues of cultural and biological continuity through the employment of racialized language. Turkish and Macedonian writers, in their attempt to deconstruct Greeks' claims to Greek territory and their cultural and linguistic heritage, resurrect Fallmerayer's 19th century racial purity theory, charging that modern Greeks are biologically unrelated to ancient Greeks and thereby discrediting Greeks' claims to the legacies and achievements of Ancient Greeks.

The Modern Greek language as a descendant of the earlier Ancient Greek language is similarly questioned. The Internet discussion groups have in the 1990s provided *fora* through which such charges are made, as Greeks, Turks, Albanians, Macedonians and others from the region "crash" each others' sites and flame each others' lists. Women's sexuality is often a prime focus in the charges that there is no continuity between modern and Ancient Greeks. In one AOL chat room discussion, for example, one Turkish discussant talked about how his own family is mixed "racially and ethnically": his mother's mother was Greek and her sister married a Turk and moved to Greece; while he has no contact with his family in Greece, he continued, another cousin also married a Greek woman and also moved to Greece. Such anecdotal stories intend to show Greeks' "impurity," as they argue that Greeks can no longer talk about a biological relation to Ancient Greeks.

During one such internet discussion in an AOL Greek Chat Room between one Turkish graduate student of political science at an American university and four Greek subscribers, the interviewer pointed out, "I find it interesting that in all three stories the woman is Greek, the man is Turkish and they move to Greece. How and why that is?" The Turkish student responded with "I have no idea what you are talking about. Greek women are beautiful and I guess Greek women find Turkish men fascinating." One of the Greek men in the room responded, "the idea is that once these men get to Greece they impregnate hundreds of Greek women thereby spreading the Turkish sperm and genes. So Greek women are f*** (sic) and dumped but the aim is to dilute Greekness and claim Turkish male supremacy. It's in the genes of course as our friend here would argue. My Turkish friend, please go and **** (sic) yourself cz (sic) u ain't gonna f*** any Greek women. Get this: Until Turks stop seeing Greeks as a people that belong under Turkish rule, we want nothing to do with you. You are a different breed of men. Your women have to put up with you but ours don't."

One of the Greek American women in the group added, "let me explain how Greek women see this. We'r (sic) a fiercely independent bunch. We have troubles with men thinking themselves superior to us bcz (sic) we're women. We have even more troubles with men who think themselves superior bcz of race. You deny us our humanity bcz we're Greek, we deny u the consideration (sic) of seeing u as potential sex partners. WE DON'T WANT YOU. You can m**** as much as u want, it only sickens us and makes u (sic) as we Greeks would say 'sihamenous.' (disgusting) Do u know that word my friend? Take your fantasy rape stories to a web site for the sexually frustrated. Last week u said Greek women are racist bcz they won't date Turkish men. Greek women will not date Turkish men bcz we don't like sleeping with men who fantasize raping us. If u r representative of ur people then ur the wrong ambassador (sic)."

Furthermore, to the extent that Greeks living in Asia Minor for thousands of years also intermarried with Turks, the argument runs, the Greek blood has interspersed with the Turkish blood. As was also pointed out in a couple of other discussion groups and sessions, this population mixing of course took place on the western coast of Turkey, the site of the City of Troy and other Hellenic cultures in the ancient times. Greeks and Greek Americans invariably respond to these charges with profanities and racialist slurs.[2]

Albanians, Turks, Macedonians, and their territorial and other interests and demands with regards to Greece thus make up the primary groups against whom the Greek or Hellenic identity is constructed. Albanians are still remembered in the popular imagination for the role they played under the Ottoman Empire, their collaboration with Hitler's invading armies in the Balkans and northern Greece. FYROM has entered the foray in claiming the name Macedonia (Macedonia being the name of a region of northern Greece) and Alexander the Great, as their own rightful legacy. Greeks are in this scenario, a besieged group in the region, as different national/racial groups from the region make territorial and cultural demands on Greece; i.e. they want to re-appropriate Greek history and Greek lands.

As Greek Americans come across other ethnic Americans at work or other public spaces, the cherished continuity thesis that forms the building bloc of modern Greek identity is questioned. New York City's other immigrant and ethnic groups, often motivated by their own home society politics pick up on such charges, transforming the work environment into a space where national politics are re-enacted and ethnic tensions intensify. One Greek born woman, working for an advertising company, described how "Americans" and "some ethnic Americans" at work, motivated by their own home society politics,

> started asking me questions about whether I could read Ancient Greek, Bible Greek. I have a replica of an ancient vase I picked up at the Athens airport on my desk. A Jewish guy . . . he visits Israel every year, he's very active in Jewish and Israeli politics . . . started hanging around it, asking me all sorts of questions, saying things like why do Geeks . . . yes, Geeks, not Greeks, he said Geeks. Why Geeks think this piece of shit is such great art. Then the language questions. I had no idea what they were talking about, I'm not too politically savvy but a Greek friend explained things . . . well, there's apparently a whole romance between Israel and Turkey for a few years now and somehow Jews committed to Israel feel they must adopt Turkey's nationalist politics. So I had to explain how a modern Greek speaker reading Ancient Greek is like a modern English speaker reading Old English. I felt violated. There was such arrogance in these

people, and after I found out their politics it made sense but there are all sorts of wierdos (sic) with narrow interests who will do anything to win their agendas. And this for me is frightening because they were questioning my very being, my very identity. Who I am, where I come from, my history. I mean, who is this person telling me that modern Greek is not related to Ancient Greece or that Turks are as much Ancient Greek as modern Greeks are. These are weird things. This is post-modernism in history, one of the ugly sides of it and it's selling.

BLACK ATHENA AND GREEK AMERICANS

These Greek or Hellenic identity and cultural legacy issues were the backdrop against which Martin Bernal's *Black Athena* (1987) was interpreted to the immigrants through community activists and non-Greek classicists that were less than versed in either archeology or American race history. Modern day American Blacks were added to the list of those who want to partake of Ancient Greek civilization and legacy. As one immigrant man said on a call-in radio program, "first the Turks, then the Albanians, then the Yugoslavs who call themselves Macedonians, now the Africans and blacks. What is going on here? Why don't they just leave us alone?" Dan Georgakas, a long time activist and historian of the Greek immigrant community tried to appease those gathered during a meeting at Hunter College in 1993 that "Bernal and African Americans aren't saying that Ancient Greeks stole everything from blacks, they're not saying that it's a Black culture, Ancient Greeks, the Ancients didn't think this way. Ancient Greeks had great respect for the Egyptian civilization. Cultures are dynamic, they borrow, they exchange, they learn from each other. He is basically arguing that we need to re-examine all these assumptions and claims that Ancient Greeks were white because these are 19th century race ideas." A few moments later he added, "our own people didn't think or talk this way of black and white."

Archeologists and historians from Greece were interviewed on Greek language radio programs. Repeatedly they made the argument that the concept and identity of Hellenism is a cultural product, it is not biological. They repeated the argument that cultures are viable entities always in interaction and interchanges and there is great proof for much exchange between Ancient Greece and the Egyptian Civilization. These ideas were drowned out by the voices of the non-Greek classicists who took a more rigid approach. This was one more instance of their on-going battle against Afro-centrism. While they agreed that Hellenism is a cultural identity, they also argued that this is a legacy that belongs only to modern day Greeks and as one woman classicist argued, "Afro-centrists are now claiming Ancient Greek civilization as their cultural heritage and this is just not so. It is unfair to do this to a people."

Bernal's *Black Athena* forced Greek Americans' formal entry into American race politics and debates. Academics long active in the politics of the community crossed discipline boundaries to talk and write about Hellenism as a heritage belonging only to Hellenes. The presentation of the issues entailed that, by definition, Greeks would side with the classicists arguing against Bernal's thesis of the need to reexamine the idea of Ancient Greece as a "white" civilization. The discussions of Bernal's *Black Athena* in Greece, did not take a "black-white" form, as archeologists discussed the ancient civilizations in terms of cultures. The *Black Athena* was a "Greek American," not a Greek affair because of the nature and history of racial politics in the two societies.

The classicists' voice and argument resounded with the immigrants. Bolstered by a larger framework of American racist ideologies claiming that civilization is a construction of the white race, immigrants situated and interpreted *Black Athena*, Greek national and territorial concerns and the Hellenic identity within the American racial framework. One activist summed up "the situation this way. Greeks were thrown into an American race battle and we weren't prepared because this thing is just not in our history. We had none of the history or context, so we got screwed and more often than not took racist positions. American race politics are still new to us."

The Greek Americans' attempts to construct a Hellenic identity through formal institutions with regards to Bernal's *Black Athena*, were set against the backdrop of Greek national issues and concerns. The classicists offered modern day Greeks an identity within the American context, which is a "skin color" "white" identity so that by default, the Hellenic identity constructed as the end-product of the *Black Athena* debate in the community became a "white" identity; i.e. Hellenes are "whites."

On a micro-level, immigrants similarly combine elements of both the country of origin's national, ethno-confessional basis of group markers and the American biologically based race ideologies in their day to day lives and thereby construct their own unique versions of racially/culturally defined national groupings. There is hardly a logical thread to this construction as immigrants change categories contextually. When confronted or working within American racial politics based on color, recent Greek immigrants will define themselves as "Europeans" or whites. Greece's entry into the European Community (in 1981) is proof enough of them being "European" and thereby "white." The American racial categories Greek immigrants, like all others, are offered with which to define themselves racially are White (i.e. of European origin), Asian, Black and Hispanic. For some Greek immigrants, these entail a regional origin so that they are within this context European and thereby white. Other immigrants define themselves as "white" in contradistinction to Blacks, Hispanics and Asians. This can take the form of deriving at a racial definition of oneself through the process of elimination, e.g. as one woman said, "well, I'm not Spanish, I'm not Asian and I'm not Black, so I guess I'm white." The answer of one's racial identity within the American context, in other words, does not always come easily and intuitively.

Greek immigrants' "racial alliance" with Europeans is more often than not an uneasy one as immigrants in silence reflect upon the role that European nations, motivated by racism, have played in Greece's recent history. One man, for example, said, "Greeks are Europeans. So that makes us whites." He dropped his eyes to his cigarette burning in the ashtray and remained silent. He continued in more somber tone, "we're not even Europeans, isn't that so. We are at the cross-roads of north and south, east and west." He then continued with a quite lengthy and quite informative ten-minute monologue on the Elgin marbles (Ancient Greek marbles removed from Greece by a British archaeologist at the end of the 19th century and held in England,) and some of Greece's more recent issues in the European Community. Some turn a blind eye to this history and on-going race based relations between Greece and northern European nations (see for example Gallant, 2002). One young woman for example, said, "I'm European, I guess that makes me white." When a couple of minutes later she was asked about England's refusal to return the Elgin marbles to Greece because Greeks are not considered capable of protecting their own history, she responded, "look, Americans don't need to know this stuff. Why would we want them to get a sniff of this? It's dirty laundry. Just tell them you're European. I get a kick out of it when I tell people I'm going to Europe for the summer. To hell with everything else, I'm here now and that's the most important thing."

Whether reflecting on Greece's national interests and its membership with the European union or Greeks' own economic and status interests here in the States, the immigrants will define themselves as "whites" because they of course must be "white" in a society that distributes resources by race. The more recent immigrants take their cues from the earlier immigrants who worked hard to exit the non-white racial category they were placed in upon their arrival in the United States. Among the college educated American born, *Helen Zeese Papanikolas'* family history is often cited and recounted as simply one of the many hardship accounts of the early immigrants. Independent of the authors' intentions, immigrants' and ethnics' stories celebrating their achievements against incredible odds become part of the folklore and ideologies which are turned on their heads and used to blame minority groups' oppression in the U.S. on the minorities themselves.

By using the national/cultural/racial ideologies they inherited from Greece, Greek immigrants understand immigrant groups outside the American racial framework. So that, while they see themselves as being a different race (*fili* or *ratsa*) from Hispanics (an American identity and label) they claim similarities between themselves and other immigrant and national groups from various continents and regions. With the exception of Puerto Ricans, one of the "biologically stigmatized" groups of NYC, Greek immigrants give Mexican, Columbian, Dominican, Nigerian, Haitian and Jamaican immigrants their own national identity. These groups also use their national identity to override the American "racial" identity. This is perhaps best reflected in the immigrants' descriptions of the individuals they work with. One immigrant woman said, "I work with a Jamaican woman;" again, "my office mate is a Haitian woman." This, national/cultural definition, however, changes, when the issue is one of intermarriage, as we will discuss later in the chapter.

The immigrants identify with and claim an affinity with other immigrant groups. This affinity is based on two dimensions. First, is the issue of the country's position in relation to super-powers, and specifically, the United States and England. During the brief war over the Falkland Islands, for example, Greek immigrants identified with and sided with Argentina rather than Britain. Despite the fact that Greece is geographically positioned within the European continent, Greek immigrants perceive non-European immigrants as arriving from countries which like Greece, have been exploited and oppressed by the United States and/or other Northern European imperial powers.

The second dimension is that of the immigrant experience. Greek immigrants identify with the common and much romanticized immigrant struggles, problems and sacrifices. Like Greeks themselves, these groups are forced to emigrate because of their home countries' economic and political exploitation. As immigrants to a strange and often unfriendly land, these groups must and do make sacrifices for the well being of their families and children. The immigrants work long hours at menial jobs with low wages. Greek Americans identify with this immigrant narrative.

The term "black" is reserved and used for American Blacks, and it is this group which immigrants place on a biologically based racial hierarchy. With respect to American Blacks, Greek immigrants are increasingly adopting the uniquely American racial dichotomous ideology that there are "blacks" and "whites" (Karpathakis, 2003, in Tastsoglou volume, 2003). This is an American created group, after all, and so is understood within the American context. But there are important differences in the language the immigrants use to describe people of color they come into contact with. Talking about her daughter's teacher at the public school, one woman said, "she's a Jamaican woman, came here with her family when she was a child." Again, "I work with some Haitian women," again, "the only person of color I ever worked with was a man from Trinidad."

Immigrants have constructed their own derogatory version of the term "Hispanics" (*Spanioloi*) and like the term "black," this term also detracts from a personal and group national/cultural identity (Thandeka, 2001). The term Spanioloi was in the 1970s used to refer to the majority Spanish speaking group in the city, namely the Puerto Ricans. Like "Blacks," Puerto Ricans had acquired negative valuations in the U.S., both groups had their own history, a language and culture. To the extent that other immigrant groups also speak Spanish, they are also at times lumped into the category of "Spanioloi" and invariably someone in the group will try to salvage the group by referring to its national/cultural origin. The term is in other words "contested," immigrants and even the American born working within the framework of national/cultural ideologies cannot and do not easily understand this label. On the one hand it is a meaningful concept because Hispanics do share a language and one overarching culture, yet on the other, they do come from different countries with different histories and local cultures. The role that Puerto Ricans play in the use of this term is seen in the following exchange between a group of immigrant women: "She's a Spaniola." "Stop it, she's not a Spaniola, she's Puerto Rican." "Those are the Spanioloi. The Puerto Ricans." "Are Mexicans Spanioloi?" "No they're Mexican." "Yes they are. They speak Spanish don't they?" "And Dominicans?" "Who are the Dominicans?" "They live in Washington Heights. Where the Greeks lived before they came to Astoria." "Where are they from? Do they speak Spanish?"

None of the monolingual Greek-speaking immigrants interviewed used the term "Asian" as an identifier. Again, this is an American label to refer to diverse national/cultural immigrant groups which the immigrants see as having a history independent of and outside the American context, i.e. their own national/cultural history. From within the national/cultural framework of identities of the immigrants, this "Asian" category is meaningless.

The term "mavros" and "mavroi" (black) has replaced the term "arapis" to refer to American born Blacks. This term of course speaks to the imputed skin tone, i.e. a biological phenomenon. The language used for American born Blacks, in other words, is one that speaks more of an undifferentiated mass of a biologically based category rather than of members of distinct cultural or national groups. "I work with some blacks." "I never hired a black." "No, no black ever worked for me." For the immigrants, this is an American group and American created label/referent. To the extent that immigrants are still largely on the political and cultural margins of the society and of course lack the historical and political understanding of American race ideologies, and since, from their own frameworks, American Blacks do share a history, a language and a culture, i.e. American, and more importantly, since there is nothing in the immigrants' political history and culture to enable them to challenge these biologically based concepts, they simply accept these categories as valid.

The "black-white" biologically based racial language is especially significant and extended to "black immigrants" by some of those in the sample, when the issue is one of interracial dating and marriage. One man, for example, talking about his

cousin's marriage to a man from Jamaica said, "my cousin married a black guy."
Again, a woman talking about her friend's interracial relationship with a Nigerian
man said, "she was dating a black guy." Again, one woman talking about her Greek
neighbor's son said, "he married a black woman." Her husband interrupted, "she
ain't black. She's Jamaican. You gotta watch your language. When you say black
people think you mean American black. This woman is Jamaican. She wasn't born
here." A few minutes later he added, "this isn't right. I meant to say that she isn't
any of those things people tend to associate with American blacks. I don't like these
things. People are people and I screwed up trying to get this woman's reputation
in order . . . I insulted a whole group of people . . . why? Why did I do it? (Raises
his voice.) Because I don't know where you stand on these things and I'm tired
of people, family, neighbors, every 'malaka' (jerk) talking about this woman as
if she's not alright because she's black. Well, she is alright and I know where my
wife comes down on this and it's all a bunch of bullshit. She's a good woman. Half
the customers in my store are black. They're fine people. They're normal people
for God's sake."

Greek immigrants' discussions of race as a biological (skin tone based)
phenomenon are riddled with contradictions. Often enough, their words contradict
their actions. One woman, for example, who often spoke of "blacks" in quite
derogatory ways, had risked losing her own job to speak on behalf of a "black"
woman at work who was being mistreated by the supervisor. One small business
owner claimed that "no black ever worked for me . . . no I don't plan on hiring any
blacks," but his wife said that he "threw out a white customer who insulted a black
delivery man." Another man, a manager of a restaurant who argued that he "voted
for Guilliani so that Dinkens wouldn't win again" is known as and respected by
his "black" employees for "sticking up for us whenever something happens." One
street vendor interfered in a street fight when two white teenagers were beating
up a black teenager and he suffered a broken nose. And yet, if one were to rely
simply on his language, one would have to infer that this man "is the biggest bigot
around" as his wife said.

When it comes to the Greek immigrants' internalization of American racist
ideologies, it is the contradiction between their words and deeds that begs an
explanation. Should we juxtapose these words and deeds with the words of "well,
I'm not Spanish, and I'm not Asian and I'm not Black" and expressions such as
"Americans don't need to know this . . . This is dirty laundry," then we also need
to examine these immigrants' racial ideologies and identifications as reflections or
manifestations of fears that they themselves may be seen as anything but "white."
For, whenever in immigrants' discussions the ghost of American white racism
surfaces, an immigrant woman invariably poses the question: "How would *you*
like it to be seen as something less than human?"

This fear of the "non-white" label is more apparent in women's attempts to "look white," i.e. "become white," through the use of cosmetics (Karpathakis, 2003). For example, one woman who takes great care to lighten her hair and in many ways "look white" was in near tears when she was told that she is not a natural blonde but rather a *melachrini* (i.e. olive complexion with black hair and dark eyes). She threw her arms in the air and raised her voice, "I'm a *melachrini* in Greece and it's ok. But things are different here. Why are you doing this to me?"

In sum thus, given the four major racial categories (white, black, Asian or Hispanic) Greek immigrants confront within the American context, Greek immigrants define themselves as white because they *must* be white, because they are not Asian, Hispanic nor black. Furthermore, the non-white options are not desirable in a society where "whites" hold the top rank in the racial hierarchy. Greek immigrants, and especially those of darker complexion, are fearful of a non-white designation, and so, through their language, even if not always through their deeds, they adamantly distinguish themselves from the non-white racial categories.

At the same time, the American born descendants of both the earlier and more recent Greek immigrant cohorts, are constructing a Hellenic identity which differs from the Hellenic identity constructed by intellectuals concerned with Greek national affairs. English language weekly and monthly magazines regularly feature articles on Hellenic themes, ranging from Antiquity to the present. The intellectuals – historians, archeologists, linguists, and others – who are engaged in national identity construction for the Greeks in Greece as well as in the Hellenic Diaspora are concerned with national, cultural, religious and linguistic criteria. Often to the dismay of the intellectuals themselves, readers of their articles often interpret this Hellenic identity within the American race-based framework. This American interpretation of Hellenic identity assumes or claims its "whiteness," for "whiteness" is a status that Americans of Greek descent *must* achieve. Thanks to its links to two greatly admired civilizations (defined as white by American society) Hellenism provides a ready-made identity for these groups. For, how better to claim one's racial equality and even superiority than to claim a direct link to the "white" civilizations of Ancient Greece and the Byzantium, the Empire that salvaged the Ancients' civilization from the ruins of Europe's Dark Ages? This Americanized Hellenic narrative is telling American "whites" that Greek Americans are the descendants of Ancient Greece and contributed to the creation of Western and American civilizations, both viewed as "white" civilizations. As a result, Greek Americans are probably even in a roundabout way superior to these "biological whites" who are simply white because of their skin tone; but have contributed little to the advancement of humanity, while Greeks are responsible for so much. Indeed, as one American born man expressed, "when my people were writing philosophy and mathematics and history and poetry, your people were living in caves and throwing their sticks at mammoths. What did you do to advance the plight of humanity?" Framed this way, the racial superiority of Hellenes over the "biological whites" of America, is of course apparent to the naked eye.

The Greek Orthodox Church is the community institution bringing together faithful of all immigrant cohorts, classes and political orientations (Karpathakis, 1994). It is here that Greek immigrants, Greek Americans and Americans of Hellenic Descent, vehemently battle out national, cultural and racial identity politics (see Karpathakis, 2001; Karpathakis & Roudometof, 2002). The Church is a microcosm of community identity politics. While the immigrants are working to maintain the church's identity as an immigrant institution, the faithful of earlier immigrant cohorts, overwhelmingly of a middle and upper middle class background, are working towards Americanizing the Church. The immigrants want the Church to maintain its ties with Greece and the Patriarchate of Constantinople (Istanbul,) the Americanizers want the Church to cut these ties and proclaim itself an American church. In the process of unraveling these conflicts, one ultimately confronts issues of national, racial, and cultural identity. The Americanizers, overwhelmingly descendants of pre-1965 immigrants, see the new immigrants as "too ethnic," more concerned with "ethnic politics" than "spiritual matters." They argue that the Church can overcome this ethnic obstacle by removing itself from Greek national affairs, establishing an Archdiocese independent of the Patriarchate of Constantinople (which is increasingly referred to as the Patriarchate of Istanbul by the groups' representatives), and changing the Church's official language from Greek to English. Many Americanizers are unhappy with the Archdiocese's compromise of using both languages in the religious services for the parishes with large numbers of English speakers.

On the other hand, immigrant laity views the language and ethnic culture as an integral element of their Church, and often complain that the Americanizers treat them as "second class citizens." "You know, the hicks, the greenhorns fresh off the boat," as one woman expressed. To the extent that immigrant status is given a lower social status in the larger society, Church membership reflects these views. Since the 1980s, in letters to editors and other publications, the Americanizers were at best condescending to the post-1965 Greek immigrants and Greek culture in general. One Americanizer responded to charges of Americanizers holding anti-Greek sentiments by writing that "I like Greek food, I like Greek music, and I even eat baklava." One priest interviewed commented on how early on in his childhood years when he looked out at the parishioners gathered, he saw "darker faces." "Now," he continued, when he looks out at the parishioners he notices how they are "lighter," they are "more American." Immigrants thus, in the eyes of the Americanizers, occupy a "less than white" status. It is precisely this status that the Americanizers are trying to overcome in their struggle to re-define the Greek Orthodox Church of America as an Orthodox Church of America, i.e. a "white" Orthodox Church of America. And so, it is not surprising that the very people who are active in the Americanization movement in the Church are also those who are outspoken on Hellenism as a cultural legacy reserved only for the Hellenes.

The Patriarchate of Constantinople has in recent years made a number of public pronouncements on the cultural nature of Hellenism and Orthodoxy. Patriarch Bartholomew has made a number of sermons as well as published a number of letters in his attempts to de-racialize Hellenic identity and define Hellenes as a cultural and religious group that crosses racial boundaries. As one parishioner in Astoria pointed out, "get on the Patriarch's website. Get on the Archdiocese website. The Orthodox are everywhere, Europe, America, Asia, Africa. I prefer to use the term that the Patriarch himself uses. *Genos*. The faithful. Hellenes are those of the Christian faith. This race stuff is a blasphemy, a sin to humanity, to God. We are Hellenes. We are Christians. Like so many other language and cultural groups are Christians under the Mother Church. God said 'go spread the word of salvation in different languages.' He said nothing about races. It's a blasphemy to think in these terms . . . The only relevant groups are linguistic and cultural groups. There are no race groups. God did not speak in these words, our Church's fathers did not speak in these words."

It is important to point out here that this man's son is married to an African American woman, the great-great granddaughter of a slave. He added, "I love my God because He accepts and loves my children and grandchildren. I love my Church because she accepts and loves my children and grandchildren. The rest, all those others are playing political self-serving games. Destructive games." Immigrants whose children married members of racial minority groups often turn to the clergy for guidance and help in having their children's spouses and grandchildren accepted into the community of faithful, i.e. into the community of Greeks and Greek Americans. One woman, whose daughter married an African American man, spoke at length about her early fears of how her daughter and family, including the grandchildren that would later come, be ostracized by Greeks in the Church. As she said, "it was a wonderful ceremony, my family, my son-in-law's family, our friends, we were all together under one God. He was baptized as a Greek Orthodox, my nephew was his godfather. Initially, I know people talked and I know they said, oh, look at so and so's daughter is marrying a black guy. But by the time of the wedding, everybody was there, celebrating with us. They all came for the children's baptisms, the children go to afternoon Greek school, they go to church. I love my God because my God loves my children."

While immigrants whose children marry outside the religious group and even "across racial lines" turn to the Church and its leaders for support in enabling their children, the spouses and grandchildren to remain within the group, parishioners do take "racial positions" in cases where the non-white faithful are either not Greek or do not inter-marry with a Greek or Greek American. One priest, with a quiet disappointment in his eyes talked about a Nigerian family, who had converted to Greek Orthodoxy back home and upon their arrival to NYC came to Church services. After lengthy pleas and hard work by him and by the laity leaders of the parish, the family left the Church because the Greek and Greek American parishioners did not accept them. "They were black. No more, no less." The family joined a nearby Baptist Church with a "black" congregation. One of the parishioners argued that "these people were not accepted because they were not Greek. Look. We have a few intermarried families. A Columbian woman, there is a Greek-African American child in the afternoon school. A Lithuanian woman. These people married Greeks. Their children are Greek. They were baptized as Greek Orthodox."

In yet another parish, a woman spoke bitterly of how she failed to gain acceptance for herself and her children because her husband "refuses to be baptized as a Greek Orthodox. He's Catholic. Why should he have to give up his religion? My children are Catholic but I want them to come to this Church . . . I'm not Greek. That's what they keep telling me in different ways." This woman is herself of mixed ancestry, her father a Greek born immigrant and her mother of Irish ancestry. "I don't want my children to learn Greek. They don't go to afternoon Greek school. That's not the role of the Church."

The Church, as the institution symbolic of Greeks' and Greek Americans' identity, the marker delineating and defining the group in relation to others, a marker rising out of Greece's War of Independence from the Ottoman Empire in the 19th and even into the 20th centuries, is riddled with the national/racial/cultural identity politics of the time. The Church is the institution that American racial identity politics are played out. The clergy have provided poor leadership in these racial and national identity politics so that Patriarch Bartholomew's pleas for the Church to unite under the idea of the *Genos* rather than be divided over race go unheeded.

CONCLUSION

While the Greek American community dates back to the late 19th century, a smaller stream of immigration in the post-war period was followed by a larger immigrant cohort arrival in the late 1960s and 1970s. These new immigrants, along with technological and transportation developments of the past three decades, have brought the Greek and Greek American societies into a "transnational field" of cultural, political and identity politics in which divergent frameworks of race play prominent roles. Greek immigrants in New York City create a variety of national/racial classification schemes existing simultaneously, each vying with the other, in totality creating a confusion of these racial classifications. Depending on immigrants' and the community's leaders frame of reference (Greek vs. American politics), the overall racial schemes used are a combination of two different historical contexts coming into one common field of politics.

NOTES

1. In 20th century discourse, the topics of biological, racial and cultural continuity received a markedly different treatment. The "continuity thesis" of the Greek historiography has provided the backdrop for all intellectual debates – it is the framework underlying the explanations of contemporary folk customs as remands from Ancient Greece (for a critique, see Danforth, 1984). But, with the exception of the Greek right and the Greek fascists, the overwhelming majority of Greek scholarship considers the 3,000 years of Greek civilization to be a matter of cultural continuity rather than a biological or racial continuity.

2. The intention of the discussion of western Turkish cities is two-fold: to redefine Ancient Greece as a Mediterranean culture and to argue that Turkey also has a rightful claim to this culture. The Greeks' response that Turks did not come to the region from the mountains of Mongolia until the 12th or 13th century goes unheeded. Turkish intellectuals, journalists as well as the tourist department advertise and sell to Americans the Ancient Greek ruins on Turkey's western coast as ruins of the Ancient Mediterranean civilization. Furthermore, an Internet map of Greater Albania (posted on an ex-U.S. congressman's home page) includes portions of land that is now part of Greece.

REFERENCES

Allen, T. W. (1994). *The invention of the white race*. London; New York: Verso.

Anderson, B. (1991). *Imagined communities*. London: Verso (2nd ed.).

Balibar, E., & Wallerstein, I. (1991). *Race, nation, class: Ambiguous identities*. London; New York: Verso.

Barber, N. (1973). *The sultans*. New York: Simon & Schuster.

Bernal, M. (1987–1991). *Black Athena: The Afroasiatic roots of classical civilization*. New Brunswick, NJ: Rutgers University Press.

Castells, M. (1996). *The rise of the network society*. London: Basil Blackwell.

Castells, M. (1998). *End of millennium*. Malden, MA: Blackwell.

Clogg, R. (1982). The Greek Millet in the Ottoman Empire. In: B. Lewis & B. Braude (Eds), *Christians and Jews in the Ottoman Empire* (Vol. 1, pp. 185–208). New York: Holmes and Meier.

Constantelos, D. J. (1999). Church and family in Greek Orthodox society from the Byzantine era to the present-day United States: Problems and Issues. In: S. J. Tsemberis, H. J. Psomiades & A. Karpathakis (Eds), *Greek American Families: Traditions and Transformations* (pp. 119–136). New York: Pella Publishers.

Danforth, L. (1984). The ideological context of the search for continuities in modern Greek culture. *Journal of Modern Greek Studies, 2*(1), 53–86.

Danforth, L. (1995). *The Macedonian conflict: Ethnic nationalism in a transnational world*. Princeton, NJ: Princeton University Press.

Featherstone, M., & Lash, S. (1999). *Spaces of culture: City, nation, world*. London; Thousand Oaks, CA: Sage.

Gallant, T. (2002). *Experiencing dominion: Culture, identity and power in the British Mediterranean*. Notre Dame, IN: University of Notre Dame Press.

Ignatiev, N. (1995). *How the Irish became white*. New York: Routledge.

Karakasidou, A. (1997). *Fields of wheat, hills of blood: Passages to nationhood in Greek Macedonia 1870–1990*. Chicago: University of Chicago Press.

Karakasidou, A. (2000). Protocol and pageantry: Celebrating the nation in northern Greece. In: M. Mazower (Ed.), *After the War Was Over: Reconstructing the Family, Nation and State in Greece, 1943–1960* (pp. 221–246). Princeton, NJ: Princeton University Press.

Karpathakis, A. (1994). Whose church is it anyway? Greek immigrants of Astoria and the Greek Orthodox church. *The Journal of the Hellenic Diaspora, 21*(1). Special Edition on Greek Americans.

Karpathakis, A. (1999). Home society politics and immigrant political incorporation: The case of Greek immigrants in New York City. *International Migration Review, 33*(1), 55–78.

Karpathakis, A. (2003). From 'Noikokyra' to 'Lady': Greek immigrant women, assimilation and race. *The Greek Review of Social Research, 110* (Issue A). Special Issue: Gender and International Migration: Focus on Greece.

Karpathakis, A., & Roudometof, V. (2002). Greek Americans and transnationalism: Religion, class and community. In: P. Kennedy & V. Roudometof (Eds), *Communities Across Borders: New Immigrants and Transnational Cultures* (pp. 41–54). London: Routledge.

Kennedy, P., & Roudometof, V. (Eds) (2002). *Communities across borders: New immigrants and transnational cultures*. London: Routledge.

Kitromilides, P. (1978). *Tradition, enlightenment, and revolution: Ideological change in eighteenth and nineteenth century Greece*. Ph.D. Dissertation, Department of Political Science, Harvard University.

Kyriakidies, S. (1955). *The northern ethnological boundaries of Hellenism*. Thessaloniki: Society for Macedonian Studies (in Greek).

Makrygiannis, I. (1947). *Apopnemoneumata kakrygianne*. Athens: Ekdoseis Historike Ereuna.

Montague, A. M. F. (1945). *Man's most dangerous myth: The fallacy of race*. New York: Columbia University Press.

Roudometof, V. (2000). Transnationalism and globalization: The Greek – Orthodox diaspora between orthodox universalism and transnational nationalism. *Diaspora, 9*(3), 361–397.

Roudometof, V. (2001). *Nationalism, globalization, and orthodoxy: The social origins of ethnic conflict in the Balkans*. Westport, CT: Greenwood.

Roudometof, V. (2002). *Collective memory, national identity and ethnic conflict: Greece, Bulgaria and the Macedonian question*. Westport, CT: Praeger.

Ryan, W. (1971). *Blaming the victim*. New York: Pantheon Books.

Sarres, N. (1990). *Ottoman reality* (2 vols.). Athens: Arsenidi (in Greek).

Sugar, P. (1977). *Southeastern Europe under Ottoman rule*. Seattle: University of Washington Press.

Tsoukalas, C. (1981). The ideological impact of the civil war. In: J. O. Iatrides (Ed.), *Greece in the 1940s: A Nation in Crisis* (pp. 319–342). Hanover, NH: University Press of New England.

U.S. Census Bureau (1998). CPH-L-149 *Selected Characteristics for Persons of Greek Ancestry.* www.census.org.

U.S. Census Bureau (2002). *Statistical abstract of the United States 2002: The national data book.* Washington DC: U.S. Census Bureau (122nd ed.).

U.S. Census Bureau (2003). 2000 *Summary File 3.* www.census.gov.

Zotos, S. (1976). *Hellenic presence in America.* Wheaton, IL: Pilgrimage.